Applied Measurement

Industrial Psychology in Human Resources Management

Applied Measurement

Industrial Psychology in Human Resources Management

Edited by

Deborah L. Whetzel
United States Postal Service

George R. Wheaton
American Institutes for Research (Retired)

LAWRENCE ERLBAUM ASSOCIATES, PUBLISHERS

2007   Mahwah, New Jersey   London

Lawrence Erlbaum Associates, Inc., Publishers
10 Industrial Avenue
Mahwah, New Jersey 07430
www.erlbaum.com

Cover design by Tomai Maridou

Library of Congress Cataloging-in-Publication Data

Applied measurement : industrial psychology in human resoruces management / edited by Deborah L. Whetzel, George R. Wheaton
    p. cm.
Includes bibliographical references and index.
ISBN 0-8058-5867-9 (cloth : alk. paper) 1. Performance standards. 2. Employees—Rating of. 3 Job analysis. 4. Psychology, Industrial—Methodology. I. Whetzel, Deborah L., 1959-II. Wheaton, George R.
HF5549.5.P35W473 2006
658.3′125—dc22

2006011745

Books published by Lawrence Erlbaum Associates are printed on acid-free paper, and their bindings are chosen for strength and durability.

Printed in the United States of America
10 9 8 7 6 5 4 3 2 1

Table of Contents

About the Authors

Lance E. Anderson, PhD is a Vice President for Caliber/ICF Consulting. He has over 15 years experience in behavioral and social science research and has directed a wide variety of projects up to five million dollars in value. Dr. Anderson has directed or conducted dozens of studies on the development and use of valid and fair selection tests. Many of these studies were conducted in litigious environments and/or under consent decrees. He has also conducted research to develop O*NET, the Department of Labor's Occupational Information Network. Other research topics and projects include demonstrating the link between illness and worker productivity, leadership development, assessment of persons with disabilities, and standards development and certification. Dr Anderson has published dozens of articles and/or book chapters on these topics.

Laura E. Baranowski is a Senior Organizational Consultant with Wachovia Corporation. She has more than eight years of professional experience providing human resources consulting services to clients in the areas of job analysis, test development and test validation. Her expertise and research, which has been published in *Personnel Psychology* and presented at national conferences, have helped to provide organizations in both the private and public sectors with innovative solutions to their personnel assessment issues. She holds an MS in industrial/organizational psychology from the University of Tennessee at Chattanooga and is a member of the American Psychological Association, the Society for Industrial and Organizational Psychology, North Carolina Industrial and Organizational Psychologists and the Personnel Testing Council of Metropolitan Washington.

Lisa W. Borden is a Partner in the Birmingham office of Baker, Donelson, Bearman, Caldwell & Berkowitz, P.C., whe test development and validation and the role of general and specific abilities in skill acquisition. He is the USAF technical representative to a NATO working group concerne worked with numerous I/O psychologists and selection professionals in a variety of contexts, including the provision of expert opinion and testimony in litigation, consultation prior to and during litigation, and the development and implementation of training programs and selection procedures in compliance with court orders. Ms. Borden received her law degree in 1989 from the Emory University School of Law in Atlanta, Georgia

Thomas R. Carretta received a PhD in psychology in 1983 from the University of Pittsburgh. Currently, he is a Research Psychologist in the System Control Interface Branch of the Human Effectiveness Directorate of the Air Force Research Laboratory (AFRL) at Wright-Patterson AFB, Ohio and conducts research regarding human factors issues in crew-system interface development. Prior to his current position, he spent over 12 years in the Manpower and Personnel Research Division of the AFRL in San Antonio, Texas working on aircrew selection and classification issues including test development and validation and the role of general and specific abilities in skill acquisition. He is the USAF technical representative to a NATO working group concerned with recruitment, selection, and training of military aircrew and a DoD-level working group concerned with military enlistment qualification. His professional interests include personnel measurement, selection, classification, and individual and group differences.

Christina K. Curnow, PhD, a Managing Associate with Caliber/ICF Consulting, has more than 10 years experience in personnel research and consulting, including job analysis and classification, test development and validation, needs assessment, skill gap analysis, design, development, and evaluation of training programs, distance learning evaluation, survey development, and assessment of individual differences. Her research skills include research design, data analysis, and technical writing. She has presented her research at numerous professional conferences and has published peer-reviewed research articles and book chapters. Dr. Curnow's consulting experiences include clients such as the U.S. Army, the Army Research Institute, the National Guard Bureau, the U.S. Office of Personnel Management, the State of Alabama, GEICO Direct, the Institute for Museum and Library Science, Joint Forces, Marine Corp, the Center for Army Leadership and Jefferson County Alabama. In addition, she has worked with personnel from a diverse range of occupations including police, judges, attorneys, accountants, inspectors, trainers, librarians, geologists, computer security personnel, water treatment personnel, sales and service supervisors, customer service representatives, EMTs, militaty officers, non-commissioned officers (NCOs) and enlisted personnel.

Patrick J. Curtin, PhD, a Senior Associate with Caliber/ICF Consulting, has 10 years of research and applied experience that includes work with non profit organizations, government agencies, the military, and private sector companies. During this time, his experiences have ranged from performing job analyses to working on large-scale organizational interventions. His areas of expertise include research methods, the development and validation of selection instruments, group and organizational processes, survey development, administration, and scoring, and organizational culture and climate. Much of his work related to selection instrument development and use has been performed in contentious legal settings. Dr Curtin is an adjunct faculty member at George Mason University, where he has taught a graduate-level course on techniques in Industrial and Organizational Psychology and a junior-level course in research methods. Dr. Curtin has also been a guest lecturer at George Washington University. He has accumulated several years of experience with research methods and advanced statistics through his own work and through teaching research methods for several years at the University of Houston. He has co-authored several journal articles, conference presentations, workshops, and technical reports related to his research interests and work experience.

Fritz Dragow received his PhD in quantitative psychology from the University of Illinois at Urbana-Champaign. He was an Assistant Professor at Yale University's School of Organization and Management and returned to the University of Illinois, where he has been an Assistant Professor, Associate Professor, and Professor of Psychology and of Labor and Industrial Relations. Dr. Drasgow's research focuses on psychological measurement and the application of quantitative methods to important practical problems. Much of his research has been concentrated on the identification of individuals who may have been mismeasured by an assessment tool. He has also studied methods for the detection of items with different measurement properties across various groups of people and languages. Computerized tests and assessments have also been the focus of much of Drasgow's research. Dr. Drasgow is a former chairperson of the American Psychological Association's Committee on Psychological Tests and Assessments, the U.S. Department of Defense's Advisory Committee on Military Personnel Testing, the Department of Defense and Department of Labor's Armed Services Vocational Aptitude Battery Norming Advisory Group, and the American Psychological Association's Taskforce on Internet Testing. Drasgow has also provided consultation on testing and measurement issues to a variety of organizations in the private sector. Drasgow is a member of the editorial review board of eight journals, including *Applied Psychological Measurement, Journal of Applied Psychology,* and *Personnel Psychology.* He is the past president of the Society for Industrial and Organizational Psychology.

Dawn L. Eubanks is a doctoral candidate in the Industrial and Organizational Psychology program at The University of Oklahoma. Prior to joining the doctoral program at The University of Oklahoma she worked as a Business Analyst at The Corporate Executive Board. After receiving her MS degree in I-O Psychology from University of Baltimore, Dawn gained experience as a consultant at Watson Wyatt Worldwide where she was involved with creation and analysis of employee satisfaction instruments. She is currently working with a team of doctoral students to create an automated process for scoring biodata items.

Daniel B. Felker, PhD specializes in several professional research areas: the analysis, design, development, and evaluation of training and instructional systems; job analysis and development of job performance assessment measures; and evaluation of educational, employment, and social programs. Dr. Felker's professional work has spanned a variety of research and development areas in business, education, the military services, and criminal justice system. Specifically, he led the Joint Services' Job Performance Measurement project for the US Army and the US Marine Corps in which a variety of work sample and performance-based job knowledge tests were developed and administered.

Jennifer L. Harvey holds a PhD in industrial/organizational psychology from the University of Akron. She is a Seniro Associate at Caliber/ICF Consulting, and has over six years of personnel research and consulting experience with private, public, and military organizations. Most of her experience has included leading and participating in job analysis, test development, and test validation projects. She has developed numerous content-valid selection instruments, including multiple-choice performance tests, structured interviews, training and experience measures, situational judgment tests, and work samples. She has conducters Award for Applied Research in the Workplace. research in applicant reactions, work motivation, job satisfaction, feedback, leadership, and emotional regulation. Dr. Harvonferences and has co-authored several book chapters.

Allen I. Huffcutt graduatedith a PhD in industrial/organizational psychology from Texas A&M University in 1992. He is now a full professor at Bradley University in Peoria, Illinois, and holds an endowed professorship from caterpillar. He has published primarily in the employment interview literature, addressing such topics as the influence of structure and the constructs that are assessed. He has published secondarily in the methods literature, in areas such as meta-analysis and outliers. His work has appeared in refereed journals, such as *Journal of Applied Psychology and Personnel Psychology.*

P. Richard Jeanneret, PhD, earned his doctorate with a major in industrial and organizational psychology from Purdue University. Dr. Jeanneret's professional career has included three and one half years of active duty as an Aviation Psychologist with the U.S. Navy and over 30 years as a management consultant. He is also an adjunct faculty member of the Rice Universiy and University of Houston Psychology Departments. In 1981 he founded Jeanneret & Associates. His areas of practice encompass the human resource management domain and include the study of work, employee selection systems, validation research, performance management, psychological assessment, organizational analysis, executive development, and compensation programs. He and his associates serve many Fortune 100 companies as well as governmental organizations and small- to medium-sized businesses. Dr. Jeanneret is internationally known for his research in job analysis, and part of his doctoral dissertation was the development of the Position Analysis Questionnaire (PAQ)-a structured worker-oriented job analysis survey. Also, he was a principal investigator and co-editor on the U.S. Department of Labor's project to replace the Dictionary of Occupational Titles with a new job analysis system, the O*NET—An occupational information System for the 21st Century. This project was recognized for its excellence by the Society for Industrial and Organizational Psychology with the 2002. M. Scott MeyeDeveloping Legally Defensible Content Valid Sele

Michael A. McDaniel, PhD is a full professor at Virginia Commonwealth University and is internationally recognized for his research and practice in personnel selection system development and validation. In 1996, he received the

Academy of Management best paper award in human resources. In 2000, he was a made a fellow of the Society of Industrial and Organizational Psychology, the American Psychological Society, and the American Psychological Association in recognition of his personnel selection research. Dr. McDaniel has published in several major journals including the *Academy of Management Journal, the Journal of Applied Psychology, and Personnel Psychology*. Dr. McDaniel is noted for his research in employment interviews, situational judgment measures, cognitive tests, reviews of education and experience, and applicant faking in non-cognitve measures. Dr. McDaniel has consulted with many organizations including international temporary firms, major electric and gas utilities, manufacturing companies, and various health care organizations.

Timothy P. McGonigle is a Managing Associate at Caliber/ICF Consulting. He received a BA (1992) in psychology from Southwestern University, MA (1995) in psychology from Stephen F. Austin State University and PhD (2000) in industrial/organizational psychology from Virginia Tech. He has conducted job analysis and test development and validation work for numerous occupations in both the public and private sectors. He has published and presented research at national conferences on job analysis and classification, test development and validation, job classification, the measurement of work experience, self-report accuracy and rater training. His professional interests include assessment development, performance measurement, and research methods. He has co-authored several journal articles, conference presentations, workshops, and technical reports related to his research interests and work experience. Dr. McGonigle teaches adjunct at George Washington University at both the Schools of Business and Education.

Ray Morath, PhD, a Project Manager with Caliber/ICF Consulting, has 16 years of basic and applied research experience. He has performed work with federal agencies, state governments, U.S. military, and private sector companies. These activities include job analyses, personnel section and promotion, test development and validation (situational judgment tests, dynamic and interactive computerized tests, training and experience exams, knowledge tests, and biodata tests), and the development and administration of managerial assessment centers that utilized role-plays and leaderless group discussions. Dr. Morath has additional expertise in the areas biodata, leadership, human error, and retention. His work in these areas has been presented at professional society conferences and has been published in peer-reviewed journals.

Michael D. Mumford is a George Lynn Cross Distinguished Research Professor at the University of Oklahoma where he is Director of the center for Applied Social Research. Dr. Mumford received his PhD from the University of Georgia in 1983 and has held positions at the Georgia Institute of Technology and George Mason University. He has received more than $20 million in grant and contract funding. Dr. Mumford has received multiple grants from the United States Department of Defense concerned with the development of background data measures. He has served as a consultant to numerous corporate clients in this regard, including Home Depot and Epredix. Dr. Mumford has published more than 160 articles on leadership, creativity, planning and integrity. The most recent of his five books in *Pathways to Outstanding Leadership: A Comparative Analysis of Charismatic, Ideological, and Pragmatic Leaders.* He currently serves as senior editor of *The Leadership Quarterly* and he sits on the editorial boards of the *Creativity Research Journal, The Journal of Creative Behavior, and IEEE Transactions on Organizational Management.* Dr. Mumford is a fellow of the American Psychological Association (Divisions 3,5, and 14), the American Psychological Society, and The Society for Industrial and Organizational Psychology. He is recipient of the Society for Industrial and Organizational Psychology's M. Scott Myers award for applied research in the workplace.

Stephen T. Murphy is a doctoral candidate in the Industrial and Organizational psychology program at The University of Oklahoma. Prior to joining the doctoral program at The university of Oklahoma he has worked as a Research Analyst at Hogan Assessment Systems. Stephen also has experience as a personnel selection specialist for the State of Tennessee and the Personnel Board of Jefferson County after receiving his MA degree in I-O Psychology from Middle Tennessee State University. He is currently working on validating a biodata measure to predict ethical decision-making in research scientists.

Scott H. Oppler received his PhD, in Industrial/Organizational Psychology from the University of Minnesota in 1990 and has spent his entire career at the American Institutes for Research (AIR) at their headquarters in Washington, DC. As Chief Methodologist for AIR's Division of Health, National Security, and Workforce Productivity, Dr. Oppler works with staff on a variety of projects, providing direction on a wide range of measurement and methodological issues. Over the past 16 years, he has conducted research on the validity and other psychometric characteristics of such instruments as the Medical College Admissions Test for the Association of American Medical Colleges, the Armed Services Vocational Aptitude Battery for the Department of Defense, the General Aptitude Test Battery for the U.S. Department of Labor, and the SAT I for the College Board. Dr. Oppler is the author or co-author of over 50 journal articles, book chapters, or conference presentations concerning the measurement or prediction of human abilities, achievement, or performance.

Norman G. Peterson is Director of Research at SPR Center, Inc in Minneapolis. He received his BA (1969) and PhD (1980) degrees from the University of Minnesota in psychology, specializing in industrial and organizational psychology. Prior to joining SPR Center, he was a research fellow at the American Institutes for Research (AIR) and Vice-President of Personnel Decisions Research Institute (PDRI). He is a fellow of the Society for Industrial and Organizational Psychology, the American Psychological Association, and the American Psychological Society.

Dr. Peterson served as the lead developer for the Project A predictors. Dr. Peterson also served as the project director to develop items for the Medical College Admission Test (MCAT). In this role, he directed the item development, item verification and equating of MCAT items. He has conducted research for a variety of public and private sector sponsors in a number of applied areas, including employee opinion and attitude surveys, occupational analysis, development and validation of measures of individual differences, employee selection and classification systems, and prediction of human performance in occupational and training settings. Dr. Peterson was the project director for the U.S. Department of Labor's project, the O*NET–An Occupational Information System for the 21st Century, designed to replace the Dictionary of Occupational Titles with a new job analysis system. This project was recognized for its excellence by the Society for Industrial and Organizational Psychology with the 2002 M. Scott Meyers Award for Applied Research in the Workplace.

Elaine D. Pulakos, PhD is Executive Vice President and Director of Personnel Decisions Research Institute's Washington DC office and Past President of the Society for Industrial and Organizational Psychology. A fellow of the American Psychological Association and Society for Industrial and Organizational psychology, she is a recognized researcher and contributor to the field of industrial and organizational psychology. She has recently co-edited books with Daniel Ilgen, titled: *The changing nature of performance: Importance for staffing, motivation, and development,* and Jerry Hedge, titled: *Implementing organizational interventions: Steps, processes, and best pratices.* She also recently published two best practices studies on performance management and selection, sponsored by the Society for Human Resources Foundation. She has served on the editorial boards of the *Journal of Applied Psychology, Personnel Psychology,* and *Frontiers in Industrial and Organizational Psychology.* Dr. Pulakos has spent her career conducting applied research in public and private sector organizations, where she has designed, developed, and successfully implemented numerous HR systems including selection systems, among other organizational interventions. Dr. Pulakos has also been extensively involved in providing expert advice on EEO-related legal matters in the areas of performance management, selection, promotion, and pay, serving as an expert witness and advisor to the Department of Justice, among others.

Malcomes James Ree completed a PhD in psychometrics and statistics at the University of Pennsylvania in 1976. His career included 25 years as a research scientist at the Air Force Research Laboratory. He retried and accepted a position as professor in the Department of Leadership Studies at Our Lady of the Lake University in San Antonio Texas. He has published more than 65 articles in referred journals, a dozen book chapters, numerous book reviews and more than 100 Air Force research reports. His interests include the role of general cognitive ability in occupational performance, statistical methodology, the history of statistics, and individual differences.

Andrew M. Rose received his PhD in experimental and cognitive psychology from the University of Michigan in 1974. From 1974 to 2006, he was at the American Institutes for Research. He was Managing Research Scientist and Chief Scientist of the Washington Research Center. In this position, he was responsible for ensuring the quality of projects and product deliverables, and for ensuring scientific rigor in the conduct of all projects. Further responsibilities included directing research and evaluation projects that focus on the analysis of communication effectiveness and performance in applied settings; and designing and conducting field studies, laboratory studies, and theoretical and applied research on communication, cognition, comprehension, and retention. Dr. Rose has been the Principal Investigator for several projects that involved complex experimental designs implemented in field settings. He helped design and administer performance tests for the Joint Services Job Performance Project, for both the US Army and for the US Marine Corps.

Teresa L. Russell, PhD is a Principal Staff Scientist with the Human Resources Research Organization (HumRRO) and has more than 20 years of experience in the personnel selection and classification field. Early in her career, she was a part of the team for the Army's Project A. She developed of some of the Project A spatial and computer-administered tests, developed performance rating scales, conducted psychometric analyses of the measures, and participated in data collections and validation of predictor measures for numerous projects. For example, she was director of a project to norm and implement valid tests used to select electrical wok apprentices nationwide. She has a broad base of experience in predictor development, including cognitive, psychomotor, and temperament measures as well as structured interviews and situational judgments tests.

James C. Sharf, PhD is an industrial psychologist with more than thirty years' experience in employee selection and appraisal. A former chief psychologist for the Equal Employment Opportunity Commission, Dr. Sharf advises human resource professionals, employment attorneys, and fellow I/O psychologists on developing, implementing, and defending selection, licensing and certification, and appraisal systems that minimize the risk of litigation. Dr. Sharf is a fellow of both the society for Industrial and organizational Psychology and the American Psychological Association.

Suzanne Tsacoumis is the Manager of the Personnel Selection and Development Program at the Human Resources Research Organization (HumRRO). She received her BA degree (1982) in psychology and sociology from Bucknell University, her MA (1984) in industrial and organizational psychology from Fairleigh-Dickinson University, and her PhD (1988) from the University of Georgia specializing in industrial and organizational psychology. Her work revolves around personnel selection, test development and validation, and assessment centers, often in a litigious environment. Suzanne has over 20 years of experience in developing content valid job simulations and assessment centers, first at the American Telephone and Telegraph Company (AT&T) and then for a variety of organizations while at HumRRo. The processes she developed have been used both for promotion into first-line supervisory and mid-level manager positions, as well as for selection into supertvisory, managerial, and executive career development programs.

George R. Wheaton is recently retired, having spent his professional career with the American Institutes for Research (AIR) in Washington, DC. He received his AB degree in psychology from Bowdin College (1961) and his MSc in clinical psychology from McGill University (1963). While at A.I.R. he conducted, directed, and managed a variety of I/O psychological research activites first as a project director, then as Vice President and Director of the Washington Research Center, and most recently as the corporation's Vice President for Quality Assurance. His research interests have included taxonomies of performance, individual differences, and application of job and task analysis methods to transfer of training phenomena and development of criterion performance measures for individuals and teams.

Deborah L. Whetzel, PhD is a Manager, Leadership Assessment, Processes and Systems at the U.S. Postal Service. Prior to joining the Postal Service, she was a Principal for Work Skills First, Inc. where she directed or conducted research on projects dealing with job analysis and competency model development, test development, research, and implementation, and performance appraisal development for both private and public sector clients. While at the American Institutes for Research, Dr. Whetzel led the item development of form assembly work for the Medical College Admission Test (MCAT). In this role, she trained item editors on how to screen and edit items and to assemble MCAT forms to be administered to examinees. She also worked on the Secretary's Commision on Achieving Necessary Skills (SCANS) in which she wrote and edited skills and their definitions for presentation to subject matter experts. Her work has been presented at professional conferences and published in peer-reviewed journals. She received her PhD from George Washington University.

Satoris (Tori) Youngcourt earned her PhD in Industrial/Organizational Psychology from Texas A&M University. An active member of the Society for Industrial and Organizational Psychology, the Academy of Management, and the American Psychological Association, she is currently a consultant at Personnel Decisions International. Her consulting activities involve leading selection and development assessments for individuals at mutiple levels within organizations across client industries, consulting on multi-rater feedback processes, and delivering training and development workshops. In addition to her applied and research interests in employment interviews, she has research interests in work-life balance issues, performance appraisal and feedback,and individual differences.

Preface

In 1997, we edited the book *Applied Measurement Methods in Industrial Psychology*. The purposes of that book were to: (a) describe the process of job analysis and test development in a hands-on way that practitioners can understand; (b) provide background about the reliability, validity, and subgroup differences of measures used to predict job performance; and (c) describe various methods for measuring job performance (e.g., ratings and work samples).

The original book received several positive reviews from academics and practitioners. Malcolm Ree, formerly of Armstrong Laboratories and currently at Our Lady of the Lakes University, reviewed the book in *Personnel Psychology* (Winter, 1998) and stated, 'When asked to review this book, I did so because of the promise held in the title and the editors. That promise has been fulfilled.... *Applied Measurement Methods in Industrial Psychology* has much to recommend it to its intended audience ... it is a useful volume with concise information and belongs in your library' (pp. 1048–1050).

Walter Borman, Personnel Decisions Research Institute, stated:

A distinguishing feature of the book is a 'how-to' emphasis that should especially help students and early practitioners to work through applied problems, develop predictor and criterion instruments, conduct validation analyses, and the like. So often, new I/O PhDs have few knowledges or skills necessary to practice I/O psychology in the real world. This book should greatly help them make this transition. (1997, personal communication)

Richard Klimoski, George Mason University, wrote:

It deals with key (but troublesome) issues in applied measurement that are encountered by those interested in promoting effective performance in work organizations: The successful identification of the individual difference constructs of interest and the translation of that knowledge into defensible predictor and criterion measures. There are very few up-to-date sources with this useful focus ... the manner in which the material is presented ... is excellent. It is neither too general to be useful nor does it get bogged down in minutia.... It is a very fine contribution indeed. (1997, personal communication)

Carol Meyers, Arizona Public Service Company, wrote in a Personnel Testing Council, Arizona newsletter:

The features of the book that make it so useful are: 1) well-written in fairly 'low-tech' lingo, 2) very well organized material that is easy to follow, 3) use of one job (electrician) as an example throughout the book, 4) written with a view to the beginning practitioner or human resource professional—a real 'how to' and applications approach, 5) excellent information tables, and 6) good summaries at the end of each chapter. (1997, p. 2)

The goal of the new book is to update the 1997 *Applied Measurement* volume. A great deal of research has been conducted since 1997 on several of the topics described in the earlier book (e.g., interviews, situational judgment tests, competency models). The purposes of the updated book remain the same: that is, to provide a single well-organized sourcebook for fundamental practices in industrial psychology and human resources management.

BOOK CHAPTERS AND AUTHORS

Like its predecessor, this book takes an applied or how-to approach to instrument development. Each chapter begins with an overview describing the job analysis or measurement method. Following this overview, the authors describe the psychometric characteristics (e.g., reliability, validity, subgroup differences) of each measurement method. Each chapter concludes with a general how-to discussion that spells out how each measurement method could be applied to any given job. As an organizing theme and for purposes of illustration, the output of each technique is provided for the job of electrician. Examples throughout the book pertain to the electrician's job so that readers can understand how job analysis data can be used to develop the broad array of measurement instruments discussed in the book.

As one can see from the list of authors, we have called on some of the most prominent researchers in the field to write chapters, including: Norm Peterson and Dick Jeanneret on deductive methods of job analysis; Malcolm Ree and Tom Carretta on cognitive ability; Allen Huffcutt on interviews; Mike Mumford on background data; Mike McDaniel on situational judgment tests; Elaine Pulakos on ratings; Fritz Drasgow and Scott Oppler on validation techniques; and Jim Sharf and Lisa Borden on methods for increasing the defensibility of systems in court. Most of these individuals are Fellows of the Society for Industrial and Organizational Psychology (SIOP) and two of them are SIOP past presidents. These authors, based on their own expertise and research, have written chapters that update the literature. For several of the chapters, we have called on other professionals with extensive practical experience to provide the updates. Not all of these individuals are academics, but they have a great deal of applied experience and many have presented their methods and the results of their research at SIOP.

DIFFERENCES BETWEEN THE NEW VOLUME AND THE FORMER BOOK

We have added three chapters, one on training and experience measures (chap. 6), one on assessment centers (chap. 10), and one on methods for increasing the defensibility of selection systems in court (chap. 14). Training and experience measures are among the most commonly used predictors, and it seemed fitting to include this approach in the new volume. Concerning assessment centers, we use a different exemplar job (supervisor or foreperson) to provide illustrative examples of the measures. The chapter on how to prepare for legal challenges is an important addition, given the increased scrutiny that selection systems are receiving, particularly in regard to issues of content validity.

We have expanded the chapter on validation strategies to include an introduction to item response theory (IRT) and a discussion of ways in which IRT can be used to refine various instruments. The chapter on measuring complex skills was deleted because it overlaps with the cognitive ability chapter and because it describes highly specialized research that is unlikely to have broad applicability. We also changed the authorship of some chapters to include individuals who have conducted more recent research in the field.

Other than these few changes, organization of chapters in the new book parallels that of the former volume. We start with chapters on job analysis that provide the foundation for the subsequent predictor and criterion development chapters.

RELATIONSHIP OF THIS BOOK TO OTHERS IN I/O PSYCHOLOGY

This book should be used in concert with other volumes on related topics. This book should not be viewed as 'the' book on testing and selection. Therefore, we do not address issues such as banding, individual assessment, and ethical issues. It is not intended to be the only I/O book the students ever read. There are other books (as there are courses) that thoroughly deal with psychometric and legal issues and we do not discuss those topics at great length in the new volume.

It is our contention, as alluded to by Walter Borman earlier, that too many PhDs leave graduate school having never written a task statement, developed questions for an interview, or developed anchors for a rating scale. It seemed useful to have a single how-to book that describes the process (i.e., starting with a job analysis that leads to the development of useful measures designed to predict and measure job performance). We also believe that such a book would be useful for practitioners.

ACKNOWLEDGMENTS

We would like to express our sincere thanks to many people who have provided assistance in this project. We would like to thank our families for their support during this process. We are extremely grateful to the authors for their enthusiasm and dedication in producing chapters that provide up-to-date research evidence as well as instructive guidance on developing or using the methods described in their chapters. The ideas represented in these chapters and the authors' cooperation in reacting to our comments on earlier drafts of their chapters made this project an extremely rewarding one. Finally, we wish to thank Anne Duffy and her colleagues at Lawrence Erlbaum Associates who have been extremely helpful throughout this process.

—Deborah L. Whetzel
—George R. Wheaton

REFERENCES

Borman, W. C. (1997). Personal communication to G. R. Wheaton, September 2, 1997.

Klimoski, R. J. (1997). Personal communication to G. R. Wheaton, August, 1997.

Myers, C. (1997, December). Applied measurement methods in industrial psychology. *Personnel testing Council/Arizona Newsletter*.

Ree, M. J. (1998). Applied measurement methods in industrial psychology (Book review). *Personnel Psychology, 51,* 1048–1050.

CHAPTER ONE

Contexts for Developing Applied Measurement Instruments

George R. Wheaton
American Institutes for Research (retired)

Deborah L. Whetzel
United States Postal Service

OVERVIEW

The primary purpose of this edited volume is to provide students and entry-level practitioners with practical, systematic guidance on how to develop and evaluate the kinds of measurement instruments frequently used in the management of human resources. The authors, therefore, take a decidedly applied or how-to approach to instrument development and evaluation. Their prescriptions are logically organized and follow the process one would actually undertake to determine the constructs to measure, the measurement techniques to use, and the reliability, validity, fairness, and legal defensibility of the resulting assessments. Accordingly, the volume contains five major sections: conducting job analyses, developing a test plan, developing measures to predict job performance, developing measures of job performance per se, and conducting studies to assess the quality and defensibility of the measurement program.

The context in which we discuss the development of applied measurement methods is the world of work. Thus, we want to assess the characteristics of job applicants to determine who would most likely excel on the job, both in the near term and in the longer run. Similarly, we periodically would want to assess employee accomplishments, as well as their strengths and weaknesses in performance, both as a basis for compensation and as a diagnostic tool for choosing

1

appropriate developmental courses of action. Measurement also might be used to assist in the planning of career trajectories, to support promotion decisions, and to design and evaluate training programs. Measurement of this latter type could be used not only to characterize how much employees have learned from exposure to selected training programs, but also to evaluate the programs themselves (e.g., by determining what facets of job performance are best trained using particular training methods).

The current text updates and expands the content of an earlier volume prepared by the same editors and many of the same authors (Whetzel & Wheaton, 1997). The updated material and associated references document progress in research on many of the book's topics. Although certainly not the last word, the book does reflect the state of the art in development and application of the methods described in each of its chapters, through the end of 2005.

The original text was expanded to include chapters on measurement of training and experience, assessment center methods, and legal issues and guidance. Other material was elaborated (e.g., an introduction to the models and uses of item response theory within the chapter on evaluation). The most difficult decision was what to exclude. For example, although reference is made to the Big 5 personality constructs as potential predictors of performance, we elected not to include a chapter on personality. Several personality measures already exist; therefore, discussion of how to create new ones did not seem warranted. Moreover, validity data from recent meta-analyses do not support their use as predictors of job performance (Hurtz & Donovan, 2000), and personality measures are highly susceptible to faking in applicant situations (Rosse, Stecher, Miller, & Levin, 1998; Stark, Chernyshenko, Chan, Lee, & Drasgow, 2001).

There is a second context, in addition to the world of work, in which to describe development, use, and evaluation of measurement techniques in support of human resources management. Applied measurement occurs within a systems context that systematically proceeds from an analysis phase, to planning the measurement approach, to development of predictor and criterion measures, to evaluation of the entire program. We cannot emphasize strongly enough the importance of conducting each phase of this process in meticulous fashion, and of documenting, in great detail, each and every step along the way. This is one of the important messages of the last chapter, "Developing Legally Defensible Content Valid Selection Procedures." Given the context of the age in which we live, many would argue that this last chapter be read first.

CONDUCTING JOB ANALYSES

Job analysis is the necessary foundation of applied measurement for the purpose of managing human resources. For example, job analysis is essential when interest lies in predicting performance on the job. When developing a test or test battery for the purpose of selecting employees from a pool of job candidates, the first step is to conduct a job analysis that identifies the most critical aspects of the job. The next step is to identify the knowledge, skills, and abilities needed to perform the critical job operations successfully. Once the knowledge, skills, and abilities have been identified, tests that measure those attributes can be selected or developed. Thus, the development of selection instruments depends on the results of job analysis. One of the methods most commonly used to parse a job into its critical tasks and to identify important worker characteristics is the job-task analysis method.

Job analysis also is used as the basis for developing performance appraisal instruments. For research purposes, measures of job performance often serve as the criteria against which selection measures are validated. For the purpose of assessing job performance operationally, job analysis can provide an empirical basis for determining the characteristics of an entire appraisal system. For example, job analysis can be used to identify the best source of information for the appraisal of different components of job performance (e.g., peers may be the best source for some components, whereas supervisors may be best for others). Job analysis might also provide information on the extent to which performance on different components of the job is constrained by factors beyond the control of individual workers (e.g., shortages in materials or personnel). One of the best job analysis methods one can use for determining the content of performance appraisals is the critical incident technique.

The results of job analysis are often used to support human engineering and usability testing studies (Dumas & Redish, 1993). The goal of both types of studies is to design machines and systems that can be easily and effectively used by humans. Job analysis can be used to detect problems with machines (e.g., critical incidents are often collected to document that a control mechanism or display has been poorly designed or inappropriately placed within a work station). Job, and especially task, analysis can also be used to describe the operations involved in using a system component (e.g., whether the task, subtask, or task element requires tracking, searching, monitoring, or decision making) and in determining the impact that design will have on system operation. Again, the job-task inventory and critical incident methods often are useful precursors to these kinds of applications.

The results of job analysis are also used for job evaluation. Job evaluation is the process by which wage rates are differentially applied to jobs. The analyst conducting the job evaluation takes a number of factors in account (e.g., duties and tasks performed, required knowledge and skills, the work environment and conditions), weights those factors, and places each job at some point along a continuum. The analyst then uses job analysis results to describe the continuum in terms of a series of classes, usually corresponding to wage categories. There are several well-known deductive job analysis methods that can be used for this purpose.

Finally, the results of job analysis are often used to support curriculum design and development. The fundamental step in designing a training program is to conduct a needs analysis that specifies a set of objectives for training. These objectives may include the provision of particular knowledge, the development of specific skills, or the formation of selected attitudes. Needs analysis consists of three separate components: organizational analysis, job and task analysis, and person or worker analysis. In this book we describe job and task analysis methods that can be used to determine instructional objectives related to particular job activities or operations. When conducting analyses to support training design and development, the question being asked is, "What skills, knowledge, and attitudes may be necessary for successful performance of the job duties being considered?"

Within this broad context of work and job performance, the fundamental building block of any measurement program designed to assess the strengths and weaknesses of personnel is a job analysis. Job analysis consists of a systematic set of procedures for determining what workers actually do on the job and for describing which aspects of worker knowledge, skill, ability, and other characteristics (KSAOs) contribute to job performance. In this book we consider four different job analysis methods.

In chapter 2, we describe deductive methods of job analysis in which jobs are analyzed to determine which variables (from standard sets of variables) apply to them. The methods are deductive in the sense that the analyst starts with a predefined taxonomy to describe job requirements. Several deductive job analysis schemes are available such as functional job analysis (Fine & Wiley, 1971), the Position Analysis Questionnaire (McPhail, Jeanneret, McCormick, & Mecham, 1991), and the Occupational Information Network (O*NET), the latest and most comprehensive of the deductive job analysis methods (Boese, Lewis, Frugoli, & Litwin, 2001). These and other deductive job analysis schemes primarily differ in terms of the standard set of descriptive variables they incorporate. In chapter 2, we discuss the circumstances under which deductive job analysis is most useful, describe several popular deductive job analysis methods that preceded the O*NET, and discuss how the database underlying the O*NET can be used to streamline deductive methods of job analysis.

In chapter 3, we describe inductive methods of job analysis in which the analyst begins by gathering detailed information about the job in terms of what workers do and what they need to know to perform the work. This information is then organized into categories and the analyst induces a higher order structure. In chapter 3, we describe the job-task analysis method in which several procedures (e.g., review of existing documentation, observations, interviews, surveys) are used to obtain information about jobs. We also describe how to assemble typical job analysis surveys, including how to define duty areas, how to write task statements, and how to describe knowledge, skills, abilities, and other characteristics. Finally, in chapter 3, we describe the critical incident technique (Flanagan, 1954), which is another inductive method having great value in uncovering important dimensions of job performance. We include guidance on how to conduct incident writing workshops and how to analyze the incidents to identify underlying dimensions of performance that can be used to construct behaviorally based rating scales, and situational judgment tests, among many other applications.

DEVELOPING A MEASUREMENT PLAN

Though quite brief, consisting of but a single chapter, this section serves as a bridge between guidance on how to conduct various types of job analysis and guidance on how to apply the results of those analyses to develop various kinds of measurement instruments. The measurement plan is a formal way of helping practitioners identify tests and other assessment tools that best satisfy the three objectives of a personnel assessment system: to maximize validity, to minimize adverse impact, and to enhance the efficiency of the measurement approach.

In chapter 4, we describe how to develop a measurement plan in the context of developing an employee selection system. The measurement plan serves as a blueprint that specifies what personnel characteristics are to be measured—as determined from job analysis—and how the targeted characteristics may best be measured to satisfy the three criteria just mentioned. Although we focus on activities in the context of employee selection, similar methods could be used for designing training. For example, a well-conceived training plan would specify the training objectives in behavioral terms and then indicate which training methods to use to achieve each objective most effectively and efficiently.

DEVELOPING MEASURES TO PREDICT JOB PERFORMANCE

When selecting employees for jobs or training programs, it is important to use predictors that are based on the requirements of the job and are valid for predicting performance on the job. Predictors can include cognitive ability tests, measures of training and experience, interviews, background data items, situational inventories, and assessment centers. Each of these possibilities is discussed in subsequent chapters along with practical advice on how to develop and implement each type of measure.

Human resource planning—for example, managing growth, downsizing, and reassignment—requires the development of predictors of job performance. To the extent that jobs are changing (e.g., jobs become more technically challenging, job requirements are redefined as a result of corporate mergers and acquisitions), the constructs that predict performance on those jobs will also change. In all of these circumstances, new predictors will be required to help determine which individuals to hire, which to retain, or which to reassign to different departments. Similarly, different kinds of selection measures can be used for career development purposes, determining which employees are most likely to thrive in particular assignments and which are likely to benefit most from specific training programs.

In this section, we describe six different methods that can be used to measure potential predictor constructs identified during a job analysis. In chapter 5, we discuss the nature of cognitive ability and offer definitions of this pervasive construct domain (e.g., Ree & Carretta, 1996, 1998). We also explore important issues surrounding the use of measures of cognitive ability as predictors of job performance, including test fairness and subgroup differences. In the how-to portion of this chapter we describe how to select an appropriate test and how to develop one should the need arise. The latter guidance includes procedures for developing test specifications, creating items, conducting sensitivity reviews, trying out items, and analyzing item data.

In chapter 6, we discuss the development and use of measures of training and experience. Although these measures have been used for many years to support a variety of personnel actions, their theoretical underpinnings have lagged behind. Recent advances in theory-based measurement (e.g., Quinones, Ford, & Teachout, 1995; Tesluk & Jacobs, 1998) are likely to improve the predictive quality of these measures, especially those that assess amounts and quality of experience rather than providing an amorphous holistic judgment. After reviewing the psychometric properties of training and experience measures, including discussion of subgroup differences and response distortion, we provide practical guidance in the development of alternative measures. These include task-based questionnaires, KSA-based questionnaires, and accomplishment records. We also describe methods for encouraging truthful responses to the questionnaires.

In chapter 7, we discuss employment interviews. In the first part of the chapter we describe what is meant by a structured interview and then consider different levels of structure and different interview formats. Following this introduction, we present research on the psychometric properties of the employment interview, including reliability and validity (Conway, Jako, & Goodman, 1995; McDaniel, Whetzel, Schmidt, & Mauer, 1994; Wiesner & Cronshaw, 1988), subgroup differences (Huffcut & Roth, 1998; Moscoso, 2000), and the incremental validity provided by interviews beyond cognitive ability (Pulakos & Schmitt, 1995; Salgado & Moscoso, 2002). In the second part of this chapter we offer guidance on how to use critical incidents to generate interview questions and response alternatives for two types of structured interviews: situational interviews and behavior description interviews.

We begin chapter 8 with a discussion of issues affecting the use of background data questions in personnel selection (Mount, Witt, & Barrick, 2000; Mumford & Owens, 1987; Owens, 1976). These issues include item relevance, faking, and item content. We then discuss the theory underlying use of background or biodata items—that past behavior is predictive of future behavior—and explore the extensive research on the psychometric properties of these predictors. In later sections of this chapter, we describe methods for generating several different types of background items, for assembling questionnaires, and for scaling and validating responses.

In chapter 9, we discuss the use and development of situational judgment tests as a form of low-fidelity job simulation. We describe what is meant by a situational judgment test, discuss what such tests measure, and review their structure and format, including video-based tests. We summarize research on the psychometric characteristics of low-fidelity simulations (e.g., McDaniel, Hartman, & Grubb, 2003) and provide guidance on building situational judgment tests. This advice includes methods for creating item stems and response options that describe potential actions that might be taken in response to a particular situation.

In chapter 10, we explore the use of assessment center methodologies to evaluate an applicant's strengths and weaknesses and to predict the applicant's potential to succeed in a given position. The high-fidelity simulations comprising assessment centers are an effective means of evaluating complex job performance including that, for example, of supervisors and managerial personnel. We begin by considering several different types of exercises that might be included in an assessment center. We then review psychometric research on validity and reliability, as well as subgroup differences. In the second half of the chapter, we present detailed guidance on how to develop assessment center exercises and rating scales. Part of this guidance consists of steps in the selection and training of assessors who will either play roles in selected exercises or be required to evaluate applicant performance during or shortly after each exercise. We outline five training modules intended to promote high levels of assessment quality.

DEVELOPING MEASURES OF JOB PERFORMANCE

One of the most common reasons for developing measures of job performance is to satisfy an organization's need to determine how well its employees are performing on the job. Operational performance appraisal systems are used to support a variety of personnel decisions, such as salary increases and promotions. When jobs are redesigned or the job requirements change, companies may have to determine which employees to retain or reassign. Measures of past performance can be useful when reaching such decisions. Operational performance appraisal systems also are used as feedback mechanisms, enabling employers to explain developmental needs to their employees.

Another purpose for developing measures of job performance is to support research efforts intended to establish the validity of selection instruments or to assess the effectiveness of training. Measures of job performance, whether based on rating scales, job knowledge tests, work sample tests, or combinations of these three, provide criteria against which to validate the kinds of predictor instruments discussed in earlier chapters. Measures of job performance can be used to evaluate training. Evaluators often use paper-and-pencil measures of job knowledge to evaluate the degree to which learning has occurred. Work sample measures are used to indicate the extent of skill acquisition and the retention of that skill over time. Rating scale data can inform evaluators about further needs for improvement of performance that can be achieved through training.

Although we have categorized various measurement instruments as predictors in one section and as performance measures in another, several instruments can be used for either purpose. This certainly is true of rating scales, job knowledge tests, work sample tests, and situational judgment tests. The use of various measurement approaches and instruments depends on the purpose of the measurement, as indicated by the study design and as specified in the measurement plan documentation.

In chapter 11, we discuss issues surrounding the development of an effective performance management system, including performance planning, ongoing feedback, and performance evaluation. Having set the broad context within which performance evaluation occurs, we then offer guidance on how to develop effective evaluation tools. Chief among these tools are rating scales, which when used to measure job performance describe typical performance, or what an employee will do, day to day. Such rating scales often serve as criterion measures against which to validate predictor instruments. We describe methods for developing rating scales that make use of critical incident data. Guidance is given on developing behaviorally anchored rating scales (Smith & Kendall, 1963), behavioral summary scales (Borman, 1979), behavior observation scales (Latham & Wexley, 1981), and mixed standard rating scales (Blanz & Ghiselli, 1972). We end the chapter by suggesting ways to improve the quality of performance ratings, especially through rater training, and by offering advice on how to implement effective performance management systems within organizations.

In chapter 12, we describe the development of measures of maximal performance. These measures focus on what an employee can do under relatively ideal testing conditions. We describe applications of job performance tests as well as their limitations, and review the psychometric characteristics of such tests. We describe procedures for sampling the job performance domain and offer sampling strategies for selecting tests. Testing techniques include both hands-on tests and the use of performance-based test items in job knowledge test development. We also offer advice on a number of scoring issues attendant to work sample testing, including product versus process scoring, the scorability and observability of tasks, pass-fail scoring versus ratings of performance, and the not inconsequential matter of testing logistics.

ASSESSING THE QUALITY AND LEGAL
DEFENSIBILITY OF A TESTING PROGRAM

In the final section of this book, we seek closure on the topics of conducting job analyses, developing a measurement plan, developing predictor measures, and developing measures of job performance for use as criteria. In this final section, we determine the quality of the selection program by considering each of its constituent parts as well as the outcomes it produces.

Consistent with the slant on personnel selection that runs throughout, in chapter 13 we describe the validation of selection instruments. In this chapter we discuss definitions of validity, raise issues that need to be addressed when developing a validation research plan, and offer advice on how to collect and analyze data. In this latter connection we also discuss the notion of test bias and how to access it. To provide how-to guidance, we use simple sets of data to demonstrate how analysis of validity data proceeds. Topics include computation of basic descriptive statistics, standard scores, and correlation coefficients, and the use of regression analysis to assess predictive bias. We describe how to assess item characteristics using both classical techniques and procedures based on item response theory (IRT). These topics are presented in a manner intended to acquaint the reader with some of the concepts involved in validation research. Throughout, we provide references to more thorough and advanced treatments. Last, but not least, we end the chapter with advice on how to document the validation research design and its results.

In chapter 14, we raise the topic of litigation and discuss steps that should be taken to develop legally defensible, content valid selection procedures. We begin with an introduction to litigation, including definitions of some of the core concepts. Next, we discuss issues involved in screening applicants on the basis of minimum qualifications and recruiting potential employees via the Internet. Finally, we describe steps that test developers should take prior to developing and evaluating selection programs. In this regard, it is essential that anyone contemplating development of selection procedures for any purpose first become familiar with the *Uniform Guidelines on Employee Selection Procedures* (1978). Adherence to these guidelines will help ensure that subsequent legal challenges are avoided or successfully countered.

ADOPTING A COMMON THEME

The advice and guidance offered in this book are based on the experiences of a large number of applied research psychologists who have developed applied measurement methods in many different contexts for many different purposes, primarily but not exclusively related to the world of work. Within the context of the workplace, these practitioners have developed measures of many different kinds of predictor constructs related to performance on many different kinds of jobs, ranging from anesthesiologists to salespersons, from insurance agents to infantry. The challenge, therefore, has been to adopt, insofar as possible, a common context within which to provide advice and offer guidance.

Toward that end, we have chosen the job of electrician as a running example throughout this volume so that the reader may better understand how measures are developed for a single job and how the various parts of the measurement process interrelate. The example is based on a large-scale project in which selection instruments were developed and validated for use in selecting candidates for a nationally based electrician apprenticeship program (Williams, Peterson, & Bell, 1994). As components of that project the researchers: (a) conducted inductive job analyses that used the job-task inventory method to identify the tasks performed by electricians and the KSAOs related to task performance, and the critical incident technique to gather incidents and specify important dimensions underlying electrician performance; (b) developed predictor instruments, including measures of cognitive ability such as reading comprehension, spatial ability, and noncognitive measures such as biodata items; and (c) developed criterion performance measures such as behavioral summary rating scales. Throughout the book, whenever possible, we make liberal use of samples of tasks, critical incidents, unused items, and other materials drawn from this project to aid the practitioner in following the guidance we offer.

REFERENCES

Blanz, R., & Ghiselli, E. E. (1972). The mixed standard scale: A new rating system. *Personnel Psychology, 25,* 185–200.

Boese, R., Lewis, P., Frugoli, P., & Litwin, K. (2001). *Summary of O*NET 4.0 Content Model and Database*. Raleigh, NC: National O*NET Consortium.

Borman, W. C. (1979). Format and training effects on rating accuracy and rating errors. *Journal of Applied Psychology, 64,* 410–421.

Conway, J. M., Jako, R. A., & Goodman, D. F. (1995). A meta-analysis of interrater and internal consistency reliability estimates of selection interviews. *Journal of Applied Psychology, 80,* 565–579.

Dumas, J. S., & Redish, J. C. (1993). *A practical guide to usability testing.* Norwood, NJ: Ablex.

Fine, S. A., & Wiley, W. W. (1971). *An introduction to functional job analysis, methods for manpower analysis* [Monograph No. 4]. Kalamazoo, MI: W. E. Upjohn Institute.

Flanagan, J. C. (1954). The critical incident technique. *Psychological Bulletin, 41,* 237–358.

Huffcutt, A. I., & Roth, P. L. (1998). Racial group differences in employment interview evaluations. *Journal of Applied Psychology, 83,* 179–189.

Hurtz, G. M., & Donovan, J. J. (2000). Personality and job performance: The big five revisited. *Journal of Applied Psychology, 85,* 869–879.

Latham, G. P., & Wexley, K. N. (1981). *Increasing productivity through performance appraisal.* Reading, MA: Addison-Wesley.

McDaniel, M. A., Hartman, N. S., & Grubb, W. L., III. (2003, April). *Situational judgment tests, knowledge, behavioral tendency, and validity: A meta-analysis.* Paper presented at the 18th annual Conference of the Society for Industrial and Organizational Psychology, Inc., Orlando, FL.

McDaniel, M. A., Whetzel, D. L., Schmidt, F. L., & Mauer, S. (1994). The validity of interviews: A comprehensive review and meta-analysis. *Journal of Applied Psychology, 79,* 599–616.

McPhail, S. M., Jeanneret, P. R., McCormick, E. J., & Mecham, R. C. (1991). *Position analysis questionnaire job analysis manual.* Logan, UT: PAQ Services.

Moscoso, S. (2000). Selection interview: A review of validity evidence, adverse impact and applicant reactions. *International Journal of Selection and Assessment, 8,* 237–247.

Mount, M. K., Witt, L. A., & Barrick, M. R. (2000). Incremental validity of empirically keyed biodata scales over GMA and the five factor personality constructs. *Personnel Psychology, 53,* 299–323.

Mumford, M. D., & Owens, W. A. (1987). Methodology review: Principles, procedures, and findings in the application of background data measures. *Applied Psychological Measurement, 11,* 1–31.

Owens, W. A. (1976). Background data. In M. D. Dunnette (Ed.), *Handbook of industrial and organizational psychology* (pp. 609–643). Chicago: Rand McNally.

Pulakos, E. D., & Schmitt, N. (1995). Experience-based and situational interview questions: Studies of validity. *Personnel Psychology, 48,* 289–308.

Quinones, M. A., Ford, K. J., & Teachout, M. S. (1995). The relationship between work experience and job performance: A conceptual and meta-analytical review. *Personnel Psychology, 48,* 887–905.

Ree, M. J., & Carretta, T. R. (1996). Central role of *g* in military pilot selection. *International Journal of Aviation Psychology, 6,* 111–123.

Ree, M. J., & Carretta, T. R. (1998). General cognitive ability and occupational performance. In C. L. Cooper & I. T. Robertson (Eds.), *International review of industrial and organizational psychology* (pp. 159–184). Chichester, England: Wiley.

Rosse, J. G., Stecher, M. D., Miller, J. L., & Levin, R. A. (1998). The impact of response distortion on preemployment personality testing and hiring decisions. *Journal of Applied Psychology, 83,* 634–644.

Salgado, J. F., & Moscoso, S. (2002). Comprehensive meta-analysis of the construct validity of the employment interview. *European Journal of Work and Organizational Psychology, 11,* 299–234.

Smith, P. C., & Kendall, L. M. (1963). Retranslation of expectations: An approach to the construction of unambiguous anchors for rating scales. *Journal of Applied Psychology, 47,* 149–155.

Stark, S., Chernyshenko, O. S., Chan, K., Lee, W. C., & Drasgow, F. (2001). Effects of the testing situation on item responding: Cause for concern. *Journal of Applied Psychology, 86,* 943–953.

Tesluk, P. E., & Jacobs, R. R. (1998). Toward an integrated model of work experience. *Personnel Psychology, 51,* 321–355.

Uniform guidelines on employee selection procedures. (1978). *Federal Register, 43,* 38290–38315.

Whetzel, D. L., & Wheaton, G. R. (1997). *Applied measurement methods in industrial psychology.* Palo Alto, CA: Davies-Black.

Wiesner, W. H., & Cronshaw, S. F. (1988). A meta-analytic investigation of the impact of interview format and degree of structure on the validity of employment interviews. *Journal of Occupational Psychology, 61,* 275–290.

Williams, K. M., Peterson, N. G., & Bell, J. A. (1994). *Job analysis of three electrical worker positions for the National Joint Apprenticeship Training Committee.* Washington, DC: American Institutes for Research.

CHAPTER TWO

Job Analysis: Overview and Description of Deductive Methods

Norman G. Peterson
Satisfaction Performance Research Center

P. Richard Jeanneret
Valtera

OVERVIEW

In this chapter, we concentrate on two traditional forms of job analysis—deductive and inductive methods—and distinguish between them. By deductive job analysis, we mean those methods that emphasize the use of existing knowledge or taxonomies of job information during analysis of the focal job. For example, use of a published, commercially available job analysis inventory such as the Position Analysis Questionnaire (PAQ; McCormick & Jeanneret, 1988) is a deductive approach to studying one or more jobs. Information collected about the job is automatically organized within the already existing system of job descriptors and can be interpreted within a database of quantitative scores on those descriptors for other jobs, providing such a database is available (as it is for the PAQ). In contrast, we define inductive job analysis methods as those that emphasize the collection of new, In this chapter, we first provide some basic definitions and discuss ways of conceptualizing the domain of job analysis methods, primarily to provide the context for our distinction between deductive and inductive job analysis. We follow this discussion with a description of the principal methods of evaluating the quality of a job analysis. In the third major section, we describe several widely used prototypical types of deductive job analysis. In the fourth and final section, we present some issues to consider when choosing a job analysis method for a particular use.

The Analysis of Work

In today's global economy the nature of work is changing and often requires adaptations to cultural settings, and to differing ways of getting work done. Furthermore, organizational climate and other contextual considerations frequently influence the nature of the job or its requirements. The Society for Industrial and Organizational Psychology (SIOP), when publishing a revised edition of the *Principles for the Validation and Use of Personnel Selection Procedures* (SIOP, 2003), recognized the importance of these changes for the more traditional forms of job analysis, and expanded the term *job analysis* to include analysis of work. This new term is intended to incorporate the traditional forms of job analysis, the study of competencies,[1] and the emerging emphasis on considering other work-related information about the work itself, the worker, the organization, and the work environment. The definition adopted by the *Principles* for the analysis of work is as follows: "Any method used to gain an understanding of the work behaviors and activities required, or the worker requirements (e.g., knowledge, skills, abilities, and other personal characteristics), and the context or environment in which an organization and individual may operate" (p. 66).

METHODS OF JOB ANALYSIS

At the outset, we provide a few definitions that will help communication in this arena. By *job* we mean a particular collection of work tasks that are reasonably stable and coherent across a number of job holders, and sometimes across organizations—though *occupation* is often used to refer to jobs that occur across more than one organization. Jobs are sometimes differentiated from positions, which usually are thought of as a particular instance of a job. Thus, Kelly Jones holds a position as an electrician (the job) for the XYZ Corporation. *Job families* are thought of as closely related jobs, such as a collection of clerical jobs. In effect, then, positions make up jobs, which make up job families. *Job descriptor*, or just *descriptor*, is a generic term for a variable or type of variable used to describe jobs. Frequently used descriptors are job duties, tasks, generalized work activities, knowledges, skills, and abilities. Sometimes, but not always, descriptors are accompanied by one or more rating scales that analysts use to indicate the importance, frequency, or some other characteristic of the descriptor. With these definitions in mind, we now consider various methods of job analysis.

There are several ways to classify job analysis methods. An elemental distinction is that between qualitative and quantitative analyses (McCormick, 1976, 1979). Qualitative analyses result in narrative descriptions of jobs, usually containing general descriptions of the primary purpose of the job, the major duties of the

---

[1]A competency is considered to be the "'successful' performance of a certain task or activity, or 'adequate' knowledge of a certain domain of knowledge or skill" (Shippmann et al., 2000, p. 707).

job, and some of the important qualifications for the job. Although such qualitative job descriptions are useful for providing a general sense of what is done on the job and what is required of a job holder, they have little use beyond that. Quantitative analyses, on the other hand, often provide numeric ratings of various types of job descriptors on scales like the importance of, time spent on, frequency of, or difficulty of performance. These numeric ratings generally are provided by job incumbents, job supervisors, persons responsible for training job holders, or other people with expert knowledge of the job generically called subject matter experts (SMEs). McCormick (1979) called these SMEs the agents of data collection, another way in which he differentiated job analysis methods.

As noted previously, the nature of variables used to describe the job—job descriptors—usually is an important dimension in categorizing job analysis methods. McCormick (1976) used job-oriented versus worker-oriented as a primary distinction. By *job-oriented* he meant descriptions of the work activities performed, usually in terms of what is accomplished, and sometimes how, why, and when the activities are accomplished. *Worker-oriented* activities included human behaviors performed in work, such as sensing, decision making, and the like. The final way in which McCormick described the job analysis process was in terms of the methods of collecting job analysis information. These methods include observing the job, interviewing individuals or groups of individuals performing or supervising the job, collecting and interpreting critical incidents (see chap. 3), administering open-ended and structured questionnaires, and reviewing various kinds of information or records relevant to the job. By using McCormick's categorization scheme, each instance of job analysis can be identified as quantitative or qualitative, using job-oriented or worker-oriented descriptors, relying on one or more methods of data collection, and using one or more types of agents to collect the information.

Although McCormick's (1976) system of categorizing approaches to job analysis is reasonably complete, some alternatives have been proposed. Peterson and Bownas (1982) used a 2 × 2 matrix to classify a special set of job analyses aimed at linking job-oriented (e.g., tasks) and worker-oriented (e.g., abilities) descriptors to one another. Classifying worker- and job-oriented descriptors as either *fixed* (a set of standard items intended to apply to all jobs) or *sampled* (generated specifically for each job or job type studied), they proposed four basic types of linkages. Type I includes the linkage of a fixed set of job tasks to a fixed set of worker abilities (the deductive approach), and they offered the Position Analysis Questionnaire as an example of this approach. Type IV includes the linkage of a sampled set of tasks to a sampled set of abilities (the inductive approach), one version of which is described in chapter 3. Types II and III include the use of sampled tasks and fixed abilities, and fixed tasks and sampled abilities, respectively. Both of these are combinations of inductive and deductive approaches.

Fleishman and Quaintance (1984) proposed a fourfold categorization of job analysis methods, labeled *behavioral description, behavioral requirements, ability requirements,* and *task characteristics*. In addition, they summarized a number of other approaches to thinking about job analysis and related taxonomies.

Harvey (1991) proposed a taxonomy of job analysis methods that uses two dimensions: behavioral-technological specificity and kind of scale metric. He posited three levels of specificity: high, medium, and low. For scale metric, he proposed three types:

- Cross-job relative—meaningful, level-based comparisons across jobs, such as an absolute frequency scale (once a year, once a month, once a week, etc.).
- Within-job relative—rating values expressed relative to the other descriptors (e.g., tasks) within a job, or on scales not anchored in terms of verifiable job behavior.
- Qualitative—no numerical ratings or other quantitative comparisons possible among jobs.

Using these two dimensions he described nine major types of job analysis methods, three of which are qualitative and six of which are all forms of quantitative analysis.

This brief review of ways of thinking about the various methods of job analysis is meant to drive home the point that there is no single best way for performing job analysis. Choice of a method depends to a large extent on the purpose for which a job analysis is being performed as well as on a consideration of the kinds of issues covered in the taxonomic schemes described earlier. The purposes for a job analysis might include the development of a simple narrative description for a job, identification of the tasks and skills to be covered in a formal training course, determination of the amount of pay appropriate for a job, or the best way to select future employees for a job. These purposes involve the consideration of the taxonomic issues and associated methods of analysis. A simple narrative description will not require elaborate information gathering or the collection of quantitative data using rating scales like time spent or importance, but rather can be completed with a few interviews and some observation of the job. Note, however, that the usefulness of this product is extremely limited. Identification of information for a training course requires a detailed, specific description about all or almost all the tasks done on a job and the skills required to complete those tasks, as well as quantitative information about the relative importance, time spent on, or other evaluative index that can be used to determine how essential each task and skill is for the job. Determining the appropriate level of pay for a job often requires a focus on aspects of a job that are more traitlike, such as decision making and span of control, and the comparison of those dimensions' scores across jobs—which may imply the use of absolute ratings.

In this book, we primarily are concerned with job analyses intended to provide information for the development of employee selection or assessment systems. With almost no exceptions, such job analyses will be quantitative. Beyond this basic distinction, we have chosen the fairly simple dichotomy of deductive versus inductive methods. The heart of this distinction lies in the use of an existing system of job descriptors intended to apply across jobs (deductive) or the development of a new, tailored system intended to be unique to a particular job or family of jobs (inductive). Generally speaking, the deductive analyses are more appropriate when a large-scale employee selection or promotion system is to be developed for a variety of jobs, and the inductive system is more appropriate when a single job or a small set of highly similar jobs is the focus (e.g., the electrician job used as an example throughout much of this book). Even here there are exceptions, however, because the use of job component or synthetic validation (Jeanneret, 1992; Jeanneret & Strong, 2003; Mossholder & Arvey, 1984) or validity generalization (Schmidt & Hunter, 1996) strategies for validating employee selection procedures might call for the use of deductive methods for a single job.

As we described earlier, if we consider purposes for job analysis outside of selection, then other factors come into play—such as the need for very detailed task and skill information for the development of training, an inductive approach; or the determination of appropriate pay levels for a set of jobs through a deductive approach because of the need to compare jobs on standard descriptors. If the outcomes of a job analysis are intended to fulfill two or more purposes, then a hybrid approach may be the most appropriate, for example, one that uses some, if not all, of the standard descriptors and rating scales from a deductive approach plus the identification of the job-specific tasks and skills through an inductive approach. Such an approach would fall in Type II or Type III in the Peterson and Bownas (1982) matrix. Some researchers advocate a more direct combining of the two approaches by using the standard descriptors from a deductive approach to guide the inductive development of job-specific descriptors for a particular job (Mumford, Sager, Baughman, & Childs, 1999). In the future, it may increasingly be the case that inductive methods of job analysis are carried out within the guiding framework of a given deductive system. Thus, the set of more general job descriptors found in a system such as the O*NET (Peterson, Mumford, Borman, Jeanneret, & Fleishman, 1995, 1999) or the PAQ might guide the identification of unique or more specific sets of job descriptors for a particular job or set of jobs.

EVALUATING THE QUALITY OF JOB ANALYSIS INFORMATION

Realizing that we are viewing job analysis as a methodology that goes beyond the narrative description and documentation of job responsibilities, requirements, and conditions, we necessarily are relying on some form of measurement. Accordingly, once we begin to measure job information in some quantitative manner, we can evaluate the quality of the actual job analysis data. This is important from two perspectives. First, knowing something about the quality of the job information provides feedback to the developer of that information. In effect, it tells the developer how good the effort was that led to the resulting job information. Second, it tells the user about the confidence that can be placed in the job analysis findings themselves, as well as the influence the findings might have if they were used for some human resource management purpose (e.g., to build a selection or performance appraisal system).

The quality of job analysis information can be assessed in many ways. In this section, we discuss reliability, validity, the effects of analyst influences, and sampling. Furthermore, it should be recognized that these are generic topics and evaluation strategies, applicable to all forms of quantitative job analysis including those discussed in chapter 3.

Theoretical Models of Reliability

The reliability of job analysis information describes the degree to which such information is consistent. We should determine the reliability of every job analysis procedure, if possible, because without knowledge of reliability, it is difficult to speak to the validity of the job analysis data or the utility of any results based on those job analysis data.

Consideration of reliability begins with a theoretical model. Two theoretical models have received most attention: classical reliability theory (Nunnally & Bernstein, 1994) and generalizability theory (Cronbach, Gleser, Nanda, & Rajaratnam, 1972). In classical reliability theory, one estimates the degree to which the job analysis information is free from error or noise. That portion of a job analysis score or index that is error-free is referred to as the *true score*. Consequently, reliability becomes the ratio of the true score variance to the observed score variance, which is comprised of both error and true score. In such calculations, the reliability coefficient is similar to a correlation coefficient ranging from 0.0 to 1.0. Thus, lower magnitude error variances result in higher ratio or reliability indices.

Generalizability theory also provides an appropriate model for determining the reliability of job analysis data. Using this model, one attempts to account systematically for the multiple sources of variance that affect observed scores rather than casting them as either error or true score. The sources of variance one might investigate include job analyst, type of organization, types of jobs, types of descriptors, and so forth, although it usually is not possible to analyze all the possible sources of variance at once. The notion of generalizability evolves from the strategy that a researcher measures and evaluates one or more specific sources of variance in one study, and then uses the results of that study to estimate the reliability in other, usually fairly similar, types of studies. Generalizability coefficients are obtained from these studies and are defined in terms of the extent to which job analysis scores can be generalized across the variables (e.g., analysts, organizations) that have been studied.

Classical Reliability Estimates

Reliability based on classical theory can be calculated in several ways. However, there are two fundamental designs that can guide measurement of a job analysis instrument's reliability. One design considers the degree to which two or more independent raters (analysts) agree on the analysis of a job at the same relative point in time. The second design evaluates consistency of job data over time. A third possibility is to examine the internal consistency of the fixed set of descriptors included in the job analysis instrument. Finally, the standard error of measurement also is an appropriate index in certain job analysis situations.

Interrater Agreement. Interrater agreement is usually calculated by determining the correlation between analysts across all the job descriptor items (or questions) on an instrument. The design can be confounded by whether a single position (or job incumbent) is analyzed by several job analysts or whether several positions (or job incumbents) having ostensibly the same job content are analyzed by different analysts. In all instances, differences in analyst agreement are considered to be error. When multiple and varied jobs are studied by a job analyst team, it also is possible to examine reliability for each job analysis item (as opposed to analyses conducted across all the items within an instrument). Using such a design, reliability is measured by the extent to which an item consistently differentiates across jobs, where the variability due to job differences is true score variance and the variability due to different analysts is error variance. A similar argument can be made if job analysis items are combined in some manner to form a dimension or component. The reliability of that component can be derived across a sample of jobs using an analysis of variance paradigm that considers job variability due to analysts as error variance.

As one develops an overall job analysis data collection strategy, it is important to consider how reliability is going to be assessed. We present the following examples to give the reader an appreciation of the options:

- Analyst pair analyzes one job—We use the term analyst to indicate individuals who complete a job analysis instrument. It is recognized that such individuals could be incumbents, supervisors, trainees, process engineers, or others who have sound knowledge of the jobs being analyzed. When two analysts independently analyze the same job, the degree to which their scores agree is interrater reliability. When there are a number of analyst pairs, their respective reliability results can be aggregated to calculate an overall interrater reliability coefficient for the job being studied.
- Many analysts analyze many jobs—Unless every analyst analyzes every job, which is unlikely and probably not very efficient, then one would calculate all possible pairwise coefficients within each job and then aggregate the data across all the jobs.

The interested reader is referred to an article by Geyer, Hice, Hawk, Boese, and Brannon (1989), who studied the reliabilities of ratings made by four experienced job analysts who independently studied 20 diverse jobs using standard U.S. Employment Service job analysis procedures (U.S. Department of Labor, 1991a). These procedures categorize job information into the *Dictionary of Occupational Titles* (U.S. Department of Labor, 1991b) format. Results indicated that reliabilities calculated using both interrater reliability and analysis of variance models were generally high (.79 to .98) for work functions, educational development, aptitudes, temperaments, and interests. Reliabilities were often moderate (.40 to .75) for physical and perceptual job demands. More recently, several studies of military occupations presented reliability estimates similar to those just described for a number of different kinds of descriptors and associated rating scales (Bennett, Ruck, & Page, 1996). Dierdorff and Wilson (2003) conducted a meta-analysis of job analysis data and found reliability for task data to be .77. For more generalized (generic) data collection methods the reliability was .61. Such research provides a benchmark that can be used to evaluate the consistency of other job analysis data, especially when obtained by deductive procedures.

Rate-Rerate Reliability. The second fundamental design for measuring the reliability of job analysis data under the classical theory examines the consistency of the job information over time. It is known as rate-rerate reliability. Assuming there is no reason for the job content to change from Time 1 to Time 2 (say, over a 4-week period), then job analysis scores produced by the same set of analysts should be in agreement across that time frame. Any differences in job analysis scores indicate error in the data. Sometimes the resulting calculation is referred to as a stability coefficient (see McCormick, 1979, p. 133). The calculations can be done using product-moment correlations of scores across the two time periods, or by using analysis of variance, just as is done for interrater agreement calculations.

Internal Consistency. A third method for estimating reliability that evolves from classical theory is known as internal consistency (Nunnally & Bernstein, 1994). Under this method, one considers as error the sampling of descriptors in a job analysis instrument. The design necessary to calculate an internal consistency index (such as coefficient alpha or a split-half coefficient) requires a job analysis instrument that uses many descriptors to measure a particular component of work, and many job analysts who rate those descriptors. Because the issue of internal consistency of the descriptors typically is not a critical one in this context, job analysts seldom attempt to assess it. Consequently, internal consistency reliability is not an especially useful index for job analysis instruments in the way that it is for various tests of individual abilities.

Standard Error of Measurement. A fourth useful statistic that reflects the consistency of certain types of job analysis data is the standard error of measurement. This index is derived, for example, when a particular job has been repeatedly analyzed, perhaps in numerous organizations with the same job analysis instrument. Calculation of a true job analysis score for each descriptor of the job (e.g., job dimension or factor) would be expressed in terms of the standard deviation and reliability of the observed scores. The standard error of measurement then establishes a confidence band (range of error) about a true score, and given a bandwidth of (±) one standard error, about 68% of the observed scores should fall within that band.

Generalizability Theory and Reliability.   As previously mentioned, estimates of reliability based on generalizability theory attempt to partition variance arising from multiple sources that may influence the quality of job analysis data. The analysis of variance design requires those developing a job analysis data collection process to consider the sources of variance that are important and should be measured, as well as the universe to which the job analysis scores will be generalized. Furthermore, not only are individual sources of variation considered, but the design also allows for the evaluation of their interactions. Perhaps the two sources of variance most often of concern would be analysts and time. Using a generalizability approach allows the inclusion of both sources in the calculation of one generalizability coefficient, unlike the separate calculations of interrater agreement and stability coefficients that are necessary when using classical reliability approaches.

Unfortunately, there are relatively few instances in which job analysts have used generalizability theory to design a reliability study. However, a comprehensive study by Van Iddekinge, Putka, Raymark, and Eidson (2005) is noteworthy. Their study examined sources of error variance in ratings of knowledge, skills, abilities and other characteristics (KSAOs) by three levels of raters (incumbents, first-level supervisors, and second-level supervisors) across five organizations for the job of customer service manager. Their customized questionnaire assessed 118 KSAOs grouped into 10 dimensions. Results indicated that most of the variance in ratings (70%–80%) was due to differences in how raters rank-ordered the KSAOs. There was little variance due to the level of the rater or the organizational setting. Practically speaking, this meant that the observed importance rating of a KSAO (i.e., its ranking with regard to the other KSAOs) accurately represented its standing across all five organizations and all raters—it mattered not if raters were incumbents or supervisors, or from which organization the raters were drawn. If, on the other hand, the type of rater and organization had accounted for significant amounts of variance, then the ranking of a KSAO would have to be computed for each type of rater for each organization. This example illustrates the value of the generalizability approach for examining specific sources of variance in job analysis data, and more directly eliminating potential error sources for a particular application.

Validity

When we ask if some set of job analysis data is valid, we want to know if the data adequately reflect and actually measure the job characteristics of interest as they in fact occur. In essence, the concept of validity requires us to examine the correctness of the information obtained with our job analysis methodology. However, it is not a process that is often completed in a very rigorous manner. That is to say, we typically assume the job analysis method asks the right questions, and we then are only concerned with observing consistent (reliable) answers. In many respects, our assumptions about validity are warranted, and it rarely is necessary to reaffirm the validity of our data through a post hoc validity study. The reasons for this assertion are described later, as we examine certain validity concepts and strategies in some detail.

Content Validity. One establishes content validity by directly sampling from the domain of interest and then incorporating the material sampled into the design of the instrument that will be used for measurement purposes. Within the field of job analysis, a content validity strategy is often followed at the time of instrument development. When inductive instruments are prepared (e.g., the Job Analysis Questionnaire described in chap. 3), they usually evolve from direct observations of the work and from interviews with SMEs. Furthermore, such instruments are often pilot tested and provide other means for respondents to be sure that the job content domain has been adequately addressed. For nomothetic or, in our vernacular, deductive instruments that are intended to have general applicability to the analysis of a broad spectrum of occupations, the job analysis items typically are based on work activities that are broadly defined and have their foundation in many, if not most, well-known or high-occupancy jobs. Most of these types of instruments are based on the incorporation of results of a large number of inductive job analyses and the use of theoretical knowledge derived from research in psychological or other relevant sciences.

If one is interested in trying to establish the content validity of job analysis findings in some methodical way, there are alternatives. One possibility is to have SMEs independently confirm the representativeness and accuracy of job analysis outputs. A second more rigorous approach may establish linkages between job analysis outcomes and objective records of productivity. For example, in many production jobs, employee time is charged to specific activity accounts for job costing purposes. Such records could be used as criteria to study the reasonableness of incumbent ratings of time spent on various job tasks or activities. Incidentally, although studies of this topic are few in number, the reported results are not always comforting. Whereas McCormick (1979) mentioned a U.S. Air Force study that was very positive in confirming job analysis results, Harvey's (1991) citations were more disconcerting.

Construct Validity. In a classical construct validity model, a new measure of a construct is compared to an established and accepted measure of that same construct and, if possible, to accepted measures of dissimilar, confounding constructs. If the degree of congruence (often measured with correlation coefficients) is high between the old and new measures of the construct, then the construct validity of the new measure has been established to an appreciable degree. The case is further strengthened if there is low congruence between the new measure and the measures of the dissimilar, confounding constructs. Although not especially efficient, it is possible to compare results from multiple methods of job analysis and determine their similarity. If one method is well established and a second method is being used for the first time, such a technique could document the construct validity of the newer measure if comparable results were achieved. One example of such a strategy was reported by Harvey, Friedman, Hakel, and Cornelius (1988), who demonstrated the comparability of data obtained with the Job Element Inventory (JEI; Cornelius & Hakel, 1978) to that collected with the *PAQ*. A more recent study (Manson, Levine, & Brannick, 2000) following a multitrait-multimethod design demonstrated a high degree of convergent validity for several different task inventory ratings (e.g., time spent, difficulty to learn).

Summary

Although it is possible to design job analysis methods so that one can evaluate the validity of the method or data resulting from application of the method, such efforts are seldom carried out. In many instances, the process could be redundant and might appear to confirm the obvious. Furthermore, scholars in the field of job analysis such as McCormick (1979) are content to rely on reliability information and assume validity is acceptable if reliability is reasonable. We add that such an assumption is more likely warranted if care has been taken in developing the job analysis method and instruments from the outset.

Other Strategies for Evaluating the Quality of Job Analysis Information

Four other strategies may be useful when evaluating certain sets of job analysis information. Again, these strategies may be applied to both deductive and inductive methodologies.

Descriptive Statistics.   The most straightforward descriptive indices can be very informative about the quality of job analysis data. One possibility is to evaluate the frequency distribution of responses (or percentage of responses) given to the various options of a descriptor scale (e.g., across the options of a frequency scale for performance of job tasks, like "once a year," "once a month," "once a week," and "once a day"). Comparisons can be made of the observed distribution to other distributions from similar studies or databases of job analytic information. Also, simply viewing the distribution in terms of reasonableness relative to rational expectations can be informative. Departures from prior findings or expectations should be investigated and clarified. There often is a special circumstance that explains the differences, but if no explanation can be found, then there may be some inadequacies with the job analysis.

Calculating the means and standard deviations for descriptor responses can be equally informative. Again, both statistics should be comparable to known indices or expectations. Furthermore, standard deviations should be viewed in terms of how much variability there might be in the content of positions that have been merged (averaged) for analytical purposes. In fact, some researchers question the advisability of routinely using mean scores to eliminate the within-job variability that typically is observed in job analysis ratings (Harvey, 1991). The basic argument that opposes aggregating to a mean score is that it really is not error variance that is being discarded. Therefore, the resulting mean score profile does not correctly represent any of the positions included within the job analysis. Although our experience is not this extreme, it certainly is more comforting if one can compare observed mean scores with an existing database of information and verify the reasonableness of one's data. Such a strategy is particularly appropriate with deductive methods that have well-established databases such as those available for the *PAQ* or the Generalized Work Inventory (GWI; Cunningham & Ballentine, 1982).

Multivariate Analyses.   Various kinds of multivariate analyses are often conducted on job analysis data. They usually are conducted to provide summaries of data at a higher level for one or another applied purpose. Factor analysis is used to identify higher level organizations of job descriptors to use in job descriptions or in other analyses. Cluster analysis is used to aggregate positions or jobs into higher level job families for any of a variety of purposes—to develop selection procedures or to form training curricula for related jobs. Discriminant analyses are used to identify job descriptors that contribute the most to differentiating among jobs. Each of these techniques has associated with it a considerable body of knowledge about its application and interpretation. From an evaluative perspective, these multivariate analyses should yield interpretable, rational results only if the underlying data are themselves meaningful. Thus, for example, if a factor analysis has been completed in a methodologically sound manner, but the outcome lacks meaning, then there is a strong likelihood that the original data were inadequate in some way. Additionally, with a factor analytic study one should be able to explain a reasonable portion of the variability of the descriptors being analyzed, and if this is not the case, there may be a concern about the representativeness of the underlying data. Similar comments apply to the other techniques. If clusters of jobs are unexpected or nonsensical, then the underlying job analysis data are probably not adequate for the purposes of the clustering and may cast doubt on the general usefulness of the data.

We raise a note of caution here, however. The use of multivariate analyses is difficult and they must be conducted with extreme care. The inappropriate choice of methods of multivariate analyses can lead to unexpected or nonsensical results, even if the underlying job analysis data are adequate. Further treatment of these topics can be found in a number of excellent sources (e.g., Aldenderfer & Blashfield, 1984; Cohen & Cohen, 1983; Harman, 1976; Harris, 1985).

Potential Influences on Accuracy of Job Analysis Information.   A third strategy is to evaluate purposefully one or more influences that might be hypothesized to alter or bias the quality of job analysis data. Morgeson and Campion (1997) postulated a number of potential social (e.g., impression management, peer influence) and cognitive (e.g., limited information processing, carelessness) sources leading to inaccuracy of job analysis data. They noted that the likelihood of these influences affecting the accuracy of the job analysis results is a function of what method is being used and how it is being implemented. The more structured and clear-cut the job analysis, the less likely there will be any negative influences.

Morgeson and Campion (1997) also noted that demographic (e.g., age, sex) variables have been studied, but stated that any differences that have been found have been small and difficult to interpret (i.e., whether the differences are due to the attribute of interest or are real cross-position differences). The reality for the user is that there are a multitude of potential sources of inaccuracy. Morgeson and Campion hypothesized 38 social-cognitive sources with their likely effects (e.g., influence on interrater reliability, completeness of job information). In a given job analysis it would be impossible to control for all of these variables. Hence, the user should consider what would be practical in a particular situation and use sound professional judgment when selecting a job analysis data collection strategy.

Sampling.   A fourth method for enhancing the quality of job analysis data is the use of sampling to exert control over analyst or other unwanted influences. When any strategy is used other than implementing a job analysis method that encompasses 100% of a defined analyst set (i.e., those who either perform the jobs or have knowledge about the jobs being studied), then some form of sampling occurs. In turn, the sampling strategy and final sample representativeness will influence the quality of job analysis data obtained regardless of the specific methodology implemented. In most job analysis studies, the sampling strategy is influenced by a number of variables. Some of the most important variables are as follows: Who comprises the job analyst set (incumbents, supervisors, some other SMEs, combinations thereof)? Is the focal job made up of a single incumbent or does it have many incumbents? If the latter, how many? What geographical and functional divisions should be considered? What shifts do job incumbents work? Are there differences in the kinds of technology and equipment used?

In consideration of these variables, a sampling plan should be designed that provides for a representative and comprehensive analysis of the jobs under study. Subsequently, after the job analysis data collection is complete, one should be able to document that the sampling plan has, in fact, been met. Generally there are not a lot of hard and fast rules that can be followed in making sampling plan decisions. McCormick and Jeanneret (1988) prepared several guidelines for sampling when studying jobs with the *PAQ* that might work well for many deductive approaches. These guidelines included the following:

- Obtain information about the organization from the top down to understand the functioning and distribution of jobs within an organizational unit.
- For a large (n = 100+) multi-incumbent job, a 10% to 20% sample should be considered.
- For a small (n = 10 to 100) multi-incumbent job, a 50% or larger sample should be considered.

- For a very small (n < 10) multi-incumbent job, a sample of as many incumbents as feasible should be obtained.
- The rule of three should be followed whenever possible, which means there should be at least three respondents completing the job analysis questionnaire if other than trained job analysts are performing the analyses.

EXAMPLES OF DEDUCTIVE JOB ANALYSIS METHODS

There are many examples of deductive job analyses that could be chosen. We present two such examples in some detail, and then identify other systems that are available.

The Occupational Information Network (O*NET)

Our first example is the Occupational Information Network (O*NET). We have chosen it because it is a national occupational database and it contains virtually all the major kinds of job descriptors. More detailed information than discussed here can be obtained from the O*NET Center Web site (http://www.onetcenter.org).

Background. The O*NET replaces the *Dictionary of Occupational Titles* (*DOT*; U.S. Department of Labor, 1991a). It was developed to implement the recommendations of the Advisory Panel for the Dictionary of Occupational Titles (1993) that was formed to review the DOT. The recommendations proposed a considerable expansion of the kinds of job descriptors included in the system, the use of an electronic database as the primary repository for the occupational information, the use of questionnaire survey methodology as the primary mode of data collection, and timelier updating and maintenance of the database. A prototype O*NET was developed and released in 1998 and its development was described comprehensively in Peterson, Mumford, Borman, Jeanneret, and Fleishman (1999). The O*NET was developed with the philosophy that a national occupational database must be continuously updated and improved, and it has undergone further development and refinement since that time.

Description and Organization. Figure 2.1 shows the job description content model as it was implemented for the prototype version of the O*NET. The first thing to notice about this model is the large number of descriptor types that it contains and the way those descriptors are organized. There are six larger domains of descriptors (e.g., worker requirements) with constituent descriptor types within each domain (e.g., basic skills within worker requirements). Each of these descriptor types is appropriate for some uses of job analysis, but not for all. For example, abilities and experiences are likely to be most useful for employee selection purposes, but of little use for training. Generalized work activities and

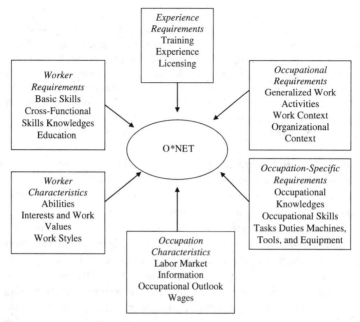

FIGURE 2.1   O*NET content model.

knowledges are likely to be useful for training purposes. Skills may be useful for both selection and training purposes. Generalized work activities and work context are likely very useful for job evaluation or pay purposes. All of the occupation-specific descriptor types would be useful for training and performance evaluation purposes. These multiple windows allow all users of job analysis information to select the appropriate type of descriptor for their purpose. The worker requirements and worker characteristics domains of the O*NET contain the kinds of descriptors referred to most often as worker-oriented, whereas the occupational requirements, occupation-specific requirements, and occupation characteristics contain the kinds of descriptors referred to as job-oriented. The experience requirements domain contains descriptors that sit between these two more general areas. All of the descriptors, with the exception of those in the occupation-specific domain, are designed to be cross-occupational—that is, they could be expected to apply to many different jobs, but in varying degrees of importance, frequency, or level required. Definitions of all the descriptor types and the individual descriptors themselves, with their associated rating scales as used in the prototype version, can be found in Peterson et al. (1999). The organizational scheme of the content model, shown in Fig. 2.1, is carried through in the electronic database that is the primary product of the O*NET.

As noted previously, further development of the O*NET has occurred since release of the prototype version and development continues to occur. The content model, as depicted in Fig. 2.1, has largely remained the same, but there have been changes in the wording of the particular descriptors within a domain, the scales used to collect data for a domain, and the presentation or display of the scales on the data collection instruments (e.g., Boese, Lewis, Frugoli, & Litwin, 2001; Hubbard et al., 2000). Moreover, the O*NET now uses the Standard Occupational Classification (Executive Office of the President, Office of Management and Budget, 2000) to identify specific occupations.

Rating Scales and Available Data.   When all the descriptors and their associated rating scales are considered, the O*NET system contains several hundred separate bits of information about each occupation. These data are collected on structured questionnaires from job incumbents, supervisors, or analysts using a variety of rating scales, including the level or complexity of a descriptor required to perform the job, the importance of the descriptor, the frequency of performance of the descriptor, and others.[2] The mean ratings, computed across all the available raters for an occupation, are the primary data entered into the O*NET database. The actual information displayed for users may be different due to transformations intended to make the information more accessible or understandable,[3] as illustrated later in the description of the O*NET database information currently made available to interested users.

There are two primary ways to use the O*NET: One way is simply to make an inquiry of the existing database about an occupational title of interest. The alternative is to complete the O*NET questionnaire(s) for a specific occupation and then examine the results. Of course, comparisons can be made between new data obtained about an occupation with the data that exist in the O*NET database. A sophisticated user also might consider collecting job analysis data using the O*NET for a number of jobs that have some communality in order to study the structure of the job family or build career ladders.

The O*NET offers what is labeled a "Details Report" for the occupation being studied. Included in the outputs are listings of tasks, knowledges, abilities, generalized

---

[2]The O*NET Center will provide generic forms of questionnaires to any user wishing to collect occupational information. These questionnaires can be modified to meet specific needs by adding or revising questions and rating scales. The O*NET Center cautions users about deleting questions.

[3]According to the O*NET Consortium Web Site, some of the original scale scores are converted according to the following formula: $S = ((O - L) / (H - L)) * 100$; where S is the standardized score, O is the original rating score on one of the O*NET scales, L is the lowest possible score on the rating scale used, and H is the highest possible score on the rating scale used. For example, an original Importance rating score of 3 is converted to a standardized score of 50 (i.e., $50 = [3 - 1] / [5 - 1] * 100$).

work activities, work context, interests, work values and work needs. For all of these descriptors the rating scale values are presented both numerically and graphically. Additionally, information on education, overall experience, and job training is contained in a report section labeled "Job Zone." Occupational examples also are provided for the zone, and distributions are presented that indicate the percentages of respondents reported for various levels of education, training, and experience. Two final items of information are included in the report: a link to wages and employment data, and a set of related occupations.

Figure 2.2 presents an abbreviated output for the occupation of electrician. These results are a summary of the individual analyses that have been included in the O*NET database for the occupation.[4] A user could compare the results of a specific job analysis of an electrician job to the profile for that job as presented in the O*NET Details Report. A user also could compare the results of various maintenance and construction jobs in an organization to study the similarities and differences. Finally, it is possible to examine the O*NET database on an individual descriptor basis. For example, one could ask for a listing of occupational titles rank-ordered on importance for a particular skill or ability. Then one could determine where the electrician occupation was located in the world of work on the particular skill or ability of interest.

It is intended that a large number of applications will be developed that use O*NET data, including job descriptions, job classification schemes for different purposes, selection, training, vocational counseling, and others. Many of these applications, like those that were created for the DOT, will undoubtedly be developed by independent vendors.

Maintenance of the O*NET Database.   One of the most valuable aspects of the O*NET is the intended continuous maintenance of the content model, as dictated by scientific advances in job analysis, and evolution of the data populating the database. The National Center of O*NET Development of the U.S. Department of Labor published a list of the occupations that will be included with future updates of the O*NET. This publication, as well as a host of other information about the development, maintenance, and future plans for the O*NET, can be found at the O*NET Web site.

Reliability.   In the initial study of the prototype O*NET, sufficient data to conduct reliability and other analyses were collected on about 30 occupations (Peterson, Borman, Hanson, & Kubisiak, 1999; Peterson et al., 1996). The primary statistic computed was the interrater agreement coefficient. There were nine questionnaires completed by incumbents, and the coefficients for the various rating

---

[4]These data were obtained on October 20, 2005. Over time these data may change as new analyses are added.

Details Report for: 47-2111.00 - Electricians

Install, maintain, and repair electrical wiring, equipment, and fixtures. Ensure that work is in accordance with relevant codes. May install or service street lights, intercom systems, or electrical control systems.

Sample of reported job titles: Electrician, Journeyman Electrician, Inside Wireman, Maintenance Electrician

Descriptor Type and Rating Scale Value	Descriptors with Definitions

Importance   **Task**

77   Assemble, install, test, and maintain electrical or electronic wiring, equipment, appliances, apparatus, and fixtures, using hand tools and power tools.

76   Diagnose malfunctioning systems, apparatus, and components, using test equipment and hand tools, to locate the cause of a breakdown and correct the problem.

76   Connect wires to circuit breakers, transformers, or other components.

75   Inspect electrical systems, equipment, and components to identify hazards, defects, and the need for adjustment or repair, and to ensure compliance with codes.

Importance   **Knowledge**

67   **Building and Construction** — Knowledge of materials, methods, and the tools involved in the construction or repair of houses, buildings, or other structures such as highways and roads.

67   **Mechanical** — Knowledge of machines and tools, including their designs, uses, repair, and maintenance.

62   **Mathematics** — Knowledge of arithmetic, algebra, geometry, calculus, statistics, and their applications.

60   **English Language** — Knowledge of the structure and content of the English language including the meaning and spelling of words, rules of composition, and grammar.

Importance   **Skill**

68   **Installation** — Installing equipment, machines, wiring, or programs to meet specifications.

64   **Active Listening** — Giving full attention to what other people are saying, taking time to understand the points being made, asking questions as appropriate, and not interrupting at inappropriate times.

64   **Reading Comprehension** — Understanding written sentences and paragraphs in work related documents.

Details Report for: 47-2111.00 - Electricians

Descriptor Type and Rating Scale Value	Descriptors with Definitions

64 — **Troubleshooting** — Determining causes of operating errors and deciding what to do about it.

Importance   **Ability**

81 — **Arm-Hand Steadiness** — The ability to keep your hand and arm steady while moving your arm or while holding your arm and hand in one position.

81 — **Problem Sensitivity** — The ability to tell when something is wrong or is likely to go wrong. It does not involve solving the problem, only recognizing there is a problem.

75 — **Finger Dexterity** — The ability to make precisely coordinated movements of the fingers of one or both hands to grasp, manipulate, or assemble very small objects.

75 — **Near Vision** — The ability to see details at close range (within a few feet of the observer).

Importance   **Work Activity**

84 — **Making Decisions and Solving Problems** — Analyzing information and evaluating results to choose the best solution and solve problems.

83 — **Communicating with Supervisors, Peers, or Subordinates** — Providing information to supervisors, co-workers, and subordinates by telephone, in written form, e-mail, or in person.

77 — **Performing General Physical Activities** — Performing physical activities that require considerable use of your arms and legs and moving your whole body, such as climbing, lifting, balancing, walking, stooping, and handling of materials.

- climb ladders, scaffolding, or utility or telephone poles
- install/string electrical or electronic cable or wiring
- move or fit heavy objects

Context   **Work Context**

96 — **Freedom to Make Decisions** — How much decision-making freedom, without supervision, does the job offer?

94 — **Spend Time Standing** — How much does this job require standing?

88 — **Contact with Others** — How much does this job require the worker to be in contact with others (face-to-face, by telephone, or otherwise) in order to perform it?

Details Report for: 47-2111.00 - Electricians

Descriptor Type and Rating Scale Value	Descriptors with Definitions

88 ▰▰▰▰▰▰   **Structured versus Unstructured Work** — To what extent is this job structured for the worker, rather than allowing the worker to determine tasks, priorities, and goals?

Occupational Interest

Interest

94 ▰▰▰▰▰▰   **Realistic** — Realistic occupations frequently involve work activities that include practical, hands-on problems and solutions. They often deal with plants, animals, and real-world materials like wood, tools, and machinery. Many of the occupations require working outside, and do not involve a lot of paperwork or working closely with others.

Importance   **Work Style**

75 ▰▰▰▰▰   **Attention to Detail** — Job requires being careful about detail and thorough in completing work tasks.

74 ▰▰▰▰▰   **Dependability** — Job requires being reliable, responsible, and dependable, and fulfilling obligations.

70   **Initiative** — Job requires a willingness to take on responsibilities and challenges.

Extent   **Work Value**

66 ▰▰▰▰▰   **Achievement** — Occupations that satisfy this work value are results oriented and allow employees to use their strongest abilities, giving them a feeling of accomplishment. Corresponding needs are Ability Utilization and Achievement.

Extent   **Work Need**

78 ▰▰▰▰▰   **Moral Values** — Workers on this job are never pressured to do things that go against their sense of right and wrong.

72 ▰▰▰▰▰   **Ability Utilization** — Workers on this job make use of their individual abilities.

62 ▰▰▰▰▰   **Activity** — Workers on this job are busy all the time.

62 ▰▰▰▰▰   **Compensation** — Workers on this job are paid well in comparison with other workers.

Job Zone Three: **Medium Preparation Needed**

Overall Experience   Previous work-related skill, knowledge, or experience is required for these occupations. For example, an electrician must have completed three or four years of apprenticeship or several years of vocational training, and often must have passed a licensing exam, in order to perform the job.

2. JOB ANALYSIS: DEDUCTIVE METHODS

Details Report for: 47-2111.00 - Electricians

Descriptor Type and Rating Scale Value	Descriptors with Definitions
Job Training	Employees in these occupations usually need one or two years of training involving both on-the-job experience and informal training with experienced workers.
Education	Most occupations in this zone require training in vocational schools, related on-the-job experience, or an associate's degree. Some may require a bachelor's degree.

FIGURE 2.2   Selected descriptor results for electrician job from O*NET database.

scales used in the nine questionnaires ranged from a low of .45 to a high of .87, based on approximately 10 raters per occupation. Estimates for the case of 30 raters, the targeted, desired number of raters, were mostly in the .90s. Aggregate scores for the O*NET descriptors were formed by computing mean values for the descriptors that were categorized into the next highest level of each domain's hierarchy. These results were very similar to those for the base-level descriptors, except that the coefficients generally were a bit higher. The analyses also showed that the level and importance scales prominently used in the O*NET were approximately equal in terms of reliability. Ratings from trained job analysts, used in the interim database, showed comparable or higher levels of interrater agreement in those O*NET domains and occupations for which both the analyst and incumbent ratings were available. The two sets of ratings showed sufficient agreement to warrant use of the trained analyst ratings on an interim basis. (The average correlations of the mean ratings of the analysts with the mean ratings of the incumbents ranged from .53 to .74 across the common O*NET domains.)

*O*NET Application.* The O*NET Center envisions a number of human resource management applications, and one of those is to identify criteria to guide selection and placement decisions. An employer would expect such criteria to be valid, as the term *valid* is used in the *Uniform Guidelines on Employee Selection Procedures* (1978) and the *Principles for the Validation and Use of Personnel Selection Procedures* (SIOP, 2003). An initial study (Jeanneret & Strong, 2003) of the O*NET generalized work activities indicated that these descriptors would be predictive of cognitive abilities (e.g., verbal and numeric aptitudes), perceptual measures (e.g., spatial aptitude, form perception), and even physical capabilities (e.g., motor coordination, finger dexterity). The importance of this research indicates that the O*NET data can directly lead to estimates of validity[5] for various measures that would be appropriate for use in employee selection.

The Position Analysis Questionnaire (PAQ)

Description.   The *PAQ*[6] was designed with the specific intent of developing a generic, worker-oriented, structured questionnaire that would provide quantitative information about a job undergoing analysis. The PAQ is generic in that it can be used to analyze virtually any job in any industry across the entire labor force. Since its inception in 1969, the PAQ has been used in hundreds of thousands of job analyses across the entire labor force, including all of the major jobs found in the *DOT*. The results of these job analyses are retained in a comprehensive database.

The PAQ is worker-oriented because it focuses on the human behaviors or requirements that are involved in work activities. This perspective is in contrast to job-oriented procedures that describe the tasks, duties, technologies, or outcomes of jobs (see McCormick, 1979, for a thorough discussion of these differences). Questions on the PAQ are organized in a format whereby the respondent job analyst uses a rating scale to analyze the involvement of each of 187 questions in the job being analyzed. Any job is analyzed with the same set of questions, although not all questions will be applicable to a given job. The PAQ provides structured information about a job, because the rating scale responses are scored with research-based algorithms that compare the results for the job of interest to the master database of jobs. In turn, the job analysis results, which are expressed in standard score and percentile forms, can be interpreted both ipsatively and normatively.

Organization of The PAQ.   The questions in the PAQ are organized into six divisions:

1. Information input: Where and how does the worker get the information that is used in performing the job?
2. Mental processes: What reasoning, decision-making, planning, and information-processing activities are involved in performing the job?
3. Work output: What physical activities does the worker perform and what types of tools or devices are used?
4. Relationships with other persons: What relationships with other people are required in performing the job?

---

[5]This form of validity is known as job component validity and is described in detail in Jeanneret and Strong (2003).

[6]The PAQ is copyrighted and trademarked by the Purdue Research Foundation. It is published by PAQ Services, Inc. (http://www.paq.com), an affiliate of the Economic Research Institute (ERI).

5. Job context: In what physical and social contexts is the work performed?
6. Other job characteristics: What activities, conditions, or characteristics other than those described earlier are relevant to the job?

The first three divisions include questions that characterize specific types of job activities within three major categories that exist in virtually every job—receiving information from the job environment, mentally processing that information (typically leading up to a decision), and taking some form of action or creating some work output. The other three divisions characterize the involvement with others, the work context, and the demands of the job.

PAQ Descriptors.   Each PAQ question describes a general work behavior or activity, work condition, or job characteristic. In most cases, examples (often job titles or major job features) illustrate the central idea of the job descriptor. However, these examples only help illustrate the intent of the descriptors and represent only a few of the possible examples that could characterize these descriptors. A job analysis manual provides extensive information on how to interpret the PAQ questions (McPhail, Jeanneret, McCormick, & Mecham, 1991).

Rating Scales for PAQ Descriptors.   A rating given by the analyst determines the relevance of a PAQ descriptor to the job being analyzed. Several different rating scales are used throughout the questionnaire, and directions are provided for each particular type of scale. The types of rating scales include extent of use, importance, time, possibility of occurrence, and applicability (i.e., a dichotomous index).

Reliability of PAQ Data.   Reliability has been determined for the ratings of each PAQ question across all 187 descriptors by having two analysts study the same job and independently complete a PAQ. The ratings were then correlated, and the averages for pairs of analysts were accumulated across a wide range of job analyses to obtain an average reliability coefficient. The average reliability coefficients have typically been in the 0.80s and even as high as 0.90 across 303 different positions. Moreover, studies have been completed regarding the rate-rerate reliability of the PAQ, and the results reveal reliabilities in the high 0.70s and 0.80s. These reliability results tend to be consistent whether the analysts are incumbents, supervisors, or independent analysts, although job incumbents and their supervisors do give higher ratings on the descriptors than do independent analysts. (For more information on the reliability of PAQ data, see Dierdorff & Wilson, 2003; McCormick & Jeanneret, 1988; McCormick, Mecham, & Jeanneret, 1977; Smith & Hakel, 1979.)

PAQ Job Dimensions.   Factor analysis (specifically, principal components analysis) has been used to derive a set of dimensions of human behaviors involved in job activities, and these dimensions can characterize the structure of work (McCormick & Jeanneret, 1988). Several independent studies have replicated the PAQ dimensions. The set of dimensions used to derive various PAQ outputs (see later discussion) is based on a sample of 2,200 jobs that characterizes the composition of the U.S. labor force. Each job analyzed with the PAQ is scored in terms of the job dimensions, and results are provided in terms of both standard scores and percentiles.

PAQ Outputs. The PAQ dimensions serve as the common denominators for comparing the similarities and differences between and among jobs, and for estimating the personal requirements and worth (job evaluation values) of jobs. Specific outputs that can be derived include the following:

- Estimates of the requirements for various mental (i.e., verbal, numerical, etc.), perceptual, psychomotor, and physical abilities.
- Estimates of the requirements for certain types of temperaments and interests.
- Estimates of the worth of a job (expressed as job evaluation points and a prestige score) and the probability that a job is exempt from the Fair Labor Standards Act (1938).
- Job families that can form career progressions or establish the basis for grouping jobs for some purpose

These outputs can be used to develop or support a number of human resource management systems. Examples include developing a selection process, designing a compensation plan, preparing a performance appraisal system, or instituting a career development and vocational counseling program. More descriptive information on the derivation and application of PAQ data can be found in Jeanneret (1988) and McCormick and Jeanneret (1988). A set of outputs for the job of electrician is presented in Fig. 2.3, including a job dimensions profile useful for salary determination, a selection report useful for identifying possible employee selection tools, and a job requirements report useful for identifying attributes needed for successful performance as an electrician. The same types of uses can be made of the PAQ profiles that were described for the O*NET.

Other Deductive Job Analysis Instruments

To provide the reader with a wide range of options that might be useful for a specific job analysis study, we have compiled information on instruments that fit our definition of a deductive job analysis method. By no means is it our position that we have identified all of the available instruments, nor is it our intention to endorse any method. In fact, it is important to recognize that we have obtained the information provided here directly from materials written by the developers or publishers. In some instances the information may not be completely up to date or otherwise may have changed. Accordingly, we would recommend contacting the developer or publisher for more detailed information about an instrument of interest before making either a positive or negative selection decision.

Table 2.1 provides the following information about each deductive job analysis instrument:

- Instrument name: full name as well as acronym, if used.
- Types of job: the categories for which the instrument is relevant.
- Types of descriptors: the types and number of questions (items) included in the instrument.
- Types of analyst: individuals whom the developer or publisher indicates should complete the instrument.
- Applications: uses the developer or publisher has intended for the job analysis results obtained with the instrument.
- Database available: whether or not a database of job analysis information is maintained.
- Year developed: the year the instrument was developed.
- Availability: name of developer or publisher who can be contacted for more information about the instrument.

ISSUES IN CHOOSING JOB ANALYSIS METHODS

To select from the number of available job analysis systems and methodologies, the user must make a series of decisions about the nature of the job analysis that is to be undertaken. In addition, comparisons must inevitably be made among particular job analysis options that meet the general requirements of the planned job analysis. There is no single way to go about this process, but there are some issues that should be considered along the way. We offer one particular set of ordered questions as an illustration. Other questions or differing orders of questions certainly are possible. We are assuming in the following that the decision has already been made to use one of the deductive methods as opposed to the inductive method. The inductive method is generally preferred when it is desirable, for whatever reason, to generate descriptors from scratch for a particular job or job family, and it is described in the next chapter.

1. What is the purpose of the job analysis? This question is offered by most authors as the single most important consideration in choosing a job analysis method. Often, though, little more is said. In general terms, the end uses of job analysis information can be job classification, employee selection or placement, performance appraisal, job evaluation, job design, disability accommodation, training development, and related human resources management programs. The person responsible for conducting a job analysis should attempt to get as complete a statement as possible about the immediate, short-term, and long-term uses of the job analysis information.

Position Analysis Questionnaire (PAQ) Output for the Job of

Electrician (DOT Code: 829.261.018)

Job Dimensions Profile

Dimension Name	Score	SEM	Percentile
Having decision, communication and general responsibility	−0.39	0.18	36
Operating machines and/or equipment	1.04	0.20	86
Performing clerical and/or related activities	−0.34	0.35	38
Performing technical and/or related activities	.068	0.34	76
Performing services and/or related activities	−1.03	0.26	17
Other work schedules vs. working regular day schedule	−1.12	0.30	15
Performing routine and/or repetitive activities	−0.32	0.29	39
Being aware of work environments	−0.60	0.22	29
Engaging in physical activities	0.07	0.33	53
Supervising/directing/estimating	−0.62	0.31	28
Public and/or customer and/or related contacts	−0.58	0.34	20
Working in an unpleasant/hazardous/ demanding environment	0.73	0.31	77
Having a non-typical schedule/ optional apparel style	−0.40	0.33	36
Information Input			
Interpreting what is being sensed	0.97	0.26	84
Using various sources of information	−0.29	0.37	40
Watching devices and/or materials for information	0.81	0.32	80
Evaluating and/or judging what is sensed	−0.26	0.32	41
Being aware of environmental conditions	−0.30	0.28	40
Using various senses	−0.50	0.25	32
Mental Processes			
Making decisions	0.59	0.30	73
Processing information	−0.61	0.35	29
Work Output			
Using machines and/or tools and/ or equipment	0.53	0.29	71
Performing activities requiring general body movement	0.46	0.37	68
Controlling machines and/or processes	−0.53	0.26	31
Performing skilled and/or technical activities	0.57	0.32	72
Performing controlled manual and/or related activities	0.96	0.25	84
Using miscellaneous equipment and/or devices	−0.36	0.20	37
Performing handling and/or related manual activities	−0.92	0.36	19

Position Analysis Questionnaire (PAQ) Output for the Job of

Electrician (DOT Code: 829.261.018)

Job Dimensions Profile

Dimension Name	Score	SEM	Percentile
General physical condition	0.25	0.38	61

Relationships with Other Persons

Communicating judgments and/or related information	−0.63	0.24	28
Engaging in general personal contact	−0.09	0.21	48
Performing supervisory and/or coordination	−0.07	0.24	49
Exchanging job-related information	0.10	0.41	54
Public and/or related personal contacts	−0.65	0.30	27

Job Context

Being in a stressful and/or unpleasant environment	1.29	0.28	91
Engaging in personally demanding situations	−0.49	0.26	33
Being in hazardous job situations	−0.21	0.33	43

Other Job Characteristics

Working non-typical vs. day schedule	−1.06	0.36	16
Working in a businesslike situation	−1.22	0.22	13
Wearing specified vs. optional apparel	−0.46	0.38	34
Being paid on a salary vs. variable basis	−0.02	0.13	51
Working on an irregular vs. regular schedule	0.21	0.23	59
Working under job-demanding circumstances	−0.45	0.32	34
Performing unstructured vs. structured work	−0.22	0.38	43
Being alert to changing conditions	0.22	0.27	59

Selection Report

GATB Tests with a High Probability of Use for This Job

GATB Construct	Probability of Use	Predicted Validity Coefficient
G–General Cognitive Ability	0.083	0.346
V–Verbal Aptitude	0.036	0.224
N–Numerical Aptitude	0.769	0.263
S–Spatial Aptitude	0.912	0.271
P–Form Perception	0.481	0.222
Q–Clerical Perception	0.303	0.213
K–Motor Coordination	0.177	0.131
F–Finger Dexterity	0.039	0.149
M–Manual Dexterity	0.492	0.143

Job Requirements Report

Attribute title and description	Percentile
Sensory Requirements	
Near Visual Acuity – ability to perceive detail at normal reading distance	82
Far Visual Acuity – ability to perceive detail at distances beyond normal reading distance	65
Body Orientation – ability to maintain body orientation with respect to balance and motion	61
Perceptual Requirements	
Aesthetic Judgment – ability to make sensitive evaluations or artistic quality	31
Visual Form Perception – ability to perceive pertinent detail or configuration in a complex visual stimulus	83
Selective Attention – the ability to perform a task in the presence of distracting stimulation or under monotonous conditions without significant loss in efficiency	31
Time Sharing – the ability to utilize information obtained by shifting between two or more channels of information. The information obtained from these sources is either integrated or used as a whole or retained and used separately.	27
Perceptual Speed – ability to make rapid discriminations of visual detail	68
Closure – ability to perceptually organize a chaotic or disorganized field into a single perception	36
Movement Detection – ability to detect physical movement of objects and to judge their direction	72
Spatial Visualization – ability to manipulate visual images in two or three dimensions mentally	82
Depth Perception – ability to estimate depth of distances or objects (or to judge their physical relationships in space)	75
Color Discrimination – ability to perceive similarities or differences in colors or in shades of the same color, or to identify certain colors	66
Spatial Orientation – the ability to maintain one's orientation with respect to objects in space or to comprehend the position of objects in space with respect to the observer's position	79
Kinesthesis – ability to sense position and movement of body members	73
Cognitive Requirements	
Numerical Computation – ability to manipulate quantitative symbols rapidly and accurately, as in various arithmetic operations	42
Arithmetic Reasoning – ability to reason abstractly using quantitative concepts and symbols	27
Long-term Memory – ability to learn and store pertinent information and selectively retrieve or recall, much later in time, that which is relevant to a specific context.	26

Job Requirements Report

Attribute title and description	Percentile
Problem Sensitivity – the ability to recognize or identify the existence of problems. This attribute does not include any of the reasoning necessary for the solution of a problem	25
Mechanical Ability – ability to determine the functional interrelationships of parts within a mechanical system	89

Psychomotor Requirements

Finger Dexterity – ability to manipulate small objects (with the fingers) rapidly and accurately	75
Manual Dexterity – ability to manipulate things with the hands	75
Arm/Hand Positioning – ability to make precise, accurate movements of the hands and arms	76
Arm/Hand Steadiness – ability to keep the hands and arms immobilized in a set position with minimal tremor	79
Continuous Muscular Control – ability to exert continuous control over external devices through continual use of body limbs.	69
Rate of Arm Movement – ability to make gross, rapid arm movements	72
Eye-Hand Coordination – ability to coordinate hand movements with visual stimuli	76
Eye-Hand-Foot Coordination – ability to move the hand and foot coordinately with each other in accordance with visual stimuli	64
Speed of Limb Movement – this ability involves the speed with which discreet movements of the arms or legs can be made. The ability deals with the speed with which the movement can be carried out after it has been initiated; it is not concerned with the speed of initiation of the movement	65
Simple Reaction Time – the period of time elapsing between the appearance of any stimulus and the initiation of an appropriate response	66
Response Integration – ability to rapidly perform various appropriate psychomotor responses in proper sequence	65
Rate Control – ability to make continuous anticipatory motor adjustments, relative to change in speed and direction of continuous moving objects	72

Physical Requirements

Dynamic Strength – ability to make repeated, rapid, flexing move-ments in which the rapid recovery from muscle strain is critical	67
Static Strength – ability to maintain a high level of muscular exertion for some minimum period of time	68
Stamina – this ability involves the capacity to maintain physical activity over prolonged period of time. It is concerned with the resistance of the cardio-vascular system to break down	62

Job Requirements Report

Attribute title and description	Percentile
Explosive Strength – ability to expend a maximum amount of energy in one or a series of explosive or ballistic acts (as in throwing, pounding, etc.)	71

Interest Requirements

Repetitive/Short-Cycle Operations – operations carried out according to set procedures or sequences	68
Dealing with Things/Objects – preference for situations involving activities which deal with things and objects rather than activities concerned with people or the communication of ideas	78
Processes/Machines/Techniques – situations which are non-social in nature, being primarily concerned with methods and procedures often of a mechanical or chemical nature	82
Scientific/Technical Activities – using technical methods or investigating natural phenomena using scientific procedures	54

Temperament

Personal Risk – risk of physical or mental illness or injury	74
Pressure of Time – working in situations where time is a critical factor for successful job performance	
Sensory Alertness – alertness over extended periods of time	44
Attainment of Set Standards – attainment of set limits, tolerances, or standards	60
Working Under Specific Instructions – i.e., those that allow little or no room for independent action or judgment in working out job problems	45
Working Alone – working in physical isolation from others, although the activity might be integrated with that of others.	38
Tangible/Physical End-Products – working with material elements or parts which ultimately result in a physical product	73
Sensory/Judgmental Criteria – arriving at generalizations, judgments, or decisions which require sensory discrimination or cognitive appraisal	35
Measurable/Verifiable Criteria – arriving at generalizations, judgments, or decisions based on known or obtainable standards, characteristics, or dimensions	42
Susceptibility to Fatigue – diminished ability to do work, either physical or mental, as a consequence of previous and recent work done	58

FIGURE 2.3   Selected descriptor results for electrician job from PAQ database.

TABLE 2.1
Deductive Job Analysis Instruments

Deductive Instrument	Types of Jobs	Types of Descriptors	Types of Analyst	Applications	Database Available	Year Developed	Availability
Essential Functions Worksheet	All	6 of the ADA criteria 100+ Essential functions	Analysts Incumbents Supervisors	Compliance with the ADA	No	1998	Ed Williams, Ph.D. (501) 447 – 3386 Ed.Williams@prsd.org
Common Metric Questionnaire (CMQ)*	All	Background Contacts with people Decision making Physical and mechanical activities Work setting (285 items)	Analysts	Job descriptions Performance appraisal	Yes	1991	The Psychological Corporation 555 Academic Court San Antonio, TX 78204 (800) 228 – 0752
Fleishman Job Analysis Survey (F – JAS)	All	50 abilities Cognitive Perceptual Sensory Physical	Incumbents Supervisors Analysts	Job descriptions Selection Classification Performance appraisal	No	1984	Management Research Institute, (MRI) 6701 Democracy Blvd. Bethesda, MD 20817 (301) 571 – 9363

TABLE 2.1
(Continued)

Deductive Instrument	Types of Jobs	Types of Descriptors	Types of Analyst	Applications	Database Available	Year Developed	Availability
Functional Job Analysis (FJA) Scales	All	Benchmark tasks organized according to three primary objects of worker behavior (i.e., data, people, things)	Analysts	Job descriptions Selection Training needs	Dictionary of Occupational Titles	1944 Revised 1991	*The Revised Handbook for Analyzing Jobs* U.S. Government Printing Office, Superintendent of Documents Mail Stop SSOP Washington,DC 20402 – 9328
General Work Inventory (GWI)	All	Sensory activities Information – based activities General mental requirements General physical requirements Physical activities Interpersonal activities Work conditions Job benefits (268 items)	Incumbents Supervisors	Job profiling Selection Placement	Yes	1981	J.W. Cunningham, Ph.D. P.O. Box 3655 Placida, FL 33946 (941) 698 – 9270 jwc – psc@msn.com

TABLE 2.1
(Continued)

Deductive Instrument	Types of Jobs	Types of Descriptors	Types of Analyst	Applications	Database Available	Year Developed	Availability
Identifying Criteria for Success (ICS)	Managers Professionals Sales Hourly Clerical	41 job dimensions	Analysts Incumbents	Selection Career planning	Yes	1990	DDI World Headquarters – Pittsburgh 1225 Washington Pike Bridgeville, PA 15017 – 2838
Job Analysis Guide (JAG)	All	Major duties Work behaviors Work conditions Machines or tools and equipment Required qualifications	Incumbents Supervisors Analysts	Americans with Disabilities Act (ADA) essential functions Job accommodation Selection	No	1992	Valtera Corp. 601 Jefferson Suite 3900 Houston, TX 77002 (713) 650 – 6535 www.valtera.com
Job Components Inventory (JCI)	Most	Tools and equipment Physical and perceptual skills Math Communications Decision – making responsibilities	Trained interviewers	Curriculum development and assessment Training design Career guidance Skill profiling	Unknown	Unknown	Manpower Services Commission Sheffield, UK

TABLE 2.1
(Continued)

Deductive Instrument	Types of Jobs	Types of Descriptors	Types of Analyst	Applications	Database Available	Year Developed	Availability
Management Position Description Questionnaire (MPDQ), now called FOCUS	Supervisory Managerial	Activities Contacts Scope Decisions Competencies Reporting relationships	Incumbents	Job descriptions Job comparisons Job evaluation Management development Performance appraisal Selection or promotion Job design	Yes	1974	Personnel Decisions Intl. 2000 Plaza VII Tower 45 S. 7th Street Minneapolis, MN 55402 (612) 373-3430
Managerial and Professional Job Functions Inventory (MP – JFI)	Management Professional	Organizational activities Leadership responsibilities Human resources management Community activities (140 items)	Incumbents Supervisors	Job hierarchies or levels Training needs	Unknown	1978	Melany Baehr, Ph.D. 5555 S. Everett #E3 Chicago, IL 60637 (312) 324 – 8190
Minnesota Job Description Questionnaire (MJDQ)	All	21 statements about work environment given in terms of occupational reinforcers	Incumbents	Vocational counseling Occupational grouping	Yes	1968	University of Minnesota Vocational Psychological Research Minneapolis, MN 55402

TABLE 2.1
(Continued)

Deductive Instrument	Types of Jobs	Types of Descriptors	Types of Analyst	Applications	Database Available	Year Developed	Availability
Multipurpose Occupational Systems Analysis Inventory-Closed Ended (MOSAIC)	All Federal occupations	Task Competencies	Incumbents Supervisors	Position description Position classification Selection	Yes	1990–2002	U.S. Office of Personnel Management Personnel Resources and Development Center Theodore Roosevelt Bldg. 1900 E Street, NW Washington, DC 20415 202-606-1800 www.opm.gov/deu/Handbook_2003/DEOH-MOSAIC.asp
Occupational Information Network (O*NET)*	All	Tasks Abilities Interests or values Work styles Skills Knowledges Education Experience	Incumbents Analysts Supervisors	Job description Job grouping Job matching Intended as a database for integrated human resources	Yes	1998, regular updates	National O*NET Consortium, www.onetcenter.org

TABLE 2.1
(Continued)

Deductive Instrument	Types of Jobs	Types of Descriptors	Types of Analyst	Applications	Database Available	Year Developed	Availability
				resources management			
Position Analysis Questionnaire (PAQ)*	All	Generalized Work activities Work Context Information Input Mental Processes Work Output Relationships with others Job context Job demands (187 items)	Incumbents Analysts Supervisors	Selection Job evaluation Job grouping Job design Performance appraisal Position classification Job matching	Yes	1969	PAQ Services, Inc. 111 Bellwether Way Suite 107 Bellingham, Washington 98665 800-292-2198 paqinfo@paq.com
Position Classification Inventory (PCI)	All	84 questions tagged to Holland's Occupational Interests categories	Incumbents	Career development Vocational counseling	Yes	1990	Psychological Assessment Resources, Inc. P.O. Box 998 Odessa, FL 33556
Professional and Managerial Position Questionnaire (PMPQ)*	Profess-ional Manage-ment Exempt	Job functions Planning Processing information Judgments Communications Interpersonal	Analysts Incumbents	Job evaluation Performance appraisal Job grouping	Yes	1976	PAQ Services, Inc. 1625 111 Bellwether Way Suite 107 Bellingham, Washington

TABLE 2.1
(Continued)

Deductive Instrument	Types of Jobs	Types of Descriptors	Types of Analyst	Applications	Database Available	Year Developed	Availability
		Technical Personal					98665 800-292-2198 paqinfo@paq.com
Secretary's Commission on Achieving Necessary Skills (SCANS)	Entry-level jobs in the U.S workforce	Basic skills Foundation skills Personal qualities Illustrative tasks	Analysts	Position description Vocational counseling Selection	No	1992	Arnold H. Packer Johns Hopkins University Institute for Policy Studies Wyman Park Building 3400 N. Charles Street Baltimore, MD 21218-2696 (410) 516-7174
Threshold Traits Analysis System (TTAS)	All	33 traits Physical Mental Learned Motivational Social	Incumbents Supervisors Other SMEs (minimum of 5 recommended)	Selection - Promotion Training needs Effectiveness Performance appraisal Job accommodation	Unknown	1970	Lopez & Associates, Inc. One Third Vista Way Port Washington, NY 11050 (576) 883-4041

TABLE 2.1
(Continued)

Deductive Instrument	Types of Jobs	Types of Descriptors	Types of Analyst	Applications	Database Available	Year Developed	Availability
Transition to Work Inventory (TWI)	Most	Physical Psychomotor Decision making Social interaction Perceptual Equipment use Context (81 items)	Analysts	Job accommodation	No	1996	The Psychological Corporation 555 Academic Court San Antonio, TX 78204 (800) 228-0752
Work Profiling System (WPS)*	Manage-rial or pro-fessional Service or admin-istrative Manual Technical	Tasks* key context factors (492 items)	Incumbents Supervisors Analysts	Selection Placement Performance appraisal Job design Job description	Yes	1986	Saville & Holdsworth, Ltd. 575 Boylston St. Boston, MA 02186
Worker Rehabili-tation Question-naire (WRQ)*	All	Same as PAQ (150 items only)	Analysts	Disability or rehabilitation	Yes	1986	David Robinson, Ph.D. Worker Rehabilitation Associates 4265 Corrienta Place Boulder, CO 80301 (303) 581 – 9778 david@worker rehab.com

*Computer analysis of data available.

Examples of statements of purpose that are inadequate are: "selection," "improve skills," and "find out why we are losing profit." Better statements are: "to develop and validate employee selection tests for every entry-level job in our company," "to find out what we need to be training our customer representatives on," or "to make it easier to transfer people across jobs with some assurance that they can perform well on the new job in a reasonable period of time." Note that each of the first set of inadequate statements is very short, very vague, or identifies an organizational outcome very distal from job analysis information. Each of the second set of statements, though not perfect, contains information about the personnel function to be implemented or changed and the range of jobs that is to be included. This usually is about as much information as persons unfamiliar with job analysis are able to provide for the general purpose of a job analysis. One very important decision to make here is whether a job analysis is even called for; some organizational problems definitely call for different research approaches or interventions. The purpose statement will often point toward particular kinds of job descriptors (e.g., abilities and skills if employee selection is the purpose of the analysis) or toward a system that has an already developed application for that purpose (e.g., a method for evaluating jobs for compensation if the development of a compensation system is the purpose). An excellent description of how to use job analysis data for the specification of the content for licensure and certification examinations was provided by Raymond (2001).

2. What is the scope of the intended job analysis? Although the definition of the purpose should illuminate the intended end use of the job analysis information, the scope of people and organizations to be included has a major effect on choosing the job analysis system. Factors affecting scope include number of positions within each job, amount of diversity of jobs, number of major job families, and number and geographic scatter of organizations or organizational sites. A very focused analysis involving a few positions within one job at one organizational site argues for the use of an interview or group interview approach and, therefore, the use of a job analysis system that can be used efficiently by interviewers or trained analysts. On the other hand, when many jobs across many organizations are involved, the use of an efficient survey questionnaire that can be completed by incumbents or supervisors may be the best bet. A related question here is the availability of SMEs for participation. That is, will job incumbents, supervisors, trainers, human resources experts, or others with expert knowledge about the job(s) be able to provide time for completion of questionnaires or to be interviewed? Less availability calls for more targeted use of job descriptors for the more immediate purposes; greater availability allows the use of a greater range of descriptors with greater potential for long-range use. Finally, if a job analysis system has a database encompassing the appropriate kind of information for the focal jobs, then it may be useful as a substitute for the planned job analysis,

for augmenting the information that will be collected, or as a means of checking the quality of the to-be-collected job information.

3. Which candidate job analysis system has the technical, legal, and practical characteristics that most closely match the purpose and scope of the planned job analysis? Given as complete a definition as possible of the purpose(s) and scope of the job analysis, there may be several deductive methods that might be appropriate. Such candidates have the appropriate descriptors, can be used by the appropriate SMEs, have appropriate end products or applications, and have an existing, appropriate database. Each should then be evaluated on its technical quality, legal defensibility, and practicality of use. By technical quality we mean the demonstrated reliability and validity of the system as described in our earlier section on the quality of job analysis data. Legal defensibility is a somewhat volatile concept, as discussed later in chapter 14. It changes with the passage of pertinent laws (e.g., the Civil Rights Acts of 1964 and 1991; the Americans with Disabilities Act of 1990), the accumulation of court decisions (e.g., Albermarle Paper Co. v. Moody, 1975; Griggs v. Duke Power Co., 1971), and changes in accepted professional practice (*Uniform Guidelines on Employee Selection Procedures*, 1978; *Standards for Educational and Psychological Testing* [American Educational Research Association, American Psychological Association, National Council on Measurement in Education, 1999] and the *Principles for the Validation and Use of Personnel Selection Procedures* [SIOP, 2003]). A demonstrated track record of accepted use by the courts and within the profession of industrial and organizational psychology provides some promise of defensibility. Practicality of use includes such considerations as training required for use by SMEs, acceptability to SMEs and end users of the job analysis instruments and products, and the cost and time required to use the data collection instruments and obtain outputs from the system. Although we have not undertaken a formal evaluative study of the available deductive systems, others have attempted to do so (e.g., Brumbach, Romashko, Hahn, & Fleishman, 1974; Gatewood & Field, 1991; Holley & Jennings, 1987; Levine, Ash, Hall, & Sistrunk, 1983). Although these studies are somewhat dated, the interested reader is referred to them for their comparative evaluations of various job analysis methods. Though the authors just cited did not compare and evaluate all of the instruments described in Table 2.1, they covered several of them. They also evaluated several methodologies (such as task analysis) that we define as inductive methods, as discussed in the next chapter.

SUMMARY

In chapter 4, the authors describe a generic test plan that guides the development of tests and assessments that are most likely to satisfy the multiple objectives of employee selection. Job analysis provides essential information for the creation of such a test plan.

Job analysis also contributes to the fulfillment of a variety of functions in human resources management. As a consequence, an understanding and specification of the purposes for job analysis are critical for selecting appropriate methods and carrying out productive analyses. Building on this basic premise, we reviewed the many ways that scholars and users of job analyses have categorized job analysis methods. Embedded in this rich context, we have made a primary distinction between deductive job analysis methods, the subject of this chapter, and inductive methods, the subject of the following chapter. The heart of this distinction lies in the use of an already existing system of job descriptors intended to apply across jobs (deductive) or the development of a new, tailored system intended to be unique to a particular job or family of jobs (inductive). Deductive analyses are generally more appropriate when a large-scale employee selection or promotion system is to be developed for a variety of jobs, and the inductive system is generally more appropriate when a single job or a small set of highly similar jobs is the focus.

We discussed several techniques for evaluating the quality of quantitative job analysis information, including estimates of the reliability, validity, and sensibility of the information. Such evaluations are essential to ensuring that job analysis data are suitable for the purposes to which they are intended.

We then presented information on two deductive job analysis systems: the O*NET, a national occupational database developed by the Department of Labor to replace the DOT, and the PAQ, a commercially available system that has a long and well-researched history. We presented tabular information about a number of other deductive systems.

In the last section of the chapter, we presented several issues that should be considered in the choice of a job analysis system. These included the purpose or purposes for the job analysis, the scope of the job analysis, and the technical, legal, and practical qualities of candidate systems that fulfill the purpose and scope of the planned job analysis.

REFERENCES

Advisory Panel for the Dictionary of Occupational Titles. (1993). *The new DOT: A database of occupational titles for the twenty-first century* (Final Report). Washington, DC: Employment and Training Administration, U.S. Employment Service, U.S. Department of Labor.

Albermarle Paper Company v. Moody, 422 U.S. 405 (1975).

Aldenderfer, M. S., & Blashfield, R. K. (1984). *Cluster analysis.* Newbury Park, CA: Sage.

American Educational Research Association, American Psychological Association, & National Council on Measurement in Education (Joint Committee). (1999). *Standards for educational and psychological testing.* Washington, DC: American Educational Research Association.

Americans With Disabilities Act of 1990, Public Law No. 101-336, 104 Stat. 328 (1990).

Bennett, J. W., Ruck, H. W., & Page, R. E. (1996). Military occupational analysis. *Military Psychology, 8,* 115–266.

Boese, R., Lewis, P., Frugoli, P., & Litwin, K. (2001). *Summary of O*NET 4.0 Content Model and Database*. Raleigh, NC: National O*NET Consortium.

Brumbach, G. B., Romashko, T., Hahn, C. P., & Fleishman, E. A. (1974). *Models for job analysis, test development, and validation procedures* (Final Report). Washington, DC: American Institutes for Research.

Civil Rights Act of 1964, 42 U.S.C. § 2000e (1964).

Civil Rights Act of 1991, 42 U.S.C. § 2000e (1991).

Cohen, J., & Cohen, P. (1983). *Applied multiple regression/correlation analysis for the behavioral sciences* (2nd ed.). Hillsdale, NJ: Lawrence Erlbaum Associates.

Cornelius, E. T. & Hakel, M. D. (1978). *A study to develop an improvised enlisted performance evaluation system for the U.S. Coast Guard*. Washington, DC: Department of Transportation, U.S. Coast Guard.

Cronbach, L. J., Gleser, G. C., Nanda, H., & Rajaratnam, N. (1972). *The dependability of behavioral measurements: Theory of generalizability for scores and profiles*. New York: Wiley.

Cunningham, J. W. & Ballentine, R. D. (1982). *The general work inventory*. Raleigh, NC: Author.

Dierdorff, E. C., & Wilson, M. A. (2003). A meta-analysis of job analysis reliability. *Journal of Applied Psychology, 88*, 635–646.

Executive Office of the President, Office of Management and Budget. (2000). *Standard occupational classification manual*. Washington, DC: Bernan Associates.

Fair Labor Standards Act of 1938 (FLSA), as amended (29 USC § 201 et seq.; 29 CFR Parts 510 to 794).

Fleishman, E. A., & Quaintance, M. K. (1984). *Taxonomies of human performance*. Orlando, FL: Academic Press.

Gatewood, R., & Field, H. S. (1991). Job analysis methods: A description and comparison of the alternatives. In J. W. Jones, B. D. Steffy, & D. W. Bray (Eds.), *Applying psychology in business* (pp. 153–168). New York: Lexington Books.

Geyer, P. D., Hice, J., Hawk, J., Boese, R., & Brannon, Y. (1989). Reliabilities of ratings available from the Dictionary of Occupational Titles. *Personnel Psychology, 42*, 547–560.

Griggs v. Duke Power Company, 401 U.S. 424 (1971).

Harman, H. H. (1976). *Modern factor analysis* (3rd ed.). Chicago: University of Chicago Press.

Harris, R. J. (1985). *A primer of multivariate statistics* (2nd ed.). Orlando, FL: Academic Press.

Harvey, R. J. (1991). Job analysis. In M. D. Dunnette & L. M. Hough (Eds.), *Handbook of industrial and organizational psychology* (2nd ed., pp. 71–163). Palo Alto, CA: Consulting Psychologists Press.

Harvey, R. J., Friedman, L., Hakel, M. D., & Cornelius, E. T., III. (1988). Dimensionality of the job element inventory (JEI): A simplified worker oriented job analysis questionnaire. *Journal of Applied Psychology, 73*, 639–646.

Holley, H., & Jennings, K. (1987). *Personnel/human resource management contributions and activities*. Hinsdale, IL: Dryden Press.

Hubbard, M., McCloy, R., Campbell, J., Nottingham, J., Lewis, P., Rivkin, D., et al. (2000). *Revision of O*NET Data Collection Instruments*. Raleigh, NC: National O*NET Consortium.

Jeanneret, P. R. (1988). Computer logic chip production operators. In S. Gael (Ed.), *The job analysis handbook for business, industry, and government* (pp. 1329–1345). New York: Wiley.

Jeanneret, P. R. (1992). Application of job component/synthetic validity to construct validity. *Human Performance, 5*, 81–96

Jeanneret, P. R., & Strong, M. H. (2003). Linking O*NET job analysis information to job requirement predictors: An O*NET application. *Personnel Psychology, 65*, 465–492.

Levine, E. L., Ash, R. H., Hall, H., & Sistrunk, F. (1983). Evaluation of job analysis methods by experienced job analysts. *Academy of Management Journal, 26,* 339–347.

Manson, T. M., Levine, E. L., & Brannick, M. T. (2000). The construct validity of task inventory ratings: A multitrait- multimethod analysis. *Human Performance, 13,* 1–22.

McCormick, E. J. (1976). Job analysis. In M. D. Dunnette (Ed.), *Handbook of industrial and organizational psychology* (pp. 651–696). Chicago: Rand McNally.

McCormick, E. J. (1979). *Job analysis: Methods and applications.* New York: Amacom.

McCormick, E. J., & Jeanneret, P. R. (1988). Position analysis questionnaire (PAQ). In S. Gael (Ed.), *The job analysis handbook for business, industry, and government* (Vol. 2, pp. 825–842). New York: Wiley.

McCormick, E. J., Mecham, R. C., & Jeanneret, P. R. (1977). *Technical manual for the position analysis questionnaire* (2nd ed.). Logan, UT: PAQ Services.

McPhail, S. M., Jeanneret, P. R., McCormick, E. J., & Mecham, R. C. (1991). *Position analysis questionnaire job analysis manual.* Logan, UT: PAQ Services.

Morgeson, F. P., & Campion, M. H. (1997). Social and cognitive sources of potential inaccuracy in job analysis. *Journal of Applied Psychology, 82,* 627–655.

Mossholder, K. W., & Arvey, R. D. (1984). Synthetic validity: A conceptual and comparative review. *Journal of Applied Psychology, 69,* 322–333.

Mumford, M. D., Sager, C., Baughman, W. A., & Childs, R. A. (1999). Occupation-specific descriptors: Approaches, procedures and findings. In N. G. Peterson, M. D. Mumford, W. C. Borman, P. R. Jeanneret, & E. A. Fleishman (Eds.), *An occupational information system for the 21st century: The development of O*NET* (pp. 227–235). Washington, DC: American Psychological Association.

Nunnally, J. C., & Bernstein, I. H. (1994). *Psychometric theory* (3rd ed.). New York: McGraw-Hill.

O*NET database. Retrieved November 11, 2005, from http://www.onetcenter.org

Peterson, N. G., Borman, W. C., Hanson, M. A., & Kubisiak, U. C. (1999). Summary of results, implications for O*NET applications, and future directions. In N. G. Peterson, M. D. Mumford, W. C. Borman, P. R. Jeanneret, & E. A. Fleishman (Eds.), *An occupational information system for the 21st century: The development of O*NET* (pp. 289–295). Washington, DC: American Psychological Association.

Peterson, N. G., & Bownas, D. A. (1982). Skill, task, structure, and performance acquisition. In E. A. Fleishman (Ed.), *Human performance and productivity: Human capability assessment* (Vol. 1, pp. 49–105). Hillsdale, NJ: Lawrence Erlbaum Associates.

Peterson, N. G., Mumford, M. D., Borman, W. C., Jeanneret, P. R., & Fleishman, E. A. (Eds.). (1995). *Development of prototype occupational information network (O*NET) content model* (Vols. 1–2). Salt Lake City: Utah Department of Employment Security.

Peterson, N. G., Mumford, M. D., Borman, W. C., Jeanneret, P. R., & Fleishman, E. A. (1996). *O*NET final technical report* (Vols. 1–3). Salt Lake City: Utah Department of Employment Security.

Peterson, N. G., Mumford, M. D., Borman, W. C., Jeanneret, P. R., & Fleishman, E. A. (Eds.). (1999). *An occupational information system for the 21st century: The development of O*NET.* Washington, DC: American Psychological Association.

Position Analysis Questionnaire. Retrieved November 22, 2005, from http://www.paq2.com

Raymond, M. R. (2001). Job analysis and the specification of content for licensure and certification examinations. *Applied Measurement in Education, 14,* 369–415

Schmidt, F. L., & Hunter, J. E. (1996). Measurement error in psychological research: Lessons from 26 research scenarios. *Psychological Methods, 1,* 199–223.

Shippmann, J. S., Ash, R. A., Battista, M., Carr, L., Eyde, L. D., Hesketh, B., et al. (2000). The practice of competency modeling. *Personnel Psychology, 53,* 703–740.

Smith, J. E., & Hakel, M. D. (1979). Convergence among data sources, response bias, and reliability and validity of a structured job analysis questionnaire. *Personnel Psychology, 32,* 677–692.

Society for Industrial and Organizational Psychology, Inc. (2003). *Principles for the validation and use of personnel selection procedures* (4th ed.). Bowling Green, OH: Author.

U.S. Department of Labor. (1991a). *Dictionary of Occupational Titles* (4th ed., rev.). Washington, DC: U.S. Government Printing Office.

U.S. Department of Labor. (1991b). *The revised handbook for analyzing jobs.* Washington, DC: U.S. Government Printing Office.

Uniform guidelines on employee selection procedures. (1978). *Federal Register, 43,* 38290–38315.

Van Iddekinge, C. H., Putka, D. J., Raymark, P. H., & Eidson, C. E. (2005). Modeling error variance in job specification ratings: The influence of rater. *Journal of Applied Psychology, 90,* 323–334.

CHAPTER THREE

Job Analysis: Gathering Job-Specific Information

Jennifer L. Harvey, Lance E. Anderson, Laura E. Baranowski, and Ray A. Morath
Caliber, an ICF International Company

OVERVIEW

Job-specific information often is used to develop or validate measurement tools used in human resources management (HRM). The manner in which that job-specific information is gathered can determine the usefulness, validity, and defensibility of the measurement tools. In this chapter, we present and discuss recommendations for gathering job-specific information to support development and use of tools for a wide variety of applications.

We describe two examples of inductive job analysis methods: the job-task analysis method and the critical incident technique. These methods of job analysis differ from the deductive approaches described in chapter 2 inasmuch as the analyst who uses them starts from scratch to conduct a highly tailored job analysis. Rather than selecting and administering an existing instrument like any of those listed in Table 2.1, the analyst goes through a number of prescribed steps to build one or more instruments designed to generate quantitative information about the job being analyzed. The analysis, resulting instruments, and outcomes are therefore unique to the job or job family under study.

The methods we describe are intended to serve as general guidelines applicable to a variety of jobs. Implementation of the methods may vary, however, according to the number of jobs being analyzed, the number of job incumbents, and the homogeneity of the population of incumbents in terms of geographic location, tasks performed, abilities required, and organizations served. Both methods are consistent with the *Uniform Guidelines on Employee Selection Procedures* (1978), the *Standards for Educational and Psychological Testing* (American

57

Educational Research Association, American Psychological Association, National Council on Measurement in Education, 1999), and the *Principles for the Validation and Use of Personnel Selection Procedures* (SIOP, 2003).

The job/task analysis method involves gathering detailed information about the job in terms of what workers do and what they need to know to perform their jobs. This detailed information often is developed into an inventory that is then administered to subject matter experts (SMEs) to generate information about what aspects of the work are most frequently performed or most critical to perform and to provide links between what workers do and what workers need to know. The resulting information is analyzed to support a variety of HRM applications, including competency profiles, selection instrument development, training development, performance management and compensation.

The critical incident technique is a flexible set of procedures for collecting and analyzing instances of actual behavior that constitute job performance. Job analysts use this procedure to develop descriptions of job performance — especially descriptions of effective and ineffective performance — and often use the incidents resulting from this process to develop rating scales to assess incumbent performance. The critical incidents serve as anchor points on such scales. Critical incidents can also be particularly useful for developing interviews (see chap. 7), situational judgment tests (see chap. 9), and assessment center exercises (see chap. 10).

BACKGROUND

Job-task analysis traces back to the beginning of the 20th century with Fredrick Taylor's studies of how workers performed their jobs (Taylor, 1911). He observed and analyzed the motions workers performed and the time it took to perform those motions on the job. In the 1920s, researchers studying jobs began to focus on more than time and motion. Several researchers began to identify the work behaviors of the job and the worker characteristics needed to perform the behaviors (Lytle, 1954). With the need to determine exempt and nonexempt work for the Fair Labor Standards Act of 1938, the emphasis on job analysis grew and received further impetus with the passage of the Equal Pay Act of 1963 and the Civil Rights Act of 1964. The Equal Pay Act mandated that jobs with a particular pay status have the same level of requirements in skill, effort, and responsibility, whereas the Civil Rights Act mandated that the worker requirements for a job be job-related. Thus, because job-task analysis defines knowledge, skills, abilities and other characteristics (KSAOs) of a job and then links those characteristics to the job's work behaviors, job-task analysis is an important component for meeting legal requirements for HRM. When developed in a manner consistent with professional and legal guidelines, job-task analysis produces reliable and content valid data to support personnel decisions.

The critical incident technique was developed during World War II by John Flanagan, who was ordered to determine the cause of high pilot failure rates during training (Flanagan, 1954). He began to focus on factual incidents embedded in reports prepared by the Army Air Force Elimination Board. The detailed observations of human behavior in the reports appeared to him to be more useful than the personality traits of "good" and "bad" trainees. He and his colleagues augmented the incident reports with behavioral observations of cadets from flight instructors and developed selection instruments using these observations that significantly reduced the failure rates. The Aviation Psychology Program subsequently went on to gather specific incidents of effective and ineffective behavior in the context of other projects, refining the process and eventually calling it the critical incident technique. Following World War II, Flanagan began to use the technique to identify KSAOs that led to success or failure on the job (Flanagan, 1957). The technique is widely used today and is even applied outside the realm of personnel research, such as to evaluate the impact of a medical information system (Lindbergh, Siegal, Rapp, Wallingford, & Wilson, 1993).

A SEVEN-STEP PROCESS

This chapter describes seven steps for conducting an inductive job analysis based on job-task analysis and the critical incident technique. There are other possible steps that may be useful for a variety of purposes, but they are outside the scope of this chapter. The steps we review in this chapter are:

- Gather background information
- Identify SMEs
- Develop work behavior, task, and KSAO statements
- Develop and administer job analysis questionnaire
- Analyze job analysis questionnaire data
- Gather critical incidents
- Analyze critical incidents

The first three steps are relevant to both methods. Steps 4 and 5 are applicable if a job analysis questionnaire is developed. Steps 6 and 7 describe the critical incident technique. Throughout the chapter we include examples derived from the analysis of one particular job family — that of electrician. Chapter 2 provided examples of outcomes from deductive job analysis methods applied to the electrician job. Chapter 4 describes how to use the job analysis information to develop a test plan.

Gather Background Information

The first step in the job analysis process is to gather all available information about the job being analyzed. The purpose of this fundamental step is to prepare for subsequent job observations and interviews, and to provide the job analyst with information required to write draft work behavior, task, and KSAO statements. Some sources that may be examined for relevant background information about the job include:

- Previous job analysis reports
- Existing job descriptions
- Training information
- The Occupational Information Network (O*NET, as described in chap. 2; O*NET Consortium, 2005)
- Professional journals
- Job analyses of similar jobs in other organizations
- College and vocational school catalogs, or high school course materials
- Organizational charts

Other sources of information may be investigated to gain a complete understanding of a job. The purpose is to locate material that will provide information on what workers do and what they need to know to perform their jobs. In addition to reviewing the various sources just listed, the job analyst should consider exploring the selection literature associated with the job.

Identify SMEs

The purpose of this step is to target individuals who, through interviews, workshops, or responses to job analysis surveys can provide the best perspective on the job requirements. Potential SMEs include incumbents, supervisors, training course instructors, and customers (e.g., representatives from client organizations). Incumbents have an important perspective because they see all aspects of the job. However, to the degree possible, different SME groups should participate in each phase of the job analysis—site observations, job analysis interviews, job analysis questionnaire completion, and obtaining and refining critical incidents. SMEs should have at least 6 months of familiarity with the job. SMEs should possess knowledge of the job and must be able to articulate job information. To the degree possible, SMEs should be representative of persons familiar with the job, and they should be diverse in regard to race, gender, duties performed, and departmental structure and size. The typical numbers of SMEs needed at various data collection points are provided in Fig. 3.1. At times, there may be a small number, or even no incumbents in a job to serve as SMEs for collecting job analysis information. If this is the case, then the first thing to do is identify other individuals who are familiar with the job who can serve in the SME capacity. SMEs that may be used in this situation include supervisors, agency or department leaders, analysts of the job, or even incumbents from other organizations or agencies.

Develop Work Behavior, Task, and KSAO Statements

One of the key steps of the job-task inventory method is to develop statements that describe the content of the job in terms of work behaviors and tasks performed, and KSAOs needed to perform those work behaviors and tasks. In this section, we describe these statements in detail and then we describe how to develop and refine these statements.

Data Collection	Purpose	What SMEs Must Do (Estimated Burden Per SME)	Typical Number of SMEs Needed
Job observations	Gather preliminary job information	Provide tour of job site. Answer questions about environmental conditions, equipment used, and key tasks and procedures. (30 Minutes)	2-3 observations per job
Job analysis interviews	Develop task and knowledge, skill, ability lists	Participate in interview by discussing tasks, and knowledge, skill, ability relevant to the job. (45 minutes)	3-10 interviews per job
Task and KSAO Workshop	Develop and refine preliminary task and KSAO lists	Generate and refine tasks, group task statements, generate and refine knowledge statements, review skill and abilities lists (4 hours)	5-8 for one work shop
Complete job analysis questionnaire	Respond to job analysis questionnaire	Respond to job analysis questionnaire (2-3 hours)	Depends on size of population of incumbents (N). If N < 50, then all incumbents need to respond.
Critical Incident Workshop	Gather additional information to support measure development or to support understanding of complex KSAOs	Write critical incidents (3-4 hours)	6-10 per workshop, depending on amount of information needed.

FIGURE 3.1 Number of SMEs needed for various job analysis activities.

Draft Initial Work Behavior and Task Statements.   Within a particular job, work behaviors (sometimes called duties) provide the highest level of description. Work behaviors are the major parts of work that are performed on a job and comprise a number of tasks. They are written at a general level and, typically, begin with a verb ending in *ing*. For example, the work behavior Installing Panels for the electrician job may include the tasks:

- Establish panel location
- Terminate wires in panel
- Label the panel

Most jobs can be broken down into 8 to 10 work behaviors. Work behaviors can either be defined before task statements are written, or task statements can be collected and later grouped into work behaviors (Williams & Crafts, 1997). For example, the electrician position can be described by 19 work behaviors, as shown in Fig. 3.2 (Williams, Peterson, & Bell, 1994).

Tasks are the basic unit of the job-task analysis. A task is a logical and necessary step performed by an employee in the performance of a work behavior and usually has an identifiable beginning and end (Gael, 1983). To ensure that task statements

1. Planning and Initiating Project
2. Establishing OSHA and Customer Safety Requirements
3. Establishing Temporary Power During Construction
4. Establishing Grounding System
5. Installing Service to Buildings and Other Structures
6. Establishing Power Distribution within Project
7. Erecting and Assembling Power Generation Equipment
8. Planning and Installing Raceway Systems
9. Installing New Wiring and Repairing Old Wiring
10. Providing Power and Controls to Motors, HVAC, and Other Equipment
11. Installing Receptacles, Lighting Systems and Fixtures
12. Installing Instrumentation and Process Control Systems, including Energy Management Systems
13. Installing Fire Alarm Systems
14. Installing Security Systems
15. Installing and Repairing Telephone and Data Systems
16. Installing, Maintaining, and Repairing Lightning Protection Systems
17. Installing and Repairing Traffic Signals, Outdoor Lighting, and Outdoor Power Feeders
18. Troubleshooting and Repairing Electrical Systems
19. Supervising Journeymen and Apprentices

FIGURE 3.2   Work behaviors of an electrician.

		Part of Task Statement	
	Verb	**Object**	**Qualifier**
Purpose	To identify the action being taken.	To describe on whom or on what the action is performed.	To describe how, why, where, or when a task is performed (Gael, 1983).
Example 1	Cut ...	high voltage cables.	—
Example 2	Grade and level ...	trench.	—
Example 3	Read ...	blueprints ...	to determine location of high voltage room or electrical closet.

Note: the Qualifier is needed only when this information is critical to understanding the job, and cannot be implied from the verb and the object.

FIGURE 3.3   Structure of task statements.

provide sufficient detail for understanding the job, it may be useful to think of tasks as having three parts: a verb, an object, and a qualifier (see Fig. 3.3). Task statements should begin with a verb and be written in the present tense and active voice (Ghorpade, 1988). The subject is understood to be the worker. The verbs should be specific and describe observable behaviors. Thus, verbs such as *review, understand,* and *consider* are not very useful as observable action verbs. The verb should refer to an object and a qualifier should be included when additional information is needed to modify the statement (Williams & Crafts, 1997). Examples of different types of qualifiers that often are used in task statements are shown in Fig. 3.4.

The level of specificity for the statements depends on the purpose(s) of the job analysis and the population for which the job analysis is applicable. If the job analysis is to be used for a classification study, then statements should be specific to highlight any possible differences in jobs. On the other hand, if the job analysis is to be used to identify core or common elements across a group of jobs for an evaluation study, then broad statements that are more likely to apply across jobs with similar requirements should be developed. If the job analysis is to be used to develop selection or performance appraisal instruments, it is useful to have statements that are specific to the job so that they will withstand legal challenge.

If the population of job incumbents is relatively homogeneous in terms of location and job performance, then statements can be specific; however, if the population is in different locations and job performance varies, then statements will

How	Establish temporary power requirements *by consulting with other crafts*
Why	Install batteries in parallel *to provide back-up power source*
Where	Install plates and covers *on receptacles and switches*
When	Complete "as built" drawings *after work is complete*
How much	Measure length of wire *needed to pull through conduit and attach to the tugging machine*

FIGURE 3.4   Qualifiers often used in task statements.

need to be broader to be applicable to all. For example, in a state government, where there are multiple agencies employing people for the same job but where there are slight differences in how the tasks are performed due to different equipment and agency procedures, statements will need to be written at a fairly broad level. The key is to consider what will happen when the statements are included in a job analysis questionnaire and provided to the job incumbents for review. If statements are too specific, there is the possibility that they will fall out as not performed or not needed when in reality they are performed by incumbents with just slight variations. In addition, less detail can provide for greater generalizability of the findings across time and organizational units, making the job analysis more useful for more people for a longer period of time. To minimize unnecessary detail, the analyst should review all tasks grouped under a given work behavior, and potentially combine any tasks that require exactly the same set of KSAOs.

Draft Initial KSAO Statements.   In addition to work behaviors and task statements to describe the content of the job, the job-task analysis method is used to identify needed characteristics (KSAOs) of workers who perform the job. Knowledges are specific types of information that people must have to perform a job (Williams & Crafts, 1997). Skills can be thought of as the competencies needed to perform a task, which can be developed over time and with exposure to multiple situations. Abilities are an individual's relatively enduring capabilities for performing a particular range of different tasks (Fleishman, Costanza, & Marshall-Mies, 1997). Other characteristics include occupational values and interests and work styles (Peterson, Mumford, Borman, Jeanneret, & Fleishman, 1997); personal preferences and interests (Holland, 1973); and individual difference variables (Jackson, 1967) that facilitate the performance of a job.

KSAO statements should be developed based on the work behaviors and task statements and reflect the KSAOs needed to perform the job tasks. KSA statements should begin with the same wording depending on the characteristic (i.e., *Knowledge of, Skill in, or Ability to*). Other characteristics should be written in a way that clearly describes the trait that is needed. Operational terms should be included as needed to express the appropriate type or level of the KSAO needed

Knowledges

Knowledge of blueprints, including symbols used
Knowledge of ladder logic diagrams
Knowledge of state and local electrical codes
Knowledge of which materials are good conductors and insulators
Knowledge of which wire/cable to use in different circumstances
Knowledge of the properties of fiberoptic cable
Knowledge of how a surge protector or lightning protector works
Knowledge of direct and alternating current

Skills

Skill at reading a wire table to determine conductor size required
Skill at programming programmable logic controllers
Skill at splicing aluminum or copper wire
Skill at splicing high voltage cable
Skill at working in rubber gloves on high voltage lines

Abilities

Ability to climb ladders and poles up to 25 feet
Ability to lift objects heavier than 25 pounds
Ability to traverse irregular surfaces while maintaining balance
Ability to bend over to get over or under objects while working on top of a
pole or tower
Ability to operate two-handed power equipment

Other Characteristics

Possesses car and valid driver's license for transportation among multiple job
sites each day
Is motivated to work under extreme temperature conditions
Works with others as a member of a team
Remains calm in an emergency situation

FIGURE 3.5   Preliminary list of KSAOs for the electrician job.

(Williams & Crafts, 1997). Figure 3.5 provides illustrative KSAOs for the electrician
job (Williams, Peterson, & Bell, 1994).

   As with the task statements, the level of specificity will depend on the intended
use of the information. Competencies are broader statements of characteristics
and often encompass multiple KSAOs. Competency modeling has been increasing

in popularity among organizations (Lievens, Sanchez, & De Corte, 2004). Competency modeling is different from traditional job-task analysis in that it makes a strong link between individual requirements and strategic business goals. Values and personality are more likely to be included with this approach and thus it is useful for widening the predictor domain (Shippman et al., 2000). However, competency modeling is less rigorous than traditional job analysis and requires a larger inferential leap from the competencies to the job (Lievens et al.; Shippman et al.). Competencies are often rated or judged on their own without any reference to or linkage with job tasks or job specifications and because of this may have more difficulty meeting the standards of the *Uniform Guidelines on Employee Selection Procedures* (1978). An integration of job analysis and competency modeling, however, may address some of those concerns and allow job analysts to have the advantages of competency modeling and hold on to the rigor of job analysis. Lievens et al. showed that the blending of competency modeling with job-task information increases both interrater reliability and discriminant validity among jobs and competencies. Higher order KSAO or competency profiles in lieu of more detailed task and KSAO statements may be more appropriate for rapidly changing jobs, such as jobs in the technological field, because they can be written to include more potential responsibilities and will require less rewriting as the jobs change.

Conduct Job Analysis Interviews or Site Observations. After conducting background research on the job, the analyst should interview job incumbents and observe work sites. Direct observation is appropriate for acquiring information on jobs that emphasize physical activity or motor behavior; however, direct observation may be insufficient for acquiring information about positions that emphasize cognitive skills. For jobs that primarily involve mental tasks, an interview may be necessary to obtain the desired information. The purpose of the interviews and site observations is to gain firsthand knowledge of what the job tasks are and how they are performed, the work conditions under which the job is performed, the KSAOs necessary to perform the job, and equipment and materials used on the job.

The number of interviews or site observations conducted depends on the job being studied. A general guide is provided in Fig. 3.1. The interviews or observations should represent all aspects of a job, including differences in geographical location, shift, or other relevant differences. In some cases, a job will not have any incumbents, so the person(s) who would ostensibly supervise that position should be interviewed. Finally, it may be necessary to interview persons who will be supervised by or who will interact with the job incumbent(s) on a regular basis.

Questions in the interviews or observations should focus on gathering information to develop a complete list of work behaviors, tasks, and KSAO statements to define and describe the job. If draft statements have been developed, incumbents should review the draft statements and then add any tasks or KSAOs that are missing and reword any statements to be more accurate and appropriate for the job. After selected SMEs have been interviewed or observed, the draft statements should be revised to include any tasks or KSAOs added by the SMEs and any changes to the statements suggested by the SMEs.

If the job class is small and all of the incumbents have been interviewed or observed, it probably is not necessary to conduct the following step. The work behavior, task, and KSAO statements can be finalized. The statements should be finalized by having supervisors review and approve them.

Conduct Job Analysis Workshop With SMEs. To further refine the information gathered in the background research and to confirm the information collected in the interviews or observations, job analysis workshops are conducted. The workshops should include groups of SMEs who are representative of all aspects of the job (e.g., geographical location, shift, or other relevant differences). The number of SMEs will depend on the job and the number of incumbents. During the workshops, the SMEs should provide input into refining the task and KSAO statements, confirming the categorization of tasks under the work behaviors, as well as ensuring that the list of KSAOs is complete and accurate. For small-sample workshops, ratings of the statements and development of linkages between tasks and KSAOs may be completed at the end of the workshops.

Prepare Final List of Work Behaviors, Tasks, and KSAOs. Following the job analysis workshops, it is desirable to have upper level management or supervisory personnel review the work behavior, task, and KSAO statements that were refined and created from the workshop and comment on their coverage of the job content domain. Professional judgment will be needed to determine how this feedback will be incorporated into the final version of the task and KSAO list. The final versions of the task and KSAO list then should be incorporated into a job analysis questionnaire.

Develop and Administer Job Analysis Questionnaire

After the work behavior, task, and KSAO lists have been developed and reviewed, and are considered complete, additional information about the lists often is gathered. The kinds of information to be collected will depend on the purpose(s) for which the job analysis is being conducted. Depending on the purpose of the job analysis and the availability of SMEs, the additional information can be gathered in a number of ways (e.g., using interviews, workshops, or both). In this section, we describe development and administration of the job analysis questionnaire (JAQ). A JAQ allows the SMEs to rate the work behaviors, tasks, and KSAOs on various dimensions, such as frequency or importance. The results of a JAQ can provide defensible data useful for activities such as competency profile or selection instrument development.

A JAQ is useful when job analysis data are collected from a large number of SMEs, and especially when the sample is geographically dispersed. Administration procedures are flexible; JAQs may be administered in person to individuals or groups, by mail, e-mail, or via the Internet. The format of a JAQ can be either unstructured or structured. Unstructured questionnaires can be developed quickly but more time may be needed to analyze the resulting data. Open-ended questions require development of content categories for coding and summarizing the variety of written responses. On the other hand, structured JAQs are usually constructed after preliminary information has been gathered from documentation, observation, and interviews, and questions are more limited in scope (e.g., ratings of task importance). There are several advantages to administering structured JAQs as part of the job analysis process. They are economical to administer to large samples because less professional staff time is required for data collection. JAQs yield data that can be readily analyzed and permit easy comparisons among many different positions in a standardized manner. In addition, JAQs provide data that represent the job over a period of time, as opposed to a specific time period (e.g., the log and observation methods). The resulting data are useful for many purposes, such as identifying training needs (Dunnette, Hough, & Rosse, 1979), identifying ability requirements for jobs (Bosshardt, Rosse, & Peterson, 1984), and establishing pay grades (Gomez-Mejia, Page, & Tornow, 1982). We next describe a method for developing a structured JAQ and analyzing the resulting data.

Develop the JAQ.   The quality of the data is significantly affected by the design of the JAQ. The format and instructions should be carefully developed so that respondents understand what they are asked to do and can provide complete and accurate data. Examples are helpful, especially for unique types of items or scales. The typical sections of a JAQ include:

- A cover page that explains in general terms the purpose and background of the project or study, the role of the JAQ and the respondents, the use of the data, and follow-up steps, and gives the name of a person for respondents to contact in case they have any questions.
- An introduction that describes the sections and structure of the JAQ.
- A task-rating section that includes a description of the steps to complete the ratings for tasks, with examples of scales and items. An example of a task-rating section is provided in Fig. 3.6.
- A KSAO-rating section that includes a description of the steps to complete the KSAO ratings, with example scales and items. An example of a KSAO-rating section is provided in Fig. 3.7.
- A KSAO-to-task linkage rating matrix that includes a description of the steps to complete the KSAO-to-task linkage ratings, with illustrative scales and items. Alternatively, a KSAO-to-work-behavior linkage rating matrix may be used. Use of this type of matrix greatly reduces the rating burden on SMEs and thus may be a good idea if SME time is limited. An example of a KSAO-to-work behavior linkage rating matrix is provided in Fig. 3.8.
- A background information page that requests basic demographic information about the respondent such as current job title, tenure in the current job, tenure in the organization, tenure in the profession, highest level of education, gender, and race or ethnicity.

All or a representative sample of SMEs should complete the JAQ. Incumbents with less than 6 months in the job should not complete JAQs due to their unfamiliarity with the job. SMEs who participated in the job observations can provide ratings on the JAQ, if needed. When only a small number of SMEs is available (e.g., fewer than 50), all may complete the JAQ. When there is a larger number of potential SMEs, a sampling strategy may be used to target a representative number of SMEs who vary on factors such as age, race or ethnicity, gender, specialty, or experience level.

Job analysis ratings such as task importance and frequency ratings, as well as KSAO importance and necessary-at-entry ratings, can be collected through the JAQ. These ratings can be collected individually or via group consensus. They may be collected from SMEs in a workshop or through other means, such as a mail-out or Internet survey in which the individuals complete the JAQ at their convenience. Typically, a JAQ will require approximately 2 hours to complete.

In addition to collecting ratings as described, KSAO-to-task linkage ratings may be collected through the JAQ. If time allows for data analysis of the task and KSAO ratings, a linkage matrix consisting of only those important and frequently performed tasks and those KSAOs that are important and necessary at entry may be developed. The SMEs will determine which tasks and KSAOs are linked by answering the question "Is this KSAO used to perform this task?" and completing the corresponding KSAO-task box. If time does not permit data analysis prior to administration of the KSAO-to-task linkage matrix, SMEs may complete the exercise using all tasks and KSAOs. Alternatively, job analysts may complete the linkage ratings (Baranowski & Anderson, 2005). This may be appropriate if there is concern that the SMEs may not understand some of the KSAOs, or how KSAOs are used to perform work. Illustrative task and KSAO rating scales as well as a rating scale that could be used by the SMEs to provide the linkage ratings are provided in Figs. 3.6 through 3.8.

Analyze JAQ Data

Typically, job analysts combine ratings from multiple raters into a single composite profile to calculate aggregate ratings. In general, the use of aggregate ratings is acceptable because the goal of job analysis is to develop a profile of the job. However, according to McGonigle (2004), there are several types of problems that may occur when using aggregate ratings from SMEs. One major problem can occur if all raters are not rating the same job. A second major problem occurs when trying to separate person and job characteristics (e.g., determining if SMEs are providing information on the job or on their performance of the job). During the job analysis, it is important to be aware of these potential problems and remind SMEs to focus on what is critical to the job that is being analyzed.

Once all of the JAQ ratings have been collected, the list of work behaviors, tasks, and KSAOs can be narrowed by setting rating cutoffs for each scale. This narrowed list can be used to develop a competency profile or to identify the

In this section, we present work behaviors and tasks that may be relevant to your job. Each work behavior is bolded. Under each work behavior, we list its associated tasks. Please rate the frequency and importance of each task for your job by placing an "x" over the appropriate number. Please refer to the following scales when making your ratings.

Task Frequency Rating Scale: *Which of the following most closely matches how often you perform this task in this job?*

0 =   *Never.*
1 =   *A few times per year.*
2 =   *Once a month.*
3 =   *Once a week.*
4 =   *Once a day.*
5 =   *More than once a day.*

Task Importance Rating Scale: *How important is this task for successfully performing this job?*

1 =   *Not important.*
2 =   *Slightly important.*
3 =   *Moderately important.*
4 =   *Very important.*
5 =   *Extremely important.*

TASKS	Which of the following most closely matches how often you perform this task in this job?	How important is this task for successfully performing this job?
	0 = Never 1 = A few times per year or less	1 = Not important 2 = Slightly important 3 = Moderately important
2 = Once a month	4 = Very Important 3 = Once a week	5 = Extremely Important
4 = Once a day	5 = More than once a day	

1.0   Work Behavior: Planning and Initiating Project

1.1   Study blueprints to determine location of high-voltage room or electrical closet.   ⓪ ① ② ③ ④ ⑤   ⓪ ① ② ③ ④ ⑤

1.2   Load, haul and unload materials and supplies.   ⓪ ① ② ③ ④ ⑤   ⓪ ① ② ③ ④ ⑤

1.3   Assemble tools and equipment.   ⓪ ① ② ③ ④ ⑤   ⓪ ① ② ③ ④ ⑤

FIGURE 3.6   Task rating section of JAQ.

test domain from which to build a selection instrument. For the task ratings, the following criticality formula may be used: Criticality Score = (2 × Importance) + Frequency Using the rating scales in Figs. 3.6, 3.7, and 3.8, examples of commonly used cutoffs include:

- Work behaviors with at least one critical (defined above) task
- Tasks with a criticality score of 5.00 or greater
- KSAOs with a mean importance rating of 3.00 or greater
- KSAOs considered to be necessary at entry (rating of 1.00)
- KSAOs that are linked with a mean rating of .67 or greater to at least one task

Once these cutoffs have been used to identify the important and frequently performed tasks and the important and needed-at-entry KSAOs, the reduced list of tasks and KSAOs can be used to inform instrument development as described later in hout this book. An example of results from a JAQ is provided in Fig. 3.9. Based on the results, two of the three tasks (1.1 and 1.3) under the work behavior Planning and Initiating Project met the criticality cutoff for tasks (i.e., a score of 5.00 or greater). Two of the four KSAOs (1 and 3) listed met the cutoff criteria. Knowledge of How to Perform an Emergency Rescue was not needed at entry (with an average rating of .5); therefore, this KSAO may be used as a criterion in performance management but should not be used as a criterion for selection. Ability to Lift Objects Weighing up to 50 Pounds did not meet the cutoff for importance (with an average rating of 2.5) and should not be used in personnel decisions because it is not critical to the job.

If only a small number of SMEs completed the JAQ, then there may not be enough data to permit meaningful statistical analysis and assessment of data quality indices, such as the standard deviation of the ratings and reliability estimates. With a limited sample size, a normal distribution cannot be assumed. In addition, jobs with a small number of incumbents often take on the characteristics of their incumbents and have many other duties.

There is a variety of potential strategies one can use when there is a small number of SMEs available for job analysis. One strategy is to identify similar positions and group those positions. Alternatively, a set of higher order KSAOs or competencies can be identified that may provide a meaningful profile for a diverse set of positions. It is possible that differences disappear when KSAOs are combined to form higher order groups (McGonigle, 2004). When there is a small number of SMEs, multiple sources of job analysis information (e.g., focus groups, interviews, observations, and background information) should be used to remove bias from any one source. Job analysis databases and existing occupational information (e.g., O*NET or the Dictionary of Occupational Titles), Internet sites (e.g., the Office of Personnel Management's General Schedule Position Classification Standards), and local or state personnel sites may serve as comparisons or checks on the job analysis information. Finally, expert judgment should be incorporated when necessary. We now turn to the second method for collecting job-specific information, the critical incident technique.

SECTION 2: KNOWLEDGE, SKILL, AND ABILITY RATINGS

In this section, we present knowledge, skills, and abilities that may be relevant to your job. Please rate the importance of each knowledge, skill, or ability for successfully performing your job by placing an "x" over the appropriate number. Then, rate whether new employees must have each knowledge, skill, or ability when they are first promoted or hired into your job. Please refer to the following scales when making your ratings.

Knowledge, Skills, Abilities, and Other Characteristics Importance Rating Scale: *How important is this knowledge, skill, ability, or other characteristic for successfully performing this job?*

1 =   *Not Important.*
2 =   *Slightly Important.*
3 =   *Moderately Important:*
4 =   *Very Important.*
5 =   *Extremely Important.*

Knowledge, Skills, Abilities, and Other Characteristics Necessary at Entry Rating Scale: *Must new employees have this knowledge, skill, ability, or other characteristic when they first start this job?*

0 =   *No.*
1 =   *Yes.*

KSAOs	How important is this knowledge, skill, ability, or other characteristic for successfully performing this job? 1= Not important 2= Slightly important 3= Moderately important 4= Very important 5= Extremely important	Must new employees have this knowledge, skill, ability, or other characteristic when they first start this job? 0= No 1= Yes
1. Knowledge of National Electrical Code	⓪ ① ② ③ ④ ⑤	⓪ ①
2. Knowledge of how to perform an emergency rescue	⓪ ① ② ③ ④ ⑤	⓪ ①
3. Skill at welding	⓪ ① ② ③ ④ ⑤	⓪ ①
4. Ability to lift objects weighing up to 50 pounds	⓪ ① ② ③ ④ ⑤	⓪ ①

FIGURE 3.7   KSAO rating section of JAQ.

Gather Critical Incidents

Critical incidents are targeted descriptions of job situations or scenarios in which job incumbents have applied specific KSAOs in performing specific work functions at various levels of proficiency (Anderson & Wilson, 1997; Flanagan, 1954). Critical incidents include three components:

- The situation, including the context or events leading up to the behavior
- The individual's behavioral response to the situation
- The outcome of the behavioral response

An example of a critical incident is presented in Fig. 3.10.

Critical incidents provide important, contextually rich examples of job behaviors. Because they provide descriptions of situations in which behaviors occur, critical incidents are particularly useful for developing situational and behavior description interviews (see chap. 7), situational judgment tests (see chap. 9), and assessment center exercises, such as in baskets and role-play or counseling exercises (see chap. 10). Similarly, because they describe behavioral responses to situations at different levels of proficiency (and the resulting outcomes of those behaviors), critical incidents also are especially useful for developing the rating scales needed to score these assessments. Finally, critical incidents are used in the development of behavioral rating scales used in performance appraisals (see chap. 11).

Extensions and adaptations of Flanagan's (1954) critical incident methodology have been widely used in job analyses. The information obtained via this methodology is more behaviorally and contextually rich than task-analytic approaches for gathering job-relevant information. Although task-based approaches focus on discrete activities of individuals performing the job, the critical incident approach and variants of this approach address factors preceding and facilitating the incident (contextual or environmental factors, preceding behaviors or tasks), the incident itself (processes, behaviors), as well as the consequences of the incident (behaviors, tasks, outcomes).

Within his taxonomy of job analysis methods, Harvey (1991) described the critical incident technique as capable of multiple levels of descriptive specificity with regard to the tasks and behaviors in a particular incident. The approach also has the capacity to provide much more explicit situation-oriented information concerning the job than behavior- or worker-oriented approaches. Although the strengths of the behavioral approaches lie in their classification of jobs based on generic, widely applicable, behavioral metrics, this quality precludes them from the level of specificity afforded by the critical incident technique.

Collect Critical Incidents. There are various methods for collecting critical incidents, including face-to-face interviews, telephone interviews, workshops, and systematic record-keeping efforts. The goal of each of these methods is to assist SMEs in providing clear and concise examples of behavior that they have observed.

SECTION 3: KSAO LINKAGES TO WORK BEHAVIORS

In this section of the questionnaire, you will be indicating whether each KSAO is used to perform each work behavior. It is best to work across a row, looking at the first KSAO and then considering whether you would need it to perform each of the work behaviors. Make sure to give an independent rating for each of the work behaviors. Please refer to the following scale to make your ratings. An example is provided below.

Knowledge, Skill, and Ability to Work Behavior Linkage Rating Scale: *Is this KSAO used to perform this work behavior?*
0 =   *No.*
1 =   *Yes.*

Example ratings:

	Work Behavior	
	1. Repairing Watches	2. Supervising employees
KSAOs		
K09 Knowledge of watch mechanics	1	0
A04 Ability to convince others of alternative views	0	1

Explanation

1. Knowledge of watch mechanics is essential for performing the work behavior "Repairing Watches," so it is rated "1."
2. Knowledge of watch mechanics is of little use for performing the work behavior "Supervising Employees" so it is rated "0."
3. Ability to convince others of alternative views is not needed to perform the work behavior "Repairing Watches," so it is rated "0."
4. Ability to convince others of alternative views is useful in order to perform the work behavior "Supervising Employees" so it is rated "1."

KSAOs	1.Planning and Initiating Project	
1. Knowledge of National Electric Code	⓪	①
2. Knowledge of how to perform an emergency rescue	⓪	①
3. Skill at welding	⓪	①
4. Ability to life objects weighing up to 50 pounds	⓪	①

FIGURE 3.8   KSAO linkages to work behaviors section of JAQ.

Tasks	Mean Criticality Score		
Work Behavior: Planning and Initiating Project			
1.1 Study blueprints to determine location of high-voltage room or electrical closet.	12.0		
1.2 Load, haul and unload materials and supplies.	4.0		
1.3 Assemble tools and equipment.	14.0		
	Mean Importance Rating	Mean Needed at Entry Rating	Mean Linkage to Work Behavior Rating
KSAOs			
1. Knowledge of National Electric Code	5	1.0	1.0
2. Knowledge of how to perform an emergency rescue	4.5	0.5	0.75
3 Skill at welding	5	1.0	1.0
4. Ability to lift objects weighing up to 50 pounds	2.5	1.0	0.75

FIGURE 3.9   Example job analysis questionnaire results.

Each of the methods has trade-offs. Face-to-face interviews involve a one-to-one exchange between the job analyst and the SME. Although this method is fairly costly and time consuming, the quality of the incidents is likely to be high because the job analyst can question the SME at the time incidents are provided. The job analyst can also probe more deeply into particular areas the SME tended to omit, and to solicit the SME to provide richness of information and detail that matches the needs of the job analysis. Telephone interviews have several of the same benefits as the face-to-face interview, and are less expensive because no travel is involved.

Workshops also are less expensive than face-to-face interviews. However, depending on the number of SMEs and how the workshop is conducted, there may be less clarification and exchange between the job analyst and each SME, especially if the workshop involves having SMEs record their critical incidents in writing. Similarly, some SMEs may be unwilling or unable to write incidents that contain sufficient detail. Workshops that are conducted to allow SMEs to share

Situation	A contractor was assigned a project that would involve determinating and removing several hundred wires, removing the conduit from the gear, relocating the gear, re-installing the conduit and wire, and finally re-terminating the wire. The only catch to the assignment was that the work had to begin at 11:00 p.m. on Thanksgiving, and had to be completed by 7:00 a.m. the following morning, which seemed nearly impossible.
Action:	The foreman chose seven of the best wiremen employed by the company to do the work. Through skillful planning and hardwork, the men worked through the night without stopping for a break and got the job done on time and with no problems.
Outcome:	The customer was extremely impressed that they got such a project completed in such a short amount of time with zero errors. As a result, the customer has chosen this contractor to do almost all of its work.

FIGURE 3.10   Example of a critical incident.

descriptions orally can compensate for potential weaknesses in individuals' description or their memory of events, and to allow others to fill in the gaps. Thus, this method provides a greater potential for synergy among SMEs and potentially greater participation. Finally, systematic record keeping on the part of SMEs can provide high quality data, because the SME does not have to recall events that happened months or even years prior to the data collection. However, record-keeping efforts must take place over an extended period of time, requiring the SME to be strongly motivated to continue the effort.

In this section, we describe the workshop method for collecting critical incidents with the aim of collecting job-level rather than KSAO-level information. (It is important to note, however, that there are other purposes for using the critical incident technique and that this method may be focused on collecting information for a particular KSAO.) In general, the workshop method entails assembling SMEs into a small group, training the SMEs on how to write critical incidents, and then having them record in writing those critical incidents relevant to the job. The steps are as follows:

Step 1:   Identify SMEs. This would be the same process as described previously. For most purposes, it is important to document the SME characteristics to ensure representativeness as well as experience with the job being analyzed.

Step 2:   Prepare for critical incident workshops. The workshops should be arranged several weeks in advance. Each workshop session should be scheduled to last about 3 to 4 hours, with 15 to 30 minutes for training, and about 2.5 hours for writing the incidents. One should schedule 6 to 10 individuals per session. Equipment and facilities that will be needed include a large room with tables and chairs for SMEs, critical incident forms, pencils, and various materials to train the SMEs on how to write critical incidents.

Step 3:   Conduct critical incident workshop. In general, the purpose of the workshop is to have individuals who are knowledgeable about the job describe instances of ineffective, average, and effective job performance. SMEs are asked to think back over the last 6 months and relate actual behaviors they have exhibited or observed others exhibit on the job. Participants are asked to record the circumstances leading up to the incident, what actions were taken by the job holder, and the outcome of the actions. The first 15 to 30 minutes of the workshop should be used to train the SMEs on how to write critical incidents. During this training, the individual conducting the workshop should review the goals of the workshop, explain the format of critical incidents, and provide some tips for writing a useable critical incident. Tips for writing critical incidents are provided in Fig. 3.11. During this review and background discussion of critical incidents, SMEs should be encouraged to ask questions. When providing examples of incidents, it may be best to use an example that is not part of the job being analyzed because a job-relevant example may unduly narrow SMEs' focus. In other words, if an example incident for the job of electrician involved reading blueprints, it is likely that a disproportionate number of incidents written in that workshop would involve reading, or not reading, blueprints.

Some job analysts opt to place additional structure on the critical incident workshop by providing dimensions of performance for which the SMEs should write incidents. The idea behind using predefined dimensions is that they ensure that SMEs write incidents on all the relevant aspects of the job. At times, this has been done by asking SMEs to "write at least one critical incident for each performance dimension." Note, however, that use of predefined performance dimensions will cause SMEs to focus on those dimensions—perhaps to the exclusion of other important, yet undiscovered dimensions. Also, the use of predefined dimensions means that the job analyst cannot use the critical incident technique to discover the underlying structure of performance, thus losing a potentially useful outcome of the critical incident method.

After the workshop leader conducts the training, the SMEs should begin to write their incidents. A form that is useful for collecting critical incidents is shown in Fig. 3.12. The form that SMEs use to write incidents should include prompts for the situation, the behavior, the outcome, and a rating of the behavior's effectiveness.

During the workshop, SMEs may have difficulty thinking of incidents. When this happens, the job analyst should probe the SMEs to stimulate recall. A typical probe is, "Think of a recent situation in which you observed an employee do something that was especially effective or ineffective on the job. What led up to the performance? What did the person do? What happened as a result?" A set of probes that may be used is shown in Fig. 3.13.

In the workshop, it should be emphasized that incidents should describe actions SMEs saw a person do, not what the SMEs inferred from the action about the skills or personal characteristics of the person. For example, rather than write that an individual "displayed loyalty," the incidents should describe what the individual did that was so effective (e.g., worked all night to finish a job, or defended the supervisor's position to a group of subordinates).

When SMEs start writing incidents, the job analyst should encourage and reinforce them. The purpose is to shape their behavior so that they write productively. The incidents should be reviewed during the workshop and as they are being handed in to ensure compliance with the instructions. If an incident does not contain important information (i.e., describes an individual knowledge, skill, or ability, rather than the behavior that occurred), the writer should be probed for more detail about the behavior that occurred. Because many individuals hesitate to write, especially in a group setting, small editorial changes should be ignored during the workshop. These changes can be made after the workshop. If, during the workshop, a participant develops a well-written critical incident, the job analyst might ask the SME's permission to read it aloud to the group. This will reinforce the writer and provide an example to other SMEs. This may be done several times during the workshop so that writers have several examples of well-written incidents. Although the number of incidents written by each SME will vary, it is reasonable to expect that an average of 5 to 10 critical incidents can be generated by each SME in a 2- or 3-hour workshop.

A critical incident written by an electrician is shown in Fig. 3.14. This particular incident is not very useful because:

- It is written in the passive voice.
- It is unclear who performed the behaviors.
- It does not refer to the actions of a single person.
- An action is not clearly presented; therefore it is unclear what led to the outcome. A well-written incident is provided in Fig. 3.15. Note that the incident:

- Discusses a specific incident in an action-oriented manner.
- Describes a complete situation, action, and result.
- Refers to the behavior of one individual rather than a team.

The number of incidents needed to adequately describe a job's performance requirements will depend on the complexity of the job. For example, it would take fewer critical incidents to describe thoroughly the effective and ineffective performance of a toll collector than it would to describe the performance of an electrician. To ensure that enough incidents are generated to fully describe the job domain, the critical incidents obtained in each workshop should be reviewed. When fewer than two or three new incidents are gathered at a subsequent workshop, it is likely that a comprehensive set of incidents has been generated. In addition, it also is usually desirable to have critical incidents depicting performance that spans the effectiveness range. Effectiveness ratings provided by the SMEs can assist in monitoring how well the range of effectiveness is represented.

---

1. Concisely describe the situation, the action taken, and the outcome. Carefully decide what information is relevant to each event.

2. Describe what the apprentice or journeyman did (or failed to do) in that specific situation. Do not describe "types of things that people do" or general traits of effective or ineffective workers. The emphasis should be on what was observed, not on interpretation of the action.

3. Focus on the actions of a single person rather than those of a team.

4. Write events in the third person (he or she) and do not use personally identifying information. Use terms such as "the apprentice," "the supervisor," etc. Even if you relate events that are things you did, please write them in the third person.

5. Keep it concise. It is important that you carefully decide what information is relevant to each event.

6. Write about actions you have taken or the actions of others that you have personally observed, not situations reported to you by someone else, because your recollection of these events will be the most vivid and accurate.

FIGURE 3.11   Tips for writing critical incidents.

Edit Critical Incidents.   After critical incidents are collected, the information is entered into a database and edited. The purposes of editing are to: (a) place each incident in a standard, readable format; (b) clarify some of the wording by correcting spelling, grammar, and punctuation; (c) group redundant or highly similar critical incidents; (d) ensure a comparable level of detail across incidents; and (e) rephrase statements as necessary to eliminate jargon that is not widely used in the SME community. This editing is usually done by a job analyst familiar with the job being studied. Guidelines for editing critical incidents are as follows:

- Incidents are written in three parts, but the writer may not have made the correct distinctions about where to record each part. All information about the background leading up to the incident should be part of the situation or context. The middle section on the actions taken should include all of the key steps taken by the actor in the incident. Sometimes writers put some of this information under the outcome. The outcome can usually be summarized in one sentence. The outcome should be as concrete as possible.
- The words of the writer should be used as much as possible. The analyst should not make interpretations about what happened, but should try to describe the incident clearly and concisely.
- Spelling, grammar, and punctuation mistakes should be corrected.

Critical Incident Form	Participant #_____

1. What was the situation leading up to the event? [Describe the context.]

2. What did the apprentice or journeyman do?

3. What was the outcome or result of the apprentice's or journeyman's action?

4. Circle the number below that best reflects the level of performance that this **event** exemplifies.

1	2	3	4	5	6	7
Highly Ineffective			Moderately Effective			Highly Effective

FIGURE 3.12   Critical incident form.

- Think of something you did in the past that you are proud of.
- Think of a time when you learned something the hard way. What did you do and what was the outcome?
- Think of a person whom you admire on the job. Can you recall an incident that convinced you that the person was an outstanding performer?
- Think of a time when you realized too late that you should have done something differently. What did you do and what was the outcome?
- Think about the last six months. Can you recall a day when you were particularly effective? What did you do that made you effective?
- Think of a time when you saw someone do something in a situation and you thought to yourself, "If I were in that same situation, I would handle it differently." What was the scenario you saw?
- Think about mistakes you have seen employees make when they are new at the job.
- Think about actions taken by more experienced employees that help them to avoid making mistakes.

FIGURE 3.13   Probes for stimulating SMEs to write critical incidents.

- Incidents should be about the actor named in the incident. Sometimes individuals will think they are writing an incident about a trainee or subordinate when the incident is really about the supervisor. One way to figure this out is to determine whose actions resulted in the outcome. If the supervisor's actions produced the outcome, then the incident is about the supervisor and, therefore, a different job.
- References to the actors should be gender neutral (unless it is somehow important to the incident). Masculine and feminine pronouns should be eliminated.
- Incidents that provide insufficient information or that do not include a plausible relationship between the person's actions and the outcomes should be discarded.

Analyze Critical Incidents

To use the critical incidents to inform instrument development, SMEs should reassign the incidents to performance dimensions and then rate the behaviors described in the incident for effectiveness. This process is known as "retranslation" (Smith & Kendall, 1963). Steps for conducting this process are described next.

Identify SMEs. SMEs can be the authors of the incidents or they can be an independent sample. Identifying an independent sample of SMEs helps accomplish an alternative goal of developing the dimensional structure using information from the broadest possible set of SMEs.

Present Dimensions and Edited Critical Incidents to the SMEs. This could be done in the context of a workshop, or in a mail-out or Internet survey. The task is to sort each incident into one dimension based on its content and then to rate the effectiveness level of that incident. A seven-point scale is often used for these ratings, where 1 = highly ineffective and 7 = highly effective performance. The performance dimensions may be gathered from the results of the job-task analysis. Appendix A provides an illustrative set of performance dimensions for the job of electrician. An example of a form that SMEs could use to do the retranslation activity is provided in Fig. 3.16.

Analyze the Data. Data should be analyzed by calculating the percentage of respondents who sorted each incident into each performance dimension and the mean and standard deviation of the effectiveness ratings given to each behavioral incident. Appendix B shows the output of a critical incident data analysis. The first column shows the dimensions into which the SMEs categorized the incidents; the second column shows the percentage of respondents who indicated that the incident should be placed in that category; the third column shows the number of SMEs, from among those participating in retranslation, who indicated that the

What were the circumstances leading up to the incident?

During the installation of a new feeder on the exterior of a building, it was decided to carry the cable up a nearby exterior stairway and push the cable down into the conduit.

What actions did the worker take that were effective or ineffective?

The cable easily went into the conduit. However, as it gained momentum all of the cable went through the conduit and out onto the ground.

What were the outcomes of these actions?

The crew had to repeat the job, but this time, the cable was tied off on the high end of the conduit.

FIGURE 3.14   An example of a critical incident that is not useful.

What were the circumstances leading up to the incident?

A journeyman was to install a new feeder on the exterior of a large 10-story building, and there was no obvious method for getting the cable through the conduit.

What actions did the worker take that were effective or ineffective?

The journeyman decided to run the cable up a nearby stairway and drop the cable in from above. He placed the bottom end of the cable into the conduit and let it go so that gravity would pull the cable through the conduit. He failed to tie off the top end of the cable to keep all of it from falling to the ground. The cable gained momentum as more and more cable went into the conduit, and the journeyman was unable to stop it when it got to the end.

What were the outcomes of these actions?

All of the cable slipped through the conduit and landed on the ground. The journeyman had to repeat the job, but this time, the cable was tied off on the high end of the conduit.

FIGURE 3.15   An example of a critical incident that is useful.

incident should be placed in that category; the fourth column shows the mean effectiveness rating of the incident; the fifth column shows the standard deviation of the effectiveness rating; and the sixth and final column shows the incident. As shown in Appendix B, the first incident was sorted into Dimension A: Planning, preparing and organizing work by 76% (16 out of 21) respondents. The mean effectiveness rating is 5.69, which is fairly high on a seven-point scale, and the standard deviation is .85, indicating a relatively high degree of agreement. Conversely, respondents appeared to have trouble categorizing the ninth incident. Eleven out of 21 (52%) respondents put the incident in Dimension A, whereas 10 out of 21 (48%) put the incident in Dimension J. The incident received fairly average effectiveness ratings in both categories (3.00 and 2.70), and the standard deviations of effectiveness were fairly large to moderate (over 1.13 and .78).

Use Results to Inform Instrument Development. The results of the preceding data analyses will reveal where and how well an incident fits into the performance structure, and how the behavior depicted in the incident fits on a continuum of effectiveness. When there is high agreement among SMEs as to the dimensional placement of an incident, it can clearly be assigned to that dimension. Those incidents with the highest agreement on category placement can be considered most representative of the dimension, and thus can be used as examples when discussing and defining performance on the dimensions. The incidents selected should have high, medium, or low mean effectiveness ratings and those ratings should have small standard deviations.

Given this information, the job analyst may choose to select incidents for use in training exercises, rating instruments, exemplars of performance, or assessment exercises. The way the incidents are to be used will affect which incidents are selected. For example, the job analyst may want to select incidents that exhibit different mean levels of effectiveness so that they can be used for behavioral anchors at low, moderate, or high levels of performance on a particular dimension. In general, however, the best incidents tend to be those where there is high agreement among SMEs on category placement and on the effectiveness ratings (as indicated by a small standard deviation).

SUMMARY

In this chapter, we described the job-task analysis process for specifying and structuring the two domains important to the world of work: the job-task domain and the KSAO domain. The goal of the process is to systematically obtain comprehensive, relevant information appropriate for the purpose(s) of the job analysis that specifies these two domains and links them together. We also described the critical incident technique, which is useful for understanding the performance of individuals, systems, and organizations. Various applications arise from this greater understanding of performance, such as training individuals, designing systems and organizations, conducting performance appraisals, developing assessment tools, and evaluating systems. The critical incident technique is particularly appropriate for analyzing complex jobs in which the behavior exhibited largely depends on the situation encountered, as opposed to routine jobs where the same behaviors are routinely performed.

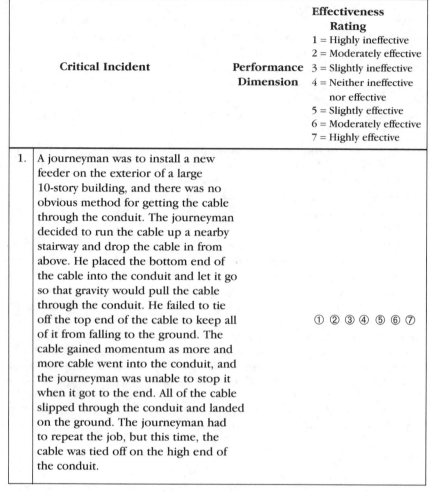

Critical Incident	Performance Dimension	Effectiveness Rating 1 = Highly ineffective 2 = Moderately effective 3 = Slightly ineffective 4 = Neither ineffective nor effective 5 = Slightly effective 6 = Moderately effective 7 = Highly effective
1. A journeyman was to install a new feeder on the exterior of a large 10-story building, and there was no obvious method for getting the cable through the conduit. The journeyman decided to run the cable up a nearby stairway and drop the cable in from above. He placed the bottom end of the cable into the conduit and let it go so that gravity would pull the cable through the conduit. He failed to tie off the top end of the cable to keep all of it from falling to the ground. The cable gained momentum as more and more cable went into the conduit, and the journeyman was unable to stop it when it got to the end. All of the cable slipped through the conduit and landed on the ground. The journeyman had to repeat the job, but this time, the cable was tied off on the high end of the conduit.		① ② ③ ④ ⑤ ⑥ ⑦

FIGURE 3.16   Retranslation activity form.

The information obtained through the job-task analysis that specifies the task and KSAO domains, supplemented by the information from the critical incident technique, provides the basis for predictor and criterion instrument development. As will be shown in the next chapters, the reduced list of tasks and KSAOs from the job-task analysis are used to develop test plans and specifications, and the contextually rich information and understanding from the critical incidents helps test developers create tests that are job-related.

REFERENCES

American Educational Research Association, American Psychological Association, & National Council on Measurement in Education (Joint Committee). (1999). *Standards for educational and psychological testing.* Washington, DC: American Educational Research Association.

Anderson, L. A. & Wilson, S. (1997). Critical incident technique. In D. L. Whetzel & G. R. Wheaton (Eds.), *Applied measurement methods in industrial psychology* (pp. 89–112). Palo Alto, CA: Consulting Psychologists Press.

Baranowski, L. E., & Anderson, L. E. (2005). Examining rating source variation in work behavior to KSA linkages. *Personnel Psychology, 58,* 1041–1054.

Bosshardt, M. J., Rosse, R. L., & Peterson, N. G. (1984). *Electric power plant study: Analysis of job activities and personal qualifications of maintenance employees in electric power generating plants* (Institute Report No. 90). Minneapolis, MN: Personnel Decisions Research Institute.

Dunnette, M. D., Hough, L. M., & Rosse, R. L. (1979). Task and job taxonomies as the basis for identifying labor supply sources and evaluating employment qualifications. *Human Resources Planning, 2,* 37–51.

Civil Rights Act of 1964, 42 U.S.C. Section 2000e.

Equal Pay Act of 1963 (Pub. L. 88-38) (EPA), as amended (29 USC §206d).

Fair Labor Standards Act of 1938 (FLSA), as amended (29 USC § 201 et seq.; 29 CFR Parts 510 to 794).

Flanagan, J. C. (1954). The critical incident technique. *Psychological Bulletin, 41,* 237–358.

Flanagan, J. C. (1957). *Research on the selection of aircrew personnel* (Research Notes. No. 13, 1-4). Washington, DC: American Institutes for Research.

Fleishman, E. A., Costanza, D. C., & Marshall-Mies, J. C. (1997). Abilities. In N. G. Peterson, M. D. Mumford, W. C. Borman, P. R. Jeanneret, & E. A. Fleishman (Eds.), *O*NET: An occupational information network* (pp. 175–195). Washington, DC: American Psychological Association.

Gael, S. (1983). *Job analysis: A guide to assessing work activities.* San Francisco: Jossey-Bass.

Ghorpade, J. (1988). *Job analysis: A handbook for the human resource director.* Englewood Cliffs, NJ: Prentice Hall.

Gomez-Mejia, L. R., Page, R. C., & Tornow, W. (1982). A comparison of the practical utility of traditional, statistical, and hybrid job evaluation approaches. *Academy of Management Journal, 24,* 790–809.

Harvey, R. (1991). Job analysis. In M. D. Dunnette & L. M. Hough (Eds.), *Handbook of I/O psychology* (2nd ed., Vol. 2, pp. 71–164). Palo Alto, CA: Consulting Psychologists Press.

Holland, J. L. (1973). *Making vocational choices: A theory of careers.* Englewood Cliffs, NJ: Prentice Hall.

Jackson, D. N. (1967). *Personality research form manual.* Goshen, NY: Research Psychologists Press.

Lievens, F., Sanchez, J. I., & De Corte, W. (2004). Easing the inferential leap in competency modeling: The effects of task-related information and subject matter expertise. *Personnel Psychology, 57,* 881–904.

Lindbergh, D. A. B., Siegel, E. R., Rapp, B. A., Wallingford, K. T., & Wilson, S. R. (1993). Use of MEDLINE by physicians for clinical problem solving. *Journal of American Medical Association, 269,* 3124–3129.

Lytle, C. W. (1954). *Job evaluation methods.* New York: Ronald Press.

McGonigle, T. (2004, April). *Measurement problems in small n job analysis projects*. Paper presented at the 19th annual conference of the Society for Industrial and Organizational Psychology, Inc., Chicago.

O*NET Consortium. (2005). *Welcome to O*NET OnLine! Making occupational information interactive and accessible for all.* Available from www.onecenter.org

Peterson, N. G., Mumford, M. D., Borman, W. C., Jeanneret, P. R., & Fleishman, E. A. (Eds.). (1997). *O*NET: An occupational information network.* Washington, DC: American Psychological Association.

Shippman, J. S., Ash, R. A., Battista, M., Carr, L., Eyde, L. D., Hesketh, B., et al. (2000). The practice of competency modeling. *Personnel Psychology, 53,* 703–740.

Smith, P. C., & Kendall, L. M. (1963). Retranslation of expectations: An approach to the construction of unambiguous anchors for rating scales. *Journal of Applied Psychology, 47,* 149–155.

Society for Industrial and Organizational Psychology, Inc. (2003). *Principles for the validation and use of personnel selection procedures* (4th ed.). Bowling Green, OH: Author.

Taylor, F. W. (1911). *Principles of scientific management.* New York: Harper & Row.

Uniform guidelines on employee selection procedures. (1978). *Federal Register, 43,* 38290–38315.

Williams, K. M., & Crafts, J. L. (1997). Inductive job analysis: The job/task inventory method. In D. L. Whetzel & G. R. Wheaton (Eds.), *Applied measurement methods in industrial psychology* (1st ed.). Palo Alto, CA: Consulting Psychologists Press Inc.

Williams, K. M., Peterson, N. G., & Bell, J. A. (1994). *Job analysis of three electrical worker positions for the National Joint Apprenticeship and Training Committee.* Washington, DC: American Institutes for Research.

APPENDIX A

Job Performance Dimensions (from Williams, Peterson, & Bell, 1994)

Reprinted with Permission

APPENDIX A

Job Performance Dimensions

A. **Planning, Preparing, and Organizing Work**

- thinking through job requirements
- ordering materials and ensuring sufficient supplies
- planning for problems that might occur
- laying out steps and procedures
- documenting or diagramming the job

B. **Working Hard, Taking Initiative, and Being Responsible**

- completing a lot of work in a short time period
- taking on more responsibility
- continuing to work in difficult circumstances
- adhering to job rules, including starting times
- not using drugs or alcohol on the job

C. **Solving Problems**

- finding new methods to complete a task when a problem occurs
- improvising using available materials
- finding a better way to do a task

D. Working Safely

- following correct safety procedures
- using tools and equipment safely
- using precautions when working with hot circuits

E. Teamwork

- communicating clearly with other workers
- helping other team members
- following the instructions given for completing a task
- asking for help if needed
- warning others of danger

F. Troubleshooting

- finding the cause of an electrical problem
- inspecting or testing equipment
- getting a system or equipment to work

G. Responding to an Emergency

- preventing a problem from worsening
- administering first aid
- keeping the public out of danger

H. Supervising

- assigning tasks to others and monitoring progress
- contributing to crew morale
- disciplining other workers
- managing project resources
- working with contractor, inspectors, and other outside people
- checking working conditions

I. Training

- providing learning opportunities for others
- demonstrating proper techniques
- giving feedback on performance
- explaining the reasons behind work procedures

J. Following Blueprints, Code, and Installation Instructions

- checking blueprints to install correctly
- making sure that an installation meets Code
- reading instructions from kits

K. Using Tools and Equipment

- using hand tools
- using machinery, including trucks
- using ladders

L. Planning and Installing Conduit

- finding a path for a duct bank or raceway
- installing a duct bank and securing the conduit
- building a raceway and supporting the conduit

M. Preparing Conduit for Installation

- cutting and threading conduit
- bending conduit

N. Pulling Wire or Cable

- measuring wire or cable
- using a fish tape, mouse, or other means to establish a pull line
- setting up a hand or machine tugger
- lubricating the pull
- tagging the wire or cable

O. Installing Panels

- establishing panel location
- terminating wires in panel
- labeling the panel

P. Installing Switches, Receptacles, Lighting, and Other Fixtures

- establishing correct location for the outlet or fixture
- making terminations
- finishing the installation

Q. Installing Buss Ducts and Switchgear

- moving switchgear into place
- making terminations
- installing and securing buss ducts

R. Installing Transformers

- checking phases
- marking wires
- connecting wires to the equipment

Example of Results from Analyses of Critical Incidents (from Williams, Peterson, & Bell, 1994)

Reprinted with Permission

Dimension	Percent of respondents placing an incident with a particular dimension	Number of respondents placing an incident with a particular dimension	Mean effectiveness rating of incidents	Standard deviation of effectiveness ratings	Critical incident
A: Planning, and organizing work	76	16/21	5.69	.85	An electrical apprentice working on the construction of a six-story hospital, was responsible for the installation of all underground conduit runs for the parking lot lighting. Before beginning to run the conduit, the apprentice ensured that there would be enough material to finish the project. After gathering all the material that was needed to successfully complete the job and organizing it in a manner that would allow the apprentice to keep easy access to it, the apprentice began the project. The result of the apprentice's organizing allowed the project to be finished in a short amount of time and the project to be completed correctly and effectively.
F: Trouble shooting	82	18/22	4.94	1.08	An apprentice was asked to troubleshoot a lighting fixture. The lighting system voltage was a 120/208 system. The

Dimension	Percent of respondents placing an incident with a particular dimension	Number of respondents placing an incident with a particular dimension	Mean effectiveness rating of incidents	Standard deviation of effectiveness ratings	Critical incident
					apprentice opened up the belly bar on the fixture and found that the voltage rating was 277/480 ballast. It was installed incorrectly from the manufacturer. The apprentice changed the ballast to the correct voltage reading.
B: Working hard, taking initiative, and being responsible.	24	5/21	6.40	0.49	A journeyman put an apprentice on a speaker system that was showing no load with a general idea as to the route of the speakers. The apprentice looked up the plans for the speaker system, better understood the job and started to troubleshoot the system using a meter. The apprentice located and fixed the problem well before the journeyman expected.
F: Trouble shooting	57	12/21	6.08	0.76	
A: Planning preparing, and organizing work	39	7/18	5.86	1.67	The foreman of a job gave a print to an an apprentice and said, "Tomorrow, lay lay this whole floor out and pipe it." The next day the apprentice realized that he did not know how to do the task and the foreman was not available. The
H: Supervising	50	9/18	5.22	1.53	

Dimension	Percent of respondents placing an incident with a particular dimension	Number of respondents placing an incident with a particular dimension	Mean effectiveness rating of incidents	Standard deviation of effectiveness ratings	Critical incident
					apprentice reviewed available documentation until he learned what he needed to know. The apprentice successfully completed the job and felt proud.
A: Planning, preparing, and supervising work	60	12/20	2.45	0.66	The job was piping school rooms for lighting. An apprentice used shallow boxes for lighting because that was all that was available at that time. The apprentice had a very hard time doing make-up in the boxes, which took extra time.
C: Solving problems	15	3/20	3.75	.043	
N: Pulling wire or cable	20	4/20	3.50	0.50	
A: Planning, preparing, and organizing work	77	17/22	6.06	0.80	Twelve workers were spread over a pharmaceutical plant with approximately 20 buildings on site. The apprentice suggested that the workers turn in material lists a day in advance, so that the apprentice could have it ready and organized. Since the apprentice took the initiative to better organize the material and demand for it, there was minimal down time for the mechanics.

Dimension	Percent of respondents placing an incident with a particular dimension	Number of respondents placing an incident with a particular dimension	Mean effectiveness rating of incidents	Standard deviation of effectiveness ratings	Critical incident
C: Solving problems	95	19/20	1.16	0.36	While pulling in a "pull line," the rope got hung up in a block. An apprentice took the bucket, set up and tried to free the "p-line" by reaching through an open wire secondary without gloves and sleeves on. The apprentice was electrocuted and died.
A: Planning, preparing, and organizing work	80	16/20	2.25	0.83	The apprentice was told to load material on the trucks before going home. The apprentice went home before finishing loading the trucks. The apprentice forgot some material the next day which delayed the job.
A: Planning, preparing, and organizing work	52	11/21	3.00	1.13	A job was to run pipe starting from an MCC to a trough 80 feet away, using the best path to run with the least amount of bends. The apprentice mounted the trough and knocked out the top before the pipe was run to it. The result was the pipe had to be offset to reach the knockout instead of waiting to see where the pipe would line up.
J: Following blueprints, code, and installation instructions	48	10/21	2.70	0.78	

CHAPTER FOUR

Measurement Plans and Specifications

Teresa L. Russell
Human Resources Research Organization

Norman G. Peterson
Satisfaction Performance Research Center

OVERVIEW

Organizations use employment tests and other assessment tools to select workers who are likely to perform well in their new jobs. In doing so, organizations hope to become more competitive by employing well-qualified staff and to save money that would otherwise be lost through poor employee performance. Even so, the validity of the selection procedure for identifying well-qualified workers, while it might be the paramount objective, is not the organization's only concern. When designing employee selection procedures, organizations attempt to balance three goals:

1. Maximize validity.
2. Minimize adverse impact (i.e., test score differences between legally or societally significant subgroups).
3. Enhance the efficiency of the procedures.

Maximizing test validity increases the likelihood that organizations will select applicants who will perform well on the job. Evidence of validity can come from correlations between employee test scores and job performance, linkages between the content of the job and the content of tests, and linkages between job-relevant worker characteristics and the tests that measure them, as well as documentation of the validity of a test for similar jobs.

Minimizing adverse impact against minorities and women is important for enhancing the diversity of the organization's workforce and for meeting professional and legal standards for employee testing (American Educational Research Association, American Psychological Association, & National Council on Measurement in Education, 1999; Society of Industrial and Organizational Psychology [SIOP], 2003). The *Uniform Guidelines for Employee Selection Procedures* (1978) recommended that employers seek valid alternatives to cognitive ability tests when such tests are found to produce substantial adverse impact. Minimizing adverse impact enhances the legal defensibility of the selection procedures.

No matter how it is done, employee selection costs time and money. Tests of underlying personnel characteristics must be selected or developed, and then administered and scored. Interview questions must be developed, interviewers must be trained, and the sessions must be conducted. Background data instruments and situational judgment tests also may be constructed, administered, and scored. The amount of time and money an organization is willing to spend developing, maintaining, and operating an employee selection program will depend on the type of job under consideration as well as available organizational resources.

This chapter describes methods that we have used to develop measurement plans that, on balance, satisfy the three objectives of employee selection, and test specifications that implement those measurement plans. A measurement plan summarizes information from a thorough job analysis and literature review. It provides a rationale for tests and assessment methods that are chosen as part of the selection procedure and for those that are not chosen. It documents the hypothesized relationships between measurement methods and worker characteristics. A measurement plan is a blueprint for development and validation of selection procedures. In turn, test specifications implement the measurement plan. They document the details (e.g., format and number of items, tasks or questions, scoring procedures, time restrictions) for each measure identified in the measurement plan.

THE MEASUREMENT PLAN

The centerpiece of a measurement plan is a matrix, shown in Fig. 4.1, that compares worker characteristics to be measured against possible measurement methods. Worker characteristics to be measured are listed along the rows; those worker characteristics should be ones resulting from a job analysis, as described in chapters 2 and 3. Possible measurement methods, derived from review of the research literature, are listed in the columns. Several alternative measurement methods are described in chapters 5 (tests of cognitive ability), 6 (training and experience measures), 7 (employment interviews), 8 (background data), 9 (situational judgment tests), and 10 (assessment centers). Judgments about the quality with which different measurement methods are likely to measure the worker characteristics appear in the cells of the matrix.

There are three primary steps for completing the matrix. The first is a thorough job analysis to identify the job-relevant worker characteristics that should be measured. Once the job analysis is complete, the second step is to identify methods

MEASUREMENT METHODS				
Worker Characteristics	*Aptitude or Achievement Tests*	*Interview*	*Self-Report*	*Simulation*
Ability to add, subtract, multiply, and divide and use formulas				
Ability to understand verbal instructions and warnings				
Ability to communicate orally with others				
Ability to read and understand graphs, charts, and diagrams				
Ability to develop alternative solutions to a problem and choose the best alternative				
Ability to work in a noisy environment				
Ability to work at heights				

FIGURE 4.1   Worker characteristics and methods of measurement matrix.

of measuring the worker characteristics—methods that are likely to prove useful given organizational constraints on resources and the goals of maximizing validity and minimizing adverse impact. The third step is to complete the matrix—make judgments about the quality of a measurement method for assessing the constructs at hand while weighing concerns about adverse impact and costs.

Identify Worker Characteristics

Worker characteristics—knowledges, skills, abilities, and other characteristics (KSAOs)—must be derived from a thorough job analysis. Chapters 2 and 3 explain job analysis methodologies that yield job-relevant worker characteristics. Generally, all job analysis methods involve soliciting job information from subject matter experts (SMEs) who may be supervisors, job incumbents, trainers, or job analysts. Regardless of the job analysis methodology, professional standards and legal guidelines (American Educational Research Association et al., 1999; *Uniform Guidelines,* 1978; SIOP, 2003) suggest that worker characteristics selected for measurement should be: (a) job relevant, (b) before-hire requirements, and (c) supported by prior research.

Job relevance means that the worker characteristic is needed to perform job activities. Evidence of job relevance can come from several sources, but usually involves judgments about worker characteristics. Two of the most frequently used judgments are: (a) the overall importance of the worker characteristics for performing the job and (b) the importance of the worker characteristic for performing critical job tasks, duties, or activities. The first judgment often is obtained from a questionnaire or focus group where SMEs are asked to judge the importance of various worker characteristics. The second judgment is usually obtained from a second exercise in which SMEs are asked to rate the importance of each of many worker characteristics for performing job activities. Both of these procedures are described in greater detail in chapters 2 and 3.

Worker characteristics used for selection into entry-level jobs should be those required before hire. Worker characteristics that can be learned in a brief orientation period after job entry are candidates for training programs, not selection methods (*Uniform Guidlines,* 1978). Evidence that the worker characteristic is one that employees should bring with them to the job is typically collected during a job analysis. This before-hire requirement may be particularly subject to differences across organizations. Some organizations may choose, as a matter of philosophy, to provide their own training for many characteristics; another may provide training for very few, only for characteristics unique to the organization.

Another factor to consider in selecting worker characteristics for measurement is prior research support. Characteristics that have demonstrated validity in previous studies of similar jobs are good candidates for inclusion.

Identify Methods for Measuring Worker Characteristics

Test designers must carefully consider different types of measurement methods, their properties, and the test-administration medium that is most likely to prove

Measurement Method	Advantages	Disadvantages/Concerns	
Achievement or Aptitude Tests			
	General cognitive ability Specific cognitive ability Knowledge or achievement Operational costs are relatively low. There is strong evidence of the validity of cognitive tests for many occupations. Reliability usually is high.		
	Racial/ethnic subgroup differences tend to be large. Interviews are appealing to organizations.	Interviews	
	Interviews have proven to be valid selection tools for some jobs, but the magnitude of the validity typically is not large. Interviewers and raters must be trained.		Operational costs are relatively high.
Self-Report			
	Biographical Data Personality Inventories		Operational costs are relatively low.

	Can predict contextual performance.		
	Can provide incremental validity over cognitive tests.		All self-report measures can be susceptible to response distortion.
	Content validation is usually not an option. Applicants may find some items offensive.		
Simulations			
	Situational Judgment Tests Work Sample Tests		
	Assessment Center Exercises There is some evidence of criterion-related validity.		Simulations can have content and face validity. Operational costs are high for high-fidelity simulations.
	Assessors often need to be trained.		

FIGURE 4.2   Characteristics of several types of measurement methods.

useful to the organization. Measurement methods can be broadly clustered into four categories—achievement or aptitude tests, interviews, self-report measures, or simulations. Each type of method offers some advantages and disadvantages as noted in Fig. 4.2.

Aptitude or Achievement Tests.   Aptitude or achievement tests include measures of cognitive ability (which are discussed in greater detail in chap. 5) and knowledge. Relative to other tests, aptitude or achievement tests are usually inexpensive to administer and score.

The chief advantage of aptitude or achievement tests lies in their excellent psychometric quality. Aptitude and achievement tests are typically highly reliable (with observed reliabilities commonly in the .80-.90 range), and there is strong evidence of their validity for most occupations (Hunter & Hunter, 1984; Schmitt,

Gooding, Noe, & Kirsch, 1984; Schmidt & Hunter, 1998). Aptitude and achievement tests are particularly useful for predicting task performance (Borman & Motowidlo, 1993; Campbell, McCloy, Oppler, & Sager, 1993) and training performance or grades (Schmitt et al., 1984).

There are average differences among racial-ethnic groups and between the genders on cognitive abilities. Those differences can lead to adverse impact on aptitude and achievement tests. Differences between Whites and African Americans are relatively uniform across a wide variety of cognitive abilities (e.g., verbal, math, spatial); there typically is about one standard deviation difference between Whites' and African Americans' scores (Department of Defense, 1982; Jensen, 1980; National Center for Education Statistics [NCES], 1994). Hispanic and Asian American differences are more difficult to estimate because sample sizes are too small in most studies. Large-scale studies of nationally administered tests, such as the Scholastic Aptitude Test (NCES, 1994), suggest that mean score differences between Hispanics and Whites are about two thirds of a standard deviation for most cognitive tests and that Asians typically score higher than Whites on mathematical ability tests, by almost half a standard deviation.

Gender differences vary with the cognitive ability construct being measured. Males typically score higher than females on tests of mathematical ability by almost half a standard deviation (Hyde, Fennema, & Lamon, 1990). Females have a small advantage, about 1/10th of a standard deviation, on measures of verbal ability (Hyde & Linn, 1988). Sex differences in spatial ability vary widely with the type of spatial measure (Voyer, Voyer, & Bryden, 1995). Measures that require three-dimensional mental rotation of objects yield the largest differences, and measures that require spatial reasoning or fitting pieces of objects together yield the smallest differences.

Interviews. Interviews are very appealing to organizations. Interview questions can be developed to tap a range of cognitive and non-cognitive skills and abilities. They often focus on communication skills, interpersonal skills, decision making, and substantive (i.e., declarative) knowledge. Chapter 7 provides additional information on types of interviews.

Interviews have proven to be valid selection tools, with validities of about .39 for job-related, structured interviews designed to predict job performance (McDaniel, Whetzel, Schmidt, & Maurer, 1994). Interviews correlate with cognitive ability measures, and interview ratings that correlate higher with cognitive ability tend to be better predictors of job performance (Huffcutt, Roth, & McDaniel, 1996). But, interviews have also been shown to provide some incremental validity over and above that obtained by cognitive tests (Cortina, Goldstein, Payne, Davison, & Gilliland, 2000; Pulakos & Schmitt, 1995).

On average, the reliability of interviews where two or more raters evaluate the applicants ranges from about .53 to .77 depending on the interview setting (Conway, Jako, & Goodman, 1995)—notably lower than that obtained by aptitude and achievement tests.

With regard to subgroup differences, a meta-analysis across 31 studies reported that African American and Hispanic American interviewees received interview ratings that were, on average, about .25 of a standard deviation lower than ratings of White interviewees (Huffcutt & Roth, 1998). In contrast, the African American and White subgroup difference on multiple-choice cognitive tests is, on average, about 1.00 standard deviation, four times as large. Of course, the reduced subgroup difference on the interview could be due to its lower reliability, range restriction from prior selection on cognitive ability (Roth, Bobko, Switzer, & Dean, 2001), its tendency to measure noncognitive as well as cognitive performance, or a combination of these factors.

Finally, interviews are relatively expensive compared to other measurement methods. Interviewers must be trained; applicants must be interviewed one at a time, often for an hour or more. For that reason, many organizations place interviews at the end of their selection process—interviewing only those applicants who have performed successfully on preceding components of the selection process.

Self-Report Measures.   Self-report measures include instruments that job applicants use to describe their experiences and personal characteristics. Like other paper-and-pencil, multiple-choice measures, these can be completed on scannable forms, making their operational costs relatively low.

Research suggests that biographical and personality variables, two commonly used self-report measures, are important predictors of contextual performance factors such as work effort and motivation (Borman & Motowidlo, 1993; Campbell et al., 1993). Although biographical and personality variables are not particularly good predictors of training or task performance, they have been shown to provide additional validity over and above that of cognitive tests in predicting overall job performance (McHenry, Hough, Toquam, Hanson, & Ashworth, 1990; Mount, Witt, & Barrick, 2000). Biographical data and personality measures differ somewhat in their patterns of prediction because biographical data can tap cognitive constructs as well as noncognitive ones. Chapter 8 discusses biographical data in more detail.

Self-report personality measures often yield little or no differences among racial-ethnic groups (Kamp & Hough, 1986); however, they do yield small to moderate differences between men and women (Feingold, 1994; Maccoby & Jacklin, 1974; Peterson, Russell, et al., 1990). Males tend to score higher than females on assertiveness and self-esteem; females score higher than males on extroversion, anxiety, trust, and nurturance (Feingold, 1994).

Unfortunately, all self-report measures can be susceptible to distortion by the job applicant. A number of studies have documented the tendency for applicants to respond in a socially desirable way (e.g., Oppler, Peterson, & Russell, 1993). Socially desirable responding reduces the variance in a measure because responses become skewed and can result in a ceiling effect. Even so, it is unclear how severely socially desirable responding affects validity; the results across studies are mixed (Reynolds, 1994). For example, Barrick and Mount (1996) found that applicants for truck driver jobs ($n = 286$) distorted their responses to a personality questionnaire, but the distortion did not attenuate the predictive validities of the personality constructs. On the other hand, Oppler et al. (1993) found that new Army recruits ($n > 40,000$) were much more likely to respond to a personality questionnaire in a socially desirable way than incumbents ($n >$ 9,000). Criterion-related validities were also substantially lower for the new recruit sample. Although other factors such as differences between the samples could have affected the validities, it is possible that response distortion had an attenuating effect.

One other drawback regarding most self-report measures is that they may lack face validity and can be difficult to justify based on content validity alone. Applicants are likely to question the relevance of background and personality items and, in some cases, applicants view the items as intrusive (Mael, Connerly, & Morath, 1996).

Simulations.   Simulations are exercises intended to faithfully represent work situations. They vary greatly in terms of their fidelity—how realistically the work situation is represented. Paper-and-pencil situational judgment tests, which are described further in chapter 9, are low-fidelity simulations; work samples, discussed in chapter 12, anchor the high-fidelity end of the simulation fidelity continuum.

Simulations also vary greatly in their costs. Paper-and-pencil measures can be relatively inexpensive to develop and administer, whereas assessment centers (see chap. 10) require one-on-one contact over a period of several hours and can be quite expensive. Also, assessors must be trained; that adds to the cost. Consequently, assessment centers, like interviews, are typically placed near the end of a hiring process to minimize the number of applicants to be assessed. To complicate the cost issue, simulations that are high in fidelity generally cover less of the job performance domain than do lower fidelity measures. A multiple-choice paper-and-pencil instrument can cover dozens of relevant job situations in an hour or two; work samples using actual equipment and realistic contexts would require days, if they could be administered at all, to cover the same number of situations.

A primary advantage of simulations is that they can have substantial face and content validity. They reflect the job and, if they are developed through solid content-validation procedures, their relevance to the job is obvious. For the same reasons, though, they may not meet the before-hire requirement.

Simulations provide moderate criterion-related validity. Situational judgment tests (SJTs) have become increasingly popular employee selection tools in recent years due to accumulating evidence of their criterion-related validity (Chan & Schmitt, 2005; McDaniel, Morgeson, Finnegan, Campion, & Braverman, 2001) and potential for incremental validity over cognitive ability (Chan & Schmitt, 2002; Clevenger, Pereira, Wiechmann, Schmitt, & Schmidt, 2001). On average, assessment center validities corrected for range restriction are about .37 (Gaugler, Rosenthal, Thornton, & Bentson, 1987). Work sample tests also yield validities in the mid .30s (Schmitt et al., 1984). Information about reliability and subgroup differences in performance on simulations is not systematically reported and is thus difficult to summarize (Gaugler et al., 1987).

Computer-Administered Measures.   Decisions about the means of administering the test should be made early in the measure selection process. Tests

Characteristic	Definition
Relevance	
Population	Extent to which the test is appropriate for the population of applicants.
Ability	Degree to which the test assesses abilities that are relevant to the job.
Psychometric	
Reliability	Degree to which the method tends to yield consistent scores as measured by traditional psychometric methods such as test-retest, internal consistency, or parallel forms reliability.
Validity	Degree of evidence supporting inferences drawn from test scores.
Subgroup Differences and Fairness	Extent to which the test minimizes differences between racial and gender subgroups' scores and the extent to which the instrument meets technical standards of fairness across subgroups.
Operational	
Applicant Acceptance	Extent to which the appearance and administration methods of the predictor enhance or detract from its plausibility or acceptability to applicants.
Consequential Validity	Extent to which use of the assessment does not have unintended negative results.
Training Implications	Extent to which applicants, assessors, and other personnel would need to be trained for the assessment to be reliable and valid.
Resistance to Compromise	Extent to which test content could be easily leaked or test responses could be coached, guessed, remembered, or distorted by examinees.
Consistency/Robustness of Administration and Scoring	Extent to which administration and scoring are standardized across administrators and locations; ease of administration and scoring.
Cost	Developmental and operational costs; costs associated with instrument and scoring system development, administration, and scoring and frequency and difficulty of developing alternative forms.

FIGURE 4.3   Examples of measurement method characteristics.

Situational Judgment Tests (SJTs) have also been called low fidelity simulations, social intelligence tests, and tacit knowledge tests. SJTs measure effectiveness in social functioning, including: conflict resolution, negotiation skills, interpersonal problem solving, communication, rewarding and disciplining, facilitating teamwork and unit cohesion, motivating others, and working with culture and or gender differences. SJTs are useful in assessing managerial and leadership abilities (Motowidlo, Dunnette, & Carter, 1990).

SJTs provide a verbal description of a scenario and a list of potential plans of action. The respondent is to read the situation and to indicate which plan of action he/she believes to be the most effective and to indicate which plan of action he/she believes to the least effective. A sample item appears below:

You volunteered to serve on the CFC committee. The person in charge of the committee frequently arrives late for meetings and complains about the work to be done.

A. Take the problem to his boss.

B. Reprimand him in front of the committee to create some peer pressure.

C. Talk to him about the importance of CFC and encourage him to have a positive attitude.

D. Tell him you would be willing to take over the chairmanship.

E. Discuss the problem with the other committee members to get their ideas.

Scoring: Test questions are generally based on critical incidents. Alternatives are generated by incumbents and supervisors. Scores are based on subject matter experts' ratings of the best and worst alternatives.

Correlations with other constructs: In Motowidlo et al. (1990) (N = 120), aptitude test measures did not correlate with the SJT, except for GPA in major ($r = .30$, $p < .05$). However, SJT ratings did correlate significantly with interview ratings of interpersonal skills ($r = .21$), communication skills ($r = .16$) and negotiation ratings ($r = .50$).

Subgroup Differences: Subgroup differences are often not reported. Motowidlo et al. (1990) reported higher scores for women than men.

Reliability: Motowidlo et al. (1990) reported an internal consistency estimate of .56 although they suggest that test-retest statistics might be a more appropriate measure of reliability because situational judgment tests are not expected to be unidimensional or homogeneous.

Validity Evidence: Motowidlo et al. (1990) reported validity estimates of .30 ($p < .01$) for overall effectiveness ratings for managers (N = 120–140). McDaniel et al. (2001) conducted a meta-analysis to determine the criterion-related validity of SJTs. McDaniel, Hartman and Grubb (2003) reanalyzed and updated the 2001 data. They showed that knowledge response instructions yielded higher validity (.33) than behavioral tendency instructions (.27).

Motowidlo, S. J., Dunnette, M. D., & Carter, G. W. (1990). An alternative selection procedure: The low-fidelity simulation. *Journal of Applied Psychology*, 75, 640–647.

McDaniel, M. A., Morgeson, F. P., Finnegan, E. B., Campion, M. A., & Braverman, E. P. (2001). Use of situational judgment tests to predict job performance: A clarification of the literature. *Journal of Applied Psychology*, 86, 730–740.

McDaniel, M. A., Hartman, N. S. & Grubb III, W. L. (2003, April). *Situational judgment tests, knowledge, behavioral tendency, and validity: A meta-analysis.* Paper presented at the 18th Annual Conference of the Society for Industrial and Organizational Psychology. Orlando.

FIGURE 4.4   Example of a literature summary for situational judgment tests.

should be pilot tested and validated in the mode (e.g., computer administered or paper-and-pencil) in which they will eventually be administered, unless literature comparing scores from the two methods already exists. Both methods have some advantages and disadvantages. For smaller organizations, the cost of computer equipment and testing processes may make paper-and-pencil testing a more viable option. For organizations that have the means, computer administration can increase the standardization of testing procedures. Testing can be continuous rather than conducted on large groups at infrequently scheduled times. Computer-administered testing allows for novel test formats and use of engaging auditory and visual stimuli.

In recent years, Internet testing has become increasingly popular (Naglieri et al., 2004). A number of test administration vendors train administration staff to follow procedures desired by the client, provide secure facilities, needed equipment, and trained staff for test administration, register examinees (if desired), score exams, provide score reports, and develop and maintain databases of test score and test-relevant information. The larger test administration firms have secure test facilities nationwide and can administer a test and report the data using standardized procedures in hundreds of locations in the United States. Naglieri et al. (2004) provided a useful discussion of factors related to Internet testing.

Complete the Measurement Plan Matrix

When complete, the worker characteristics and methods of measurement matrix, illustrated in Fig. 4.1, provides a solid basis for the measurement plan. The rows of the matrix list job-relevant worker characteristics that are not likely to be learned in a brief job orientation period—characteristics that the worker should bring to the job. The measurement methods defining the columns of the matrix should be based on a literature review identifying possible methods for measuring the worker characteristics. The cells of the matrix contain judgments about the quality of the various methods for measuring each worker characteristic.

Assembling Objects Test (AO)

Construct Measured: General Spatial Ability—Spatial Visualization

Short Description of Test:

Subjects visualize how an object will look when its parts are put together or assembled according to instructions. In part one, the items in the picture are labeled with letters and the subject must visually put the parts together according to the letters. In part two, pieces in the pictures fit together like a puzzle. Subjects must determine which figure from 4 alternatives is the correct shape when the parts are all put together.

Number of Items: 36   *Time Limit: 18 minutes*

Psychometrics:

Scoring: The score is the total number of correct answers.

Correlations with other constructs: Assembling Objects correlates with Object Rotation r = .41, .46; MAZE r = .51, .51; Orientation r = .46, .50; Reasoning r = .56, .56; Map test r = .50, .52, all N's = 9332, 6941 respectively (Peterson, Russell, et al., 1990). Factor analytic research suggests that Assembling Objects is a good marker test for general spatial ability (Russell, Humphreys, Peterson, & Rosse, 1992).

Subgroup Differences: Gender differences tend to be rather small with effect sizes ranging from −.02 to .08 in large samples (Peterson, Russell, et al. 1990). Whites tend to score higher than African Americans with effect sizes ranging from .78 to .83. Whites tend to score higher than Hispanics with effect sizes .15, .24, and .25 (Peterson, Russell, et al., 1990).

Reliability: Cronbach alphas of .88 (N = 6754); .90 (N = 9332); .92 (N = 290). Test-Retest Reliability: .70 (N = 499); .74 (N = 97).

Practice and Coaching Effects: Test performance on spatial ability tests is to some degree malleable; test scores improve with practice (Lohman, 1988). However, the gains are not substantially larger than those observed for tests of other abilities (Russell et al., 1994). There also is some evidence that gains from practice are larger for speeded tests than for power tests (Dunnette, Corpe, & Toquam, 1987). Gains from practice on the Assembling Objects test have been low in two studies. With a one-week interval between testing sessions (N = 100), subjects' scores went up .08 sd from testing 1 to testing 2 (Peterson, 1987). With one month between testing sessions (N = 473) subjects' scores again went up .06 sd from testing 1 to testing 2 (Toquam, Peterson, Rosse, Ashworth, Hanson, & Hallam, 1986). Busciglio and Palmer (1992) studied the effects of practice and coaching on three spatial tests, one of which was Assembling Objects. Practice effects were significant for all three tests. The effects of coaching on Assembling Objects were negligible.

Validity Evidence: In Project A, McHenry et al. (1990) combined six Project A spatial tests to form one composite score. The spatial score yielded modest incremental validity (beyond that afforded by the ASVAB) for predicting technical proficiency in Army enlisted MOS and hands-on performance. Similar results were obtained for a longitudinal validation sample.

Mayberry and Hiatt (1990) found that Assembling Objects was the best new predictor of the job knowledge criterion; corrected incremental validities were .02 for four military jobs. Carey (1992) examined incremental validities (over the ASVAB) for several tests. Assembling Objects added the most incremental validity to the cognitive test for predicting the hands-on performance criterion in automotive and helicopter mechanic samples.

FIGURE 4.5   Example of a literature summary for a spatial ability test.

Specify Measurement Methods in the Columns.   A thorough literature review of methods for measuring each of the worker characteristics resulting from the job analysis is an important step when identifying measurement methods for consideration. Before beginning the literature review, it is useful to list and define all the selection program characteristics that are important for the organization and the situation. Figure 4.3 provides a list of characteristics based on the *Standards* (American Educational Research Association et al., 1999), the *Principles* (SIOP, 2003), and the *Uniform Guidelines* (1978) that we have used and tailored for particular research projects over the years (cf. Ford, Campbell, Campbell, Knapp, & Walker, 1999; Peterson & Wing, 2001; Russell, Norris, & Goodwin, 2000). Additional, or more specific, characteristics for particular situations might include incremental validity over an existing measure, construct validation support, usefulness for classifying people into jobs, and so on.

The list of characteristics structures and guides the literature review, which culminates in a written summary of each measurement method. Short summaries of two different measures, situational judgment tests and a test of spatial ability, appear in Figs. 4.4 and 4.5.

As the literature review proceeds, measurement methods, tests, and scales will emerge as viable candidates for test development or validation. The level of detail specified in the columns of the matrix will vary depending on the purposes of the selection test battery and the needs of the organization. For example, if the organization wishes to use published test batteries in its selection system, it is best to review the merits of each published test specifically under consideration, for example, the Wonderlic (Hanna, 1998; Schmidt, 1985; Schoenfeldt, 1985) and the Bennett Mechanical Comprehension Test (Ghiselli, 1966; Guilford & Lacey, 1947), against the worker characteristics. Even if the organization plans to develop its own tests, it is a good idea to include some published tests in the matrix as markers for the new tests to be developed. Also, if the measurement methods include scales from tests that have subscales (e.g., Emotional Stability from the Guilford-Zimmerman Temperament Survey [Guilford, 1959; Guilford & Zimmerman, 1956]

MEASUREMENT METHODS						
WORKER CHARACTERISTICS	Aptitude or Achievement Tests	Interview	Self-Report	Simulation	Situational Judgment Test	Work Sample
	The Basic Math Test	The Test of Verbal Comprehension	The Skilled Trades Selection Interview	The Environmental reactions Biographical Inventory		
Ability to add, subtract, multiply, and divide and use formulas						
Ability to understand verbal instructions and warnings						
Ability to communicate orally with others						
Ability to develop alternative solutions to a problem and choose the best alternative						
Ability to work in a noisy environment						
Ability to work at heights						
.....						

FIGURE 4.6 Example of a page from a worker characteristics and methods of measurement matrix.

111

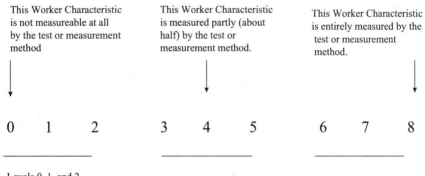

FIGURE 4.7   Example of an extent of measurement rating scale.

or Work Orientation from the California Personality Inventory [Gough, 1985; Megargee, 1972]), each scale should be listed separately in a column to facilitate comparison of scales across instruments. An example of a page from a worker characteristics and measurement methods matrix structured in this fashion appears in Fig. 4.6.

Complete the Cells of the Matrix.   The cells of the matrix indicate which measurement methods are likely to be valid measures of the worker characteristics. The matrix can be completed by one expert in an organization or by many experts or testing professionals as part of a team. The entries can be checkmarks, qualitative descriptions (e.g., high, low), or numeric ratings. The level of formality needed for a given situation depends on the degree of novelty and complexity of the worker characteristics and measurement methods. If there is little research information on which to base decisions, if the measurement method is a newly emerging technology, or if the worker characteristics are of a clinical nature (e.g., resistance to stress and anxiety), it often is desirable to carry out more formal expert judgments to link constructs to methods. Prior research suggests that psychologists can reliably make these judgments (e.g., Russell et al., 1995). Studies typically report reliabilities in the .80 to .90 range for experts' judgments of relationships among constructs (Peterson & Bownas, 1982; Peterson, Owens-Kurtz, Hoffman, Arabian, & Whetzel, 1990; Wing, Peterson, & Hoffman, 1984). Indeed, experts can make reasonably accurate estimates of empirical validities for tests (Schmidt, Hunter, Croll, & McKenzie, 1983).

WORKER CHARACTERISTICS	Aptitude or Achievement Tests — The Basic Math Test	Interview — The Test of Verbal Comprehension	Self-Report — The Skilled Trades Selection Interview	Simulation — The Environmental reactions Biographical Inventory	Situational Judgment Test	Work Sample
Ability to add, subtract, multiply, and divide and use formulas	X					
Ability to understand verbal instructions and warnings		X	X			X
Ability to communicate orally with others		X	X			
Ability to develop alternative solutions to a problem and choose the best alternative			X		X	X
Ability to work in a noisy environment				X		
Ability to work at heights				X		
Expected Reliability	High	High	Moderate	Moderate	Moderate/High	Moderate/Low
Expected Subgroup Differences	High	High	Low	Low	Moderate	Moderate
Expected Development Cost	None	None	Moderate	None	Moderate	Moderate

FIGURE 4.8 Example of a page from a completed worker characteristics and methods of measurement matrix.

Expert judgment exercises have used a variety of scales—asking experts for judgments of validity, measurement efficiency, and so on (Peterson & Bownas, 1982). The most important judgment to obtain is a judgment about the extent to which the test, scale, or measurement method measures the worker characteristic. An example of an extent-of-measurement rating scale that has been used in a number of studies (Peterson & Bownas 1982; Russell et al., 1995) appears in Fig. 4.7.

Figure 4.8 shows a completed matrix after judgments have been made. Entries (i.e., Xs in this example) in different cells of the matrix represent instances where experts have judged that the measurement method is likely to be a valid measure of the worker characteristic. Thus, the Basic Math Test is unlikely to predict Ability to Understand Verbal Instructions and Warnings; however, it is more likely to predict Ability to Add, Subtract, Multiply, and Divide and Use Formulas.

Evaluate Measurement Methods.   The next step is to evaluate the measurement methods against the characteristics that were defined during the literature review (see Fig. 4.3). As with the other evaluations in the matrix, this evaluation may be made by one expert in an organization or by many testing professionals as part of a team, depending on the situation. The summary evaluations are added to the bottom rows of the worker characteristics and methods of measurement matrix as shown in Fig. 4.8.

Select Measures for Development or Inclusion in the Selection Procedure.
When selecting tests for an experimental battery, it is wise to err on the side of inclusiveness. Even well thought out and conscientiously developed tests do not always yield adequate validity. To the extent possible, therefore, the experimental battery should include a couple of measures of some of the most important worker characteristics. If the battery includes highly experimental measures with little research support, then it would be prudent to include fall-back measures anticipated to have high validity.

A host of other practical questions also enter the equation. How many tests or measures can the organization afford to develop? How will the tests be validated and what length (in time) can an experimental test battery be before it becomes burdensome? What types of facilities and equipment will be available for testing? Which tests require special settings? Will the testing, interviewing, or assessing take place at a few locations or many? How many interviewers, test administrators, or assessors will have to be trained?

Two mechanisms for organizing and designing a test battery help establish balance among the competing concerns. One involves organizing the selection tests or measurement methods into a series of hurdles. Multiple-hurdle approaches can reduce costs by placing more expensive selection procedures near the end of the selection process. Multiple-hurdle approaches also affect the overall level of adverse impact and validity in a selection system (Sackett & Roth, 1996). Generally, multiple-hurdle approaches increase the relative effect of each measure (in terms of both validity and adverse impact) over that of more compensatory approaches like those mentioned in the next paragraph (where all measures are administered to all applicants and combined via some formula).

The other mechanism is the whole-job measurement approach. That is, most jobs require a wide range of worker characteristics including cognitive abilities, interpersonal skills, and so on. The whole-job measurement approach concentrates on predicting the entire range of job performance by assessing and combining a wide array of relevant worker characteristics. The intent is to maximize the validity of the entire selection procedure by using a variety of measures each contributing validity over and above that provided by the other measures.

As an example, if we were to use the matrix shown in Fig. 4.8 to select a set of predictors for the job of apprentice electrician, we would probably consider each of the predictors listed in the columns. The Basic Math Test is the only predictor listed here that measures the Ability to Add, Subtract, Multiply, and Divide and Use Formulas. There are no development costs because it can be purchased off the shelf; there are low operational costs because individual responses can be optically scanned; however, it may have a high degree of adverse impact. Experts indicated that the Test of Verbal Comprehension measures two worker characteristics: Ability to Understand Verbal Instructions and Warnings, and Ability to Communicate Orally with Others. Like the Basic Math Test, there are no development costs because it can be purchased off the shelf, and there are low operational costs because responses are optically scanned. But, it may have high adverse impact.

According to the experts in our example, the selection interview measures Ability to Understand Verbal Instructions and Warnings, Ability to Communicate Orally with Others, and Ability to Develop Alternative Solutions to a Problem and Choose the Best Alternative. Even though the development cost is moderate and the operational cost is high, the interview could be an attractive predictor because the anticipated adverse impact of this method is low. Use of this predictor could help offset the adverse impact of the first two predictors, but it is important to remember that the interview is likely to be less reliable and valid than the other two tests. Also, interviewers must be trained in order to make an interview process work validly; if the organization is highly decentralized and has little control over interviewer training, the interview may not be advantageous.

Self-reports, often measured using background data questionnaires, are useful because they can get at constructs that are difficult to measure otherwise (i.e., Ability to Work in a Noisy Environment and Ability to Work at Heights). This is a good alternative predictor because it may have low adverse impact and because development and operational costs would be low. In spite of these advantages, one must be concerned with face validity and user acceptance of the questions asked.

Simulations also are useful predictors. An SJT could be developed to measure the Ability to Develop Alternative Solutions to a Problem and Choose the Best Alternative. The adverse impact of this measure is likely to be low, the cost of development is moderate, and the cost of using the method is low because it typically is administered as a pencil-and-paper exercise. The work sample kind of simulation also measures Ability to Develop Alternative Solutions to a Problem and Choose the Best Alternative, as well as Ability to Understand Verbal Instructions and

1. **Measure name:** The Skilled Trades Selection Interview

2. **Measure purpose:** Scores on this interview will be used to select [job title] for [employer]. It will assess examinee's ability on KSAOs relevant to this job. Applicants who have passed a paper and pencil test battery will be interviewed.

3. **Briefly describe the measure and provide key citations from the published literature:** A number of external contextual features of the interview are important for limiting potential sources of bias and enhancing consistency across applicants. These features are consistent with best practices in interviewing (Campion, Palmer, & Campion [1997]). They include security and structure, panel composition and training, limitations on ancillary information, and independent ratings on anchored rating scales.

4. **How much testing time will this interview require (e.g., 1 hour, 3 hours)-** 45 minutes.

5. **How will the interview be administered (individual or group administration)?** Individual applicants will be interviewed by panel of three trained interviewers.

6. **Will any special equipment be needed for interview administration?** No.

7. **Who will administer the interview?** A panel of three trained interviewers.

8. **Will the interview have a time limit?** No.

9. **How will the interview be scored?** Immediately after the interview, each panel member will independently rate the applicant using detailed, anchored rating scales that accompany the interview questions. The applicant's score on the interview will be the mean score computed across scales and raters.

10. **Will any special training be required for test administrators, interviewers, or scorers on this measure?** All interviewers will attend a training workshop.

11. **How much time will be needed for this training (e.g., a one-day workshop)?** 2 days.

12. **Will the applicant have to read any materials?** If so, what reading level is appropriate for this test (e.g., 10th grade) and how was that level determined? The interview will not require reading.

13. **What materials will need secure storage (e.g., manuals, questionnaires, scoring guides)?** The interview and the rating scales will require secure storage. Manuals will be designed such that they do not require secure storage.

FIGURE 4.9   Example of an external contextual factors worksheet completed for a selection interview.

Warnings. Similar to the SJT, the adverse impact is moderate and the development costs are moderate. However, the operating costs of work samples are high because tests typically are administered individually and scorers need to be trained. If one were to eliminate a predictor due to testing time or costs, the work sample predictor might be viewed as one that could be omitted from the battery because the constructs it measures are assessed by other predictors at lower cost.

In summary, the final measurement plan describes the tests to be developed, their hypothesized relationships with worker characteristics derived from the job analysis, and the mode of administration to be used. It is a blueprint for development and validation of personnel selection procedures.

TEST SPECIFICATIONS

Test specifications implement the measurement plan and guide the development of each selection tool. They specify external contextual factors such as the testing time, security procedures, mode of administration, and the population for whom the measure is appropriate, as well as the internal attributes of the measure such as the format of items, tasks, or questions; the content and distribution of content across items; and desired psychometric characteristics. Requirements for specifications documents are set forth in the *Standards* (e.g., see *Standards* 3.2-3.5, 3.7, and 3.11 in American Educational Research Association et al., 1999) and standardize the testing procedures. Specifications provide all of the information that developers need to generate items, tasks, or questions, and that administrators need to plan and set up test administration.

There is no set structure for test specifications, and specifications vary in detail. The format and content will depend on the issues that are relevant to the measurement method and setting. In this section, we provide examples of tools and worksheets we have used to develop test specifications. We encourage the reader to refer to other sources for additional information. Excellent discussions of specifications are provided in Millman and Greene (1989), Roid and Haladyna (1982), and Childs, Baughman, and Keil (1997).

Describe External Contextual Factors

External contextual factors are the constraints on the selection setting and the processes necessary for administration, scoring, and maintenance of the measure. Often the constraints are a function of organizational resources (e.g., availability of computers, anticipated number of applicants, and staff availability). Processes ensure the integrity and security of the measure. Selection interviews, for example, require well thought out processes (e.g., number and training of interviewers) designed to enhance the quality of the interview scores within the constraints of the organization's resources. We have found it useful to follow a worksheet in specifying the external contextual factors for the measurement method. The worksheet addresses questions such as:

- What is the name, purpose, and description of the measure?

1. **Based on the measurement plan, list the knowledges, skills, abilities, and other characteristics that this test is expected to measure:** *Ability to understand verbal instructions and warnings, Ability to communicate orally with others, and Ability to develop alternative solutions to a problem and choose the best alternative.*

2. **List everything that needs to be developed for this test:** *Interview questions, interview rating scales, and interviewer training.*

3. **Name the specific sources of content that will be used (e.g., list math textbooks, describe SME input, expert judgment/ experience):** *Critical incidents and interview notes from the job analysis and experience from other interviews of similar KSAOs.*

4. **How will the items be distributed among content components?** *See chart below.*

Important KSAOs to be Measured	Interview Questions				
	1	*2*	*3*	....	*17*
Ability to understand verbal instructions and warnings	X				
	X				
Ability to communicate orally with others	X	X	X	X	
Ability to develop alternative solutions to a problem and choose the best alternative			X	X	

5. **What types of item formats will be used?** *The interview questions will be behavior-based. They will ask the applicant to describe past behavior in situations relevant to apprenticeship. Behavioral questions are based on the notion that past behavior is the best predictor of future behavior in a similar situation, and this type of question has repeatedly demonstrated empirical validity (e.g., Campion, Campion, & Hudson [1994], Pulakos & Schmitt [1995]). Seven-point behaviorally anchored rating scales will accompany the interview. There will be one rating scale for each ability and one overall rating scale.*

6. **How many items will be produced?** *The first draft will contain 17 questions. The final interview will have 7–8 questions.*

7. **What item writing rules, guides, or principles will be followed?** *Best practices described by Campion, Palmer, and Campion (1997).*

8. **What psychometric characteristics of the items are desired (e.g., number of multiple choice items at different difficulty levels, desired point biserial)?** *The scores on each rating scale should have good inter-rater agreement/reliability and discriminate among ratees.*

9. **How will the items be evaluated and selected?** *Twenty five current apprentices will be interviewed and rated by three-member panels. Items will be selected based on their psychometric properties and input from the interview panels regarding how well the questions worked.*

10. **How will the test items be arranged and sequenced?** *According to the abilities to be assessed.*

11. **How will the items/test be scored (e.g., holistically, on dimensions, sum of item scores)?** *Scores will be averaged across abilities and then across panel members to form one mean score for the interview.*

12. **What psychometric properties of the test are desired?** *Agreement among panel members on the mean score should be high. Subgroup differences in mean scores should be low.*

13. **How will passing scores be set?** *Only applicants who have achieved a passing score on a test battery will be interviewed. Applicants will be rank-ordered based on their interview scores and will be selected in a top down fashion for apprenticeship.*

FIGURE 4.10 Example of test specifications for a reading comprehension test.

- How will the measure be administered (e.g., individual or group administration) and how much time will be required?
- Will examinees use any special equipment (e.g., calculators, keyboards, joysticks)?
- Who will administer the measure and what training will administrators receive?
- Who will score the measure? Describe the scoring process.
- What security procedures are required for the measure?
- What retesting policy will be followed? How often will items or forms be replaced?

An example of a worksheet completed for a selection interview appears in Fig. 4.9.

Describe Internal Attributes

The internal attributes of the test specifications refer to the number, distribution, psychometric properties, and format of the items and the creation, scaling, and use of the test score. Worksheets for addressing internal attributes might include the following questions:

- Based on the measurement plan, what attribute(s) is this measure expected to measure?

- How many items will the measure contain? How will the items be distributed among content components?
- What types of item formats will be used (e.g., multiple-choice, open-ended, past behavioral interview questions)?
- Will alternate forms or large item pools be developed? If so, how?
- What item-writing rules, guides, or principles will be followed?
- What psychometric characteristics of the items are desired (e.g., number of multiple-choice items at different difficulty levels, desired point biserial)?
- How will the items be evaluated and selected?
- How will the test items be arranged and sequenced?
- How will the items or test be scored (e.g., holistically, on dimensions, sum of item scores)? How will the test score be scaled (e.g., number correct, stanines, t-scores, z-scores)? Will test scores be normed, equated, or both? If so, how?
- What psychometric properties of the test score are desired?
- How will the scores be used? Will the score be combined with scores from other measures? Will examinees be rank-ordered according to scores? Will a passing score or set of standards be set? Explain the method to be used.

An example of an internal attributes worksheet completed for a selection interview appears in Fig. 4.10.

The distribution of content across items—sometimes referred to as the test blueprint, the item budget, or the weighting plan—is a particularly important internal attribute. Clearly, when content relevance is the primary source of validity evidence, the blueprint is the key documentation of inferences between job and test content. This blueprint lists proportions, weights, or numbers of items assigned to content categories (e.g., abilities, tasks). Judgmental and empirical methods of determining the distribution of content usually involve transforming or summarizing the job analysis ratings for tasks, KSAOs, or both to create weights for content areas (cf. Raymond, 2001, 2002). They can involve mapping the number of test items against the number of important KSAOs or tasks, combining job analysis ratings from different scales into composites (Arthur, Doverspike, & Barrett, 1996), using judged linkages between tasks and KSAOs (e.g., Wang, Schnipke, & Witt, 2005), or fairly sophisticated schemes for scaling and weighting job analysis data (e.g., Spray & Huang, 2000).

Another key component of measurement planning has to do with how the scores on the measure will be used (e.g., top-down selection, pass-fail, standard setting, or banding). If passing scores or standards are to be set, a number of operational and procedural concerns should be addressed early in measurement planning because they can affect item writing and test content (Millman & Greene, 1989). That is, inferring a particular level of competence from the test score might require a sufficient number of items written at a particular difficulty level or could require expert judgment about the extent to which an item reflects the intended level of competence. There is a relatively large body of literature on standard setting. Some useful starting points include articles on methodologies for standard setting: contrasting groups (Jaeger, 1989), holistic examination

External Attributes

Test Name. Reading Comprehension

Test Purpose. Scores on this test are used in combination with scores on other tests to select among applicants for skilled trades apprenticeships.

Description. This paper-and-pencil test consists of three passages. Eight multiple choice items accompany each passage. The time limit is 30 minutes. It is administered in group sessions by a trained test administrator who has successfully completed a test administrator training course. Test administrators use timing devices to time the test. Otherwise, no special equipment is needed. Examinees mark their responses on optical scanning sheets that are, computer scored.

Internal Attributes

Relevant Job Analysis KSA. Ability to read and comprehend complex technical materials.

Passage Length. Reading comprehension passages are 400 to 600 words in length. They have several paragraphs so that they are not too dense to read.

Passage Readability Level. Passages are at the 10th grade reading level using the Flesch-Kincaid Grade Level statistic.

Source Material. The content of the passage must be written for this test (i.e., not excerpted from existing sources). Ideas come from magazine or encyclopedia articles.

Appropriate Topics. The content of the passages is conceptually relevant to technical and scientific topics. The test does not contain work samples or training materials. The test is designed to assess the applicant's ability to read and comprehend technical materials, not the applicant's knowledge of skilled trades topics.

The content of the passage resembles material high school students are likely to encounter. General topic areas include physical sciences, earth sciences, mechanics, life sciences, crafts, technology, and study habits. Examples of passage topics are: The Metric System, How Diamonds are Made, How Clocks Work, History of the Camera, The Effect of El Nino in North America.

Passage Fairness/Sensitivity. Passages do not address topics that are likely to arouse strong feelings (e.g., abortion, violence, suicide, religion) or are likely to be confusing to or offensive to people of different cultures. Passages

Passage Timeliness. Select topics that are not likely to become outdated within the next 10 years.

Passage Format. Please type your passage and items in Word, Times New Roman 12.

Number of Items. Write 10 items for each passage.

Number of Response Options. Each item has four response options lettered A through D.

General Guidelines. Follow the general guidelines for item development provided in Childs, Baughman, & Keil (1997).

Classes of Items. There are four general classes of items: (1) comprehension, (2) evaluation, (3) application, and (4) incorporation of new information. These are described further in a separate handout. Draft passages should have 10 items: eight comprehension items and two items representing any of the other three classes of items.

Psychometric Properties of Items. The items on this test vary in difficulty, but on average they should be relatively easy. Difficulties range from .20 to .95 with a mean of .75. Point-biserials are higher than .20 with a mean of .48. The overall reliability for the test is KR-20 of .80.

Test Scores. The test score is a count of the number of correct items.

Psychometric Properties of the Test. On average, applicants get 17 out of the total 24 items correct. The overall reliability for the test is KR-20 of .80.

Passing Score. The passing score was set on the total test battery composite score.

FIGURE 4.11   Example of test specifications for a reading comprehension test.

(Jaegar & Mills, 2001), and bookmarking (Mitzel, Lewis, Patz, & Green, 2001); discussions of operational concerns (e.g., Muchinsky, 2004, p. 193); and professional guidance (i.e., the *Standards,* 1999, Standard 4.19-4.21, and the *Principles,* 2003, pp. 46–48).

   Over the years, a number of general item formatting guides have been developed for multiple-choice tests (cf. Childs et al., 1997; Millman & Greene, 1989). We have found that additional format rules are needed for some item types. For example, the font and spacing rules are critical for mathematical formulas; deviations from format can make items confusing to examinees and create unwanted error variance. Also, graphically displayed items require rules about figure and line sizes and so on. Some of the more common format rules that apply to most four-option multiple-choice tests are:

1. Response order: The four responses in an item should be logically arranged, if appropriate (as with a numerical sequence). If not dictated by logic, the order should be random.
2. Key position: The position of the correct response should vary. The number of correct As, Bs, and so on in a complete unit should be approximately the same.
3. Response consistency: The responses must be consistent with the stem, and all responses should have the same grammatical structure. That is, if the key is a phrase, the distractors should also be phrases; if the key is a name, the distractors should also be names. No response should vary drastically in length from the other responses.
4. "All of the above": Avoid using "all of the above" as a response. If an examinee recognizes two of the four responses as correct, logic dictates that the all-inclusive response is correct, whether or not the examinee recognizes the correctness of the remaining alternatives. Conversely, if the examinee recognizes one of the alternatives as false, then the all-inclusive response is immediately eliminated. That is, the item fails to offer a true choice of four responses.
5. "None of the above": The response "none of the above" also is undesirable. In effect, it creates a different test item for each examinee by requiring the generation of a hypothetical, ideal response and the comparison of that self-generated response with the alternatives presented.
6. Independence of items: Each item must be independent of all other items; one item must not contain information that helps examinees to answer other items.
7. Style of stem: Item stems should be direct and concise. Questions should be written that examinees who have understood the question will be able to answer correctly. Questions that include negatives in both stem and response should not be used.
8. Completeness of stem: All stems should ask complete questions. The stem should tell examinees exactly what they are being asked.
9. Uniqueness of key: Each item must have one and only one response that is correct or clearly better than all the other choices. No distractor should be so close to the correct answer that it can legitimately be defended as correct. Furthermore, all choices must be mutually exclusive. That is, no choice can include the answer provided by another choice.
10. Effectiveness of distractors: Distractors are effective to the extent that they attract examinees who have not understood the question or are computing the answer incorrectly. The best approach is to create distractors that correspond to major errors examinees could make. Responses that are

glaringly wrong are not appropriate. Any distractor that an examinee can reject solely on the basis of prior knowledge of the subject also is unacceptable.

Examples of additional format rules for math items include the following:

1. Unknowns should be in lower caps and italicized (e.g., x = 3).
2. There should not be a space within a division or multiplication operation (e.g., 4x = 3x + 4). Do not use an asterisk or an x for multiplication.
3. There should be one space before and after the sign in an addition or subtraction operation (4x = 3x + 4).
4. Place one space before and one space after an equal sign (e.g., x = 3).
5. Exponents should be Word superscripts with no spaces between the superscript and the variable. The superscript should not be italicized (e.g., x2).

Update Test Specifications

Test specifications evolve over the life cycle of a measure. When a measure is first drafted, the test specifications may describe draft item formats and will not contain psychometric information. As the measure is pilot tested, revised, and finalized, the test specifications evolve to describe the final form and its psychometric properties. The final test specifications facilitate the development of large item pools for the measure, the development of parallel forms, and form equating. Figure 4.11 provides an example of final test specifications for a Reading Comprehension Test.

SUMMARY

A measurement plan helps measurement specialists identify tests and other assessment tools that, on balance, maximize validity, minimize adverse impact, and use resources efficiently. It summarizes information from a thorough job analysis and literature review and forms a blueprint for test development and validation. It provides a rationale for tests and assessment methods that are chosen for a selection test battery and for those that are not chosen.

A measurement plan can be conceptualized as a matrix where the rows are worker characteristics derived from a job analysis and the columns list measurement methods. The cells of the matrix document the hypothesized relationships between measurement methods and worker characteristics.

Although the matrix facilitates decision making about tests to be developed or validated, a host of other concerns must also be considered in creating the final measurement plan. Minimizing adverse impact and making efficient use of resources are two of those concerns. Many other practical constraints also will affect the organization's final measurement plan.

Test specifications help implement the measurement plan by converting job analysis data and the overall measurement plan into specifics about the number, format, content, administration, and psychometrics of items. The worksheets provided in this chapter are useful tools for addressing the internal and external issues surrounding test development.

REFERENCES

American Educational Research Association, American Psychological Association, & National Council on Measurement in Education. (1999). *Standards for educational and psychological testing*. Washington, DC: American Educational Research Association.

Arthur, W., Doverspike, D., & Barrett, G. V. (1996). Development of a job analysis-based procedure for weighting and combining content-related tests into a single test battery score. *Personnel Psychology, 49*, 971–985.

Barrick, M. R., & Mount, M. K. (1996). Effects of impression management and self-deception on the predictive validity of personality constructs. *Journal of Applied Psychology, 81*, 261–272.

Borman, W. C., & Motowidlo, S. J. (1993). Expanding the criterion domain to include elements of contextual performance. In N. Schmitt & W. C. Borman (Eds.), *Personnel selection in organizations* (pp. 71–98). San Francisco: Jossey-Bass.

Busciglio, H. H., & Palmer, D. R. (1992, August). *An empirical assessment of coaching and practice effects on three Army tests of spatial aptitude*. Paper presented at the annual meeting of the American Psychological Association, Washington, DC.

Campbell, J. P., McCloy, R. A., Oppler, S. H., & Sager, C. E. (1993). A theory of performance. In N. Schmitt & W. C. Borman (Eds.), *Personnel selection in organizations* (pp. 35–70). San Francisco: Jossey-Bass.

Campion, M. A., Campion, J. E., & Hudson, J. P., Jr. (1994). Structured interviewing: A note on incremental validity and alternative question types. *Journal of Applied Psychology, 79*, 998–1002.

Campion, M. A., Palmer, D. K., & Campion, J. E. (1997). A review of structure in the selection interview. *Personnel Psychology, 50*, 655–702.

Carey, N. B. (1992, August). *New predictors of mechanics' job performance: Marine Corps findings*. Paper presented at the annual meeting of the American Psychological Association, Washington, DC.

Chan, D., & Schmitt, N. (2002). Situational judgment and job performance. *Human Performance, 15*, 233–254.

Chan, D., & Schmitt, N. (2005). Situational judgment tests. In N. Anderson, A. Evers & O. Voskuijil (Eds.), *Blackwell handbook of selection* (pp. 219–242). Oxford, England: Blackwell.

Childs, R. A., Baughman, W. A., & Keil, C. T. (1997). Tests of cognitive ability. In D. L. Whetzel & G. R. Wheaton (Eds.), *Applied measurement methods in industrial psychology* (pp. 143–183). Palo Alto, CA: Davies-Black.

Clevenger, J., Pereira, G. M., Wiechmann, D., Schmitt, N., & Schmidt, H. V. (2001). Incremental validity of situational judgment tests. *Journal of Applied Psychology, 86*, 410–417.

Conway, J. M., Jako, R. A., & Goodman, D. F. (1995). A meta-analysis of interrater and internal consistency reliability of selection interviews. *Journal of Applied Psychology, 80*, 565–579.

Cortina, J. M., Goldstein, N. B., Payne, S. C., Davison, K. H., & Gilliland, S. W. (2000). The incremental validity of interview scores over and above cognitive ability and conscientiousness scores. *Personnel Psychology, 5*, 325–351.

Department of Defense. (1982). *Profile of American youth: 1980 nationwide administration of the Armed Services Vocational Aptitude Battery.* Washington, DC: Office of the Assistant Secretary of Defense.

Dunnette, M. D., Corpe, V. A., & Toquam, J. L. (1987). Cognitive paper-and-pencil measures: Field test. In N. G. Peterson (Ed.), *Development and field test of the trial battery for Project A* (ARI TR-739, pp. 1–13). Alexandria, VA: U.S. Army Research Institute for the Behavioral and Social Sciences.

Feingold, A. (1994). Gender differences in personality: A meta-analysis. *Psychological Bulletin, 116,* 429–456.

Ford, L. A., Campbell, R. C., Campbell, J. P., Knapp, D. J., & Walker, C. B. (1999). *21st century soldiers and noncommissioned officers: Critical predictors of performance* (FR-EADD-99-45). Alexandria, VA: U.S. Army Research Institute for the Behavioral and Social Sciences.

Gaugler, B. B., Rosenthal, D. B., Thornton, G. C., & Bentson, C. (1987). Meta-analysis of assessment center validity [Monograph]. *Journal of Applied Psychology, 72,* 493–511.

Ghiselli, E. E. (1966). *The validity of occupational aptitude tests.* New York: Wiley.

Gough, H. G. (1985). A work orientation scale for the California Psychological Inventory. *Journal of Applied Psychology, 69,* 233–240.

Guilford, J. P. (1959). *Personality.* New York: McGraw-Hill.

Guilford, J. P., & Lacey, J. I. (Eds.). (1947). *Printed classification tests* (AAF Aviation Psychology Program, Research Reports, Rep. No. 5). Washington, DC: U.S. Government Printing Office.

Guilford, J. P., & Zimmerman, W. S. (1956). Fourteen dimensions of temperament. *Psychological Monographs, 70*(10, Whole No. 417).

Hanna, G. S. (1998). Review of the Wonderlic Basic Skills Test. In J. C. Impara & B. S. Plake (Eds.), *The thirteenth mental measurements yearbook* (pp. 1136–1140). Lincoln, NE: Buros Institute of Mental Measurements.

Huffcutt, A. I., & Roth, P. L. (1998). Racial group differences in employment interview evaluations. *Journal of Applied Psychology, 83,* 179–189.

Huffcutt, A. I., Roth, P. L., & McDaniel, M. A. (1996). A meta-analytic investigation of cognitive ability in employment interview evaluations: Moderating characteristics and implications for incremental validity. *Journal of Applied Psychology, 81,* 459–473.

Hunter, J. E., & Hunter, R. F. (1984). Validity and utility of alternative predictors of job performance. *Psychological Bulletin, 96,* 72–98.

Hyde, J. S., Fennema, E., & Lamon, S. J. (1990). Gender differences in mathematics performance: A meta-analysis. *Psychological Bulletin, 107,* 139–155.

Hyde, J. S., & Linn, M. C. (1988). Gender differences in verbal ability: A meta-analysis. *Psychological Bulletin, 104,* 53–69.

Jaeger, R. M. (1989). Certification of student competence. In R. L. Linn (Ed.), *Educational measurement* (3rd ed., pp. 485–514). New York: Macmillan.

Jaeger, R. M., & Mills, C. (2001). An integrated judgment procedure for setting standards on complex, large-scale assessments. In G. J. Cizek (Ed.), *Setting performance standards: Concepts, methods, and perspectives.* Mahwah, NJ: Lawrence Erlbaum Associates.

Jensen, A. R. (1980). *Bias in mental testing.* New York: Free Press.

Kamp, J. D., & Hough, L. M. (1986). Utility of temperament for predicting job performance. In L. M. Hough, J. D. Kamp, & B. N. Barge (Eds.), *Utility of temperament, biodata, and interest assessment for predicting job performance: A review and integration of the literature* (pp. 1–72). Minneapolis, MN: Personnel Decisions Research Institute.

Lohman, D. F. (1988). Spatial abilities as traits, processes, and knowledge. In R. J. Sternberg (Ed.), *Advances in the psychology of human intelligence* (Vol. 4, pp. 181–248). Hillsdale, NJ: Lawrence Erlbaum Associates.

Maccoby, E. E., & Jacklin, C. N. (1974). *The psychology of sex differences.* Stanford, CA: Stanford University Press.

Mael, F. A., Connerly, M., & Morath, R. A. (1996). None of your business: Parameters of biodata invasiveness. *Personnel Psychology, 49,* 613–650.

Mayberry, P. W., & Hiatt, C. M. (1990). *Incremental validity of new tests in prediction of infantry performance* (CRM 90-110). Alexandria, VA: Center for Naval Analyses.

McDaniel, M. A., Hartman, N. S., & Grubb, W. L., III. (2003, April). *Situational judgment tests, knowledge, behavioral tendency, and validity: A meta-analysis.* Paper presented at the 18th annual conference of the Society for Industrial and Organizational Psychology, Orlando, FL.

McDaniel, M. A., Morgeson, F. P., Finnegan, E. B., Campion, M. A., & Braverman, E. P. (2001). Use of situational judgment tests to predict job performance: A clarification of the literature. *Journal of Applied Psychology, 80,* 730–740.

McDaniel, M. A., Whetzel, D. L., Schmidt, F. L., & Maurer, S. D. (1994). The validity of employment interviews: A comprehensive review and meta-analysis. *Journal of Applied Psychology, 79,* 599–616.

McHenry, J. J., Hough, L. M., Toquam, J. L., Hanson, M. A., & Ashworth, S. (1990). Project A validity results: The relationship between predictor and criterion domains. *Personnel Psychology, 43,* 335–354.

Megargee, E. I. (1972). *The California Psychological Inventory handbook.* San Francisco: Jossey-Bass.

Millman, J., & Greene, J. (1989). The specification and development of tests of achievement and ability. In R. L. Linn (Ed.), *Educational measurement* (3rd ed., pp. 335–366). New York: Macmillan.

Mitzel, H. C., Lewis, D. M., Patz, R. J., & Green, D. R. (2001). The Bookmark procedure: Psychological perspectives. In G. J. Cizek (Ed.), *Setting performance standards: Concepts, methods, and perspectives.* Mahwah, NJ: Lawrence Erlbaum Associates.

Motowidlo, S. J., Dunnette, M. D., & Carter, G. W. (1990). An alternative selection procedure: The low-fidelity simulation. *Journal of Applied Psychology, 75,* 640–647.

Mount, M. K., Witt, L. A., & Barrick, M. R. (2000). Incremental validity of empirically keyed biodata scales over GMA and the five factor personality constructs. *Personnel Psychology, 5,* 299–323.

Muchinsky, P. M. (2004). When the psychometrics of test development meets organizational realities: A conceptual framework for organizational change, examples, and recommendations. *Personnel Psychology, 55,* 175–209.

Naglieri, J. A., Drasgow, F., Schmit, M., Handler, L., Prifitera, A., Margolis, A., et al. (2004). Psychological testing on the internet. *American Psychologist, 59,* 150–162.

National Center for Education Statistics. (1994). *Condition of education 1993.* Washington, DC: Author.

Oppler, S. H., Peterson, N. G., & Russell, T. L. (1993). Basic validation results for the LVI sample. In J. P. Campbell & L. M. Zook (Eds.), *Building and retaining the career force: New procedures for accessing and assigning Army enlisted personnel. Annual report, 1991 fiscal year* (pp. 155–193). Alexandria, VA: U.S. Army Research Institute for the Behavioral and Social Sciences.

Peterson, N. G., & Bownas, D. A. (1982). Skill, task structure, and performance acquisition. In M. D. Dunnette & E. A. Fleishman (Eds.), *Human performance and productivity* (Vol. 1, pp. 49–105). Hillsdale, NJ: Lawrence Erlbaum Associates.

Peterson, N. G., Owens-Kurtz, C., Hoffman, R. G., Arabian, J. M., & Whetzel, D. L. (1990a). *Army synthetic validity project: Report of Phase II results: Volume I* (Tech. Rep. No. 892). Alexandria, VA: U.S. Army Research Institute for the Behavioral and Social Sciences.

Peterson, N. G., Russell, T. L., Hallam, G., Hough, L. M., Owens-Kurtz, C., Gialluca, K., et al. (1990). Analysis of the experimental predictor battery: LV sample. In J. P. Campbell & L. Zook (Eds.), *Building and retaining the career force: FY 1990 annual report* (ARI-FR-PRD-90-6, pp. 73–199). Alexandria, VA: U.S. Army Research Institute for the Behavioral and Social Sciences.

Peterson, N. G., & Wing, H. (2001). The search for new measures: Sampling from a population of selection/classification predictor variables. In J. P. Campbell & D. J. Knapp (Eds.), *Exploring the limits in personnel selection and classification* (pp. 53–70). Mahwah, NJ: Lawrence Erlbaum Associates.

Pulakos, E. D., & Schmitt, N. (1995). Experience-based and situational interview questions: Studies of validity. *Personnel Psychology, 48*, 289–308.

Raymond, M. R. (2001). Job analysis and the specification of content for licensure and certification examinations. *Applied Measurement in Education, 14*, 369–415.

Raymond, M. R. (2002). A practical guide to practice analysis for credentialing examinations. *Applied Measurement in Education, 21*, 25–37.

Reynolds, D. (1994). Personality, interest, and biographical attribute measures. In T. L. Russell, D. H. Reynolds, & J. P. Campbell (Eds.), *Building a joint-service classification research roadmap: Individual differences measurement* (AL/HR-TP-1994-0009, pp. 71–100). Brooks Air Force Base, TX: Armstrong Laboratory.

Roid, G. H., & Haladyna, T. M. (1982). *A technology for test item writing.* Orlando, FL: Academic Press.

Roth, P. L., Bobko, P., Switzer, F. S., & Dean, M. A. (2001). Prior selection causes biased estimates of standardized ethnic group differences: Simulation and analysis. *Personnel Psychology, 54*, 591–617.

Russell, T. L., Crafts, J. L., Peterson, N. G., Rohrback, M. R., Nee, M. T., & Mael, F. (1995). *Development of a roadmap for Special Forces selection and classification research.* Alexandria, VA: U.S. Army Research Institute for the Behavioral and Social Sciences.

Russell, T. L., Humphreys, L., Rosse, R. L., & Peterson, N. G. (1992, October). *The factor structure of a spatial test battery.* Paper presented at the 34th annual conference of the Military Testing Association, San Diego, CA.

Russell, T. L., Norris, D. G., & Goodwin, G. F. (2000). *Literature review: Alternative methods of measuring CPA knowledge and skill.* Washington, DC: American Institutes for Research.

Russell, T. L., Reynolds, D. H., & Campbell, J. P. (1994). *Building a joint-service classification research roadmap: Individual differences measurement* (AL/HR-TP-1994-0009). Brooks Air Force Base, TX: Armstrong Laboratory.

Sackett, P. R., & Roth, L. (1996). Multi-stage selection strategies: A monte carlo investigation of effects on performance and minority hiring. *Personnel Psychology, 49*, 549–572.

Schmidt, F. L. (1985). Review of the Wonderlic Personnel Test. In J. V. Mitchell, Jr. (Ed.), *The ninth mental measurements yearbook* (pp. 1755–1757). Lincoln, NE: Buros Institute of Mental Measurements.

Schmidt, F. L., & Hunter, J. E. (1998). The validity and utility of selection methods in personnel psychology: Practical and theoretical implications of 85 years of research findings. *Psychological Bulletin, 124*, 262–274.

Schmidt, F. L., Hunter, J. E., Croll, P. R., & McKenzie, R. C. (1983). Estimation of employment test validities by expert judgment. *Journal of Applied Psychology, 47*, 590–601.

Schmitt, N., Gooding, R. Z., Noe, R. A., & Kirsch, M. (1984). Meta-analyses of validity studies published between 1964 and 1982 and the investigation of study characteristics. *Personnel Psychology, 37*, 407–423.

Schoenfeldt, L. F. (1985). Review of Wonderlic Personnel Test. In J. V. Mitchell, Jr. (Ed.), *The ninth mental measurements yearbook* (pp. 1757–1758). Lincoln, NE: Buros Institute of Mental Measurements.

Society of Industrial and Organizational Psychology, Inc. (2003). *Principles for the validation and use of personnel selection procedures* (4th ed.). College Park, MD: Author.

Spray, J. A., & Huang, C. (2000). Obtaining test blueprint weights from job analysis surveys. *Journal of Educational Measurement, 37,* 187–201.

Toquam, J., Peterson, N. G., Rosse, R. L., Ashworth, S., Hanson, M. A., & Hallam, G. (1986, March). *Concurrent validity data analyses: Cognitive paper-and-pencil and computer-administered predictors.* Paper presented at the Project A Scientific Advisory Group, Minneapolis, MN.

Uniform guidelines on employee selection procedures. (1978). *Federal Register, 43,* 38290–38315.

Voyer, D., Voyer, S., & Bryden, M. P. (1995). Magnitude of sex differences in spatial abilities: A meta-analysis and consideration of critical variables. *Psychological Bulletin, 117,* 20–270.

Wang, N., Schnipke, D., & Witt, E. A. (2005). Use of knowledge, skill and ability statements in developing licensure and certification examinations. *Educational Measurement: Issues and Practices, 24,* 15–22.

Wing, H., Peterson, N. G., & Hoffman, R. G. (1984, August). *Expert judgments of predictor-criterion validity relationships.* Paper presented at the annual American Psychological Association Convention, Toronto, Canada.

CHAPTER FIVE

Tests of Cognitive Ability

Malcolm James Ree
Our Lady of the Lake University, San Antonio, TX

Thomas R. Carretta[1]
Air Force Research Laboratory, Wright-Patterson Air Force Base, OH

OVERVIEW

This chapter consists of six sections. The first section briefly reviews the historical foundation of the concept of cognitive ability and early attempts to measure it. The second section reviews modern theories of the structure of cognitive ability and the emergence of the concept of general cognitive ability. Section three introduces the concepts of specific knowledge, skills, abilities, and other characteristics. Section four discusses psychometric characteristics of tests including reliability, validity, and subgroup differences. The fifth section reviews the issues to be considered when deciding whether to choose from among commercially available tests or develop a test. Example questions to help in test construction are provided. The final section contains a general summary.

HISTORICAL FOUNDATIONS

The concept of cognitive ability can be traced back over 2,500 years. Zhang (1988) reported that in the 6th century B.C., the great Chinese philosopher Confucius divided people into three groups based on intelligence: people of great wisdom, people of average intelligence, and people of little intelligence. Another Chinese

[1]The views expressed are those of the authors and not necessarily those of the United States Government, the Department of Defense, or the United States Air Force.

philosopher, Mencius (4th century B.C.), likened intellectual measurement to measurement of physical properties. Within a century, the Han dynasty (202 B.C.–200 A.D.) had heeded Confucius and Mencius and implemented a system of civil service tests in China.

Zhang (1988) reported on the custom of testing children at 1 year of age beginning in the 6th century A.D. in China, particularly in southern China. This was described in the writings of Yen (531–590 A.D.). Zhang (1988) also noted that the use of puzzles to test cognitive ability was popularized during the Song dynasty (960–1127 A.D.). One example consisted of several geometric shapes that could be manipulated and fit into a variety of designs. The test was designed to measure creativity, divergent thinking, and visual-spatial perception. Another popular Chinese puzzle test designed to measure reasoning ability consisted of interconnected copper rings mounted on a bar with a rod running through their center. The goal of the test was to remove the bar from the center of the rings.

In the West, Aristotle made a distinction between ability (*dianoia*) and emotional and moral capacity (*orexis*) in the 4th century. Following the Dark Ages, the examination of human cognitive abilities was taken up by religious philosophers. In the 16th century A.D., Descartes (1998), the French secular philosopher, regarded ability as *res cogitans,* the thing that thinks.

In 1575, Juan Huarte published in Spanish a treatise on work and human ability called *Examen de Ingenios*. It was later published in English as *The Examination of Men's Wits: Discovering the Great Differences of Wits Among Men and What Sort of Learning Suits Best With Each Genius* (Peiro, & Munduate, 1994).

The modern scientific study of human cognitive abilities, however, is often attributed to Binet in France and to the World War I Army Alpha and Beta tests in America.

GENERAL COGNITIVE ABILITY

The English polymath, Sir Francis Galton (1869), invented the construct of general cognitive ability, calling it *g* as shorthand. Charles Spearman (1927, 1930) made the concept of *g* more accessible to psychology through his two-factor theory of human abilities, which proposed that every measure of ability had two components, a general component (*g*) and a specific component(*s*).

Whereas the general component was measured by every test, the specific component was unique to each test. Though each test might have a different specific component, Spearman (1927, 1930) also observed that *s* could be found in common across a limited number of tests. Therefore, the two-factor theory allowed for a spatial factor or other factor that was distinct from *g* but could be found in several tests. These factors shared by tests were called "group factors." Spearman (1927) identified several group factors and noted (Spearman, 1937) that group factors could be either narrow or broad. He further observed that *s* could not be measured without measuring *g*. As we have written elsewhere (Ree & Carretta, 1996, 1998), to be accurate, we should call mathematics not M but:

$$g + M$$

with g written large to indicate its contribution to the variance of the factor (Ree & Carretta, 1996, p. 113). In fact, tests that do not even appear to measure g do so as illustrated by Rabbitt, Banerji, and Szymanski (1989), who demonstrated a strong correlation (.69) between Space Fortress, a psychomotor task that looks like a video game, and an IQ test.

Controversy about g has not abated despite Spearman's early assertion (1930) that g was beyond dispute. In contrast to Spearman's model, Thurstone (1938) proposed a multiple-ability theory. Thurstone allowed no general factor, only seven "unrelated abilities" that he called "primary." Spearman (1938) reanalyzed Thurstone's data noting that g had been submerged through rotation. He then demonstrated the existence of g in Thurstone's tests. This finding was independently confirmed by Holzinger and Harmon (1938) and finally by Thurstone and Thurstone (1941).

Despite empirical evidence for the existence of g, theories of multiple abilities held sway (Fleishman & Quaintance, 1984; Gardner 1983; Guilford, 1956, 1959; Sternberg, 1985). This was particularly true in psychometrics, where these theories led to the construction of numerous multiple-ability tests such as the Differential Aptitude Test, General Aptitude Test Battery, Armed Services Vocational Aptitude Battery, Air Force Officer Qualifying Test, Flanagan Aptitude Tests, Flanagan Industrial Tests, and others. But cleaving to the empirical data, other researchers continued to study g (Arvey, 1986; Gottfredson, 1986, 1997; Gustafsson, 1980, 1984, 1988; Jensen, 1980, 1993, 1998; Schmidt & Hunter, 1998, 2004; Thorndike, 1986; Vernon, 1950, 1969). Although measures of g may be comprised of verbal, math, spatial, reasoning, and other item types, it would take a greater number of items to reliably measure verbal ability, math ability, reasoning, and spatial ability separately. The validity of these abilities would not be any greater than g alone as a measure of g would be included in the verbal, math, reasoning, spatial, or other ability scores.

SPECIFIC ABILITY, KNOWLEDGE, AND NONCOGNITIVE CHARACTERISTICS

The measurement of specific knowledge, skills, abilities, and other characteristics often has been proposed as crucial for understanding human characteristics and occupational performance. Ree and Earles (1991) demonstrated the lack of predictiveness for specific abilities over and above g, whereas Ree and others (Olea & Ree, 1994; Ree, Carretta, & Doub, 1998–1999; Ree, Carretta, & Teachout, 1995; Ree, Earles, & Teachout, 1994) demonstrated the predictiveness of job knowledge.

McClelland (1993), for example, suggested that under some circumstances noncognitive characteristics such as motivation may be better predictors of job performance than cognitive abilities. Sternberg and Wagner (1993) proposed the use of measures of tacit knowledge and practical intelligence in lieu of measures of "academic intelligence." They defined tacit knowledge as "the practical know how one needs for success on the job" (p. 2). Practical intelligence is defined as a more general form of tacit knowledge. Schmidt and Hunter (1993), in a review of Sternberg and Wagner, noted that their concepts of tacit knowledge and practical intelligence are redundant with the well-established construct of job knowledge. Additionally, Ree and Earles (1993) pointed out the lack of rigorous empirical evidence to uphold the assertions of McClelland, Sternberg, and Wagner as well as other critics.

The construct of emotional intelligence (Goleman, 1995) was proposed as another facet that is more important than ordinary cognitive ability. Although its proponents (e.g., Mayer, Salovey, & Caruso, 2002) consider it to be a distinct construct, Schulte, Ree, and Carretta (2004) demonstrated that it is not much more than a combination of the existing constructs of cognitive ability and personality.

PSYCHOMETRIC CHARACTERISTICS OF COGNITIVE ABILITY MEASURES

Courses in statistics and research methods are common for human resources management and personnel specialists and there are established guidelines for conducting studies of personnel measurement and selection (American Educational Research Association, American Psychological Association, & National Council on Measurement in Education, 1999; Society for Industrial and Organizational Psychology, 2003). Reliability, validity, and subgroup differences are core concepts that must be considered whether choosing a commercial test or developing a test from scratch.

Reliability

Reliability is best defined as precision of measurement, that is, how much of the measurement is true and how much is error. In this statistical context, *error* does not mean wrong. Rather, error means random fluctuation that happens per force and cannot be avoided, although it can be minimized. From this basic definition flow the other popular definitions of reliability such as stability over time and consistency across test forms, as well as internal consistency. (See chap. 2 for a discussion of reliability and some alternative ways of evaluating it.)

Two widely used cognitive ability tests are the Wonderlic Personnel Test (1999) and the Watson-Glaser Critical Thinking Appraisal (1980). According to research cited in the Mental Measurements Yearbook (Hanna, 1998), the Wonderlic's test-retest and alternate form reliabilities range from .83 to .93. Similarly high levels of reliability are noted for the Watson-Glaser Critical Thinking Appraisal Manual (Form S; Geisinger, 1998). The internal consistency reliability (coefficient alpha) of the measure was .81. Test-retest reliability was .81 for a sample of 42 employees. The data from these two well-known and frequently used tests show that cognitive ability is a reliably measured construct.

For a test to be reliable there must also be consistent administration, consistent collection of answers, and objective scoring. Test administration procedures must not vary from examinee to examinee and the data collection methods must be consistent. For example, Ree and Wegner (1990) showed that apparently minor changes in machine-scored answer sheets could produce major changes in test scores, particularly in speeded tests. This issue looms larger as we consider placing a selection test on a computer where the presentation could vary by screen size, contrast, and font type. Additionally, when different modes of administration or response collection are necessary, it is essential to develop statistical corrections for the scores (Carretta & Ree, 1993). The use of tests of poor reliability to make decisions about excluding applicants from a training program, especially applicants near the minimum cutting point, is bad practice and may lead to indefensible consequences in court, should a legal challenge arise.

Scoring must be objective. A correct answer must be counted correct by all scorers. Deviation from this standard will cause scores to vary by who did the scoring and will reduce reliability of the test, leading to reduced validity and possibly to an indefensible position in court. This is less of a problem for multiple-choice tests where the answer is presented and must be identified from among answers presented. It is more of a problem for essay-type exams where the answer must be produced and evaluated.

There are several methods to measure cognitive ability reliably. However, as Thompson (2003) has pointed out, the reliability to be considered is the reliability in the sample currently being investigated, not that from previous test administrations or the normative sample: "It is important to evaluate score reliability in *all* studies, because it is the reliability of the data in hand that will drive study results, and not the reliability of the scores described in the test manual" (Thompson, p. 5).

Validity

The important question about validity is whether a test measures what it claims to measure. Although it is convenient to distinguish several types of validity (see chap. 2 for additional discussion), the argument can be made that all validity studies are really construct validity studies. If the test can be shown to be valid, it is shown to be measuring the targeted construct and, therefore, its construct validity is bolstered.

However, a caveat must be offered here. A measure can have predictive validity in cases where it is assumed that it measures a certain construct, but it in fact measures a different construct. For example, in a validation of a structured pilot candidate selection interview, Walters, Miller, and Ree (1993) reported validity for training performance. At first glance, it appeared that the validity of the interview came from measuring motivation and job knowledge. However, the interview also correlated with measures of cognitive ability collected earlier and unavailable to the interviewer. These conditions suggested that its lack of incremental validity over a cognitive ability test was because the interview, at least to some extent, was a measure of cognitive ability. The same may be cited for the example of the psychomotor test Space Fortress (Rabbitt et al., 1989). It did not look like a cognitive ability test but, on analysis, was found to be a cognitive ability measure. Elsewhere (Walters et al.), we identified this as the "topological fallacy."

Schmidt and Hunter (1998) reported on the validity of cognitive ability from a very large meta-analytic study conducted for the U.S. Department of Labor (Hunter, 1980; Hunter & Hunter, 1984). The database for the meta-analysis included over 32,000 employees in 515 widely diverse civilian jobs. Similar to reliability, validity can be assessed using correlations. The resulting validity coefficients can range from +1.0 to -1.0. They found that the validity of cognitive ability for predicting job performance was .58 for professional-managerial jobs, .56 for high-level complex technical jobs, .51 for medium-complexity jobs (which comprise 62% of all jobs in the U.S. economy), .40 for semiskilled jobs, and .23 for completely unskilled jobs. In summary, the research evidence for the validity of cognitive ability measures for predicting job performance is very strong.

Subgroup Differences

There are several issues that must be addressed when measuring ability in gender and ethnic groups. One of these is that the same factors should be measured for all groups. Another concerns the predictive fairness of a test. These issues are discussed next.

Fairness and Similarity: Near Identity of Cognitive Structure.   McArdle (1996), among others, advocated that factorial invariance (i.e., equality of factor loadings) should be demonstrated before other group comparisons (e.g., mean differences) are considered. McArdle stated that if factorial invariance is not observed, the psychometric constructs being measured may be qualitatively different for the groups being compared, obscuring the interpretation of other group comparisons.

Several studies of cognitive factor similarity have been conducted. Comparing the factor structure of World War II U. S. Army pilot selection tests for African Americans and Whites, Michael (1949) found virtually no differences. Humphreys and Taber (1973) also found no differences when they compared factor structures for high and low socioeconomic status boys from Project Talent. Although the ethnicity of the participants in Project Talent was not specifically identified, they expected that the ethnic composition of the two socioeconomic groups would differ significantly.

Using 15 cognitive tests, DeFries et al. (1974) compared the structure of ability for Hawaiians of either European or Japanese ancestry. They found the same four factors and nearly identical factor loadings for the two groups.

These studies all examined common factors, which are factors that appear in more than one test such as verbal or math. Using a hierarchical model, Ree and Carretta (1995) examined the comparative structure of ability across gender and ethnic groups. They observed only small differences on the verbal math and speed factors. No significant differences were found for g on ability measures.

Carretta and Ree (1995) compared aptitude factor structures in large samples of young Americans. The factor model was hierarchical including g and five lower order factors representing verbal, math, spatial, aircrew knowledge, and perceptual speed. The model showed good fit and little difference for both genders and all five ethnic groups (White, African American, Hispanic, Asian American, and Native American). Correlations between factor loadings for the gender groups and for all pairs of ethnic groups were very high, approaching $r = 1.0$. Comparisons of regression equations between pairs of groups indicated that there was no mean difference in loadings between males and females or among the ethnic groups. These and previous findings present a consistent picture of near identity of cognitive structure for sex and ethnic groups.

Predictive Fairness.   Several decades of individual research studies have shown that Whites achieve higher mean cognitive ability scores than African Americans (Gordon, 1986; Gottfredson, 1988; Herrnstein & Murray, 1994; Jensen, 1985; Sackett & Wilk, 1994). In a large-scale meta-analysis, White job incumbents achieved significantly higher mean cognitive ability test scores than African Americans ($d = .90$, $k = 13$, $N = 50,799$; Roth, BeVier, Bobko, Switzer, & Tyler, 2001).

As a result of this research regarding subgroup differences, several researchers have conducted studies of predictive fairness of cognitive ability tests. Jensen (1980, p. 514) noted that numerous large-scale studies provided no evidence for predictive unfairness. He concluded that predictive bias did not exist, although intercept differences could be observed and were likely due to sampling error or differences in reliability for the two groups.

Putting a finer point on it, Carretta (1997) demonstrated that even when intercept differences were observed in statistical tests of differences of regression equations for two groups, the differences were due solely to differing reliability found in the two groups.

Hunter and Schmidt (1979) investigated 39 studies of African American and White validity and found no evidence of differential prediction for the groups. Schmidt and Hunter (1982) illuminated pitfalls in assessing the fairness of regressions using tests of differences in (linear) regression models. In these two studies, the authors concluded that artifacts accounted for the apparent differential prediction and that no predictive bias was present. Carretta (1997) and Jensen (1980) provided clear statistical explanations of the issues. In summary, no evidence exists that cognitive ability tests are unfair.

HOW TO SELECT OR DEVELOP A COGNITIVE ABILITIES TEST

Selection or development of a test begins with job analysis. The goal of job analysis, as discussed in chapters 2 and 3 and elsewhere (e.g., Cascio, 1991; Gael, 1988; McCormick, 1976, 1979), is to establish job, task, and cognitive requirements or knowledge, skills, abilities, and other requirements (KSAOs). A job analysis must be conducted whether one ultimately selects a cognitive ability test from among commercially available tests or develops a test. Job and task analysis can be accomplished in many different ways. The authors of chapters 2 and 3 describe three such methods and Cascio discussed others. Results of the job analyses lead to development of a test plan and test specification requirements (e.g., test content, reading level, item difficulty, item discriminability), as described in chapter 4.

Once a job analysis has been completed and a particular set of KSAOs has been identified as necessary for successful job performance, the next step is to decide whether to select an existing test or develop one to measure those KSAOs. To make a reasoned decision, testing professionals should obtain information about several factors, including:

- Test development documentation such as theoretical basis, normative sample, and test development procedures.
- Psychometric characteristics, such as reliability, validity, and test bias.
- Information regarding administration, including materials, procedures, instructions, reasonable accommodation for applicants with disabilities, and special training requirements.
- Test interpretation aids such as normative data, expectancy charts, or cut scores.
- Scoring options, including whether the test is hand scored, computerized, or machine scored and the qualifications for scorers.
- Ongoing research and refinement of the test.
- Time requirements.
- Credentials and expertise of the test developers.
- Total costs, including materials, fees, and test development costs.

The following sections discuss factors that affect the decision to select an existing test or develop one for use in personnel measurement and selection and the associated human resource management activities. The job of an entry-level electrician is used throughout as an example. In particular, we assume that a worker characteristic and methods of measurement matrix has been completed as in Fig. 4.8. We further assume that some of the identified worker characteristics include cognitive abilities such as the "ability to comprehend written instructions and warnings."

Selecting an Existing Cognitive Ability Test

Reasons for Selecting an Existing Cognitive Ability Test. Use of commercially available tests often is an attractive alternative. Two common reasons for this choice are to (a) avoid the costs associated with test development and maintenance and (b) gain ready access to normative and psychometric data. The level of effort, technical expertise, and other resources often required for test development and maintenance may not be available to many human resource professionals.

For example, test development activities include development of test specifications and item pools, conduct of technical and sensitivity reviews, creation of test administration procedures and instructions, try-out of items and analysis of item-level data, assembly and production of the test, and preparation of test documentation such as test manuals. Test development costs may be further increased because of the need to develop new test forms periodically (e.g., to combat test compromise, to update test content). The availability of normative data (e.g., population and subgroup performance) and psychometric data (e.g., reliability, content validity, construct validity, criterion-related validity) for commercially available tests provides a valuable context within which to interpret test results (e.g., comparison to other groups).

Identifying Candidate Cognitive Ability Tests. The first step in selecting a commercially available cognitive ability test is to identify candidate tests. There are several helpful sources of information and much information is now available via the Internet (e.g., Buros Institute of Mental Measurements, http://www.unl.edu/ buros; Educational Testing Service, http://www.ets.org; and Pro-Ed, http://www. proed-inc.com). Example publications include the *Mental Measurement Yearbooks* (Spies & Plake, 2005), *Tests in Print* (Murphy, Plake, Impara, & Spies, 2002), and *Test Critiques* (Keyser & Sweetland, 1997). The *Mental Measurement Yearbooks,* a set of volumes covering many decades, include descriptive information, professional reviews, and references. Each volume only includes information about tests that are new, revised, or in wide use since the previous edition. *Tests in Print* is a comprehensive bibliography of all known commercially available tests in print in the English language. It provides information about the purpose of the test, what it measures, author, publisher, publication date, in-print status, cost, intended test population, and administration time. *Test Critiques* includes tests used in business, education, and psychology. It provides information regarding practical applications and uses, guidelines for administration, scoring, and interpretation, psychometric data (norms, reliability, validity), and critical reviews. Professional organizations such as the American Psychological Association (APA) and the Educational Resources Information Center (ERIC) are other valuable sources of information about commercially available tests. The APA neither endorses nor sells tests, but provides information about tests and their proper use (http://www.apa.org/science/faq-findtests. html). The same is generally true for the American Psychological Society (http:// www.psychologicalscience. org/) and the Society for Industrial and Organizational Psychology (http://www. siop.org/ Workplace/default.htm). The Association of Test Publishers (http: //www. testpublishers.org/), a nonprofit organization representing providers of assessment tools, tests, and related services, is yet another source of information.

Evaluating the Information about Candidate Tests. Once a set of candidate tests has been identified, the next step in selecting a test is to evaluate the available information. A variety of issues should be considered when tests are to be used in an employment context, including:

- The appropriateness of the test for its intended use.
- Administrative procedures (individual vs. group, paper-and-pencil vs. computerized, administration time, need for special equipment or setting, training of administrators).

- Interpretability of test scores (norms).
- Cost.
- Usefulness of supporting materials (administrative and technical manuals).
- Psychometric properties (error of measurement, reliability, validity, lack of bias).

Fortunately, this information is available from the sources just described. Naturally, although the reviews of published tests are useful, the final evaluation of a particular test's usefulness must be postponed until the test has been obtained, the materials studied, and the test has been administered and validated. Due to the technical nature of the material in test reviews and manuals, it is important to obtain professional assistance in interpreting test information.

Consider an example regarding the evaluation of applicants for an entry-level electrician job training program. A review of the job analysis results (e.g., see Fig. 4.6), as required by law, will guide us regarding both the specific abilities required (e.g., verbal comprehension, mathematics, spatial reasoning) and their level (e.g., 10th grade or higher for verbal comprehension and 12th grade or higher for mathematics and spatial). A review of the information provided in the *Mental Measurement Yearbooks, Tests in Print*, and *Test Critiques* will allow us to identify candidate tests that already exist and whether they are appropriate for use in the current context.

Looking in the references cited earlier, we find several tests that meet the content requirements. Among these tests are the Armed Services Vocational Aptitude Battery, Differential Aptitude Tests, and the Wonderlic Personnel Test. All are professionally developed and have acceptable psychometric properties (i.e., reliability, validity, norms). The Armed Services Vocational Aptitude Battery is not available for commercial purchase. Both the Differential Aptitude Tests and the Wonderlic Personnel Test are available commercially and can be group administered. For purposes of the entry-level electrician job, the Wonderlic Personnel Test offers the advantage of lower costs and shorter administration time. If the job analysis had revealed worker KSAOs measured by the Differential Aptitude Tests but not by the Wonderlic Personnel Test, then the Differential Aptitude Tests or other similar tests would have been a proper choice.

Obtaining the Test. Once an appropriate test has been identified, the next step is to obtain copies of the test, answer sheets if necessary, test manuals, and permission to reproduce or use the test. Requirements for the purchase and use of tests vary across test publishers (Eyde et al., 1993). Some test publishers will only permit potential test users to purchase the test manual, for use in further evaluating the suitability of the test prior to making a final purchase decision. To qualify for test purchase, some test publishers require the purchaser to have an advanced degree in psychology, education, or a related field; to have completed specialized training in test administration, methodology, and use; and to possess a professional license.

Trying Out the Test. After the test has been obtained, it must be tried out on a sample of the intended applicant group, which includes assessing its reliability and validity. Reliability can be estimated if appropriate assumptions about the applicant group can be met (Cronbach, 1951).

The general standards for validity studies are described in §1607.5 of the *Uniform Guidelines on Employee Selection Procedures* (1978). During this stage, predictor and criterion measures are identified, data are collected on an appropriate sample, and predictive validity is examined. In a predictive validity design, the appropriate sample is a large group of applicants (i.e., several hundred). The selection instruments are administered during application and the criteria are collected after those selected have completed training or been on the job for some period. A correlation may be computed from the data collected on the predictor test and the criterion. Because this correlation is likely downwardly biased due to preselection, a correction for range restriction (Hunter & Schmidt, 2004; Ree, Carretta, Earles, & Albert, 1994) should be applied to determine what the validity would be in the full applicant sample.

In addition to the selection test's usefulness for identifying those likely to be successful, there are other important considerations in evaluating the test for personnel selection. For example, it is important to determine whether the way the test is used differentially qualifies members of different subgroups (i.e., adverse impact). Cutting or qualification scores or combining the weighted test scores with other selection information defines the selection decision. The selection decision, in turn, defines whether groups qualify at differing rates, which may indicate adverse impact.

Another important factor to consider is whether the test predicts training and job performance equally well for members of different gender and ethnic-racial groups (i.e., predictive bias). Information about studies conducted to examine adverse impact and predictive bias may be available in the test documentation.

Developing a Cognitive Ability Test

Reasons for Developing A Cognitive Ability Test. Despite the availability of off-the-shelf commercial cognitive ability tests with acceptable psychometric properties, there are several reasons why it may be desirable for organizations to develop new tests. Some reasons are: (a) a proprietary test is desired, (b) alternate forms are required but not available for the commercial test, (c) test content becomes outdated, and (d) there is a need to measure a newly hypothesized or highly specialized ability identified as a result of the deductive or inductive job analyses described in chapters 2 and 3.

Proprietary tests are desirable when organizations want to control test content, administration and scoring procedures, and testing policy (e.g., test-retest). A well-known example is the Armed Services Vocational Aptitude Battery (ASVAB), which is used for U.S. military enlistment qualification. Despite careful efforts to control test exposure, commercially available ASVAB study guides are readily available and there is a constant threat of compromising test content.

Alternative forms include parallel forms (different items, but equivalent content and score distributions) and forms administered in different formats (paper-and-pencil, computer-administered, and computerized adaptive tests). Alternative forms are useful when retests are allowed and they can help to combat possible test compromise. In the case of retests, when alternate forms are available applicants can be retested on a form with different, but construct and psychometrically equivalent, items to reduce retest gains due to prior exposure to test items.

Test content may become outdated for several reasons. Two examples are when word usage patterns change or when test content focuses on technological areas that change rapidly. New words enter common usage and others drop out over time. An example of outdated test content might be items from a 1960s vintage electrical knowledge test that included questions about vacuum tubes and audio output transformers. These items clearly would not be appropriate for measuring knowledge about state-of-the-art electrical technology.

Sometimes it is desirable to develop test content based on newly hypothesized abilities if they are found in the job analysis (e.g., procedural knowledge, working memory capacity) or on specialized KSAO content not represented in commercial off-the-shelf cognitive tests. Specialized technical content tests are common in the U.S. military. For example, the ASVAB includes subtests that measure knowledge of electricity and electronics, mechanical and physical principles, automobile terminology and technology, and tools and shop terminology and practices. If similar commercial tests are unavailable and information cannot be found in the testing sources cited earlier, then the required test(s) must be developed.

Test Development Procedures

The level of effort and technical expertise required by an organization to develop and maintain its own cognitive ability test may be prohibitive for many organizations. Test development activities include development of test specifications and item pools, technical and sensitivity reviews, creation of test administration procedures and instructions, trying out items, analyzing item-level data, assembling the test, and preparing test documentation (Childs, Baughman, & Keil, 1997). Nevertheless, test development may be necessary and will entail the following steps and considerations. The reader who would like more detailed information about test development procedures should consult such classic works as Cronbach (1984) and Nunnally (1978).

Develop Test Specifications.   Test specifications are required to guide test development activities (see chap. 4). Because reading technical information (e.g., manuals) is required for electricians, a verbal comprehension test for applicants for the apprentice electrician job could be used. Test specifications for such a measure include an operational definition of the construct to be measured, content taxonomy, item reading level, item difficulty level, item format, item homogeneity, and number of items.

Construct definition: A clear operational definition of the construct to be measured must exist prior to beginning test content development. The construct definition should include a label, a brief definition, and information that distinguishes the construct (e.g., verbal comprehension) from related constructs (e.g., verbal reasoning, word knowledge).

Content taxonomy: After the construct has been specified, the particular content used to measure the construct must be specified. The content for a verbal comprehension test can be described by grammar, word knowledge, making inferences, finding facts, seeing relationships, and identifying the main idea of the text.

Reading and difficulty levels: The appropriate reading and item content difficulty levels should be identified prior to test development during the job analysis. For cognitive ability tests used in employment settings, appropriate reading and item difficulty levels depend on the job requirements, the ability level of the intended applicant population, and the ability of the items to differentiate among applicants' ability level. For example, a 10th-grade difficulty level would be appropriate if the results of the job analysis support it and if the target population consists of high school graduates with little or no college. A higher level would be appropriate if job requirements were more demanding and the target population was college graduates. For tests not requiring verbal ability (e.g., numerical memory, spatial reasoning) and intended for the general population, a lower reading level might be appropriate. If too high a reading level is used, differences in performance on test content might be obscured by differences in reading skill.

Item format: Although multiple-choice formats are widely used, cognitive ability test items may take other forms, including essay, true-false, and short answer. The Educational Testing Service, for example, recently added essay questions to the SAT because several colleges and universities wanted an indicator of applicants' ability to express themselves. Regardless of which format is used, the item content should be representative of the cognitive processes the test is intended to measure (construct validity).

For multiple-choice tests, items are composed of a stem and response alternatives. The correct response is called the keyed response; all other response alternatives are distractors. Childs et al. (1997) noted several issues that should be considered when developing multiple-choice test items. Items should be well organized and clearly written, using familiar words and brief, direct statements. Item stems should be complete and provide enough information so the question is clearly stated. It should not be necessary for the examinee to have to read the response alternatives to understand the test question. The response alternatives should be logically and grammatically consistent with both the item stem and the other response alternatives. Each item should have a single key. That is, there should be only one alternative that is clearly superior to the others. None of the distractors should be close enough in meaning to the keyed response that they could be justifiably defended as the correct response. Although the distractors should not be close enough in meaning to the item key that they can be justifiably defended as correct, they should be plausible enough to be effective. On the surface, well-written distractors should appear plausible in order to attract examinees who only superficially read the alternatives or who do not know the content. The response alternatives also should be written to be mutually exclusive. That is, no response alternative should logically contain another (e.g., "none of the above"). Finally, all items should be independent from one another. Neither the item stem nor the response alternatives should include information that suggests the correct answer to another item. An example might be an item such as "Ohm's Law defines the relations between what variables?" followed by another question that includes information about the relationships among power, voltage, current, and resistance.

Item homogeneity: Item homogeneity is inversely related to the breadth of the ability being measured. Tests designed to measure narrowly defined cognitive abilities such as verbal comprehension will be comprised of very similar items. In contrast, a test of a more broadly defined concept such as verbal ability may contain items with varied content (verbal comprehension, verbal reasoning, verbal working memory, written expression). Regardless of the specificity or breadth of the ability being measured, the items should: (a) be representative of the ability they are intended to measure and not measure other abilities as well and (b) not contain content that may confound measurement of the targeted ability.

Number of items: The number of items will be a function of the breadth of content, item format, and response format. For example, we may decide that in addition to questions focusing on comprehension, our test of verbal comprehension also should include items that measure grammar and word knowledge. It should be decided how many items of each type are desired prior to beginning to write test items. Detailed specification of the number and types of items for a test facilitates test construction and helps ensure comparability across forms, when multiple forms of a test are to be developed.

Figure 5.1 provides an example of a passage and questions that could be used to assess verbal comprehension of applicants to an entry-level electrician job training program.

Note that the content of the passage, about Thomas Edison's many inventions, is of potential interest to applicants and is likely to increase applicant acceptance of the test (i.e., face validity). Verbal comprehension passages need not be so lengthy as this example. Items from the ASVAB Paragraph Comprehension subtest consist of short passages each followed by a single question.

Figures 5.2 and 5.3 provide examples of test questions that could be used to assess math and spatial perception for applicants to an entry-level electrician job training program. Detailed item-writing guidelines are available elsewhere. See, for example, Millman and Greene (1989) and Roid and Haladyna (1982).

Thomas Edison took out his first patent when he was 21 years old. It was for an electronic vote counter, which he intended for use in the United States House of Representatives. Although the machine worked perfectly, Congress would not buy it. The congressmen did not want the vote counting to be done too quickly. The roll call vote often was used to delay the voting process. Political groups relied on these delays to influence and change the opinions of their colleagues. Edison learned a valuable lesson from this experience; that is, "First be sure a thing is wanted or needed, then go ahead."

Born in 1847, Edison was the 7th and last child of Samuel Edison, Jr. and Nancy Elliot Edison. At an early age, he developed hearing problems that may have motivated him in the development of several of his inventions. To compensate for his deafness, Edison became an avid reader. Although Edison was inquisitive and imaginative, he had difficulty in school due to his hearing problems and only attended a total of 434 days over a five-year period.

Edison created the first industrial laboratory in Menlo Park, NJ. At age 29, Edison began work on the carbon transmitter, which ultimately helped make Alexander Graham Bell's "articulating" telephone audible enough for practical use. In 1879, disappointed that Bell had beaten him in the race to patent the first authentic transmission of the human voice, Edison invented the first commercially practical incandescent electric light bulb. Edison tested over 3,000 filaments before he came up with his particular version of a practical light bulb.

Many of Edison's inventions were in response to specific demands for new products or for improvements. However, he also had a gift for exploring unexpected direction's when they were presented. Such was the case with the phonograph. The telephone was considered to be a variation of acoustic telegraphy. As with the telegraph, Edison was trying to develop a method to transcribe the signals as they were received. The recorded voice would then be retransmitted as a telegraph message. (The telephone was not yet conceived of as a general purpose method for person to person communication). In 1877, Edison used a stylus tipped carbon transmitter to make impressions on a strip of paraffin coated paper. To Edison's surprise, the barely visible indentations produced a vague reproduction of sound when the strip of paper was pulled back beneath the stylus. Edison subsequently replaced the paraffin covered paper with a cylinder wrapped in tinfoil. The device was universally acclaimed and Edison became known as the "Wizard of Menlo Park." It would be another decade, however, till the phonograph moved from the laboratory to become a commercial product.

Perhaps Edison's greatest invention, however, was a practical and complete model for a standardized centralized electrical power system and its supplementary components. This revolutionary breakthrough influenced the design, development, and success of all later power plants. Edison's design featured a unique transformer controlled three wire feeder grid. It was the first design to guarantee that electrical energy could economically power and light small, medium, and large communities worldwide. Despite its importance, the significance of this invention has largely been ignored and forgotten.

At the time of his death at age 84, Edison either singly or jointly had patented 1,093 inventions, including the incandescent light bulb, alkaline storage battery, phonograph, and motion picture projector. He also improved on the original design of other inventions such as the stock ticker, telegraph, and telephone. He believed in hard work, sometimes working 20 hours a day. This strong work ethic is reflected in a quote attributed to him that "Genius is one percent inspiration and 99 percent perspiration."

1. According to the passage, Congress decided not to purchase Edison's electronic vote counter because

    A. it was too expensive to implement

    B. of potential errors in vote counting

    C. they preferred the roll call vote

    D. electronic voting would lead to delays

2. According to the passage, Edison's work on the carbon transmitter contributed to the development of the:

    A. stock ticker

    B. telegraph key

    C. feeder grid

    D. articulating telephone

3. According to the passage, the phonograph was:

    A. a response to demand from the entertainment industry

    B. developed to record voice messages from telephones

    C. preceded by the development of the telephone

    D. an immediate commercial and financial success

4. According to the passage, Edison originally recorded sound on a:

    A. strip of paraffin covered paper

    B. paraffin covered paper cylinder

    C. cylinder covered with tinfoil

    D. solid wax covered cylinder

5. According to the passage, Edison:

    A. was known as the "Wizard of Wall Street" due to his shrewd knack for investments

    B. held patents in diverse areas, including the light bulb, phonograph, and automobile

    C. was credited with creating the first industrial laboratory in Menlo Park, NJ

    D. attended Princeton University where he earned a master's degree in science

6. According to the passage, Edison's greatest invention was the:

    A. affordable incandescent light bulb

    B. portable electric powered phonograph

    C. first practical articulating telephone

    D. model for a centralized power system

FIGURE 5.1 Example of a passage and test questions designed to access verbal comprehension for applicants to an entry-level electrician job training program.

Conducting Technical Reviews. Technical reviews are formal procedures in which subject matter experts (SMEs) and testing experts review test materials prior to field testing. The purpose of the SME review is to ensure the technical accuracy of the test items. For example, SMEs would determine that the item key is correct and that the item distractors are incorrect and are not ambiguous. The purpose of the review by testing experts is to make sure that the test items follow the item development guidelines described earlier and that the item content reflects an appropriate level of the ability being assessed, as was determined in the job analysis.

Conducting Sensitivity Reviews. Sensitivity reviews are formal procedures in which representatives from various demographic groups review test materials to ensure they do not contain content that may be viewed as potentially offensive. As a rule, sensitivity reviews focus on three issues. These are whether the items: (a) include assumptions, stereotypic descriptions, or objectionable or demeaning characterizations of subgroups; (b) give one subgroup an advantage over others; and (c) contain content about potentially sensitive topics. Some examples of content that might give one group an unfair advantage over another include topics typically more familiar to one gender group (e.g., fashion, sports trivia), activities that are more accessible to members of higher socioeconomic status groups (e.g.,

1. An electrician doing the wiring for a building estimates that 1,600 feet of electrical cable will be needed. Four spools contain 1,000 feet of cable. How many spools should the electrician purchase?

    A. 2

    B. 4

    C. 6

    D. 7

2. A contractor wants to purchase electrical insulating material for the area shown in the figure below. How many square feet of insulating material are needed to cover the entire area?

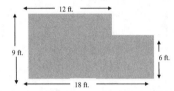

    A. 108

    B. 144

    C. 162

    D. 216

3. What is the volume of a cylinder designed to hold electrical equipment that is 8 inches tall and has a 1 inch radius? (Use $\pi = 3.14$)

    A. 24.00 cubic inches

    B. 25.12 cubic inches

    C. 50.24 cubic inches

    D. 78.88 cubic inches

4. The reciprocal of 10 is:

    A. 0.05

    B. 0.01

    C. 0.10

    D. 1.00

FIGURE 5.2   Examples of test questions designed to access mathematics knowledge for applicants to an entry-level electrician job training program.

The following test items are designed to measure your ability to solve spatial problems. For each problem, you will be given three rules that will determine how four cubes are to be combined to form a larger figure. The cubes are grouped into two sets as follows:

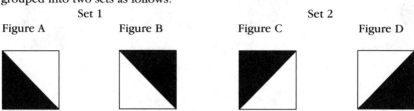

Set 1   Set 2

Figure A   Figure B   Figure C   Figure D

Consider the following example:

Rule #1: "Figure B precedes Figure A" yields

Rule #2: "Figure D does not follow Figure C" yields

Rule #3: "Set 1 is below Set 2" yields

    Set 2

    Set 1

Combining the results of all three rules to create a larger figure yields:

Use the following figures to solve all of the remaining problems:

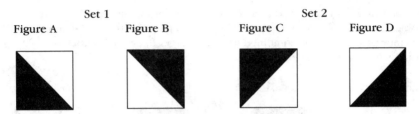

Set 1   Set 2
Figure A   Figure B   Figure C   Figure D

1. Use the following three rules to create a larger figure:

Rule #1: Set 2 is not below Set 1

Rule #2: Figure B does not follow Figure A

Rule #3: Figure C precedes Figure D

Choose the correct solution from the following alternatives.

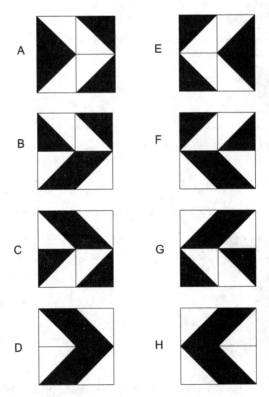

FIGURE 5.3   Examples of test questions that could be used to assess spatial perception for applicants to an entry-level electrician job training program.

equestrian, golf, possession of a private pilot's certificate), and local or regional knowledge (local or regional geography, history, or customs). Examples of potentially sensitive topics include religion, sex, and politics. These topics should be avoided. Furthermore, items should not include offensive terms or language.

Creation of Test Administration Procedures and Instructions. Standardization of test administration procedures and instructions is necessary to ensure that the test-taking experience is as similar as possible for all examinees. Standardization provides administrators with a process to control potentially extraneous factors (e.g., physical testing conditions) that may affect examinees' performance and to ensure that test scores are comparable across test administrations.

Test administration procedures should include detailed instructions regarding the need for specialized training or certification for test administrators, setting up the test room, handling test materials, timing the test, and scoring completed tests. Test administration instructions should clearly describe standards for the physical testing environment (e.g., light, noise, temperature) and include information about how administrators should respond to examinees' questions. Test administration guidelines may go so far as to provide answers to clarifying questions that are frequently asked by examinees.

Trying Out Test Administration Procedures and Test Items. It is important to try out test administration procedures and test items prior to their operational administration. This is essential for newly developed tests where there are few, if any, prior data. Pilot testing provides an opportunity to refine administration procedures such as timing. For example, if a 45-minute time limit has been set for a verbal comprehension test, but most examinees complete it in less than 30 minutes, the time limit might be reduced. Another example is if one were developing a speeded test, where item content is very easy and test performance is mostly a function of response speed. If the time limit is set too long and most participants are finishing all of the items, the test may not be achieving its objective of measuring response speed and differentiating among applicants.

Sometimes in an ongoing testing program in a routine test administration, it is desirable to administer new unscored items along with those that are scored. The new items can either be embedded in the test with the scored items or presented in a separate section. These new items do not contribute to examinees' scores. They are used solely to determine the item characteristics (reliability, validity, difficulty, discrimination) and may become candidates for inclusion in a subsequent form of the test.

Analyzing Item-Level Data. Pilot studies provide a valuable source of data to conduct statistical analyses of item-level characteristics. Item-level statistical analyses focus on determining the difficulty level and discrimination index of the test items and help to guide test construction (e.g., number of items needed to reach a target reliability level):

Item difficulty: Item difficulty usually is measured by the proportion of examinees that correctly answers an item (p). Determining the appropriate range and mix of item difficulties is a crucial step in test construction. Consider two extreme examples. Suppose a test is constructed where all examinees answer some very easy items correctly ($p = 1.00$) and all examinees answer a different set of very difficult items incorrectly ($p = 0.00$). Clearly, neither the very easy nor the very difficult test items are informative. They do not provide information that permits discrimination (i.e., make distinctions) among examinees on the targeted ability or to predict some external criterion (e.g., training or job performance). A test without variance cannot predict any criterion.

Items that provide the best discrimination among examinees, from a psychometric standpoint, are items that are answered correctly by about half of those taking the test. If the goal were to maximize the number of distinctions among the examinees with respect to the targeted ability, the best approach would be to develop a test where the average proportion of correct responses is about .50 across a range of item difficulty levels. This frequently is accomplished by using items with difficulty values ranging from .20 to .80. However, if the goal were to increase the probability of screening for a particular ability level, that might require the use of a minimum qualifying (or cutting) score, then the best strategy would be to select items such that the average proportion of correct responses was equal to the selection ratio (i.e., number of openings/number of applicants). For example, if there were 300 applicants for the apprentice electrician job training program and 75 openings, the best test would be one that identified the top 75 applicants. For this example, the best test would be one where the average p value for the test items was .25. The difficulty level would be such that only about 25% of the examinees would obtain a qualifying score.

Item discrimination: Item discrimination typically is measured by the point-biserial correlation coefficient (Crocker & Algina, 1986). The point-biserial correlation indicates the degree to which performance on the test item is related to overall test performance. A test item discriminates between good and poor overall test performance to the extent that examinees who answer an item correctly also do well on the entire test. One common guideline is to retain items where the point-biserial correlation for the correct response (key) is .20 or greater. The point-biserial correlations for item distractors (incorrect options) should be negative. That is, those choosing the incorrect option should also obtain a lower score on the test as a whole. Some test constructors prefer to use the biserial correlation rather than the point-biserial correlation. The biserial correlation is not a Pearson correlation, but can be tested for significance and does not have the limitation of the point-biserial correlation with respect to extremely difficult or extremely easy items. A useful guideline is to retain items with a biserial correlation of .30 or greater.

Item bias: When examining item-level data, it also is informative to compute indices of item bias (Holland & Wainer, 1993). For example, indices of differential item functioning (DIF; see chap. 13) can provide information about whether individuals from different subgroups (e.g., gender, ethnic, or socioeconomic groups), when matched on overall test performance, perform differently on individual test items. Analyses based on item response theory (IRT; see chap. 13) also can provide information about item difficulty, discrimination, and potential bias. Items that show signs of being problematic, statistically speaking, should be reviewed carefully to determine possible structural and content-related sources that may contribute to the problem (e.g., distractors that are too close to the item key, unintentional cues to the correct answer).

Item banking: Commercial item banking programs are available. These programs allow the test constructor to keep records about specific test items on a computer and manipulate test content. Also, many spreadsheet-type programs can be used for item banking as they allow both numeric (item difficulty, item discrimination, sample size, etc.) and character (stems, keyed responses, distractors) data. Additionally, these programs allow sorting and filtering of data as well as statistical computations.

Assembling the Test. Several sources of information enter into the determination of the final set of items that will appear on a test. The results of the item-level analyses play a major role in the decision to include or exclude items. For example, item difficulty should be considered in order to achieve an appropriate range of item difficulty and overall test difficulty. In addition, point-biserial (or biserial) correlations should be considered to attain internal consistency. Furthermore, test specifications should be consulted that stipulate the number, type, and content of test items. Other sources of information that should be considered when assembling the tests include the similarity of item content to other items. Items should not be included that are redundant or provide information that may cue examinees regarding the correct answer to other items.

Although the results of the item analyses from the pilot test data provide much useful information when initially assembling the test, it is essential to conduct additional item-level analyses once the test has been operationally implemented. Test items may perform differently in an operational setting than they do during test development. There are several reasons why this may occur, including differences in administration procedures, examinee ability level and motivation, and position of the test items in the test. Therefore, it is good practice to conduct additional item-level analyses once a test has been administered operationally.

Preparing Test Documentation. Test documentation materials should include a detailed summary of the pilot test results. For instance, pilot test results may include information about areas of needed improvement (e.g., test administration procedures) and the results of such changes. This summary also should specify the number of test items that meet the predefined standards for inclusion in the operational test. Other useful information that should be provided includes distributions of surviving items sorted by difficulty level and point-biserial (or biserial) correlations.

CHECKLIST FOR _____

Item	Comment
1. Test theoretical basis	_____
2. Normative sample	_____
3. Test development procedures	_____
4. Reliability	_____
5. Validity	_____
6. Test bias	_____
7. Administration procedures	_____
Materials	_____
Instructions	_____
Reasonable accommodation	_____
Special training required	_____
8. Normative data	_____
Expectancy charts	_____
Suggested cut scores	_____
9. Scoring options and the qualifications for scoring _____	
10. Existing or planned research/refinement of the test _____	
11. Testing time requirements _____	
12. Qualifications of the test developers _____	
13. Total costs including life-cycle costs _____	

FIGURE 5.4   Checklist for evaluating and comparing candidate cognitive ability tests.

SUMMARY

High-performing individuals are important to organizations. Campbell, Gasser, and Oswald (1996) examined the productivity of individuals with high and low job performance. Using a conservative method, they estimated that the top 1% of workers produces a return 3.29 times as great as the lowest 1% of workers.

Furthermore, depending on the variability of job performance, Campbell et al. estimated that the value may range from 3 to 10 times the return. Job performance makes a difference and one of the best predictors of job performance is cognitive ability (Schmidt & Hunter, 1998).

Cognitive ability has a long history in the management of personnel resources. Measures of cognitive ability have been used to assess human capability and job qualification for centuries. The decision to select or develop a test begins with job analysis and chapters 2 and 3 in this volume provide handy references.

Throughout this chapter, we have stressed the complexity of the decision process in purchasing or developing a cognitive ability test. Information about a test should include: (a) a test's theoretical basis, normative sample, and test development procedures; (b) estimates of psychometric characteristics; (c) administration procedures, including reasonable accommodation for applicants with disabilities; (d) normative data; (e) scoring options; (f) research and refinement of the test; (g) testing time requirements; (h) qualifications of the test developers; and (i) total costs including life-cycle costs. A checklist is provided in Fig. 5.4. Use the first line to enter the name of the test and write comments about the status of the 'item.' Multiple checklists can be used for comparisons.

The responsibility for defending the use of a cognitive ability test ultimately falls on the organization that uses it. Thus, it is crucial that the theoretical basis of the test be well understood, that it has acceptable psychometric properties, and that the test be administered, scored, and interpreted in an appropriate manner. Decisions made, even in part, on the basis of applicants' performance on cognitive tests have real-world consequences that affect individuals' lives (e.g., entrance into a training or educational program, employment, promotion). Those who are screened out for entrance into training, hiring, or promotion based on their performance on a cognitive ability test may have little recourse. Furthermore, they may not have the opportunity to demonstrate other competencies (e.g., job knowledge, motivation, skills) that may compensate for low cognitive test scores. Their only recourse may be in the courts.

REFERENCES

American Educational Research Association, American Psychological Association, & National Council on Measurement in Education (Joint Committee). (1999). *Standards for educational and psychological testing.* Washington, DC: American Educational Research Association.

Arvey, R. D. (1986). General ability in employment: A discussion. *Journal of Vocational Behavior, 29,* 415–420.

Campbell, J. P., Gasser, M. B., & Oswald, F. L. (1996). The substantive nature of job performance variability. In K. R. Murphy (Ed.), *Individual differences and behavior in organizations* (pp. 258–299). San Francisco: Jossey-Bass.

Carretta, T. R. (1997). Group differences on U.S. Air Force pilot selection tests. *International Journal of Selection and Assessment, 5,* 115–127.

Carretta, T. R., & Ree, M. J. (1993). Basic Attributes Test (BAT): Psychometric equating of a computer-based test. *International Journal of Aviation Psychology, 3,* 189–201.

Carretta, T. R., & Ree, M. J. (1995). Near identity of cognitive structure in sex and ethnic groups. *Personality and Individual Differences, 19,* 149–155.

Cascio, W. F. (1991). *Applied psychology in personnel management* (4th ed.). Englewood Cliffs, NJ: Prentice Hall.

Childs, R. A., Baughman, W. A., & Keil, C. T., Jr. (1997). Tests of cognitive ability. In D. L. Whetzel & G. R. Wheaton (Eds.), *Applied measurement methods in industrial psychology* (pp 143–183). Palo Alto, CA: Davies-Black.

Crocker, L., & Algina, J. (1986). *Introduction to classical and modern test theory.* Fort Worth, TX: Harcourt Brace Jovanovich.

Cronbach, L. J. (1951). Coefficient alpha and the internal structure of tests. *Psychometrika, 16,* 297–334.

Cronbach, L. J. (1984). *Essentials of psychological testing* (4th ed.). New York: Harper & Row.

DeFries, J. C., Vandenberg, S. G., McClearn, G. E., Kuse, A. R., Wilson, J. R., Ashton, G. C., et al. (1974). Near identity of cognitive structure in two ethnic groups. *Science, 183,* 338–339.

Descartes, R. (1998). *Discourse on method* (D. A. Cress, Trans.). Indianapolis, IN: Hackett.

Eyde, L. E., Robertson, G. J., Krug, S. E., Moreland, K. L., Robertson, A. G., Shawan, C. M., et al. (1993). *Responsible test use: Case studies for assessing human behavior.* Washington, DC: American Psychological Association.

Fleishman, E. A., & Quaintance, M. K. (1984). *Taxonomies of human performance: The description of human tasks.* Orlando, FL: Academic Press.

Gael, S. (1988). *The job analysis handbook for business, industry, and government* (Vols. 1–2). New York: Wiley.

Galton, F. (1869). *Hereditary genius: An inquiry into its laws and consequences.* London: Macmillan.

Gardner, H. (1983). *Frames of mind: The theory of multiple intelligences.* New York: Basic Books.

Geisinger, K. F. (1998). Review of the Watson-Glaser Critical Thinking Appraisal (Form S). In J. C. Impara & B. S. Plake (Eds.), *The thirteenth mental measurements yearbook* (pp. 1121–1124). Lincoln, NE: Buros Institute of Mental Measurements.

Goleman, D. (1995). *Emotional intelligence.* New York: Bantam Books.

Gordon, R. A. (1986). Scientific justification and the race-IQ-delinquency model. In T. F. Hartnagel & R. A. Silverman (Eds.), *Critique and explanation: Essays in honor of Gwynne Nettler* (pp. 91–131). New Brunswick, NJ: Transaction Books.

Gottfredson, L. S. (1986). Societal consequences of the *g* factor in employment. *Journal of Vocational Behavior, 29,* 379–410.

Gottfredson, L. S. (1988). Reconsidering fairness: A matter of social and ethnical priorities. *Journal of Vocational Behavior, 33,* 293–319.

Gottfredson, L. S. (1997). Why *g* matters: The complexity of everyday life. *Intelligence, 24,* 79–132.

Guilford, J. P. (1956). The structure of intellect. *Psychological Bulletin, 53,* 267–293.

Guilford, J. P. (1959). Three faces of intellect. *American Psychologist, 14,* 469–479.

Gustafsson, J. E. (1980, April). *Testing hierarchical models of ability organization through covariance models.* Paper presented at the annual meeting of the American Educational Research Association, Boston.

Gustafsson, J. E. (1984). A unifying model for the structure of intellectual abilities. *Intelligence, 8,* 179–203.

Gustafsson, J. E. (1988). Hierarchical models of individual differences in cognitive abilities. In R. J. Sternberg (Ed.), *Advances in the psychology of human intelligence* (Vol. 4, pp. 35–71). Hillsdale, NJ: Lawrence Erlbaum Associates.

Hanna, G. S. (1998). Review of the Wonderlic Basic Skills Test. In J. C. Impara & B. S. Plake (Eds.), *The thirteenth mental measurements yearbook* (pp. 1136–1140). Lincoln, NE: Buros Institute of Mental Measurements.

Herrnstein, R. J., & Murray, C. (1994). *The bell curve.* New York: Free Press.

Holland, P. W., & Wainer, H. (Eds.). (1993). *Differential item functioning.* Hillsdale, NJ: Lawrence Erlbaum Associates.

Holzinger, K. J., & Harmon H. H. (1938). Comparison of two factorial analyses. *Psychometrika, 3,* 45–60.

Humphreys, L. G., & Taber, T. (1973). Ability factors as a function of advantaged and disadvantaged groups. *Journal of Educational Measurement, 10,* 107–115.

Hunter, J. E. (1980). *Validity generalization for 12,000 jobs: An application of synthetic validity and validity generalization to the General Aptitude Test Battery (GATB).* Washington, DC: U.S. Department of Labor, Employment Service.

Hunter, J. E., & Hunter, R. F. (1984). Validity and utility of alternative predictors of job performance. *Psychological Bulletin, 96,* 72–98.

Hunter, J. E., & Schmidt, F. L. (1979). Differential validity of employment tests by race: A comprehensive review and analysis. *Psychological Bulletin, 86,* 721–735.

Hunter, J. E., & Schmidt, F. L. (2004). *Methods of meta-analysis* (2nd ed.). Thousand Oaks, CA: Sage.

Jensen, A. R. (1980). *Bias in mental testing.* New York: Free Press.

Jensen, A. R. (1985). The nature of black-white differences on various psychometric tests: Spearman's hypothesis. *Behavioral and Brain Sciences, 8,* 193–264.

Jensen, A. R. (1993). Spearman's g: Links between psychometrics and biology. *Annals of the New York Academy of Sciences, 702,* 103–129.

Jensen, A. R. (1998). *The g factor: The science of mental ability.* Westport, CT: Praeger.

Keyser, D. J., & Sweetland, R. C. (Eds.). (1997). *Test critiques* (Vol. 11). Austin, TX: Pro-ED.

Mayer, J. D., Salovey, P., & Caruso, D. R. (2002). *Mayer Salovey Caruso Emotional Intelligence Test.* North Tonawanda, NY: MHS.

McArdle, J. J. (1996). Current directions in structural factor analysis. *Current Directions in Psychological Science, 5,* 11–18.

McClelland, D. C. (1993). Intelligence is not the best predictor of job performance. *Current Directions in Psychological Science, 2,* 5–6.

McCormick, E. J. (1976). Job and task analysis. In M. D. Dunnette (Ed.), *Handbook of industrial and organizational psychology* (pp. 651–696). Chicago: Rand McNally.

McCormick, E. J. (1979). *Job analysis: Methods and applications.* New York: AMACOM.

Michael, W. B. (1949). Factor analyses of tests and criteria: A comparative study of two AAF pilot populations. *Psychological Monographs, 63,* 55–84.

Millman, J., & Greene, J. (1989). The specification and development of tests of achievement and ability. In R. L. Linn (Ed.), *Educational measurement* (3rd ed., pp. 335–366). Washington, DC: American Council on Education.

Murphy, L. L., Plake, B. S., Impara, J. C., & Spies, R. A. (Eds.). (2002). *Tests in print IV: An index to tests, test reviews, and the literature on specific tests.* Lincoln: University of Nebraska Press.

Nunnally, J. C. (1978). *Psychometric theory* (2nd ed.). New York: McGraw-Hill.

Olea, M., & Ree, M. J. (1994). Predicting pilot and navigator criteria: Not much more than g. *Journal of Applied Psychology, 79,* 845–851.

Peior, J. M., & Munduate, L. (1994). Work and organizational psychology in Spain. *Applied Psychology, 43,* 231–274.

Rabbitt, P., Banerji, N., & Szymanski, A. (1989). Space fortress as an IQ test? Predictions of learning and of practiced performance in a complex interactive video-game. *Acta Psychologica, 71,* 243–257.

Ree, M. J., & Carretta, T. R. (1995). Group differences in aptitude factor structure on the ASVAB. *Educational and Psychological Measurement, 55,* 268–277.

Ree, M. J., & Carretta, T. R. (1996). Central role of g in military pilot selection. *International Journal of Aviation Psychology, 6,* 111–123.

Ree, M. J., & Carretta, T. R. (1998). General cognitive ability and occupational performance. In C. L. Cooper & I. T. Robertson (Eds.), *International review of industrial and organizational psychology* (pp. 159–184). Chichester, England: Wiley.

Ree, M. J., Carretta, T. R., & Doub, T. (1998–1999). A test of three models of the role of g and prior job knowledge in the acquisition of subsequent job knowledge. *Training Research Journal, 4,* 1–16.

Ree, M. J., Carretta, T. R., Earles, J. A., & Albert, W. (1994). Sign changes when correcting for range restriction: A note on Pearson's and Lawley's selection formulae. *Journal of Applied Psychology, 79,* 298–301.

Ree, M. J., Carretta, T. R., & Teachout, M. S. (1995). Role of ability, and prior job knowledge in complex training performance. *Journal of Applied Psychology, 80,* 721–730.

Ree, M. J., & Earles, J. A. (1991). Predicting training success: Not much more than g. *Personnel Psychology, 44,* 321–332.

Ree, M. J., & Earles, J. A. (1993). g is to psychology what carbon is to chemistry: A reply to Sternberg and Wagner, McClelland, and Calfee. *Current Directions in Psychological Science, 2,* 11–12.

Ree, M. J., Earles, J. A., & Teachout, M. S. (1994). Predicting job performance: Not much more than g. *Journal of Applied Psychology, 79,* 518–524.

Ree, M. J., & Wegner, T. G. (1990). Correcting differences in answer sheets for the 1980 Armed Services Vocational Aptitude Battery reference population. *Military Psychology, 2,* 157–169.

Roid, G. H., & Haladyna, T. M. (1982). *A technology for test-item writing.* Orlando, FL: Academic Press.

Roth, P. L., BeVier, C. A., Bobko, P., Switzer, F. S., & Tyler, P. (2001). Ethnic group differences in cognitive ability in employment and educational settings: A meta-analysis. *Personnel Psychology, 54,* 297–330.

Sackett, P. R., & Wilk, S. L. (1994). Within group norming and other forms of score adjustment in preemployment testing. *American Psychologist, 49,* 929–954.

Schmidt, F. L., & Hunter, J. E. (1982). Two pitfalls in assessing fairness of selection tests using the regression model. *Personnel Psychology, 35,* 601–607.

Schmidt, F. L., & Hunter, J. E. (1993). Tacit knowledge, practical intelligence, general mental ability, and job knowledge. *Current Directions in Psychological Science, 2,* 8–9.

Schmidt, F. L., & Hunter, J. E. (1998). The validity and utility of selection methods in personnel psychology: Practical and theoretical implications of 85 years of research findings. *Psychological Bulletin, 124,* 262–274.

Schmidt, F. L., & Hunter, J. E. (2004). General mental ability in the world of work: Occupational attainment and job performance. *Journal of Personality and Social Psychology, 86,* 162–173.

Schulte, M. J., Ree, M. J., & Carretta, T. R. (2004). Emotional intelligence: Not much more than g and personality. *Personality and Individual Differences, 37,* 1059–1068.

Society for Industrial and Organizational Psychology, Inc. (2003). *Principles for the validation and use of personnel selection procedures* (4th ed.). Bowling Green, OH: Society for Industrial and Organizational Psychology.

Spearman, C. (1927). *The abilities of man: Their nature and measurement.* New York: Macmillan.

Spearman, C. (1930). 'G" and after: A school to end schools. In C. Murchison (Ed.), *Psychologies of 1930* (pp. 339–366). Worcester, MA: Clark University Press.

Spearman, C. (1937). *Psychology down the ages* (Vol. 2). London: Macmillan.
Spearman, C. (1938). Thurstone's work reworked. *Journal of Educational Psychology, 39,* 1–16.
Spies, R. A., & Plake, B. S. (Eds.). (2005). *The sixteenth mental measurements yearbook.* Lincoln: University of Nebraska Press.
Sternberg, R. J. (1985). *Beyond IQ: A triarchic theory of human intelligence.* New York: Cambridge University Press.
Sternberg, R. J., & Wagner, R. K. (1993). The g-ocentric view of intelligence and job performance is wrong. *Current Directions in Psychological Science, 2,* 1–5.
Thompson, B. (2003). Understanding reliability and coefficient alpha, really. In B. Thompson (Ed.), *Score reliability* (pp. 3–30). Thousand Oaks, CA: Sage.
Thorndike, R. L. (1986). The role of general ability in prediction. *Journal of Vocational Behavior, 29,* 322–339.
Thurstone, L. L. (1938). *Primary mental abilities.* [Psychometric Monograph No. 1]. Chicago: University of Chicago Press.
Thurstone, L. L., & Thurstone, T. G. (1941). *Factorial studies of intelligence.* [Psychometric Monograph No. 2]. Chicago: University of Chicago Press.
Uniform guidelines on employee selection procedures. (1978). *Federal Register, 43,* 38290–38315.
Vernon, P. E. (1950). *The structure of human abilities.* New York: Wiley.
Vernon, P. E. (1969). *Intelligence and cultural environment.* London: Methuen.
Walters, L. C., Miller, M. R., & Ree, M. J. (1993). Structured interviews for pilot selection: No incremental validity. *International Journal of Aviation Psychology, 3,* 25–38.
Watson, G., & Glaser, E. M. (1980). *Watson-Glaser critical thinking appraisal manual.* San Antonio, TX: Harcourt Brace Jovanovich.
Wonderlic Personnel Test Manual and Scoring Guide. (1999). Chicago: Wonderlic, Inc.
Zhang, H. (1988). Psychological measurement in China. *International Journal of Psychology, 23,* 101–117.

C H A P T E R   S I X

Measures of Training and Experience

Timothy P. McGonigle and Christina K. Curnow
Caliber, an ICF International Company

OVERVIEW

In this chapter we describe the use of measures of training and experience to support personnel management decisions. We begin by briefly summarizing the history of using information about applicants' training and background to screen them in employment decisions. Though popular, these methods produce a number of psychometric concerns that must be addressed if training and experience measures are to be used reliably, validly, and with minimal adverse impact. In subsequent sections of the chapter, we discuss alternative data collection procedures and scoring approaches. The alternatives include task-based questionnaires, KSAO-based questionnaires, and accomplishment records. We next describe procedures for developing each type of measure, including steps to reduce self-report bias. We conclude the chapter by summarizing the major considerations in developing and using measures of applicant training and experience.

BACKGROUND

Measures of training and experience (T&E) are among the most commonly used personnel selection methods (Gatewood & Feild, 2001). The main objective of T&E evaluation is to screen applicant backgrounds according to specific job requirements. T&Es differ from biographic inventories in their use of weighting systems based on judgment rather than on empirically derived scoring keys (McDaniel, Schmidt & Hunter, 1988a), and their use of verifiable training, education, and experience indices. In addition, biographic inventories measure individuals' experiences with a wide range of life events whereas T&Es focus on experience with specific, job-related tasks.

T&Es typically require applicants to report their level of experience performing— or education pertaining to—particular job tasks and are presumed to be valid based on the theory of behavioral consistency (Ash, Johnson, Levine, & McDaniel, 1989; Guion, 1998; Owens, 1976; Schmidt & Hunter, 1998; Wernimont & Campbell, 1968). This theory posits that the best predictor of future performance is past performance in a similar setting. Researchers have studied the relationship between experience and performance in a variety of public-sector occupations, and in other less common occupations such as crisis counselors (Elkins & Cohen, 1982) and surgeons (Sutton, Wayman, & Griffin, 1998). However, many researchers and practitioners traditionally consider T&Es to be poor predictors of job performance. However, recent evidence suggests that it is possible to overcome the psychometric limitations of T&Es.

T&Es have been widely used in public-sector employment (McDaniel & Schmidt, 1985). As the size of the federal government's workforce grew rapidly during the early 1900s, efforts were made to hire civil servants based on merit rather than the patronage of a particular individual or political party. The purpose of merit-based selection was to ensure a stable workforce that operated regardless of politics. In addition, the increasing size of the federal government attracted large volumes of applicants, thereby necessitating a cost-effective method of screening applicants. T&Es were found not only to be cost effective and consistent with merit-based hiring, but they also required little staff training or oversight to implement. As a result, T&Es were used with increasing frequency and are still used to make many staffing decisions. With the advent of automated prescreening systems, T&Es remain as popular as ever.

Despite their administrative ease, relatively little consideration has been given to whether T&Es are valid predictors of job performance. In fact, early research suggested that T&Es were poor predictors of job performance (Hunter & Hunter, 1984). Schmidt et al. (1979) explained experience questionnaires' lack of validity by discussing some assumptions of the method. Specifically, because measures of experience are estimated to correlate .40 with knowledge, skill, and ability (KSA) requirements and KSAs are estimated to correlate .50 with job performance, the authors argued that the validity of experience questionnaires is limited to about .20 (i.e., .40 × .50). More recent research suggests that modifications in the measurement mode of T&Es can produce much larger validity coefficients (McDaniel, Schmidt, & Hunter, 1988a, 1988b; Quinones, Ford, & Teachout, 1995; Schmidt & Hunter, 1998; Tesluk & Jacobs, 1998). Such modifications are presumed to increase the correlation between the measure of experience and the KSAs.

Only recently have researchers (e.g., Quinones et al., 1995; Tesluk & Jacobs, 1998) begun to develop a theory of experience. Quinones et al. (1995) provided a theoretical model of work experience that categorizes experience in terms of both measurement method and specificity. The model specifies three measures of experience—amount, time, and type—and three levels of experience specificity— experiences with tasks, jobs, and organizations. After fully crossing both dimensions to create nine types of experience measures (e.g., amount of task experience, time

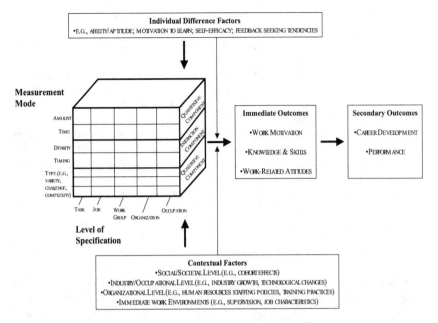

FIGURE 6.1   A model of work experience. Reprinted with permission.

spent in a specific job), the authors conducted a meta-analysis to identify the relationship between each type of experience measure and job performance. They
reported corrected correlations up to .43. More recently, Tesluk and Jacobs (1998)
expanded the Quinones et al. (1995) model by theorizing multidimensional medi-
ators, criteria, individual differences, and contextual factors that moderate the
experience-performance relationship, as well as two additional measurement
methods and two additional levels of experience specificity (see Fig. 6.1). These
models provide a theoretical foundation for experience measurement that has
been lacking for decades.

MEASURES OF TRAINING AND EXPERIENCE

Many forms of T&Es have been developed, including holistic judgments résumé
screens, point methods, task methods, and accomplishment records. Most T&E
measures have been administered to make both entry-level selection and promotion decisions. When used for entry-level positions, T&Es typically focus on determining if an applicant has the requisite KSAs to perform the job. On the other
hand, when used for the purpose of selecting employees for promotions or hiring job applicants into non-entry-level positions, T&Es help to determine whether
applicants have experience performing tasks that are similar to those performed
in the position or job class to which they are applying. T&Es have been administered as prescreens in a multiple hurdle selection system and as one instrument

in a compensatory test battery. The most common use of the T&E as a prescreening device is as a minimum qualification screen, where applicants must show that they have a certain amount of job-related experience, training, or education to proceed within the selection process.

With the exception of the accomplishment record, virtually all T&E methods can be organized according to two dimensions—data collection procedures and scoring procedures. Data collection procedures generally include application blanks and résumés, checklists, and constructed response forms. Scoring procedures generally include holistic judgment, point methods, and analyst ratings. The creation of specific T&E methods (e.g., improved point method) involves combining a data collection method (e.g., checklist) and a scoring procedure (e.g., scoring algorithm). In the next sections, we describe common data collection and scoring procedures and the accomplishment record.

Data Collection Procedures

Application Blanks and Résumés

Perhaps the most ubiquitous T&E data collection method is the application blank. Application blanks are used to collect specific information about an applicant's work history and educational background. Résumés can be substituted for an application blank and may describe the major duties associated with each position in the work history, specific coursework, special skills and credentials, and other qualifications. Typically, an analyst makes a holistic judgment about the applicability of the information provided on the application or résumé. Although these methods of data collection allow applicants to provide information on their background, they provide very little information about the quantity or quality of the applicants' qualifications.

Checklists

T&E checklists ask applicants to complete a rating form or checklist indicating their experience with a variety of work behaviors or tasks (Gatewood & Feild, 2001). On a typical task-based questionnaire (TBQ), applicants indicate whether they have performed the tasks, how often they have performed the tasks, or how much time they have spent performing the tasks (Lyons, 1984). On some forms, applicants may rate how effectively they have performed the tasks, how closely they were supervised in performing the tasks, whether they have received training directly related to the tasks, or whether they have trained others on the task (Anderson, Warner, & Spencer, 1984; Ash, 1981; Farrell, 1979; Malinowski, 1981; Ocasio, 1983). Checklist methods may also ask applicants to provide information about their work experience, educational background, or specific skills that might have prepared them to perform each task.

An alternate approach to the checklist method is the improved point method (McGonigle & Curnow, 2002; Swander & Shultz, n.d., cited in Ash et al., 1989) or KSA-based questionnaire (KSABQ). To develop a KSABQ, subject matter experts

(SMEs) identify activities that applicants could have performed that would indicate their proficiency with each job-relevant KSA. Applicants indicate their level of experience with each activity and receive 1 point for each activity they have undertaken. As a result, the improved point method is a less arbitrary approach to assigning point scores on experience questionnaires and is more likely to comply with the *Uniform Guidelines on Employee Selection Procedures* (1978), because it measures experience with behaviors that are indicative of each KSA.

Scoring Procedures

Holistic Judgment

Holistic judgment is the most common method used to evaluate applicant training and work experience. This particular method is not a formally scored T&E evaluation method but rather provides a general evaluation of an applicant's credentials. An example of the use of this method begins when a hiring authority receives a set of résumés from applicants for a particular position. The hiring authority assesses each application as a whole and makes a subjective decision about how to distinguish between qualified and unqualified applicants according to the hiring authority's individual standards. Then, the hiring authority selects several résumés and those individuals are contacted for further evaluation, typically through an in-person interview (e.g., see chap. 8). As might be expected, this method lacks both structure and objectivity. In addition, many judgments based exclusively on an applicant's résumé are confounded with information gained through interaction with the applicant. Consequently, this method can lead to very subjective selection decisions.

Point Methods

The point method is the most prevalent formal T&E evaluation technique. It consists of a mechanical formula in which applicants receive a prescribed number of points for each month or year of relevant training, education, and experience. In some cases, the number of points assigned varies by the type and duration of experience. Applicants are either rank ordered or are grouped based on specific education and experience requirements for the target job.

Although this method of T&E scoring is much more structured than the holistic judgment method, research shows it does little to improve the validity of the resulting scores (Ash et al., 1989; McDaniel et al., 1988b; Schmidt & Hunter, 1998) perhaps due to the dubious job-relatedness and specious precision of the scoring protocol. As discussed by Ash et al. (1989), the weak validity coefficients might also be due to the large amounts of measurement error introduced by a focus on the quantity of applicants' experiences rather than on their quality. Furthermore, because of its primary focus on the quantity of experience, the traditional point method can also result in adverse impact (Ash et al., 1989). There also is evidence to suggest that two individuals with equal amounts of job tenure can differ drastically in the number and types of tasks they have performed (Ford, Quinones, Sego, & Sorra, 1992; Schmitt & Cohen, 1989).

Accomplishment Records

The accomplishment record (AR) is a means of gathering self-reported and verifiable descriptions of experience on relevant behavioral job dimensions (Hough, 1984). Methodologically, the AR draws on the critical incident technique (Flanagan, 1954; Guion, 1998; also see chap. 3) and written sentence-completion protocols (Loevinger & Wessler, 1970). The goal of this method is to rank order applicants based on the types of achievement behaviors that are necessary for successful performance in the target job. The focus of an AR is on the quality of previous experience rather than on the quantity of experience. In a typical AR, applicants provide written descriptions of accomplishments that demonstrate their level of proficiency with job-related KSAs. Analysts then rate each accomplishment using a behaviorally anchored rating scale and the ratings are used to compute a total score.

PSYCHOMETRIC CHARACTERISTICS OF MEASURES OF TRAINING AND EXPERIENCE

In this section, we describe the reliability, validity, and subgroup differences in measures of training and experience. In addition, we discuss the issue of response distortion and describe methods for reducing this problem.

Reliability

The reliability of T&Es varies depending on the particular data collection and scoring procedures. Due to their unstructured nature, data collected through application blanks or résumés and subjected to holistic judgments are likely to have little to no reliability. Task-based methods have reliabilities in the .80s (Ash & Levine, 1985; Schmidt et al., 1979) and above (Sneed, Vivian, & D'Ocasta, 1987), primarily due to the straightforward nature of the scoring. Although only a few studies report on the reliability of the AR, there is evidence that it demonstrates reliabilities by dimension ranging from .75 to .85 (Hough, 1984; Hough, Keyes, & Dunnette, 1983). Sadowski and Hess (1994) reported a reliability of .84 when using an AR to evaluate teaching performance. Finally, past research showed interrater reliability estimates of T&E ratings to be around .80 (Gatewood & Feild, 2001).

Validity

Several meta-analyses reported validity coefficients for T&Es (McDaniel et al., 1988b; Quinones et al., 1995; Schmidt & Hunter, 1998). These meta-analyses show that behavioral consistency (i.e., AR) measures are the most valid ($r = .45$), followed by self-ratings of KSA proficiency ($r = .20$), self-ratings of task proficiency ($r = .15$), and the point method ($r = .11$). Quinones et al. (1995) report a correlation of .43 between amount of task experience (i.e., number of times performing a task) and job performance, although most traditional T&Es do not measure experience in this way.

There is a limited amount of evidence about the validity of ARs, although available research indicates that they are valid measures of performance with validity as high as .45. Hough (1984) and Hough et al. (1983) obtained significant correlations between ARs and supervisory ratings of performance for attorneys. Hough (1984) and Hough et al. (1983) also found AR scores to correlate significantly with pay grade, but not with other traditional predictors such as grades, or scores on tests of law aptitude, knowledge, and achievement. Therefore, the use of ARs could increase the validity of a selection system.

At least four factors contribute to the typically low validity coefficients associated with T&Es (McDaniel, Curnow, & McGonigle, 2003). First, there are relatively few studies of T&E validity, so the meta-analytic validity coefficients cited earlier are likely to be unstable. Second, most T&Es do not account for individual differences in what is gained from training and experience. At least three factors influence whether an individual gains skill from experience (McGonigle & Curnow, 2003):

- Individual differences such as cognitive ability (Kanfer & Ackerman, 1989), conscientiousness, openness to experience, and extraversion (Barrick & Mount, 1991).
- Situational characteristics such as opportunities to perform tasks (Alexander, 1997).
- Motivation to pursue available opportunities (Kanfer & Ackerman, 1989).

Third, due to the fact that all applicants who complete and return a T&E are likely to have some relevant experience, T&Es suffer from range restriction. Finally, in many cases the relationship between experience and performance is nonlinear. Ackerman (1988) demonstrated that task consistency and complexity moderate the validity of the experience-skill acquisition relationship, with early career experience typically yielding the greatest improvements in job knowledge. To the extent that these factors can be controlled through data collection and scoring procedures, the validity of T&Es can be expected to improve.

Subgroup Differences

There is no evidence of subgroup differences on T&Es. In fact, one author suggested that an explanation for the popularity of T&Es is their perceived lack of subgroup differences (Aramburu-Zbala-Higuera, 2001). However, education and experience may reflect subgroup differences. Specifically, T&Es may reflect the adverse impact of different rates of graduation between African Americans and Whites. Greene and Winters (2005) noted that in 2002, about 78% of White students graduated from high school with a regular diploma, compared to 56% of African American students and 52% of Hispanic students. The *Journal of Blacks in Higher Education* (2002) noted that the nationwide rate of college graduation for African American students is 42% whereas the graduation rate for White students is 62%. Consequently, T&Es will likely reflect these different rates in their measures of education. In terms of experience, the extent to which a group is under- or overrepresented in the workforce also will foster adverse impact. For example, according to the Office of Personnel Management's *Federal Civilian Workforce Statistics Fact Book* (2004), in 2003, 79.5% of clerical employees were women. Thus, for experience in clerical jobs, women will likely obtain higher T&E scores than men when applying for such jobs.

In addition, T&Es may reflect the subgroup differences of other selection procedures when an applicant's acquisition of experience is considered. When using TBQs to select employees, the probability of being selected will necessarily increase with previous experience. If the opportunity to perform tasks (i.e., gain experience) is earned as a result of being selected using methods that were not free of subgroup differences in prediction, as described earlier, T&Es could perpetuate these differences (Roth, Bobko, Switzer, & Dean, 2001). The same effect would be seen if managers used inherently biased procedures to assign individuals to tasks.

Response Distortion

A concern about T&Es is that they rely on the integrity of the applicant. Applicants applying for jobs may be tempted to overestimate the amount of education or experience they have had to obtain a higher score and increase their chances of getting a job. There are methods that can help reduce fallacious reporting of education and experience. For example, warnings to applicants suggesting that responses will be verified tend to reduce falsification of information (Lautenschlager, 1994). Other procedures can be used to identify inaccurate responses and minimize their occurrence. For example, Pine (1995) reported that relative frequency scales produced more incidents of false reporting on task inventory statements than absolute scales. The inclusion of bogus tasks as part of a lie scale can be used to identify applicants with a propensity to provide inaccurate information. For example, Green and Stutzman (1986) reported that 57% of the respondents in a sample indicated that they spent time performing bogus tasks and 72% indicated that these bogus tasks were at least somewhat important aspects of their job. Green and Veres (1990) used a similar method in three different samples using a variety of response scales and found the percentage of respondents endorsing bogus items ranged from 12.6% to 70.3%. A potential concern with using bogus tasks is the similarity of such tasks to real tasks. People may claim to perform tasks using nonexistent pieces of equipment, not because they are lying, but because they do not know the technical name of the equipment and believe that the bogus piece of equipment sounds similar to the real one.

By taking appropriate steps during the development of T&E measures, these difficulties can be overcome. It is possible to develop measures that possess adequate reliability and validity, and that minimize adverse impact.

HOW TO DEVELOP MEASURES OF TRAINING AND EXPERIENCE

In the previous sections, we discussed the many forms of T&Es and their associated psychometric characteristics. In this section, we discuss the two major steps for developing T&Es: select the type of T&E and develop T&E forms and scoring system.

Select the Type of T&E

After conducting a thorough job analysis and determining which KSAs will be measured using a T&E (e.g., see chaps. 2, 3, and 4), it is necessary to determine which type of T&E measure to use: task based, KSA based, AR, or some combination of these possibilities. Questions that can help guide this decision are shown in Figure 6.2.

In answering these questions, consider the typical applicants' experience: Is it an entry-level job? Are applicants likely to have experience performing the tasks on the job? Are applicants likely to have varied experiences? For example, applicants for a first-line supervisory position may have performed some of the technical tasks in a previous job, but may not have experience with the supervisory tasks. For entry-level jobs and jobs in which previous experience is unlikely, a KSA-based T&E is most appropriate. For promotions and for jobs in which applicants are expected to have previous experience with the specific job tasks, a task-based T&E or an AR is appropriate. If applicants are expected to vary in their experiences (e.g., if there are numerous feeder jobs), it may be difficult to develop items that are applicable across the applicant pool.

Also consider some of the characteristics of the job: Does the job require writing? How many skilled incumbents are there? If the job does not require writing, it is advisable to avoid the AR due to its reliance on constructed (i.e., written) responses. If there are not a large number of job incumbents (i.e., at least 30) available to serve as SMEs and help with test development, then it is advisable to use a task or KSA checklist rather than an AR.

Develop T&E Forms and Scoring System

Task-Based Questionnaire

Developing TBQs involves four steps:

- Determine whether each task is needed at entry.
- Create a response form.
- Create a scoring algorithm.
- Develop a methodology to encourage truthful responses.

SMEs play a role in each of these activities. We describe each step next.

Determine Whether Each Task Is Needed at Entry.   To ensure that a TBQ only includes those tasks that applicants need to be able to perform upon entry into

Question	TBQ	KSABQ	AR
"Is it an entry-level job?"	No	Yes	No
Are applicants likely to have experience? performing the tasks required on the job?	Yes	No	Yes
Are applicants likely to have varied achievements?	No	No	Yes
Does the job require writing?	No	No	Yes
Is there a sufficient incumbent pool to assist with test development?	No	No	Yes

FIGURE 6.2   Selecting a type of T&E instrument. TBQ = task-based question-naire; KSABQ = knowledge-, skills-, and abilities-based questionnaire; AR = accomplishment record.

the job, it is important to collect job analysis data on whether the ability to perform the task is needed on the first day of the job. The majority of SMEs should rate a task as needed at entry to the job for it to be included in the TBQ. In addition, the T&E developer should remove or revise any tasks that require knowledge that can only be gained on the job in question (e.g., knowledge of a specific form or procedure). Next, to ensure that experience on each task in the TBQ demonstrates one or more qualifying KSAs, it is important to have SMEs indicate which qualifying KSAs are needed to perform each of the selected tasks. Only tasks that are linked to at least one KSA by the majority of SMEs should be included in the TBQ.

Create a Response Form.   Two examples of response forms that could be used for a variety of electrician tasks are shown in Fig. 6.3. Both forms require applicants to estimate the number of times they have performed each task rather than simply the duration of experience (Quinones et al., 1995). On the first form, applicants indicate the duration of their experience with each task in years and months as well as the frequency of their experience (i.e., daily, weekly, monthly, quarterly, yearly) during that time period. An analyst can use that information to calculate the number of times each applicant has performed each task. For example, if applicants indicate that they performed a task quarterly for 3 years and 6 months, the applicants would have performed the task 14 times. The advantage of this form is that it provides applicants with a structure within which to estimate their experience. It collects memorable elements of their experience that can be systematically combined by an analyst.

One disadvantage of the first form in Fig. 6.3 is that it does not account for variation in experience over time. For example, it would be difficult for applicants who performed a task monthly for 2 years and then weekly for 1 year to accurately represent their level of experience. The second form is designed to accommodate varying frequency of experience. On this form, applicants select the option that is closest to the number of times they have performed each task and provide the name of someone who can verify their experience. To help applicants make more accurate judgments of their experience, the form also provides examples of how long it would take to amass each amount of experience assuming that applicants performed the task daily, weekly, or monthly.

Create a Scoring Algorithm. The scoring algorithm is designed to take into account applicants' experience on each task. As workers perform a task, they generally become more effective at it, although improvement in performance associated with more experience is likely to diminish at greater levels of experience (McDaniel et al., 1988a; Schmidt, Hunter, & Outerbridge, 1986). To ensure that scores on the TBQ reflect this relationship between experience and performance, the scoring algorithm should award points for increasing amounts of experience performing each task. However, when experience with each activity reaches the point at which additional experience is not expected to improve performance (i.e., the performance asymptote), the algorithm should award no additional points.

Identification of the performance asymptote is a judgment-based process similar to setting a cutoff score. For each task, SMEs are asked to judge the number of times that an individual would need to perform the task to reach the performance asymptote. The SMEs should be instructed to judge the performance asymptotes individually and then come to consensus about the appropriate performance asymptote for each activity. Alternatively, SMEs could be asked to estimate the probability that an applicant with specific amounts of experience performing each task would perform well on the job.

In the two examples shown in Fig. 6.3, the resulting frequency of task performance scores can range from 0 to 5. A score of 0 is assigned when applicants indicate that they have no experience with a task. A score of 5 is assigned when applicants have performed a task at least the number of times indicated by the performance asymptote. Scores from 1 through 4 are assigned for linear increases in experience. In Fig. 6.3, the asymptote for the task "interpreting residential electrical plans" is 50. This means that after interpreting residential electrical plans 50 times, one is not likely to become more proficient at this task.

Develop a Methodology for Encouraging Truthful Responses. There are three techniques that can be used in concert to reduce false or exaggerated responses. First, the form can require applicants to sign a statement certifying the accuracy of their responses and describing the consequences of inaccurate responses. Second, the form can require applicants to identify one or more individuals who can attest that the applicants performed the task. Finally, the form can include a series of bogus tasks (i.e., tasks that would be impossible for applicants

Skill in performing residential electrical work				
Please rate your experience with each of the activities below:	How much work experience do you have performing this activity?			Who can verify your work experience with this activity?
	Duration		Frequency*	
	Years	Months		
1. Installing a ceiling mount fixture.			⓪①②③④⑤	①②③④⑤ ⑥⑦⑧⑨⑩
2. Installing a three-way switch.			⓪①②③④⑤	①②③④⑤ ⑥⑦⑧⑨⑩
3. Interpreting residential electrcal plans.			⓪①②③④⑤	①②③④⑤ ⑥⑦⑧⑨⑩

*0 = No experience; 1 = Yearly; 2 = Quarterly; 3 = Monthly; 4 = Weekly; 5 = Daily

Skill in performing residential electrical work					
Activity	Frequency	Examples			Verifier(s)
	Which option is closest to the number of times you have performed this activity?	To perform this activity the number of times listed in the option to the left, you'd have to perform the task...			Who can verify your work experience with this activity?
		every day for about...	or every week for about...	or every month for about...	
Interpreting residential electrical plan.	a. 0 times	- -	- -	- -	① ⑥ ② ⑦ ③ ⑧ ④ ⑨ ⑤ ⑩
	b. 10 times	2 weeks	2 months	1 year	
	c. 20 times	4 weeks	5 months	1½ years	
	d. 30 times	6 weeks	7 months	2½ years	
	e. 40 times	8 weeks	9 months	3½ years	
	f. 50 times or more	10 weeks	1 year	4 years	

FIGURE 6.3   Examples of T&E rating scales; on a different part of this instrument, respondents indicated people who can verify their experience with the activities listed and those individuals were labeled "1" through "10"; thus, response options 1 through 10 refer to individuals who can verify experience.

to have experience performing). Applicants should be informed that these bogus tasks are randomly placed throughout the form to help alert scorers when applicants falsify or exaggerate their level of experience. Taken together, these features discourage false or exaggerated responses and provide ways to detect such instances when they occur. To develop bogus tasks, one can create statements that sound plausible but are not performed on any job. One method for developing these tasks is to create a statement using words that might be relevant to the job in question when taken alone, but not when put together. It is important to have SMEs review the bogus tasks to make sure they could not be performed and are not obviously bogus. For example, the real tasks "install batteries in parallel to provide backup power source" and "splice high-voltage cable to establish service to a residential building" could be used to produce the following bogus task: "Splice high-voltage cable to provide backup power source." It is unlikely that any qualified applicant would indicate experience performing the bogus task. As mentioned previously, candidates may endorse a bogus task because they perceive it to be a legitimate task, not necessarily to falsify their application. Including several bogus tasks, some of which do not sound similar to real tasks, may serve to reduce this error.

KSA-Based Questionnaire

Developing KSABQs is similar to developing TBQs. The largest difference involves developing the item content. The process of determining whether each task is needed at entry to the job, creating a response form, creating a scoring algorithm, and developing a methodology to encourage truthful responses is identical to that for a TBQ.

KSABQs are designed to measure applicants' experience with job-relevant KSAs without assuming that applicants have direct job-related task experience. Therefore, it is important that applicants can describe their experiences with behaviorally oriented, observable activities measuring job-related KSAs. Activities are behaviors that represent qualitatively different levels of proficiency with each skill or ability. In addition, the activities are designed to measure experience related to each skill or ability even if the applicant has no direct experience performing the job tasks. For example, although applicants may not have experience with a specific task (e.g., "measure length of wire needed to pull through conduit and attach to the tugging machine"), they may have experience performing other activities that require the same underlying skills or abilities (e.g., "measure the length of wire needed to install receptacle").

To generate activities, SMEs should identify the types of non-job activities they themselves might have performed to develop proficiency with each KSA. For example, if people are applying for the job of an entry-level electrician, it is possible that they have wired or rewired household appliances. The resulting activities should be retained only if the SMEs agree that they are related to the KSA in question and applicants could be expected to have performed them. Much like developing any high-quality test items, the process of activity generation is likely to involve iterative review and revision of item content.

Accomplishment Record

The process for developing an AR consists of four basic steps:

- Conduct job analysis.
- Develop the inventory.
- Administer the inventory.
- Develop rating scales and rating principles.

Step 1 involves conducting an accurate job analysis, which is a crucial step in developing a reliable and valid AR. To support an effective AR, the job analysis data should specify job dimensions or competencies. Once the job analysis is complete, the AR inventory can be developed (Step 2). An AR inventory provides targeted performance dimension definitions and typically requests specific information for each competency or job dimension listed, including: a general statement of the accomplishment, a precise description of exactly what was done, a time period, a description of any formal recognition that resulted from the accomplishment, and contact information of one person who can verify the accomplishment. Applicants are instructed to write about their most meritorious accomplishment for each work performance dimension. An example of a completed accomplishment statement is shown in Fig. 6.4.

Once the AR has been developed, Step 3 involves administering it to current job incumbents to collect examples of accomplishments and to test the usability of the AR instructions. Incumbents are instructed to complete the AR based on their experiences prior to their current jobs. However, collecting accomplishments from job incumbents may result in a set of accomplishments that are all highly rated. Alternatively, non-incumbents with similar experience to potential applicants could complete the AR inventory. However, non-incumbents participating in the development process would be precluded from subsequently applying for that particular job.

Step 4 is to develop the AR rating scales and rating benchmarks. This involves a four-part process of evaluating dimensionality of the accomplishments, gathering expert ratings, inducing the principles underlying the rating process, and selecting benchmarks. The discussion of the critical incident technique in chapter 3 explains key parts of the process in more detail.

Part 1. The first step in developing the AR scoring key is to evaluate the accomplishments to ensure that they comprise clearly differentiable dimensions. To do this, raters classify accomplishments generated in Step 3 (with no identifying competency information) into competency categories. The accomplishments are presented to raters without information about the dimensions for which

---

WRITTEN COMMUNICATION

Definition: Communicates technical and nontechnical information in writing, using correct English grammar and sentence structure that can be understood by the intended audience.

Time Period: 2006–2007

General Statement of what you accomplished:

In conjunction with another I/O psychologist in my office, I co-authored a training manual on how to conduct job analysis.

Description of exactly what you did:

There is a wide range of methods for how to conduct job analysis. Within my organization we decided that it would be best to use one consistent method. So, a co-worker and I wrote a training manual on how to conduct job analysis. I wrote two sections of the manual: conducting job observations and collecting job analysis ratings. This manual is still being distributed to all of our new staff on an almost daily basis. We have requested several printings—we are currently on about our fourth printing of the manual. I have received a great deal of positive feedback about the helpfulness of the manual to workers. Many supervisors have commented on how quickly they are able to get new hires up to speed on our job analysis process now that they have the training manual.

Award or Recognition:

None

The information can be verified by:

Joan Q. Supervisor, (123) 456–7890

FIGURE 6.4   Example of an accomplishment record response for written communication.

they were originally written. Accomplishments that were written for one dimension and classified by raters into another dimension are considered misclassifications. Any misclassifications can be assessed and the job dimensions can be reviewed to determine if they should be combined or eliminated. Raters can be experts in job analysis and test development or SMEs.
Part 2. The next step is to gather expert ratings on the effectiveness of accomplishments for each competency. SMEs rate the accomplishments within each dimension on a 5- or 6-point scale. Parts 1 and 2 can be combined and both

classification and ratings can be done at the same time. For parts 1 and 2, a minimum of three raters has been suggested (Hough, 1984). In operational scoring, responses to AR questions can be very diverse and can tax the ability of scorers to achieve rater agreement. By using multiple independent raters and averaging their ratings for each candidate, the developer can increase the reliability of the ratings.

Part 3.Next, the accomplishments are ordered from high to low within each dimension based on mean SME ratings. A research team should analyze the content of the accomplishments in the high range to identify the themes or principles that SMEs used to judge the incidents. Repeat the content analysis at the middle and low levels of the scale and for each performance dimension. These themes specify the elements that raters will look for when rating achievement level.

Part 4.Means and standard deviations of expert ratings are then calculated. Accomplishments with standard deviations lower than 1.0 can be chosen as benchmarks at various points on the scale (Hough, 1984). An example of the benchmarks appears in Fig. 6.5.

SUMMARY

Despite their dubious ability to predict performance, measures of training and experience have been among the most commonly used selection tools for decades due to their conceptual appeal, low cost, and ease of administration. However, more recent theoretical work has provided a foundation for improving the measurement of training and experience. By using theory-based measurement techniques, the accuracy and quality of the resulting data are likely to be improved, as is the validity of the resulting decisions. Specifically, T&Es that collect amounts of experience (i.e., number of times having performed a task) or quality of experience (i.e., ARs) show fairly strong levels of validity, whereas holistic judgment-based procedures such as resume screens and application blanks show almost no validity. There is little evidence of subgroup differences on T&Es; however, T&Es could perpetuate differences in opportunity to perform tasks (i.e., gain experience) as well as differences in educational degrees received.

There are two steps to developing T&Es: (a) selecting the type of T&E and (b) developing T&E forms and the scoring system. In selecting a type of T&E, it is important to consider the typical applicant's level and type of experience as well as characteristics of the job in question. TBQs are most appropriate when applicants are expected to have some opportunity to gain experience with the job tasks; otherwise KSABQs are more appropriate. ARs are most appropriate for professional jobs that require significant writing ability (e.g., attorney). Developing TBQs involves identifying the most appropriate tasks from the job analysis, whereas developing KSABQs involves developing activity statements exemplifying the types of experiences applicants might be expected to have. Developing ARs involves identifying the critical performance dimensions for which applicants must describe their accomplishments. Scoring TBQs and KSABQs should take into account the fact that the improvement in performance associated with more

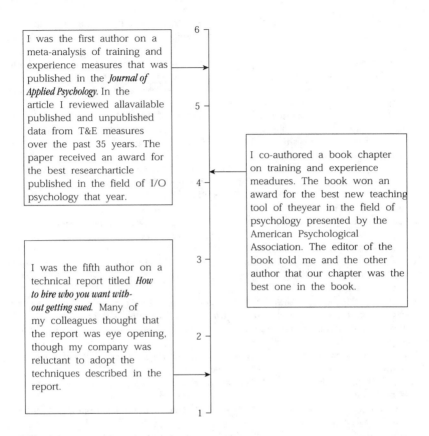

FIGURE 6.5   Accomplishment record rating scale for written communication.

experience is likely to diminish at greater levels of experience. Scoring ARs involves developing behaviorally anchored rating scales for each performance dimension.

REFERENCES

Ackerman, P. L. (1988). Determinants of individual differences during skill acquisition: Cognitive abilities and information processing. *Journal of Experimental Psychology: General, 117,* 288–313.

Alexander, P. A. (1997). Mapping the multidimensional nature of domain learning: The interplay of cognitive, motivational, and strategic sources. *Advances in Motivation and Achievement, 10,* 213–250.

Anderson, C. D., Warner, J. L., & Spencer, C. C. (1984). Inflation bias in self-assessment examinations: Implications for valid employee selection. *Journal of Applied Psychology, 69,* 574–580.

Aramburu-Zbala-Higuera, L. (2001). Adverse impact in personnel selection: The legal framework and test bias. *European Psychologist, 6*(2), 103–111.

Ash, R. A. (1981). Comparison of four approaches to the evaluation of job applicant training and work experience. *Dissertation Abstracts International, 42,* 4606B.

Ash, R. A., Johnson, J. C., Levine, E. L., & McDaniel, M. A. (1989). Job applicant training and work experience evaluation in personnel selection. In K. M. Rowland & G. R. Ferris (Eds.), *Research in personnel and human resources management* (Vol. 7, pp. 183–226). Greenwich, CT: JAI Press.

Ash, R. A., & Levine, E. (1985). Job applicant training and work experience evaluation: An empirical comparison of four methods. *Journal of Applied Psychology, 70,* 572–576.

Barrick, M. R., & Mount, M. K. (1991). The Big Five personality dimensions and job performance: A meta-analysis. *Personnel Psychology, 44,* 1–26.

Black student college graduation rates remain low, but modest progress begins to show. (2002). *Journal of Blacks in Higher Education, 50.* Retrieved April 14, 2006, from http://www.jhbe.com

Elkins, R. L., & Cohen, C. R. (1982). A comparison of the effects of prejob training and job experience on nonprofessional telephone crisis counselors. *Suicide and Life-Threatening Behaviors, 12*(2), 84–89.

Farrell, B. (1979). *Task performance self-evaluation: An alternative selection procedure to traditional experience and training ratings.* Minneapolis: Selection Research Unit, Minnesota Department of Personnel.

Flanagan, J. C. (1954). The critical incident technique. *Psychological Bulletin, 51,* 327–358.

Ford, J. K., Quinones, M., Sego, D., & Sorra, J. (1992). Factors affecting the opportunity to perform trained tasks on the job. *Personnel Psychology, 45,* 511–527.

Gatewood, R., & Feild, H. (2001). *Human resource selection* (3rd ed.). Fort Worth, TX: Harcourt Brace.

Green, S. B., & Stutzman, T. (1986). An evaluation of methods to select respondents to structured job analysis questionnaires. *Personnel Psychology, 39,* 543–564.

Green, S. B., & Veres, J. (1990). Evaluation of an index to detect inaccurate respondents to a task analysis inventory. *Journal of Business and Psychology, 5,* 47–61.

Greene, J. P., & Winters, M. A. (2005). *Public high school graduation and college-readiness rates: 1991–2002* (Education Working Paper No. 8). New York: Center for Civic Innovation at the Manhattan Institute.

Guion, R. M. (1998). *Assessment, measurement, and prediction for personnel decisions.* Mahwah, NJ: Lawrence Erlbaum Associates.

Hough, L. M. (1984). Development and evaluation of the "accomplishment record" method of selecting and promoting professionals. *Journal of Applied Psychology, 69,* 135–146.

Hough, L. M., Keyes, M. A., & Dunnette, M. D. (1983). An evaluation of three "alternative" selection procedures. *Personnel Psychology, 36,* 261–275.

Hunter, J. E., & Hunter, R. F. (1984). Validity and utility of alternate predictors of job performance. *Psychological Bulletin, 96,* 72–98.

Kanfer, R., & Ackerman, P. L. (1989). Motivation and cognitive abilities: An integrative/attribute-treatment interaction approach to skill acquisition. *Journal of Applied Psychology, 74,* 657–690.

Lautenschlager, G. J. (1994). Accuracy and faking of background data. In G. S. Stokes, M. D. Mumford, & W. A. Owens (Eds.), *Biodata handbook: Theory, research, and use of biographical information in selection and performance prediction* (pp. 391–419). Palo Alto, CA: CPP Books.

Loevinger, J. S., & Wessler, R. (1970). *Measuring ego development I: Construction and use of a sentence completion test*. San Francisco: Jossey-Bass.

Lyons, T. J. (1984). *Development and validation of the unassembled clerical exams for clerk typist (GS-4) and clerk stenographer (GS-5): A status report*. Washington, DC: U.S. Office of Personnel Management.

Malinowski, F. (1981). Job selection using task analysis. *Personnel Journal, 60,* 288–291.

McDaniel, M. A., Curnow, C. K., & McGonigle, T. P. (2003, March). *Experience measures: Current theory and practice*. Paper presented at the Personnel Testing Council of Metropolitan Washington, Washington, DC.

McDaniel, M. A., & Schmidt, F. L. (1985). *A meta-analysis of the validity of training and experience ratings in personnel selection* (OSP-85-1). Washington, DC: U.S. Office of Personnel Management.

McDaniel, M. A., Schmidt, F. L., & Hunter, J. E. (1988a). Job experience correlates of job performance. *Journal of Applied Psychology, 73,* 327–330.

McDaniel, M. A., Schmidt, F. L., & Hunter, J. E. (1988b). A meta-analysis of the validity of methods for rating training and experience in personnel selection. *Personnel Psychology, 41,* 283–314.

McGonigle, T. P., & Curnow, C. K. (2002). Development of a modified improved point method experience questionnaire. *Applied H.R.M. Research, 7,* 15–20.

McGonigle, T. P., & Curnow, C. K. (2003, May). *Current theory and practice on the measurement of experience*. Paper presented at the Mid-Atlantic Personnel Assessment Consortium, Rehoboth Beach, DE.

Ocasio, B. P. (1983). *Validation of the custodial unassembled examination procedure*. Washington, DC: U.S. Postal Service.

Office of Personnel Management. (2004). *Federal civilian workforce statistics fact book*. Retrieved April 14, 2006, from www.opm.gov/feddata/factbook

Owens, W. A. (1976). Background data. In M. D. Dunnette (Ed.), *Handbook of industrial and organizational psychology* (pp. 609–643). Palo Alto, CA: Consulting Psychologists Press.

Pine, D. (1995). Assessing the validity of job ratings: An empirical study of false reporting in task inventories. *Public Personnel Management, 24,* 451.

Quinones, M. A., Ford, K. J., Teachout, M. S. (1995). The relationship between work experience and job performance: A conceptual and meta-analytical review. *Personnel Psychology, 48,* 887–905.

Roth, P. L., Bobko, P., Switzer, F. S., & Dean, M. A. (2001). Prior selection causes biased estimates of standardized ethnic group differences: Simulation and analysis. *Personnel Psychology, 54,* 591–616.

Sadowski, C. J., & Hess, A. K. (1994). A modified accomplishment record approach to evaluating teaching effectiveness under the talent development model. *Journal of Personnel Evaluation in Education, 8,* 41–46.

Schmidt, F. L., Caplan, J. R., Bemis, S. E., Decuir, D., Dunn, L., & Antone, L. (1979). *The behavioral consistency method of unassembled examining* (TM-79-01). Washington, DC: U.S. Office of Personnel Management.

Schmidt, F. L., & Hunter, J. E. (1998). The validity and utility of selection methods in personnel psychology: Practical and theoretical implications of 85 years of research findings. *Psychological Bulletin, 124,* 262–274.

Schmidt, F. L., Hunter, J. E., & Outerbridge, A. N. (1986). The impact of job experience and ability on job knowledge, work sample performance, and supervisory ratings of job performance. *Journal of Applied Psychology, 71,* 432–439.

Schmitt, N., & Cohen, S. (1989). Internal analyses of task ratings by job incumbents. *Journal of Applied Psychology, 74,* 96–104.

Sneed, J., Vivian, V., & D'Ocasta, A. (1987). Work experience as a predictor of performance: A validation study. *Evaluation and the Health Professions, 10,* 42–57.

Sutton, D. N., Wayman, J., & Griffin, S. M. (1998). Learning curve for oesophageal cancer surgery. *British Journal of Surgery, 85,* 1399–1402.

Tesluk, P. E., & Jacobs, R. R. (1998). Toward an integrated model of work experience. *Personnel Psychology, 51,* 321–355.

Uniform guidelines on employee selection procedures. (1978). *Federal Register, 43,* 38290–38315.

Wernimont, P. F., & Campbell, J. P. (1968). Signs, samples, and criteria. *Journal of Applied Psychology, 52,* 372–376.

C H A P T E R   S E V E N

Employment Interviews

Allen I. Huffcutt
Bradley University

Satoris S. Youngcourt
Texas A & M University

OVERVIEW

In this chapter, we review the employment interview, the single most widely used selection method (other than perhaps application blanks). We begin with a discussion of what constitutes an interview, with a particular focus on the medium. Then we discuss the issue of what constitutes structure, and the general relationship between level of structure and validity. Following that, we talk about the two most popular structured formats, the situational interview and the behavior description interview, and how their validity compares to that of the typical unstructured interview. Then we address the important issue of incremental validity, specifically whether structured interviews can be combined with other tests to increase overall validity. Following the discussion of incremental validity, we look at moderators of structured interview validity and subgroup differences. Finally, we present step-by-step information on how to create a structured interview.

BACKGROUND

Few selection techniques have as long or as colorful a history as the employment interview. Throughout its history, it has been heralded, criticized, challenged, studied, and remade. Through all that, the interview has remained the single most utilized selection approach (other than perhaps application blanks). The purpose of this chapter is to review this intriguing and multifaceted technique. We begin with a discussion of what constitutes an employment interview.

In days past, the definition of an employment interview was clear and widely acknowledged. It was a face-to-face interaction conducted to determine the qualifications of a given individual for a particular open position. The main purpose of the employment interview has not changed. It remains a means to assess the qualifications of a given individual for an open position.

What has changed is the medium. Today, we no longer limit interviews to a face-to-face, verbal interaction. Because applicants come from more diverse locations than in the past (even from different countries or continents), the costs associated with transporting, housing, and feeding candidates has led some employers to turn to alternate media. Perhaps the most popular alternative is the telephone interview. In this case, an appointment is made, and then at the appointed time, the interviewer calls and conducts the interview over the phone.

Research comparing telephone interviews to face-to-face interviews has revealed somewhat mixed findings. Silvester, Anderson, Haddleton, Cunningham-Snell, and Gibb (2000), for example, found that applicants tended to be rated lower in telephone interviews. In contrast, Straus, Miles, and Levesque (2001) found that applicants fared more favorably in telephone interviews, especially applicants who were less attractive physically. Blackman (2002) found that interviewers tended to rate interviewees higher on traits conveyed via nonverbal means, such as being cheerful, warm, and socially at ease, and that interviewers were more accurate in their judgments about applicant personality when a face-to-face format was used. In terms of applicant reactions, Chapman, Uggerslev, and Webster (2003) found that face-to-face interviews were perceived as more fair than telephone interviews, and led to higher acceptance intentions, whereas Straus et al. (2001) found no difference.

A more recent alternative, one that is a product of our modern technology, is videoconferencing. Based on emerging technologies, such as Internet 2, it is now possible to conduct a "virtual" interview in which the interviewer and the interviewee see and respond to each other in real time without the distortions and glitches that have plagued previous forms of this technology. Given the expense of the equipment required, this medium for conducting interviews is in its infancy. However, one can easily foresee its increased use in coming decades.

Although research has suggested that individuals perceive candidates in videoconference interviews as being at a disadvantage relative to candidates in face-to-face interviews (Chapman & Webster, 2001), researchers have found that interviewers do not actually evaluate applicants less favorably by videoconference (Straus et al., 2001). Instead, evidence suggests a possible bias in favor of videoconference applicants (Chapman & Rowe, 2001). Nevertheless, videoconference interviews are typically seen as being less fair than face-to-face interviews (Chapman et al., 2003; Straus et al., 2001).

Occasionally, researchers have attempted to conduct interviews entirely in written form (e.g., Little, Shoenfelt, & Brown, 2000). The main question here is whether such a format really constitutes an interview. Our view is that if the written questions and responses are used subsequently as the basis for a personal interaction between the interviewer and the interviewee, one in which the interviewer reviews and inquires about the interviewee's responses, then written questions could be considered the first part of an interview. However, without the follow-up interaction, written questions remain closer to a paper-and-pencil questionnaire than to an interview.

Just to be thorough, we should mention that one could conceive of a live, Internet-based interview (similar to a "chat room") where the interviewer writes a series of questions online and the interviewee writes a response to each question as it is presented. Although written, this medium retains the interactive nature that frequently is associated with interviews.

We close this section by reformulating the definition of an employment interview. Clearly, the requirement of being physically face to face is no longer applicable. However, the boundary condition of being personally interactive still applies. Thus, one could define an employment interview as "an interactive discussion between an interviewer and a potential job candidate conducted for the purpose of determining that candidate's suitability for a given employment position." Now let us turn our attention to the types of interviews that can be conducted.

TYPES OF STRUCTURED INTERVIEWS

As an introduction to the various types of structured interviews, we first define various levels of structure. Then, we describe basic interview formats, specifically situational interviews and behavior description interviews.

Definition of Structure

At the outset, it is important to address the question of what constitutes a structured interview, or at least what the term *structure* means. Perhaps the most conceptual definition available comes from Huffcutt (1992), who defined structure in terms of a reduction in procedural variability. In unstructured interviews, interviewers are not overly constrained by what questions they can ask, and not surprisingly, there tends to be considerable variation across interviewers in the type and content of their questions. Moreover, the process of rating responses does not tend to be very detailed and specific in unstructured interviews (e.g., a general set of graphic rating scales or even a simple hire or not-hire decision), resulting in the potential for considerable diversity across interviewers in the manner in which they rate responses (e.g., what information is attended to and how it is combined and weighted). The same response to a given question, for instance, could be rated high by one interviewer and low by another.

Accordingly, structure can be defined as any process or procedure that reduces interviewer-to-interviewer variation in the type and content of the questions asked or in the criteria used to evaluate responses to those questions. Under this definition, it is obvious that interviews vary by degree in terms of structure rather than being simply structured or unstructured.

In a classic meta-analysis of studies in this area, Huffcutt and Arthur (1994) identified various levels of standardization with respect to both the questions and the evaluation process, specifically four levels of question structure and three levels of response evaluation structure. They then combined the resulting combinations into four overall levels of structure, and computed the mean corrected validity for each level. Level 1 was the lowest possible level and was characterized by no formal constraints on the questions and a global evaluation of responses (e.g., a single, summary scale). Across 15 of these studies with a total sample size of 7,308, they found a mean corrected validity of 0.20. Level 2 was the next highest level and included limited constraints on the questions through specification of the topics that had to be covered and some degree of structure on the manner in which the responses were evaluated (typically by having interviewers rate candidates on a set of specific dimensions after the interview, e.g., motivation, problem solving). Across 39 of these studies with a total sample size of 4,621, they found a mean corrected validity of 0.35.

Continuing, Level 3 required prespecification of the questions asked (although interviewers typically could choose which questions to ask which applicants) and, similar to Level 2, responses were typically rated through a specified set of dimensions after the interview (although these scales tended to be better defined). Across 27 of these studies with a total sample size of 4,358, they found a mean corrected validity of 0.56. Finally, Level 4 was similar to Level 3 in that the questions were prespecified, but now the interviewers were not given any flexibility and had to ask all applicants the same questions. Moreover, unlike Levels 2 and 3, responses to each question were rated individually using a customized scale with benchmark answers. Across 33 of these studies with a total sample size of 2,365, they found a mean corrected validity of 0.57.

What do we learn from the Huffcutt and Arthur (1994) meta-analysis? As one would expect, validity tends to increase progressively with the level of structure. However, these results suggest that there is a ceiling effect, a point beyond which additional structure does not continue to result in higher validity, and that this effect appears to occur at Level 3. Thus, although it does appear necessary to prespecify the interview questions, it does not appear absolutely necessary to require interviewers to ask the same exact questions to all applicants, nor does it appear necessary to prohibit interviewers from probing the responses (at least in a limited way). Similarly, whereas it does appear necessary to use detailed and multifaceted rating scales to evaluate responses, it does not appear absolutely necessary to rate responses individually by question.

Common Structured Interview Formats

Two structured formats in particular have become dominant over the past few decades. One is referred to as a "situational interview" or SI (Latham, Saari, Pursell, & Campion, 1980). In an SI, interviewers present applicants with a series of hypothetical job scenarios and ask them to indicate how they would respond. Weekley and Gier (1987), who developed an SI for a jewelry store sales position, provided the following classic example of a question using this format: "A customer comes into the store to pick up a watch he had left for repair. The repair was supposed to have been completed a week ago, but the watch is not back yet from the repair shop. The customer becomes very angry. How would you handle this situation?" (p. 485).

As part of the situational format, a customized rating scale is developed for each question, typically a 5-point scale with verbal anchors provided at the 1, 3, and 5 points. Whereas the 2 and 4 points on the scale are not anchored, they are used for answers that are better than one anchored level but not quite as good as the next highest anchored level. Weekley and Gier (1987, p. 485) also presented the following rating scale for the preceding question:

1—Tell the customer it isn't back yet and ask him or her or to check back with you later.

2—

3—Apologize, tell the customer that you will check into the problem and call him or her back later.

4—

5—Put the customer at ease and call the repair shop while the customer waits.

As explained in more detail later, situational questions typically are developed from critical incidents that are collected from people who are incumbents in or are at least very familiar with the position in question. Theoretically, SIs are grounded in goal setting, namely that intentions are the immediate precursors of actions (see Latham, 1989). In regard to the Huffcutt and Arthur (1994) framework, SIs fall in the Level 4 category of structure.

The other structured format can be referred to as a behavior description interview or BDI, although it has gone by several labels in the literature. Motowidlo et al. (1992), for instance, called their technique a "structured behavioral interview," whereas Pulakos and Schmitt (1995) denoted their version as "experience based." Despite the varying terminology, all three terms should be considered synonymous. In this format, interviewers ask candidates to relate situations from their own past that illustrate attributes important for the position (Janz, 1982). To illustrate, a parallel BDI question for the Weekley and Gier (1987) SI question might be something like: "Tell me about a time in your life when you had to deal with an angry and irate person. Describe the situation, your actions in that situation, and the outcome."

As initially devised by Janz (1982), responses to BDI questions are scored after the interview using a set of dimensional rating scales representing important aspects of the position (e.g., attention to detail, ability to motivate). However, some researchers have chosen to develop a customized rating scale for each question, as is done with the situational format (e.g., Campion, Campion, & Hudson, 1994). Either way (i.e., dimensional scales or question-specific rating scales) appears to be acceptable, although the latter does appear to have higher reliability (see Conway, Jako, & Goodman, 1995). Thus, BDIs can fall under either Level 3 or Level 4 in the Huffcutt and Arthur (1994) framework.

As with SIs, BDIs are typically developed from critical incidents. The main difference is in the temporal direction of the wording, with the situational format looking to the future (i.e., what would you do) and the behavior description format looking to the past (e.g., what did you do). Behavior description interviews also have a theoretical basis, which is behavioral consistency (i.e., the past is the best predictor of the future; Janz, 1989).

There is one additional format that has been used extensively in the field of education, but only rarely in business and industry. It is a technique summarized by Schmidt and Rader (1999) and is best described as being theme based. In this technique, the interview developer begins by reviewing the job description and by observing a group of employees performing the job. Then, the developer conducts in-depth interviews with outstanding performers nominated by the organization and identifies behavioral tendencies (i.e., themes) that appear to characterize these select employees. A large number of questions are written for the various themes (often over 100), and then the questions are empirically tested by comparing the ratings received by a group of outstanding performers to the ratings received by a group of unsatisfactory performers. Questions that show a significant difference are retained, whereas questions that do not are dropped. We believe that this technique merits further investigation and study in business and industry, although we do not address it again in this chapter.

PSYCHOMETRIC CHARACTERISTICS OF EMPLOYMENT INTERVIEWS

In this section of the chapter, we describe the psychometric characteristics of the interview, including reliability, validity, incremental validity over cognitive ability, and subgroup differences.

Reliability

Not surprisingly, structured interviews tend to be considerably more reliable than unstructured interviews. The classic work in this area is Conway et al.'s (1995) meta-analysis of 111 interrater reliability coefficients. They found a mean interrater correlation of 0.34 for the lowest level of structure (i.e., totally unstructured interviews). In contrast, they found a mean correlation of 0.67 for a much higher level of structure where the questions were specified exactly in advance, although some probing of responses was allowed. (These findings apply to individual interviews; panel interviews had somewhat higher reliabilities overall.)

Validity

Whereas there are a number of ways in which interviews can vary (e.g., number of questions, type of questions, medium, number of interviewers), the most important characteristic of interviews (at least in terms of reliability and validity) appears to be structure. Several large-scale meta-analyses have confirmed that structured interviews yield average validity coefficients that are substantially larger than those typically found for unstructured interviews. Wiesner and Cronshaw (1988), for example, investigated interview validity across 150 validity studies with a total sample size of 15,459. They found substantially higher validity for structured interviews (ones where the questions and the manner of evaluating responses were specified in advance) than for unstructured interviews. The corrected validity of structured interviews in fact was twice that of unstructured interviews (0.62 versus 0.31).

Similarly, McDaniel, Whetzel, Schmidt, and Maurer (1994) cumulated 245 validity studies comprising a total sample size of 86,311. They found a mean corrected validity of 0.44 for structured interviews, compared to a mean corrected validity of 0.33 for unstructured interviews. However, as Huffcutt and Arthur (1994) noted, the criterion they used to differentiate between structured and unstructured interviews might have been less stringent than the criterion used in the Wiesner and Cronshaw (1988) study, and thus they may have mixed studies with intermediate levels of structure in both their structured and unstructured categories. A clearer estimate of structured interview validity from the McDaniel et al. study comes from their finding for SIs, where the mean corrected validity was 0.50.

Whereas the Wiesner and Cronshaw (1988), McDaniel et al. (1994), and Huffcutt and Arthur (1994) meta-analyses provided information on structured interviews in general, the validity of SIs and BDIs has been investigated in more recent research. Not surprisingly, results suggest that both of these formats provide exceptional validity. Latham and Sue-Chan (1999), for instance, found a mean corrected validity of 0.47 across 20 situational studies. Taylor and Small (2002) found a mean corrected validity of 0.45 across 30 SI studies and 0.56 across 19 BDI studies. Finally, Huffcutt, Conway, Roth, and Klehe (2004) found a mean corrected validity of 0.43 across 32 SI studies and 0.51 across 22 BDI studies.

Collectively, this empirical research for both validity and reliability strongly suggests that interview developers should use structured interviews rather than unstructured interviews when devising their selection systems. The standardization afforded by structured interviews tends to make the process more job related and more consistent, and helps to filter out the typical information-processing tendencies (e.g., contrast, similarity) that plague low-structure interviews (Latham, Wexley, & Pursell, 1975; Wexley, Sanders, & Yukl, 1973).

Incremental Validity

Companies frequently include multiple measures in their selection process. For example, it is common for organizations to combine a structured interview with a mental ability test or a personality test. A question that naturally emerges from such a union is the incremental effectiveness of one approach over the other.

For our purposes, the main consideration is the degree to which the structured interview and other tests overlap. If there is substantial overlap, then little is achieved by giving applicants both measures, as one is not likely to have incremental validity over the other. On the other hand, if the overlap is relatively low, then considerable potential exists to increase the overall accuracy of the selection process by including both measures.

In one of the most comprehensive analyses available, Salgado and Moscoso (2002) analyzed the correlation between structured (e.g., SI, BDI) interviews and several other tests including mental ability and personality. Across 22 studies, they found a mean correlation of 0.14 between behavioral interviews and general mental ability tests (0.28 corrected). For personality, they found mean correlations between behavioral interviews and Big 5 personality dimensions ranging from 0.04 for emotional stability (0.08 corrected; 10 studies) to 0.10 for extraversion (0.21 corrected; 7 studies).

In a similar analysis, Huffcutt, Roth, and McDaniel (1996) analyzed the relationship between structured interview ratings and scores on a mental ability test. Across 10 studies, they found an average correlation of 0.21 between ratings on an SI and scores on a mental ability test. After correcting for range restriction in the interview, measurement error in the ability test, and measurement error in the interview, the correlation increased to 0.32. Across seven studies, they found an average correlation of 0.12 between ratings on a BDI and scores on a mental ability test (0.18 corrected).

In summary, it would appear that structured interview formats, such as SIs and BDIs, do not correlate highly with mental ability and personality tests. Thus, there appears to be considerable potential for companies to increase the overall accuracy of their selection process by combining a structured interview with a mental ability or a personality test.

A note of caution is warranted however. The previous results represent general trends and any one structured interview could have noticeably higher correlations. In a study of pulp mill workers, for instance, Campion et al. (1994) found an uncorrected correlation of 0.49 between their future (i.e., SI) interview questions and a mental ability test composite, and a correlation of 0.61 between their past (i.e., BDI) interview questions and a mental ability test composite.

In addition, there are many types of selection tests available besides those for mental ability and personality. Assessment centers and work samples, for example, are more behaviorally oriented and potentially have greater overlap with behavioral interviews. Unfortunately, little is known at present regarding the relationship between structured interviews and these other selection approaches.

Moderators of SI and BDI Validity

Moderating characteristics, such as use of panel versus individual interviews, type of criterion (e.g., administrative vs. research; performance vs. training), and type of job analysis (e.g., formal, less formal, or none), have been studied extensively in relation to interviews in general, as well as in relation to structured interviews in general (see McDaniel et al., 1994; Wiesner & Cronshaw, 1988). However, considerably less research has specifically looked at moderators of the validity of SIs and BDIs.

Taylor and Small (2002) looked at the use of detailed rating scales (i.e., ones with benchmarks used to evaluate responses to individual questions) and job complexity. Not surprisingly, they only found one situational study that did not use detailed rating scales, and thus were unable to make a meaningful assessment. However, they did find a much better mix with BDIs. Across 11 BDI studies that did use question-specific rating scales and 8 BDI studies that did not (i.e., they used more general dimensional scales that were rated after the interview), they found a mean corrected validity of 0.63 for the former and 0.47 for the latter. Thus, their results would suggest that use of detailed, question-specific rating scales appears to improve the validity of BDIs.

Huffcutt et al. (2004) investigated the moderating influence of job complexity on SI and BDI validity. For BDIs, they found very consistent validity across three levels of job complexity, with mean corrected validities of 0.48 for low complexity, 0.51 for medium complexity, and 0.51 for high complexity. For SIs, they found higher mean corrected validity for low-complexity (0.44) and medium-complexity (0.51) positions than for high-complexity positions (0.30). Their explanation was that developing an SI for positions of high complexity is fairly difficult, and the interview needs to be carefully pretested (something that has not been consistently done in the studies available in the literature).

Huffcutt et al. (2004) also investigated the moderating influence of study format (i.e., predictive vs. concurrent) on SI and BDI validity. They found that, across both SI and BDI studies, predictive studies had a mean validity that was 0.10 lower on average than that for concurrent studies. Their results appear to support Schmitt, Gooding, Noe, and Kirsch's (1984) hypothesis that, with many predictors, the indirect restriction assumed to occur in concurrent designs (through attrition and promotion) may be less severe on average than the direct restriction of range that commonly occurs with predictive designs. More recent investigations appear to provide further support for their hypothesis, such as Hough's (1998) finding that the mean validity for concurrent personality inventory studies was 0.07 higher than the mean validity for predictive personality inventory studies.

Several important conclusions emerge from the research cited in this section, all of which support the general idea that validity is not necessarily constant for all SIs and BDIs. Rather, it would appear that: (a) higher overall BDI validity results when detailed, question-specific rating scales are used instead of dimensional scales rated after the interview; (b) whereas BDI validity seems relatively robust in relation to job complexity, SI validity is more sensitive with positions of high complexity and careful development (including pretesting) is strongly advised; and (c) interview developers can expect noticeably lower validity for both the SI and BDI formats if a predictive design is used and if a correction for range restriction is not made.

Note that use of panel versus individual interviews was not mentioned in this section. This is because there is no empirical research currently available comparing them specifically for SIs and BDIs. Given the exceptional interrater reliability typically observed for situational interviews (Buchner, 1990; Latham, 1989; Weekley & Gier, 1987), we would predict little difference between panel and individual interviews. Given the lower reliability typically observed for BDIs in which dimensional ratings are made after the interview (Moscoso & Salgado, 2001; Motowidlo et al., 1992), use of an interview panel could make more of a difference.

Subgroup Differences

The subgroup difference benchmark by which selection predictors are measured is mental ability tests, because they exhibit very large subgroup differences. As noted in the book *The Bell Curve: Intelligence and Class Structure in American Life* (Herrnstein & Murray, 1994), the difference between majority and minority racial groups on mental ability test scores tends to run about one standard deviation (see also Hunter & Hunter, 1984; Sackett & Wilk, 1994; Schmitt, Clause, & Pulakos, 1996). Such a difference is extensive and can have a profound impact on hiring outcomes. A difference of one standard deviation, for instance, results in the standing where the average person in the minority group (i.e., one at the 50th percentile) has a test score that is equivalent to a person at the 16th percentile in the majority group.

So how do structured interviews fare in terms of group differences? Moscoso (2000) wrote an excellent narrative review on the topic. Across a relatively small but definitive body of research, she noted a general consensus that subgroup differences are associated with employment interviews, but not at the same level as with ability tests. In an empirical investigation, Huffcutt and Roth (1998) found that minority members received ratings on an SI that on average were 0.20 standard deviations lower than those for majority members (eight studies) and ratings on behavior description interviews that on average were 0.10 standard deviations lower than those for majority members (six studies).

Subgroup differences are influenced by the placement of the measure in the selection process. Interviews are typically the last step in a multi-step selection process. Applicants eligible to be interviewed have already survived several selection hurdles (e.g., cognitive ability testing, assessment center). This prescreening prior to the interview results in much smaller subgroup differences in the interview. If the interview were moved to an earlier part of the process, the magnitude of subgroup differences would likely be substantially larger (Roth, Van Iddekinge, Huffcutt, Eidson, & Bobko, 2002).

Clearly, SIs and BDIs appear to be attractive with regard to subgroup differences. They provide essentially the same level of validity as mental ability tests, but do so with smaller subgroup differences. Thus, from legal and societal perspectives, there is much to recommend use of these approaches in employment selection. However, it should be noted that placing the interview at the end of a multiple-hurdle selection procedure might mask subgroup differences that may exist. Also, these are general trends and any one study could exhibit a much larger level of subgroup differences.

HOW TO CREATE STRUCTURED INTERVIEW QUESTIONS

In this section, we describe a basic methodology for developing structured interview questions, regardless of whether they are SIs or BDIs. We then describe unique procedures for SIs and BDIs. We recognize that there are other approaches to developing structured interviews; the procedures described here have been used successfully by numerous researchers and practitioners.

Basic Methodology

This section describes the basic methodology for developing structured interview questions. Please note that we do not address the issue of how many questions to write for a given position, because that depends on contextual factors such as the type of position and the amount of time targeted for the interview. Nor do we address the issue of differential weighting across questions. Most structured interviews are scored by giving all questions equal weight (e.g., a simple sum). Differential weighting may make sense in certain situations, especially if there are differences in the relative importance of the knowledge, skills, and abilities (KSAs) associated with a given position, but it will not be addressed in this chapter.

Structured interview questions usually are developed from the results of some type of formal job analysis, particularly using the methodologies described in chapter 3. Feild and Gatewood (1989) provided two reasons to use job analysis data when developing a structured interview for selection: (a) The use of job analysis results serves to enhance the effectiveness of the interview as a selection tool and (b) the use of a content-related development strategy aids in compliance with legal guidelines for measures used in personnel selection.

Critical incident job analysis (Flanagan, 1954; described in chap. 3) is frequently used to identify and define the behavioral dimensions around which interview questions are organized. Using this method, large numbers of critical incidents describing effective and ineffective performance are collected. These incidents are then sorted, by similarity of behavior, into categories that comprise and define performance dimensions.

However, there are two potential limitations with using just critical incidents. One is that only relatively few of them will actually be used to form interview questions. The other is that there may not be critical incidents (or at least suitable ones) for some of the dimensions of performance. For both of these reasons, there is the potential for inadequate coverage of the performance domain. By developing and including additional interview questions using other kinds of job analysis information (e.g., KSAs or tasks), the interview can be structured to cover the entire job domain more adequately. Job analysis procedures for identifying tasks, for determining required KSAs, and for linking these domains also are described in chapter 3.

Accordingly, Feild and Gatewood (1989) suggested a job content method that combines the use of KSAs with critical incidents to ensure adequate coverage of job requirements. In their approach, once tasks and KSAs are defined (see chap. 4), KSAs are selected according to three criteria. Each KSA must be: (a) rated by subject matter experts (SMEs) as important for job performance; (b) acknowledged by a majority of SMEs as essential for a newly hired employee on job entry; and (c) linked to the performance of at least one critical job task. KSAs meeting all of these criteria are used to define the content of the interview. Critical incidents are then collected in the context of these KSAs.

Feild and Gatewood (1989) suggested a four-step method for generating critical incidents that can, in turn, be used to develop structured employment interviews. First, a panel of SMEs who have had opportunities to observe individuals performing the job is assembled. The SMEs review the KSAs (those that meet the previous criteria) to be assessed during the interview as well as the tasks associated with those KSAs. Then they describe, in writing, incidents of effective and ineffective job behaviors they have seen that reflect the KSAs and associated tasks. The second step consists of having a second group of SMEs read each incident and allocate it to the one KSA they believe the incident best represents. Incidents that are not allocated to the same KSA by a certain percentage of the SMEs (e.g., 75%) are eliminated. This process of "retranslation," or testing a performance structure, is described in chapter 3.

The third step consists of writing questions from the incidents retained in the second step, and specific steps for how to do this with SIs and BDIs are provided in subsequent sections. The fourth and final step consists of having SMEs think of persons whose performance on the job they would rate as outstanding, average, and poor, and provide written narratives describing how those persons would respond to each question. SMEs then rate the simulated responses and those responses on which there is a high degree of rater agreement are retained as anchors for the rating scale.

Situational Interviews

Latham et al. (1980) and Latham (1989) noted that the underlying assumption of the SI is that intentions are related to future behavior. Accordingly, the purpose of the SI is to identify potential employees' intentions by presenting them with a series of hypothetical job-related incidents and asking what they would do in each situation. There are six specific steps involved in developing an SI:

1. Conduct a job analysis using the critical incident (and possibly other) techniques and group the incidents into clusters (or dimensions) based on similarity of behavior (Flanagan, 1954). Methods for collecting and analyzing critical incidents are described in chapter 3.
2. Select one or more incidents from each cluster or dimension that exemplify performance in that cluster.
3. Turn each critical incident into a "What would you do if ..." question.
4. Review the questions for comprehensiveness in terms of covering material identified in the job analysis.
5. Develop a scoring guide to facilitate agreement among interviewers on what constitutes a good, acceptable, or unacceptable response to each question.
6. Conduct a pilot study to eliminate questions to which all applicants give the same answers (i.e., the questions do not differentiate among applicants), or where interviewers do not agree on the scoring.

As noted earlier, a panel of SMEs is created typically to accomplish the previous steps, particularly for Steps 2 through 5. SME panels often consist of job incumbents and supervisors with at least 6 months of experience or with adequate knowledge of the job requirements. The SME panel examines critical incidents collected from a job analysis. Then, for each dimension, SMEs choose an incident that they believe best represents the behavior identified in that dimension (Step 2), and turn that incident into a question (Step 3). The amount of time allocated for the interview may dictate the number of questions actually used. Typically, this is done by selecting the best question(s) for each dimension, as determined by the SMEs. For jobs with large numbers of dimensions, the most important dimensions may need to be identified prior to generating questions.

The five critical incidents shown next were collected as part of a job analysis for the job of apprentice electrician. The percent of SMEs who sorted each incident into the "Working Hard, Taking Initiative, and Being Responsible" dimension is shown in brackets after each incident:

1. An apprentice was working on site lighting. The journeyman did not show up for work that day, so the foreman did not have anyone to help the apprentice. The apprentice said there was enough work to do that day and that no one needed to provide help. The apprentice had a very productive day and got a lot done. The foreman thanked the apprentice for the effort and said it was a great job. [82%]
2. The wiring of a department store was in the beginning stages. During the winter, the temperature was between 0 and 20 degrees below 0 for about 2 weeks. The apprentice was running feeders out of the main distributor in a building that had no roof. The apprentice worked each day wearing weather protective clothing and was able to keep a respectable pace and the job was finished 1 week early. [89%]
3. An apprentice was hired by a foreman and told to be on time for work every day. The apprentice showed up for work late 3 days in a row and always had an excuse. The foreman did not say anything, but docked the apprentice on the next paycheck. The apprentice was never late again. [70%]
4. An apprentice was busy working one day and several journeymen decided to start pitching quarters to a wall (gambling). They invited the apprentice to join them. The apprentice gave in and decided to pitch quarters with them. The apprentice lost over $6 in quarters, but still got paid for a full day. The employer lost almost a half-day of work. [84%]
5. A ditch was being trenched to supply power for a new building. It was a hot summer with frequent showers adding to the delay in the work that was already running behind schedule. Two apprentices were piping six parallel runs of 4-inch PVC under the supervision of a journeyman. While in the ditch, one of the apprentices constantly encouraged coworkers by having a positive attitude and remaining upbeat. The project was moved closer to completion through the apprentice's attitude benefiting the project by encouraging the others to remain constantly at work. [92%]

Four of the preceding five critical incidents were allocated to the "Working Hard, Taking Initiative, and Being Responsible" dimension by more than 75% of the SMEs, and therefore they were available for use as interview questions. Although Critical Incident 4 was not the incident with the highest percentage of SME agreement, it did garner more than 75% agreement and consequently could be used as the basis for an interview question. A situational question that might be developed using this incident is: "You have been assigned to a job with several journeymen. While still on the job, you notice several of them goofing off. You know that you are falling behind on the schedule to complete the project. What would you do?" After several questions are created for each performance dimension, the questions are read aloud to the group to ensure the SMEs agree that the questions fit the dimension and will elicit responses that differentiate among applicants. Through group consensus, one or two interview questions are selected for each dimension to ensure comprehensiveness of coverage (Step 4).

To create a scoring guide for each question (Step 5), each SME independently assigns benchmarks to each answer. That is, experienced SMEs are instructed to assign a "5" to responses they have actually seen demonstrated by outstanding employees (or heard them say in an interview), a "1" to responses they have seen or heard from people who were very poor performers, and a "3" to responses they have seen or heard from people who were mediocre performers. Alternately, if SMEs have not seen or heard an employee in a particular situation, which does happen periodically, they are instructed to think of people they know who are outstanding, poor, and mediocre on the job and to indicate how they think the person would respond if they were in that situation. Each person then reads their benchmarks to the other group members. After group discussion, consensus is reached on the benchmarks that will actually be used. Using these benchmark answers, rating scales are constructed. Figure 7.1 shows a rating scale in which SMEs described how employees at various levels of competence might answer the question posed earlier using Critical Incident 4 to assess the "Working Hard, Taking Initiative, and Being Responsible" dimension.

After the questions and rating scales are developed, a pilot study (Step 6) is conducted to ensure that the questions yield useful responses. Sometimes, SMEs with a lot of job experience develop questions that an applicant could not answer without some amount of job knowledge. Therefore, questions need to be tested on individuals with characteristics similar to those of potential applicants (e.g., similar amounts of job experience).

Behavior Description Interviews

Development of BDI questions closely parallels that of SI questions. There are two major differences, however, which relate to Steps 3 and 5, respectively. These differences are discussed next.

Step 3 in the situational section was to turn each critical incident into a "What would you do if ..." question. Given the past rather than future focus associated with BDI questions, this step would now be to turn each critical incident into a "Tell me about a time when you ..." question.

LOW	MEDIUM	HIGH
Interviewee indicated that he or she would join the journeymen because they have been around longer and know the "ins and outs" of how to get the job done in a hurry and if it's okay for the journeymen to goof off occasionally, then it should be okay for the apprentices.	Interviewee said that he or she would watch the journeymen and see if they got in trouble. He or she would continue to work on the job and probably would not tell the foreman about the situation later.	Interviewee said that he or she would not join the journeymen and would tell the foreman about the situation later. They were clearly losing money due to lower productivity and he or she did not want to be a part of it.
1	2 3 4	5

FIGURE 7.1   Example of a rating scale for scoring situational interviews on the dimension working hard, taking initiative, and being responsible.

Step 5 in the situational section was to develop a scoring guide for each question, typically with benchmarks at the 1, 3, and 5 scale points. As originally devised by Janz (1982), responses to BDI questions are not rated individually. Rather, responses to clusters of questions for a given dimension (e.g., leadership) are rated collectively using a more general rating scale that typically does not have behavioral anchors. In more recent times, some researchers have developed a standardized scale with benchmarks for each BDI question (e.g., Campion et al., 1994), in which case responses would be rated individually by question as is done with the situational format.

There is one additional difference between SIs and BDIs that should be discussed, and that is probing. As originally devised by Janz (1982) and Latham et al. (1980), interviewers typically do not probe responses to situational questions but can probe responses to behavior description questions. Results of the Huffcutt and Arthur (1994) meta-analysis suggest that either approach works fine, although more recently some interview developers have not allowed probing with behavior description questions either, in order to standardize the two formats (e.g., Campion et al., 1994).

To illustrate the BDI process, a critical incident written by a SME during a job analysis is shown here. The incident was sorted by 85% of SMEs into a dimension called "Ability to Plan and Organize Tasks to Meet Deadlines":

An experienced journeyman and apprentice were given a job to terminate about 32,500-kc mil cables in the back of a 2,000-amp switchgear. The foreman was pushing the men to get as much work done as possible in the least

LOW	MEDIUM	HIGH
Responses showed limited use of potential human and material resources. Answers suggested that respondent may work harder, but that work may not be completed to specifications and would involve little cooperation with other employees to complete the job more efficiently.	Responses suggested some use of human and material resources, but the work may have been somewhat inefficient. Responses involved some limited cooperation with others. Work was of average quality.	Responses indicated a great deal of resourcefulness in terms of both human and material resources. The respondent cooperated with supervisors and peers to accomplish work in an efficient, timely manner. Work was of high quality.
1	2 3 4	5

FIGURE 7.2   Example of a rating scale for scoring behavior description interviews on the dimension ability to plan and organize tasks to meet deadlines.

amount of time. Before beginning the job, the journeyman planned what to do and explained to the apprentice how to lay the cables efficiently. The journeyman terminated the cables first, working carefully and taking time to be neat, then supervised the apprentice. The job was done in enough time to satisfy the foreman and the finished product was electrically safe. The apprentice also learned the importance of having a good plan before jumping into a big project.

A structured behavior description question using this critical incident might be: "Tell me about a time when you were given a tight deadline for a project you were working on. What did you do?"

If an interviewee provides insufficient information about an incident in response to this question, interview probes might be: "What did you do then?" (this probe is designed to solicit the action, if the applicant only describes the situation), or "What was the result of what you did?" (this probe is designed to solicit the outcome, if the applicant describes the situation and the action but does not describe the result).

As noted earlier, responses to behavior description questions can be rated either individually using anchored scales similar to those used in SIs or they can be rated collectively by job dimension. Figure 7.2 shows an anchored scale that could be used to rate responses on the dimension "Ability to Plan and Organize Tasks to Meet Deadlines."

SUMMARY

In summary, there is much to recommend both of these structured interview formats. Both have a demonstrated track record of validity, both are grounded in theory, and both can be constructed to assess the same job dimensions (e.g., Morgeson, Reider, & Campion, 2002). Two caveats to this rosy picture come from the results of the Huffcutt et al. (2004) study. One is that researchers should exert caution when interpreting results in a predictive design because the resulting validity could be an underestimate (at least relative to a concurrent design). The other is that for positions of high complexity, development of situational questions should be done with a certain degree of rigor or there could be a resulting drop in validity.

REFERENCES

Blackman, M. C. (2002). The employment interview via the telephone: Are we sacrificing accurate personality judgments for cost efficiency? *Journal of Research in Personality, 36,* 208–223.

Buchner, L. M. (1990). Increases in interrater reliability of situational interviews as a function of the number of benchmark answers. *Applied H.R.M. Research, 1*(2), 27–31.

Campion, M. A., Campion, J. E., & Hudson, J. P., Jr. (1994). Structured interviewing: A note on incremental validity and alternate question types. *Journal of Applied Psychology, 79,* 998–1002.

Chapman, D. S., & Rowe, P. M. (2001). The impact of videoconference technology, interview structure, and interviewer gender on interviewer evaluations in the employment interview: A field experiment. *Journal of Occupational and Organizational Psychology, 74,* 279–298.

Chapman, D. S., Uggerslev, K. L., & Webster, J. (2003). Applicant reactions to face-to-face and technology-mediated interviews: A field investigation. *Journal of Applied Psychology, 88,* 944–953.

Chapman, D. S., & Webster, J. (2001). Rater correction processes in applicant selection using videoconference technology: The role of attributions. *Journal of Applied Social Psychology, 31,* 2518–2537.

Conway, J. M., Jako, R. A., & Goodman, D. F. (1995). A meta-analysis of interrater and internal consistency reliability estimates of selection interviews. *Journal of Applied Psychology, 80,* 565–579.

Feild, H. S., & Gatewood, R. D. (1989). Development of a selection interview: A job content strategy. In R. W. Eder & G. R. Ferris (Eds.), *The employment interview: Theory, research, and practice* (pp. 145–157). Thousand Oaks, CA: Sage.

Flanagan, J. C. (1954). The critical incident technique. *Psychological Bulletin, 51,* 327–358.

Herrnstein, R. J., & Murray, C. (1994). *The bell curve: Intelligence and class structure in American life.* New York: Free Press.

Hough, L. M. (1998). Personality at work: Issues and evidence. In M. Hakel (Ed.), *Beyond multiple choice: Evaluating alternatives to traditional testing for selection* (pp. 131–166). Hillsdale, NJ: Lawrence Erlbaum Associates.

Huffcutt, A. I. (1992). *An empirical investigation of the relationship between multidimensional degree of structure and the validity of the employment interview.* Unpublished doctoral dissertation, Texas A&M University, College Station.

Huffcutt, A. I., & Arthur, W. (1994). Hunter and Hunter (1984) revisited: Interview validity for entry-level jobs. *Journal of Applied Psychology, 79,* 184–190.

Huffcutt, A. I., Conway, J. M., Roth, P. L., & Klehe, U. C. (2004). The impact of job complexity and study design on situational and behavior description interview validity. *International Journal of Selection and Assessment, 12,* 262–273.

Huffcutt, A. I., & Roth, P. L. (1998). Racial group differences in employment interview evaluations. *Journal of Applied Psychology, 83,* 179–189.

Huffcutt, A. I., Roth, P. L., & McDaniel, M. A. (1996). A meta-analytic investigation of cognitive ability in employment interview evaluations: Moderating characteristics and implications for incremental validity. *Journal of Applied Psychology, 81,* 459–473.

Hunter, J. E., & Hunter, R. F. (1984). Validity and utility of alternative predictors of job performance. *Psychological Bulletin, 96,* 72–98.

Janz, T. (1982). Initial comparisons of patterned behavior description interviews versus unstructured interviews. *Journal of Applied Psychology, 67,* 577–580.

Janz, T. (1989). The patterned behavior description interview: The best prophet of the future is the past. In R. W. Eder & G. R. Ferris (Eds.), *The employment interview: Theory, research, and practice* (pp. 158–168). Thousand Oaks, CA: Sage.

Latham, G. P. (1989). The reliability, validity, and practicality of the situational interview. In R. W. Eder & G. R. Ferris (Eds.), *The employment interview: Theory, research, and practice* (pp. 169–182). Thousand Oaks, CA: Sage.

Latham, G. P., Saari, L. M., Pursell, E. D., & Campion, M. A. (1980). The situational interview. *Journal of Applied Psychology, 65,* 422–427.

Latham, G. P., & Sue-Chan, C. (1999). A meta-analysis of the situational interview: An enumerative review of reasons for its validity. *Canadian Psychology, 40,* 56–67.

Latham, G. P., Wexley, K. N., & Pursell, E. D. (1975). Training managers to minimize rating errors in the observation of behavior. *Journal of Applied Psychology, 60,* 550–555.

Little, J. P., Shoenfelt, E. L., & Brown, R. D. (2000, April). *The situational versus the patterned-behavioral-descriptive interview for predicting customer-service performance.* Paper presented at the 15th annual conference of the Society for Industrial and Organizational Psychology, New Orleans, LA.

McDaniel, M. A., Whetzel, D. L., Schmidt, F. L., & Maurer, S. D. (1994). The validity of employment interviews: A comprehensive review and meta-analysis. *Journal of Applied Psychology, 79,* 599–616.

Morgeson, F. P., Reider, M. H., & Campion, M. A. (2002). *Selecting individuals in team settings: Comparing a structured interview, personality test, and teamwork ability tests.* Unpublished manuscript.

Moscoso, S. (2000). Selection interview: A review of validity evidence, adverse impact and applicant reactions. *International Journal of Selection and Assessment, 8,* 237–247.

Moscoso, S., & Salgado, J. F. (2001). Psychometric properties of a structured behavioral interview to hire private security personnel. *Journal of Business and Psychology, 16,* 51–59.

Motowidlo, S. J., Carter, G. W., Dunnette, M. D., Tippins, N., Werner, S., Burnett, J. R., et al. (1992). Studies of the structured behavioral interview. *Journal of Applied Psychology, 77,* 571–587.

Pulakos, E. D., & Schmitt, N. (1995). Experience-based and situational interview questions: Studies of validity. *Personnel Psychology, 48,* 289–308.

Roth, P. L., Van Iddekinge, C. H., Huffcutt, A. I., Eidson, C. E., Jr., & Bobko, P. (2002). Corrections for range restriction in structured interview ethnic group differences: The values may be larger than researchers thought. *Journal of Applied Psychology, 87,* 369–376.

Sackett, P. R., & Wilk, S. L. (1994). Within-group norming and other forms of score adjustment in preemployment testing. *American Psychology, 49,* 929–954.

Salgado, J. F., & Moscoso, S. (2002). Comprehensive meta-analysis of the construct validity of the employment interview. *European Journal of Work and Organizational Psychology, 11,* 299–234.

Schmidt, F. L., & Rader, M. (1999). Exploring the boundary conditions for interview validity: Meta-analytic validity findings for a new interview type. *Personnel Psychology, 52,* 445–464.

Schmitt, N., Clause, C. S., & Pulakos, E. D. (1996). Subgroup differences associated with different measures of some common job-relevant constructs. *International Review of Industrial and Organizational Psychology, 11,* 115–139.

Schmitt, N., Gooding, R. Z., Noe, R. A., & Kirsch, M. (1984). Meta-analyses of validity studies published between 1964 and 1982 and the investigation of study characteristics. *Personnel Psychology, 37,* 407–422.

Silvester, J., Anderson, N., Haddleton, E., Cunningham-Snell, N., & Gibb, A. (2000). A cross-modal comparison of telephone and face-to-face selection interviews in graduate recruitment. *International Journal of Selection and Assessment, 8,* 16–21.

Straus, S. G., Miles, J. A., & Levesque, L. L. (2001). The effects of videoconference, telephone, and face-to-face media on interviewer and applicant judgments in employment interviews. *Journal of Management, 27,* 363–381.

Taylor, P., & Small, B. (2002). Asking applicants what they would do versus what they did do: A meta-analytic comparison of situational and past behavior employment interview questions. *Journal of Occupational and Organizational Psychology, 75,* 277–294.

Weekley, J. A., & Gier, J. A. (1987). Reliability and validity of the situational interview for a sales position. *Journal of Applied Psychology, 72,* 484–487.

Wexley, K. N., Sanders, R. E., & Yukl, G. A. (1973). Training interviewers to eliminate contrast effects in employment interviews. *Journal of Applied Psychology, 57,* 233–236.

Wiesner, W. H., & Cronshaw, S. F. (1988). A meta-analytic investigation of the impact of interview format and degree of structure on the validity of employment interviews. *Journal of Occupational Psychology, 61,* 275–290.

CHAPTER EIGHT

Background Data

Michael D. Mumford
University of Oklahoma

Deborah L. Whetzel
United States Postal Service

Stephen T. Murphy and Dawn L. Eubanks
University of Oklahoma

OVERVIEW

Background data items, in which individuals are asked to recall and report their typical behaviors or experiences in a referent situation likely to have occurred earlier in their lives (Mumford & Owens, 1987), represent a standardized paper-and-pencil technique for collecting life history information (Nickels, 1994). An item might ask, "How many books have you read in the last year?" or "How often have you fixed broken appliances?" To answer these questions, people choose the answer from a predefined list of alternatives that provides the best description of their past behavior and experiences.

Background data questions have been extensively used in personnel selection (Owens, 1976). Reviews by Ghiselli (1973), Hunter and Hunter (1984), Mumford and Owens (1987), Reilly and Chao (1982), Robertson and Smith (2001), and Schmidt and Hunter (1998) indicate that background data measures are effective predictors of job performance, typically yielding criterion-related validity coefficients in the .40 to .50 range. In addition, as Mitchell (1994) and Mount, Witt, and Barrick (2000) pointed out, background data scales appear to have incremental validity over traditional aptitude and ability measures. Furthermore, recent research has demonstrated the generalizability of biodata across situations (Dalessio, Crosby, & McManus, 1996), organizations (Carlson, Scullen, Schmidt, Rothstein, & Erwin, 1999), and gender (Wilkinson, 1997).

Background data items often are used for purposes other than personnel selection. For example, Gessner, O'Connor, Clifton, Connelly, and Mumford (1993) and Gessner, O'Connor, Mumford, Clifton, and Smith (1995) have shown how background data items can be used to identify developmental events that lead to destructive tendencies and life situations likely to provoke expression of these tendencies. Other studies by Schaefer and Anastasi (1969), Mumford, O'Connor, Clifton, Connelly, and Zaccaro (1993), and Oswald, Schmitt, Kim, Ramsay, and Gillespie (2004) indicated that these items can also be used to examine the development of leadership, creativity, and college student performance.

In this chapter, we describe the development and use of background data items in the context of personnel selection. In the first section, we discuss personnel selection issues and describe different types of item content, the kinds of questions that stimulate accurate recall, and different methods of scaling items. In the second section of this chapter, we discuss the psychometric characteristics of background data items. Finally, in the last two sections we explain how to generate background data items and how to scale items after pretesting.

PERSONNEL SELECTION ISSUES

In this section of the chapter, we describe the relevance of various items to the job, the potential for examinees to use these measures to present themselves in a favorable light (i.e., faking), various kinds of item content, the ability of examinees to recall life experiences, alternative formats for background data items, and various scaling methods.

Item Relevance

When background data items are used for personnel selection, a variety of issues needs to be considered. Background data items should be developed that describe situations to which all groups of applicants have had potential exposure (Stone, Stone-Romero, & Eddy, 1995). Restrictive situations, to which only a privileged few would have been exposed, create the perception of bias and are of little use in comparing applicants (e.g., questions about yacht clubs). Furthermore, items should be written in a way that minimizes social stereotyping. For example, questions such as "To what extent do you enjoy knitting?" or "To what extent do you enjoy football?" are inappropriate. In personnel selection, the concern is the individual, not the individual's environment (Guion, 1966). Therefore, it is common practice to focus on behavior and experiences that are under the individual's control (e.g., things a person did rather than things done to the person; Gandy, Dye, & McLane, 1994; Mael, Connerley, & Morath, 1996).

Faking

When applying for a job, there is a tendency to present oneself in the best way possible. Thus, applicants may respond to questions in a way that they think an employer would consider favorable to obtain a higher score (i.e., faking). Although the extent to which faking affects the validity of background data measures is unclear, the need to obtain an accurate appraisal of life histories has led to a number of attempts to minimize faking (Kluger & Colella, 1993; Lautenschlager, 1994). One way to control for the effects of faking is through the use of statistical techniques. For example, Norman (1963) showed how items can be weighted to control for faking. The weighting essentially assigns mean scores to deceptive answers.

Another method of controlling faking concerns the items themselves. For example, including impossible life event items (e.g., "Did you ever win a [nonexistent] award?") is a strategy used to control for faking. Kilcullen, White, Mumford, and Mack (1995) found that background data items are less likely to be subject to faking than personality items requiring projections about future behavior. Klein and Owens (1965) found that applicants were less likely to fake when they had an incomplete picture of the job and items that could not readily map onto this idealized picture. Other work by Shermis, Falkenberg, Appel, and Cole (1996) found that faking can also be reduced by writing items that meet the following criteria: The items should be objective, have low to moderate social desirability, reference time periods that are neither vague nor overly specific, and have noncontinuous response options. To support this claim, Mumford (1994), in a study of foreign service applicants, found that faking was reduced when applicants could not find obvious "right" and "wrong" answers to background data items. Faking on background data items also might be minimized by avoiding the use of "loaded" items that are linked to stereotypic ideas of the job. A related issue concerns minimizing the use of items that are likely to elicit socially desirable responses. Appropriate and inappropriate items that address these issues are shown in Table 8.1.

The type of faking controls just described are appropriate when the construct being measured requires subjective judgment. In many cases, background data items can be written to capture verifiable, factual aspects of life history. Asher (1972) and Mael and Hirsch (1993) stated that objective and potentially verifiable items are less likely to be faked when applicants believe that their responses might be verified. An example of a verifiable item would be: "What was your grade-point average in high school?"

In recent years, research has been conducted in the area of social desirability and answer elaboration. An alternative approach was suggested by Schmitt and Kunce (2002). They argued that asking participants to elaborate on answers to non-cognitive test items results in lower scores. In their study, four forms of a new selection instrument were distributed to examinees for a federal civil service position. In the first form, no elaboration was required. In the second form, respondents were asked to elaborate on 17 items scattered throughout the first half of the form. In the third form, elaboration was requested for 18 items scattered

TABLE 8.1
Examples of Appropriate and Inappropriate Items That Address Faking Issues

Faking Issues	Appropriate Items	Inappropriate Items
Restrictive	How many of the following activities have you participated in during the past year? 1. Sky diving 2. Scuba diving or snorkeling 3. Hiking 4. Camping	How often have you been scuba diving in the past year
Social Stereotyping	How important has it been for you to have co-workers who showed an interest in your projects?	How often have you enjoyed working with women who were very nurturing?
Controllability	When choosing houses or apartments, how likely are you to look in uncrowded suburbs or in the country?	What was the size of the town in which you grew up?
Job Relevance	How many days per week do you typically stay late to finish something at work?	How many times per month do you go to church?
Verifiable	What was your average pay raise over the last five years?	Are you typically seen as a better performer than your peers?
Social Desirability	How often have you gone out of your way to spend time with unpopular colleagues?	How important has it been for you to be friends with your co-workers?
Loaded	How often have you continued to put in extra time on a project to compensate for mistakes made by management?	How hard have you worked on assignments?

throughout the second half of the form. The fourth form required elaboration on the 35 items in the second and third forms. Schmitt and Kunce (2002) found that asking applicants to elaborate their answers to a non-cognitive item resulted in a reduction of socially desirable responding by approximately .60 standard deviation units. Similar findings were reported by Schmitt et al. (2003). Schmitt and Kunce (2002) also found that when items were embedded among those that were elaborated and when these elaborated items were presented in the first half of the test, lower scores were observed.

Item Content

Background data measures represent an assessment technique in which items are defined by the nature and structure of people's lives as they unfold over time (Mumford, Reiter-Palmon, & Snell, 1994). Most theorists suggest that people's life histories unfold as a dynamic interaction between characteristics of the individual and the situations to which the individual has been exposed (Caspi, 1987; Lerner & Tubman, 1989; Magnusson, 1988; Schooler, 1990). Thus, individual characteristics influence perceptions of the environment, the kinds of situations encountered, behavior in these situations, and the outcomes of situational exposure (Mumford, Costanza, Connelly, & Johnson, 1996). The outcomes of this interaction, through mechanisms such as learning, memory, and cognition, lead to changes in individual development. These changes, however, often tend to be self-reinforcing as people seek out situations in which their existing characteristics will contribute positively to performance.

Expanding on the idea of an interaction between individual characteristics and situational influence, Ligon (2004) argued that select life events, for example, turning point and anchoring events (McAdams, 2001), will influence narrative construction and thus the course of people's careers. In a study of outstanding leaders they found that these narrative, or self-definitional, life events could predict leader performance across a wide variety of dimensions.

In addition to positive biodata items, in which items are generated to reflect positive instances of behavior in non-threatening situations, recent research has demonstrated that reactions to negative life experience may provide potential for developing biodata item content (Hough & Oswald, 2000). For instance, Dean, Russell, and Muchinsky (1999) argued that life experience learning, through learning aids, time, and failures, helps the individual to respond effectively to negative life events and constitutes important steps in development.

Background data items specify situations likely to have occurred in a person's life, and then ask about that person's typical behavior in the situation (Allworth & Hesketh, 1999; Mumford & Owens, 1982). Eight types of questions are typically asked: (a) situational exposure, (b) situational choice, (c) behavior in a situation, (d) reactions to a situation, (e) other people's reactions to a situation, (f) outcomes of situational exposure, (g) life narratives (turning point events), and (h) negative life experiences. Examples of these eight types of item content that assess the constructs of Openness to Experience and Achievement Motivation are shown in Table 8.2.

Because people's lives are complex and varied, one could develop thousands of background data items to predict performance for any given job. To develop a

TABLE 8.2
Eight Types of Background Data Item Content

Item Type	Openness to Experience	Achievement Motivation
Situational exposure	How many times did your family move while you were in grade school and high school?	How much encouragment did your parents give you when you were trying to do something new?
Situational choice	How often have you taken a class simply to learn something new?	How many difficult classes did you take in high school?
Behavior in situation	How often have you looked for a new way to complete an assignment?	How often have you put aside other tasks to complete a difficult assigment?
Reactions to a situation	How much have you enjoyed meeting new people at parties?	To what extent have you felt proud after completing a difficult assignment?
Others' reactions to a situation	How often have people described your approach to problems as different or unusual?	How often has your supervisor thanked you for putting in extra time on a project?
Outcomes associated with situational exposure	How many times has a project you worked on resulted in a patent or publication?	How often have you been asked to step in when someone else was having difficulty finishing a piece of work?
Life narratives (turning point events)	How often has your work role significantly changed?	How many times have you had a dramatic increase in work responsibility?
Negative life experiences	How many times have you been involved in a merger, acquisition, or downsizing?	How many times have you fallen short of your goals?

manageable number of items, background data items are typically generated that tap specific predictor constructs thought to underlie performance (Stokes & Cooper, 2001). Such constructs usually are identified through job analysis (Allworth & Hesketh, 1999; Mount et al., 2000; Schmitt & Pulakos, 1998; Stokes & Searcy, 1999; West & Karas, 1999), as described in chapter 2, by having subject matter experts brainstorm lists of knowledges, skills, abilities, and other characteristics (KSAOs). Thus, items may be generated to assess Openness to Experience if we are interested in predicting the performance of behavioral scientists; items examining Attention to Detail may be useful for predicting performance in clerical jobs; and items examining Willingness to Work in Extreme Weather Conditions may be useful for predicting performance in outdoor jobs, such as apprentice electrician.

Background data items do not directly ask individuals to evaluate their relative standing on a particular construct. Instead, such items ask how a construct might have manifested itself in different situations (Mumford, 1999). Because people behave differently from one situation to the next, the situational bounding of background data items is a critical consideration in developing reliable and valid background data measures. Questions typically examine how the variable manifests itself across a range of situations (e.g., work, school, leisure activities, family, and friends; Epstein & O'Brien, 1985). Responses to a particular background data item are of little use; it is the pattern of responses across different situations that enables valid and reliable prediction (Mumford et al., 1996). Thus, most background data inventories contain between 10 and 30 questions to assess a given construct. The number of constructs measured using background data items depends on the testing time allowed, as well as other measures in a battery that assess similar constructs. Chapter 4 describes the development of test plans, in which the measurement methods for assessing various constructs are specified.

To interpret responses to background data items, relevant questions must be asked about life situations. Because the situations individuals are exposed to change over time, and because people from different backgrounds may be exposed to different types of situations (Ferguson, 1967; Revo, 1976), different items may need to be written to measure a construct (e.g., achievement motivation) for different age groups and organization levels (e.g., apprentice electricians vs. journeymen electricians). It is essential to tailor item content to the situations to which members of the applicant pool are likely to have been exposed. Two sets of example items measuring Conscientiousness follow. In the first set, the construct is assessed for two different age groups; in the second set, the construct is assessed for two different kinds of jobs. All four questions are of the item type Behavior in a Situation (see Table 8.2).

Age groups:
Adolescence: How important was it for you to get As and Bs in your high school classes?
Adulthood: How important has it been for you to get ratings of "excellent" on your performance evaluations?

Different kinds of jobs:
Apprentice electrician: How important has it been for you to inventory your tools at the end of the day?
Journeyman electrician: How frequently have you been able to complete construction projects on time and within budget?

Recall of Life Experiences

Because responding to background data items relies on individual memory, it is important to consider what people remember about their lives and how those memories are retrieved (Asher, 1972). A number of studies have examined the nature and structure of autobiographical recall (Barsalou, 1988; Conway, 1990; Kolodner, 1984; Odegard, Lampinen, & Wirth-Beaumont, 2004; Reiser, Black, & Abelson, 1985; Robinson & Swanson, 1990). These studies indicate that autobiographical memory is organized and recalled in terms of categories reflecting different types of goal-relevant events (e.g., taking a vacation). These event categories provide summary information about key actions and relevant goals and include information about participants, locations, outcomes, and affect. Both temporal sequencing and event similarity may be used to organize the event summaries that provide the working raw material for autobiographical memory (Clifton, Mumford, & Baughman, 1999; Koriat, Goldsmith, & Pansky, 2000).

Several studies have documented the ability to recall prior behavior and experiences using background data items. In one study, Shaffer, Saunders, and Owens (1986) asked undergraduates to complete 118 background data items. The undergraduates' parents were also asked to describe their children using the same items. Generally, a high level of agreement was observed between the undergraduates' and parents' responses, although somewhat greater agreement was found when people were asked to report about observable behavior rather than subjective feelings. Other studies by McCrae and Costa (1988) and Roberts, Block, and Block (1978) also provide evidence for the surprising accuracy of autobiographical recall, at least when there is no motive for faking.

Accurate recall is facilitated when background data items are structured to be consistent with the nature of autobiographical memory. Clifton (1994) found that more accurate recall was observed on background data items written to capture summaries of past behavior than on items written to capture summaries of discrete, somewhat atypical events. He found that background data items linked to the goals and outcomes of people's actions were associated with better recall than items that asked people to report past behavior out of context. Clifton et al. (1999) found further support demonstrating that people could consistently recall and accurately report general summaries of activities and reactions to a selected task. More specifically, the basic working components of autobiographical memory are event summaries, reflecting multiple instances of goal-related behavior.

Several conclusions can be drawn about the nature of effective background data items. These conclusions stem from research on the nature of autobiographical memory. First, good items should seek to assess event summaries, not narrowly defined behaviors. Second, items should reflect goal-relevant behavior and experiences, rather than behavior and experiences taken out of context. Third, it may be useful to provide temporal or event organizers (e.g., in high school). Fourth, items should focus on salient, developmentally significant events, rather than on routine events. Fifth, items should focus on recent events (i.e., those occurring in the last few years), rather than on events that occurred some time

TABLE 8.3
Examples of Background Data Items That Encourage
Good and Poor Levels of Recall

Item Types	Good Recall	Poor Recall
Event summaries	How often were you able to improve your grades in a class when you did poorly on the first test?	How much did you improve your grade on your algebra test?
Goal relevant	How often have you been angry with someone who took advantage of a coworker?	How often have you been angry?
Event organizers	When meeting new people, how easy is it for you to introduce yourself?	How easy is it for you to introduce yourself?
Relevant events	How difficult was it for you to learn calculus in college?	How difficult was it for you to learn addition in elementary school?

ago. Examples of background data items that encourage good and poor levels of recall are shown in Table 8.3.

Alternative Formats

Although background data items are commonly used in personnel selection to assess differential characteristics of people, background data items may also be developed with a number of other applications in mind. For example, Mumford et al. (2005) sought to identify the career events shaping the performance of biological, physical, social, and life scientists. They found that background data items could be written to capture significant life events shaping scientific careers such as exposure to mentors (e.g., in the case of electricians, an event may involve family members showing one how to work with electrical equipment in high school). The findings obtained by Mumford et al. (2005) indicate that these types of items may be effective predictors of long-term career achievement.

Mumford, Connelly, Helton, Strange, and Osburn (2001) examined the ability of background data items to capture work experiences that influence the development and expression of performance potential. They developed items to measure exposure to work context variables that would influence integrity. For example, a typical integrity item might ask, "How many job sites have you worked on where people regularly borrowed tools to complete personal projects?" They found that these work context exposure items were effective predictors of integrity-related decisions as assessed in a job-simulation exercise.

Scaling Methods

After items are pretested on a sample of examinees, the item data are used to group items into categories or scales. The psychometric characteristics of four methods for scaling items are described in the next section, and methods for actually scaling items are described later in this chapter. We provide a brief description here to introduce each scaling method.

Empirical scaling procedures typically are used to select and weight items on the basis of their ability to differentiate membership in higher and lower performing criterion groups (Hogan, 1994; Mount et al., 2000). Rather than understanding constructs that account for prediction, predictive efficiency is established through demonstrated prediction of criterion performance. In the *rational scaling* approach, the test developer identifies and defines an individual difference variable (based on job analysis, as described in chap. 2) and writes questions to elicit information regarding the manifestation of the characteristic (Hough & Paullin, 1994). Item inclusion is based on the test developer's judgment of the relevance of the item to the characteristic or constructs (Allworth & Hesketh, 1999). The *factorial scaling* approach assumes that some basic structure of individual differences exists and that this structure can be discovered through factor or cluster analysis (Burisch, 1984). As such, the internal structure of the item pool determines the placement of an item with a particular scale and its direction of keying (Schoenfeldt, 1999). *Subgrouping* procedures identify groups of individuals whose prior behavior and experiences are similar enough to be summarized with little loss of information about individual group members (Hein & Wesley, 1994). Subgroups are defined by the items through the application of profile similarity measures (e.g., distances and correlations) and clustering algorithms.

Recent research, such as West and Karas (1999) and Gammie (2000), has attempted to combine methods for scaling biodata items. Items were rationally developed and then selected for use in the final biodata measure through empirical keying. Using this approach, validities in the range of .23 to .56 were obtained with similar cross-validities. Stokes, Toth, Searcy, Stroupe, and Carter (1999) combined rational and factorial scaling to develop a Salesperson Biodata Questionnaire (SBQ). The SBQ scales yielded validities in the range of .16 to .25 with appropriate criteria. However, care must be taken when combining methods to ensure that consideration of the weaknesses and strengths of each of the approaches is balanced.

PSYCHOMETRIC CHARACTERISTICS OF BACKGROUND DATA ITEMS

Background data measures have a number of psychometric characteristics that make them useful for predicting job performance. First, background data measures are highly reliable (Shaffer et al., 1986). Second, background data measures have acceptable levels of validity (Brown, 1994). Third, background data measures demonstrate adequate generalizable validity across situations (Carlson et al., 1999). Fourth, background data measures have less adverse impact on minority groups than many other types of measures commonly used to predict performance (Mumford & Owens, 1987). Following are discussions of these four characteristics.

Reliability

Empirical Scales. For empirical scales, in which items are weighted to the extent that they differentiate between desirable and undesirable criterion groups, test-retest is an important measure of reliability. The few studies that report test-retest reliability describe values ranging from .60 to .96, with the level being partially determined by time between testing sessions and by item type (Brush, 1974; Chaney, 1964; McManus & Mitchell, 1987). Mount et al.'s (2000) 138-item biodata instrument yielded an estimated internal reliability coefficient alpha ranging from .54 to .81 across four scales.

Rational Scales. Internal consistency reliability is a major concern when developing rationally based or homogeneous scales. Research shows that rational scaling procedures yield reliable background data scales. Mumford et al. (1996) found that scales developed using these procedures produce internal consistency coefficients and in the low .70s (Douthitt, Eby, & Simon, 1999). Stricker's (1989) final five biodata-based personality scales yielded coefficient alpha reliability estimates of .66 to .78. Goldberg (1972) found internal consistency reliability values for 22 homogeneously developed scales ranging from .48 to .88, with a mean of .74. Karas and West's (1999) scale of 139 items measuring six constructs produced coefficient alpha reliability estimates ranging from .70 to .96 for incumbent and applicant groups.

Factorial Scales. In factorial approaches, in which dimensions are discovered empirically through factor analysis, it is important that the resulting dimensions be internally consistent. Results of internal consistency analyses by Baehr and Williams (1967), Owens (1976), and Schoenfeldt (1999) suggest that typical dimension reliabilities are in the .70s range. A concern related to reliability is the consistency of factor structures when applied to new samples. Research suggests that different factor structures are likely for men and women (Owens, 1976) and for different age groups (Mumford et al., 1983). Given such differences, one might expect there to be different factor structures for different racial and ethnic groups, which can be problematic for applied selection purposes.

Subgrouping. This approach to biodata keying is based on the belief that people grouped on the basis of the pattern of their prior experiences will behave similarly in the future (Brown, 1994). The purpose of this method is to identify cohesive groups of people based on the similarity of their responses to biodata items. Concerning reliability, cluster analysis results will only be stable if the measures that are clustered are reliable. A concern with this approach involves the reproducibility of the subgroups in a new setting. Research reported by Mumford and Owens (1987) suggests relatively positive results for the subgrouping approach.

Validity

Empirical Scales. This approach to scaling biodata items tends to yield validity estimates that often are higher than other approaches (Asher, 1972; Henry, 1966; Mumford & Owens, 1987; Owens, 1976; Reilly & Chao, 1982; Schuh, 1967). For selection into the U.S. civil service, Gandy, Outerbridge, Sharf, and Dye (1990) reported the cross-validity (the predictor-criterion correlations that resulted from application of the scoring keys developed on each sample half to the independent half) of the Individual Achievement Record (IAR) to be .33 and .32. Little shrinkage occurred in the validity coefficients and in the cross-validities, providing strong support for the robustness of the empirical keys developed on large samples ($N = 13,000$).

Rational Scales. Mumford et al. (1996) found that when rationally developed background data scales were used to predict performance, they yielded initial validities in the low .40s, which, when cross-validated, shrank by roughly .05 to .10 points. Mumford and his colleagues indicated that the resulting scales showed construct validity, yielding theoretically meaningful patterns of relationships with external reference measures (Kilcullen et al., 1995; Mumford, Baughman, Threlfall, Costanza, & Uhlman, 1993). These validity coefficients are comparable to those obtained from empirical keys, and support the idea that rational scales and empirical keys are equally effective predictors of job performance (Hough & Paullin, 1994; Stokes & Searcy, 1999). Furthermore, Schoenfeldt (1999) found that rational scales resulted in less shrinkage in cross-validation than empirically developed scales. As Mumford and his colleagues pointed out, however, rational scales maintain the constructs underlying initial item generation. As a result, it becomes possible to accrue a wider range of construct validation evidence for rational scales, using techniques such as convergent and discriminant validation.

Factorial Scales. A concern when validating factorial scales is the likely difference in responses between applicant and incumbent samples. Basing development efforts on an employee sample could yield scales that are only appropriate for current employees. Research suggests that validities can be substantial, though typically lower than those associated with empirical approaches (Fuentes, Sawyer, & Greener, 1989; Mitchell & Klimoski, 1982; Mumford & Owens, 1987). On the other hand, Schoenfeldt (1999) found evidence for the validity and cross-validity of factorially developed scales. The study yielded multiple correlations in the .25 range with little shrinkage in the cross-validation group. Because items are scaled in terms of empirically identified constructs, a variety of construct validation analyses can be conducted that often are useful for theory development.

Subgrouping. This technique involves clustering people together who have similar life histories. Responses are scaled by assigning respondents to the group that is most similar to their pattern of item responses. Research reported by Mumford and Owens (1987) has shown subgroup status to be a valid predictor in 80% to 90% of the studies conducted, using criteria such as academic achievement, and vocational interests.

Generalizability of Biodata

The ability of biodata items and measures to generalize across situations (e.g., organizations) is an important consideration. At first glance it would seem that biodata would be situation specific. However, research has demonstrated that the validity of biodata measures is stable over time (Reiter-Palmon, 1996), across situations (Dalessio et al., 1996), and across ethnic and gender groups (Costanza & Mumford, 1993; Gonter, 1979; Wilkinson, 1997). Furthermore, there is evidence that biodata measures generalize for empirical scales (Dalessio et al., 1996), rational scales (Stokes & Searcy, 1999), and factorial scales (Reiter-Palmon, 1996).

Schmidt and Rothstein (1994) conducted a meta-analysis using 79 validity coefficients and found a mean true validity of .36 with ratings on "Ability to Perform," and .34 with ratings on "Performance of Duties." The standard deviations of true validities were .082 and .104, respectively; and the 90% credibility values were .26 and .20, respectively. These findings show that valid biodata scales can be developed for multiple settings. Results of studies by Rothstein, Schmidt, Erwin, Owens, and Sparks (1990) and Harvey-Cook and Taffler (2000) suggest that biodata validity may not be specific to a particular organization and that validity may not be moderated by age, sex, race, education, tenure, or previous experience. They cautioned that their results do not indicate that the level of generalizability they found can always be expected from biodata, and that given conventional methods of biodata instrument construction, these results likely represent the exception rather than the rule.

Dalessio et al. (1996) examined the stability of a biodata scoring key and the underlying factor structure across two situations (United States and United Kingdom or Republic of Ireland). They concluded that the scoring key was equally valid across situations and the underlying dimensional structure of the instrument and the validity of these dimensions were transportable. Carlson et al. (1999) developed and keyed a biodata measure within a single organization and tested whether the measure and key could generalize to a different organization. Their results indicated that the validity of the biodata measures and the scoring key can be generalized.

Carlson et al. (1999) argued that the generalizability of biodata measures is contingent on three key considerations. First, is there adequate theory to assume that the biodata instrument could generalize to other populations? Second, is there a relevant bank of questions to be used? Third, does an adequate development sample exist that is diverse?

Subgroup Differences

Mumford and Owens (1987) and Pulakos and Schmitt (1996) indicated that background data measures exhibit smaller subgroup differences than many other types of measures commonly used to predict performance. To further support this point, recent research on specific applications of biodata, such as administration via an interactive voice response (IVR) system, indicated that this application did not result in subgroup differences (Van Iddekinge, Eidson, Kudisch, & Goldblatt, 2003).

Reilly and Chao (1982) reviewed 11 background data studies that reported ethnic subgroup data and found significant mean differences in three cases. They concluded that for empirically keyed forms, a relationship exists between criterion mean differences and background data mean differences. Mean differences on background data will be smaller where criterion mean differences are smaller. This means that when there are relatively large differences in criteria (e.g., job performance), there will be greater adverse impact than when there are smaller differences in criterion performance.

Research on the IAR (Gandy et al., 1990) indicated that, on average, females scored slightly higher than males. In addition, Whites scored higher on average than African Americans and Hispanics; however, the differences in score levels between Whites and minority groups were small relative to those typically found on ability tests. No statistically significant differences in subgroup validities were found and comparisons of subgroup standard errors, regression slopes, and intercepts (Cleary, 1968) failed to indicate any unfairness to minorities and gender groups (Wilkinson, 1997).

HOW TO GENERATE BACKGROUND DATA ITEMS

To develop background data items that provide a fair and accurate portrayal of an individual's life history, one must identify how various characteristics of the individual, particularly those differential characteristics likely to affect job performance, have manifested themselves in the individual's daily life. To do this, two key steps are required (Mumford et al., 1996). First, one must identify constructs that predict job performance. In chapter 2, we described how to identify KSAOs. After a list of KSAOs is developed, one must determine the appropriate method for measurement, as described in chapter 4. Second, hypotheses must be developed about why a given behavior or experience in a situation might serve as an appropriate marker of the target construct using our understanding of the construct and available psychological theory (Messick, 1995).

There are two broad frameworks for identifying constructs leading to the development of background data items. In the person-oriented approach, constructs such as spatial ability and reading skills are used to develop background data items. For example, one might try to assess mechanical ability by asking, "Did you ever build a model airplane that flew?" This item, along with a number of other items intended to assess mechanical ability, might then be used to predict performance on a variety of jobs (e.g., electrician, engineer, computer programmer, automotive repairer) in which mechanical ability is known to be an important determinant of performance. Illustrations of this approach may be found in Mumford, O'Connor, et al. (1993), DuBois, Loevinger, and Gieser (1952), and Stokes et al. (1999).

In contrast, the job-oriented approach leads to the creation of items that focus on prior behavior similar to that found on the job. These questions center on the performance of duties and their associated tasks. Methods for identifying duties and tasks were described in chapter 3. Illustrations of the job-oriented approach to item development may be found in Hough (1984), Pannone (1984), and Stokes and Cooper (2001). For example, to assess organizational skills for journeyman electricians, one might ask, "To what extent do you take extra time to order enough materials to ensure sufficient supplies are on hand for a job?" Although this job-oriented approach typically yields items that have face validity, it may not be useful for entry-level positions in which most applicants lack relevant job experience. Because behaviorally oriented items tend to be highly loaded, care must be taken to minimize faking. Despite these concerns, the job-oriented approach, like the person-oriented approach, requires explicit hypotheses to generate background data measures likely to result in good prediction. In addition to considering the person-oriented and job-oriented approaches to generating items, it is important to consider the interaction between individuals and the situations to which they are exposed (Caspi, 1987; Lerner & Tubman, 1989; Magnusson, 1988; Schooler, 1990). Each individual has a different framework in which they operate in the world. Each outcome of an interaction leads to changes in the individual that will in turn affect future interactions. Students of adult development argue that this interaction has implications for item generation. First, this interaction enables identification of situations early in an individual's life that exhibit a certain construct. Second, items can be developed that reflect differences in expression of a construct across situations. These items should then be aggregated across multiple situations to assess the different ways a predictor construct is expressed.

The remainder of this section describes four methods for generating background data items. We then describe item response formats and suggest methods for assembling a background data questionnaire. These procedures reflect practices that have resulted in demonstrably valid background data measures. Other methods may be feasible, depending on the purpose for which such measures are developed.

Construct-Based Item Generation

Once a set of constructs has been identified and defined, background data items can be developed. A procedure frequently used to develop items was described by Mumford et al. (1996), Mumford and Stokes (1992), and Stokes and Cooper

(2001). The procedure begins by assembling a group of five or six psychologists, drawn from diverse backgrounds, who have some formal training and experience in developing background data measures. Typically, multiple sessions are needed to generate items. During the course of a 2-hour session, panel members usually can generate items for two to three constructs. Prior to starting item generation, panel members review the job analysis, in which the constructs are identified. They then review available research that describes the nature of the constructs, their development, and the ways in which these characteristics influence performance in various situations. For example, for the construct Achievement Motivation, one might review McClelland (1975) and Atkinson and Raynor (1974). Additionally, panel members are given a description of the population to which these measures will be applied and are asked to think about job-relevant situations that most individuals in the population would have encountered.

At the beginning of an item-generation session, panel members are given a definition of a relevant construct and are asked to discuss its importance for predicting performance in the population. For approximately 15 to 20 minutes, panel members write items that they think reflect how the construct might manifest itself in people's interactions with situations they are likely to have encountered. Although no constraints are placed on item content, panel members generate item types described previously: (a) situational exposure, (b) situational choice, (c) behavior in the situation, (d) reactions to the situation, (e) others' reactions, and (f) the outcomes of behavior in this situation. In addition, panel members are asked to keep in mind the nature of autobiographical memory. For example, a key to writing biodata items is that they should be written to capture events that reflect significant goals in a person's life. This is positively related to the ability to recall a particular memory (Clifton et al., 1999). When people have trouble recalling an event, they tend to respond in a socially desirable manner.

After writing the items for a particular construct, panel members read their items aloud. If the hypothesis underlying an item is not immediately apparent to other panel members, the panel member reading an item states the hypothesis underlying the item. The other panel members review the proposed item for its appropriateness for the construct and for the population, the feasibility of developing an objective scoring system for the item, and the appropriateness of the item for use in personnel selection. Items that lack adequate construct relevance, are not under the individual's personal control, are highly loaded, or appear to be unfair with respect to situational exposure and stereotypes are eliminated. Other problems pointed out by panel members, such as social desirability, are noted and an attempt is made to rewrite the item. These procedures typically yield 50 to 60 candidate items that might be used to measure a construct.

Once the candidate items have been generated, psychologists familiar with the job review the items to ensure that a full range of potential item content is covered. During this review, the psychologists edit items for clarity and develop response options for each item consistent with the question being asked. The questions are then presented to job incumbents, who assess item clarity and relevance and identify any potentially sensitive items for the target population.

TABLE 8.4
Examples of Construct-Based Items for the Constructs Initiative and Integrity

Initiative	*Integrity*
How often have you worked late to finish a construction project?	How important is it to you that your fellow electricians play by the rules?
How often have you suggested to someone that he or she should try a different way to solve a problem?	How often have you become angry with people who took advantage of their position?
How often have you been the one who had to deliver the "bad news" to a journeyman or foreman?	How often have you pulled someone aside who was "taking things out" on someone you know?
How many times have you volunteered to help someone finish a project?	To what extent have you been embarrassed when someone has praised your work, but not the work of your coworkers?
How much do you enjoy discussing new material that you had to learn on your own?	How likely are you to report that someone has taken credit for work that really was done by someone else?

Studies have shown that construct-based item generation tends to produce scales that have both content and construct validity (Mumford et al., 1996). Examples of items resulting from this procedure for the constructs Initiative and Integrity developed for the apprentice electrician job are shown in Table 8.4.

Behavioral Consistency Item Generation

One alternative to construct-based item generation is the behavioral consistency approach advocated by Fine and Cronshaw (1994), Hough (1984), Pannone (1984), and Schmidt et al. (1979). The behavioral consistency approach assumes that past performance is the best predictor of future performance. Thus, this approach is often used to predict performance in populations in which people have prior experience working on tasks similar to those that they will confront on the job.

As with the construct-based approach, it is essential that a thorough and comprehensive job analysis be available for describing the work itself and the conditions under which the work is performed. This job information may be collected using a variety of techniques, including task analysis and critical incidents, described in chapter 3. Job analysis results are provided to a panel of three or four psychologists who have some familiarity with the job. Each panel member is asked to identify prior behaviors and experiences that reflect good performance in situations similar to those found on the job. For example, if the electrician job is found to require organizational skills, then panel members would be asked to write background data items that reflect prior performance in organizing activities. Thus, one might develop background data items asking, "How often did you set goals or milestones for construction projects?," "How frequently did you complete projects on time?," or "Did you ever receive a raise or bonus that was based on the quality of the project you completed?"

Items written by one panel member are reviewed by other panel members and necessary revisions are made. Unlike construct-based item generation, however, the behavioral consistency approach assumes prior performance opportunities. As a result, all items should be reviewed to ensure that: (a) most applicants would have had opportunities to engage in the situations suggested in the item(s) and (b) the questions have a clear relationship to job performance (Karas & West, 1999). Following are examples of job-oriented behavioral consistency items developed to predict performance of electrician apprentices:

1.   How difficult has it been for you to work outside on a cold day?
2.   How difficult has it been for you to install electrical appliances (e.g., dishwashers)?
3.   How many times have you repaired electrical appliances around your home?
4.   Relative to other people you know, how much do you enjoy working outdoors?
5.   How frequently have you assembled pieces of electrical equipment (e.g., radios)?

Although the behavioral consistency approach is most appropriate for predicting the performance of applicants who have prior job experience, this approach can be extended to settings where such experience is lacking. One strategy, described by Fine and Cronshaw (1994) and illustrated by Keinan, Friedland, Yitzhaky, and Moran (1981), involves identifying life situations in the past that have similar performance demands to the construct of interest. Thus, for the construct Organizational Skills, one might ask, "To what extent do you prepare to go on a long trip?"

In contrast to construct-based item generation, the behavioral consistency approach yields items with greater job relevance, thereby minimizing negative applicant reactions. However, these items are somewhat transparent, making it easier for applicants to fake good responses. As a result, when the behavioral consistency approach is used, it is necessary to develop items that can be verified (Karas & West, 1999).

Career History Item Generation

A third approach to developing background data items is the career history approach. This is similar to the behavioral consistency approach because it focuses on performance in a particular setting. However, generating these items involves identifying the experiences and behaviors that contribute to the development of

TABLE 8.5
Examples of Career History Items Developed to Predict the Performance of Apprentice Electricians

- How many jobs have you had where you had to work with people who did not share your goals?
- How much have you enjoyed getting a new idea into shape so someone could work with it?
- How important has it been for you to be able to learn from more experienced persons?
- To what extent have you learned from projects that were not completed on time?
- How often have you collaborated with people on two or three different projects at the same time?
- How often have disagreements with other co-workers improved the quality of your work?
- How much have you enjoyed working with people who had a clear idea of what they wanted to do?

performance capabilities, rather than past performance. Biodata have been applied to occupations such as clerical jobs in the private sector (Mount et al., 2000), accountants (Harvey-Cook & Taffler, 2000), mechanical equipment distributors (Stokes & Searcy, 1999), managers (Wilkinson, 1997), and naval ratings (Strickler & Rock, 1998). One method for developing career history items relies on the performance of successful individuals who are asked to write essays describing their lives, or incidents that were key events in shaping their careers (Russell, Mattson, Devlin, & Atwater, 1990). An example might be to ask people to write about key events such as a particularly rewarding day at work, or an especially stressful situation (Mumford, 1999). The essays, typically drawn from at least 20 to 40 successful individuals, are reviewed by psychologists who identify: (a) key themes or dimensions in the essays and (b) the prior behaviors and experiences related to performance. For example, based on information from the essays, it might be found that successful journeyman electricians were mentored and were given challenging construction projects. Thus, items might be written asking, "In the course of your career, have you worked closely with senior-level journeyman electricians?" or "How often have you been asked to take over a project that had run into problems?" Examples of career history questions that can be developed to predict performance in a variety of occupations, including apprentice electrician, are shown in Table 8.5.

There are several possible variations of this approach. For example, one might obtain essay or interview information from both successful and unsuccessful individuals and then use the content differences observed between these groups as a basis for item generation. Alternatively, prior research may be used to specify key developmental issues (Russell & Domm, 1990; Russell & Kuhnert, 1992). Regardless of the method for developing career history items, an item content review should be conducted if the items are used in making selection or promotion decisions.

There are practical issues that should be considered when using this approach for generating items. First, career history items often reflect things done to the individual and limited personal control may make it difficult to justify using such items. Second, items typically are generated to predict performance in a career field rather than performance on a particular job, so evidence will be needed to ensure job relevance. Attempts have been made to use these kinds of biodata items to predict vocational interests (Wilkinson, 1997). For example, Wilkinson (1997) found that biodata instruments with the following criteria in common would produce predictors of vocational interest equally well in men and women: (a) criterion is a unidimensional person-specific attribute, (b) attribute is measured objectively, (c) biodata items exclude job-specific items, and (d) developmental group is as diverse as possible.

Archival Item Generation

The three item-generation approaches described earlier require a substantial amount of time and energy to develop an adequate item pool. This has led many investigators to consider using previously developed, or archived, background data items. As such, this actually is an item selection, rather than an item development, strategy.

The archival approach begins with a literature review to identify existing background data items used to predict performance. This review focuses on studies in which background data items were used to predict performance in the target job, or in a similar job. Items are selected that yield high correlations with the criterion or are found to measure constructs that predict performance, or both.

When using an archival approach, it is important to remember that background data items developed for one population may not apply to other populations. Thus, items must be reviewed for a given population by a panel of psychologists familiar with that population. Inappropriate items should be eliminated or rewritten to increase relevance to the target population. Because substantial revisions may be required if archival items are used, revised items should be reviewed by a new panel of psychologists to ensure the appropriateness of item content. To the extent that item content is revised, it may be necessary to consider the impact of such revisions on item validity and internal consistency estimates. Examples of items that were developed for a civilian population and then edited to make them appropriate for a military population are shown in Table 8.6.

Item Response Formats

It is crucial that response formats be consistent with item content and the nature of the target population. Item response options using a 5-point ordinal scale (e.g., 1 = Strongly Disagree; 5 = Strongly Agree) are recommended for several reasons. First, items using such response options are more reliable than items using other

TABLE 8.6
Examples of Items Developed for a Civilian Population and Edited to Be Made Appropriate for a Military Population

Civilian	Military
How much have you enjoyed having a job that let you do things your own way?	How important has it been for you to have supervisors who would listen to your suggestions?
How important has it been for you to be friends with the people working for you?	How important has it been for you to know when subordinates are having personal problems?
How successful have you been persuading people to see things differently?	To what extent have you been able to avoid giving orders?

kinds of response options (Owens, 1976). Second, scoring items on an underlying continuum enables a wider range of analyses to be conducted. Third, although 400 subjects are sufficient for scaling and validating continuum-type items, larger sample sizes of up to 2,000 subjects are required when non-continuous items are used because each response option is treated as an item (Mumford & Owens, 1987).

Assembling a Questionnaire

After the items and item response options have been developed, one may assemble the background data questionnaire for pretesting. Typically, the questionnaire begins with a few verifiable, job-related items. This presentation strategy helps induce an honesty set and minimizes negative applicant reactions. After the first 10 to 15 items, however, items should be presented in random order. Use of random ordering is necessary because it is easier for people to guess at the scoring protocol if all items for a given construct are presented together. People can answer three or four background data items per minute; thus, questionnaires typically contain 300 to 400 items (Mumford et al., 1996). After all the data are collected from the pretest sample, item characteristics are assessed. Some items may require minor revision in wording to make them more understandable. If the revisions are substantial (i.e., likely to result in changed statistical characteristics), the items will need to be pretested again prior to operational use. Following is a description of methods for analyzing item characteristics and developing scales consisting of appropriate items.

HOW TO SCALE AND VALIDATE BACKGROUND ITEMS

The purpose of scaling is to identify items to be incorporated in the final version of a background data questionnaire because they measure the constructs of interest or they predict job performance, or both. Usually only one third of the items administered to a pretest sample are retained in the final version of a background data questionnaire. Four general strategies are commonly used for scaling background items: (a) empirical keying, (b) rational scaling, (c) factorial scaling, and (d) subgrouping (Mumford, 1999; Mumford & Owens, 1987). These strategies are described next. These four scaling methods were introduced in our earlier discussion of biodata issues that arise in the course of personnel selection.

Empirical Keying

Three methods frequently used for empirical keying of background data measures are the correlational method (Lecznar & Dailey, 1950), the differential regression method (Malone, 1978), and the weighted application blank (England, 1971). The first two methods are most appropriate when continuous response options (e.g., 5-point Likert scales, where 5 = Strongly Agree and 1 = Strongly Disagree) are used.

The correlational method involves using the magnitude and direction of the correlation between the item and the criterion to determine the item's weight. Item weights may be the actual correlation coefficients or unit weights, depending on the statistical significance of the item correlation (e.g., plus or minus 1 for $p < .05$; Stokes & Searcy, 1999). Techniques can also include phi coefficient and point-biserial correlation when using correlations between each item response option and a binomial criterion or continuous criterion as response option weights (Dean et al., 1999; Lefkowitz, Gebbia, Balsam, & Dunn, 1999). As a general rule of thumb, a minimum correlation of .10 to .15 has been suggested for inclusion of items on a scale (Mumford & Owens, 1987). The differential regression method uses least squares regression analysis to develop a model that maximizes explained criterion variance. Items are selected based on the increment in criterion variance accounted for over and above that which is explained by items already in the equation. It is important to note that variance maximizing procedures are likely to capitalize heavily on chance, making cross-validation (using weights from one sample to predict performance for a different sample, and vice versa) very important. The weighted application blank method involves weighting alternative response options on the basis of differences in option selection for different criterion groups. Criterion groups that are well differentiated are needed to produce differential weights and these groups need to be large enough to produce stable weights. There are several studies that suggest that unit weights produce scales with validities that are nearly equal to those produced with differential weights (Dawes, 1971). This approach has been shown to be useful for professional entry-level selection where the goal is to reduce a large number of applicants to a smaller, more manageable set (Harvey-Cook & Taffler, 2000).

In summary, the empirical keying approach requires that items be retained for the final version of the questionnaire based solely on their ability to predict performance on a criterion (Mumford & Owens, 1987). To develop empirical keys, scores of a criterion group (people who are good performers on the criterion) are compared to the scores of a reference group (population of job applicants). Mean differences (when items are scored on a continuum) or percent response differences (when response options are scored) are obtained reflecting the differences between these groups (Dean et al., 1999). Items are retained if they discriminate between criterion group and reference group members; items that fail to distinguish between these groups are eliminated. Retained items are weighted based on the magnitude of the differences observed between the groups (Hogan, 1994).

An empirical keying strategy maximizes the ability of background data items to predict performance on the criterion of interest. In addition, evidence suggests that empirical keys may be less sensitive to faking than other alternative scaling procedures (Russell & Kuhnert, 1992). However, empirical keys suffer from a number of limitations. As Wernimont (1962) and Lefkowitz et al. (1999) pointed out, empirical keys tend to be unstable, requiring cross-validation studies if one is to obtain an adequate estimate of their predictive validity (Schoenfeldt, 1999). Moreover, the reliability or construct validity of empirical keys is difficult to assess because of the heterogeneity of items. As a result, after deciding on an empirical key, researchers sometimes rationally calibrate the key to ensure interpretability of scoring weights (Mount et al., 2000).

The most important problem associated with empirical keys is that scaling is based on a single criterion measure. As a result, the empirical key can be no better than the criterion used to define performance. If the criterion measure is biased or contaminated, these deficiencies may also appear in the resulting background data measures (Mumford & Owens, 1987). Thus, whenever an empirical keying strategy is used to develop background data scales, evidence must be provided that the criterion measure is a valid, reliable, and unbiased measure of performance.

Rational Scaling

Rational scaling is another technique for scaling background data items. Using this approach, items are scaled according to the constructs the items are intended to measure. Scores on construct-oriented scales are then used to predict performance on various criteria of interest. Thus, constructs, rather than items, serve as predictors in the rational scaling approach.

One clear advantage of rational scaling is that the problems associated with poor criterion measures do not contaminate the background data items. Another advantage of this approach is that the scales can be used to predict performance of different criteria in different settings (Hough & Paullin, 1994; Wilkinson, 1997), assuming there is reason to believe that the constructs are relevant as indicated by a job analysis (Stokes & Cooper, 2001). The ability to generalize to different settings and criteria, however, is not the most important characteristic of rational scales. Rational scales preserve the substantive framework underlying initial item generation. As a result, rational scales allow a greater range of validation tests, particularly the kind of theoretically driven construct validation tests that provide the best evidence for the meaningfulness of the measures (Lawshe, 1985; Messick, 1995; Mumford et al., 1996). When background data measures are developed using this approach, they often provide a vehicle for theory development as well as serving as a selection tool (Mumford, Baughman, Uhlman, Costanza, & Threlfall, 1993; Mumford, Gessner, Connelly, O'Connor, & Clifton, 1993).

The procedures used to develop rational scales are straightforward (Mumford & Owens, 1987; Mumford & Stokes, 1992; Mumford, Uhlman, & Kilcullen, 1992). Initially, all items that measure a construct are identified and a total construct score is obtained by summing scores for each construct. Individual items are then correlated with total construct scores and the reliability of each scale is established by examining the internal consistency of the items included in the scale (Stokes & Cooper, 2001; Stokes & Searcy, 1999).

Variations of this procedure include assigning items to multiple scales if the initial hypothesis underlying item development suggests that the item is complex, in the sense that it marks multiple constructs and the resulting item-total correlations justify inclusion in multiple scales. Another variation of the approach, suggested by Mael (1991), Mumford et al. (1992), and Mumford and Owens (1982), involves examining item-criterion correlations as well as inter-item correlations when forming scales. This approach involves some elements of empirical keying and rational scaling, and is useful when there is some ambiguity about the way constructs manifest themselves in performance. However, problems with generalizability and construct measurement may arise if an adequate criterion is not available. Additionally, researchers have combined factor analysis with rational procedures to ensure that items factor together under the rational constructs (Allworth & Hesketh, 1999; Stokes et al., 1999). Factor analysis bolsters the rationale for the items used to measure a construct or scale in the biodata measure (Karas & West, 1999; Mumford, 1999).

Factorial Scaling

The approach used to develop factorial scales is similar to the approach used to develop rational scales inasmuch as items are retained to form construct scales based on observed correlations. In factor analytic scaling, however, items are not assumed to measure a particular construct. Instead, constructs are induced from the data using factor analysis to group items together that yield similar patterns of responses (Stokes & Searcy, 1999). Typically, items are retained if they yield correlations above .30 with a particular factor (Chait, Carraher, & Buckley, 2000). Factor scores are obtained by summing scores on the items assigned to a factor (Schoenfeldt, 1999).

Factor analysis is used when there is no theory about a set of constructs that provides the basis for scaling. This does not mean that one should factor analyze any collection of background data items. Items should be systematically developed and factoring should be used to articulate the kind of constructs accounting for item responses (Schoenfeldt & Mendoza, 1994). Factoring is most frequently used when a theory does not define the constructs of concern, as is often the case when the career history approach has been used to develop background data items (Mumford, Stokes, & Owens, 1990). An extended discussion of factor analysis, as applied to background data items, is beyond the scope of this chapter. Interested readers should consult Schoenfeldt and Mendoza (1994).

Subgrouping

The fourth major scaling technique used to develop background data measures is subgrouping (Owens, 1968, 1971; Owens & Schoenfeldt, 1979). Subgrouping is more closely related to empirical keying than to rational or factorial scaling. Like empirical keying, in which scaling is based on the identification of groups of people who are high performers, subgrouping strategies attempt to identify naturally occurring groups of people. Rather than defining groups based on performance on a particular criterion measure, groups are defined by clustering together people who have similar responses on a number of background data items. Subgrouping attempts to identify types of people who have similar life histories. Responses are scaled by assigning respondents to the group that is most similar to their pattern of item responses. Group membership—defined by the type of life history on the background data items—then provides the basis for making predictive statements about a person.

Subgrouping techniques are still in their initial stage of development and, with a few notable exceptions (e.g., Brush & Owens, 1979), are not commonly applied in performance prediction. Over the years, a systematic research program conducted by Owens and his colleagues (Mumford et al., 1990; Mumford & Owens, 1984; Mumford, Snell, & Reiter-Palmon, 1994; Owens & Schoenfeldt, 1979; Stokes, Mumford, & Owens, 1989) has provided some understanding of the nature of subgrouping. Subgroups appear to capture people's models of themselves and their world that guide their behavior in a variety of situations. Because subgroups appear to capture these broad organizing structures, they are more useful in predicting long-term outcomes and making classification or placement decisions than in predicting performance for a particular job (Gustafson & Mumford, 1995; Katzell, 1994). For the purpose of personnel selection, care must be taken that the subgrouping strategy does not result in different keys or clusters for protected groups. For legal reasons, different keys may be viewed as providing an advantage to subgroups, even if that is not the intention of background item developers.

SUMMARY

In this chapter, several issues concerning the development and scaling of background data items for predicting job performance have been discussed. However, little effort has been made to describe many other potential applications of background data measures. For example, we only briefly touched on the application of background data measures to the study of adult development (Gessner et al., 1993; Morrison, 1994), the classification and assessment of qualitative individual differences

(Gustafson & Mumford, 1995; Mumford, Snell, & Hein, 1993), selection of vocation (Wilkinson, 1997), and student college performance (Oswald et al., 2004).

There are several important conclusions about the development of background data measures, as related to personnel selection, that need to be emphasized. First, the development of background data items is a difficult and time-consuming task. One must have an understanding of adult development and its implications for appropriate item content, and items must be written in such a way that they permit accurate recall of past experiences. Furthermore, items must be appropriate for use in personnel selection (i.e., they cannot refer to issues regarding marital status or gender- and race-related issues). Item development also requires an understanding of the nature of the constructs of interest and the ways in which they influence people's behavior and experiences.

Second, item writers need to understand both the job, which requires a thorough job analysis, and the ways in which relevant constructs manifest themselves in people's lives. Scoring strategies and validation procedures must be carefully planned, taking into account both the nature of the items and the intended applications of the measure. Indeed, one should expect to devote substantial resources to item development as well as to scaling and validation efforts.

Third, gains in validity are only one reason for applying background data measures. The use of background data items inherently is a contextual assessment technique in which performance is examined in the context of the situations to which people have been exposed. As such, background data measures show less adverse impact than other types of measures.

Fourth, because of the contextual nature of biodata items, it is important to revalidate them every 5 to 7 years. Revalidation is essential because the life history characteristics of job applicants may change, resulting in the need for new kinds of background data items. In addition, scoring keys may be compromised, resulting in the need for new selection measures. In fact, whenever possible, it is desirable to develop two or three alternative forms of a background data inventory and carefully monitor changes in applicants' mean scores to ensure that the test has not been compromised.

As is the case with any assessment, the value of the resulting inferences about performance can be no better than the kinds of questions asked. This chapter has provided some initial guidelines for framing these questions and developing background data measures that can be used to predict performance in a number of different settings.

REFERENCES

Allworth, E., & Hesketh, B. (1999). Construct-oriented biodata: Capturing change-related and contextually relevant future performance. *International Journal of Selection and Assessment, 7,* 97–111.

Asher, E. J. (1972). The biographical item: Can it be improved? *Personnel Psychology, 25,* 251–264.

Atkinson, J. W., & Raynor, J. O. (1974). *Motivation and achievement.* Washington, DC: Winston.

Baehr, M. E., & Williams, G. B. (1967). Underlying dimensions of personal background data and their relationship to occupational classification. *Journal of Applied Psychology, 51,* 481–490.

Barsalou, L. W. (1988). The content and organization of autobiographical memories. In V. Reisser & E. Winograd (Eds.), *Remembering reconsidered: Ecological and traditional approaches to the study of memory* (pp. 143–243). Cambridge, England: Cambridge University Press.

Brown, S. H. (1994). Validating biodata. In G. S. Stokes, M. D. Mumford, & W. A. Owens (Eds.), *Biodata handbook: Theory, research and use of biographical information in selection and performance prediction* (pp. 199–236). Palo Alto, CA: Consulting Psychologists Press.

Brush, D. (1974). *Predicting major field of college concentration with biographical and vocational interest data: A longitudinal study.* Unpublished master's thesis, University of Georgia, Athens.

Brush, D. H., & Owens, W. A. (1979). Implementation and evaluation of an assessment and classification model for manpower utilization. *Personnel Psychology, 32,* 369–383.

Burisch, M. (1984). Approaches to personality inventory construction: A comparison of merits. *American Psychologist, 39,* 214–227.

Carlson, K. D., Scullen, S. E., Schmidt, F. L., Rothstein, H., & Erwin, F. (1999). Generalizable biographical data validity can be achieved without multi-organizational development and keying. *Personnel Psychology, 52,* 731–755.

Caspi, A. (1987). Personality in the life course. *Journal of Personality and Social Psychology, 53,* 1203–1213.

Chait, H. N., Carraher, S. M., & Buckley, M. R. (2000). Measuring service orientation with biodata. *Journal of Managerial Issues, 12,* 109–120.

Chaney, F. B. (1964). *The life history antecedents of selected vocational interests.* Unpublished doctoral dissertation, Purdue University, West Lafayette, IN.

Cleary, T. A. (1968). Test bias: Prediction of grades of Negro and White students in integrated colleges. *Journal of Educational Measurement, 5,* 155–124.

Clifton, T. C. (1994). *Background data and autobiographical memory: Effects of item types and task characteristics.* Unpublished doctoral dissertation, George Mason University, Fairfax, VA.

Clifton, T. C., Mumford, M. D., & Baughman, W. A. (1999). Background data and autobiographical memory: Effects of item types and task characteristics. *International Journal of Selection and Assessment, 7,* 57–71.

Conway, M. A. (1990). Associations between autobiographical memory and concepts. *Journal of Experimental Psychology: Learning, Memory, and Cognition, 16,* 749–812.

Costanza, D. P., & Mumford, M. D. (1993). *Prediction of state department assessment center performance using biodata dimension scales.* Fairfax, VA: Center for Behavioral and Cognitive Studies.

Dalessio, A. T., Crosby, M. M., & McManus, M. A. (1996). Stability of biodata keys and dimensions across English-speaking countries: A test of the cross-situational hypothesis. *Journal of Business and Psychology, 10,* 289–296.

Dawes, R. (1971). The robust beauty of improper linear models in decision making. *American Psychologist, 37,* 571–582.

Dean, M. A., Russell, C. J., & Muchinsky, P. M. (1999). Life experiences and performance prediction: Toward a theory of biodata. In G. R. Ferris (Ed.), *Research in human resources management* (Vol. 17, pp. 245–281). Elsevier Science.

Douthitt, S. S., Eby, L. T., & Simon, S. A. (1999). Diversity of life experiences: The development and validation of a biographical measure of receptiveness to dissimilar others. *International Journal of Selection and Assessment, 7,* 112–125.

DuBois, P. H., Loevinger, J., & Gieser, G. C. (1952). *The construction of homogeneous keys for a biographical inventory.* Lackland Air Force Base, TX: Air Force Human Resources Laboratory.

England, G. W. (1971). *Development and use of weighted application blanks* (Bulletin No. 55). Minneapolis: University of Minnesota, Industrial Relations Center.

Epstein, S., & O'Brien, E. J. (1985). The person-situation debate in historical and current perspective. *Psychological Bulletin, 48,* 513–537.

Ferguson, L. W. (1967). Economic maturity. *Personnel Journal, 46,* 22–26.

Fine, S. A., & Cronshaw, S. (1994). The role of job analysis in establishing the validity of biodata. In G. S. Stokes, M. D. Mumford, & W. A. Owens (Eds.), *Biodata handbook: Theory, research and use of biographical information in selection and performance prediction* (pp. 39–64). Palo Alto, CA: Consulting Psychologists Press.

Fuentes, R. R., Sawyer, J. E., & Greener, J. M. (1989, August). *Comparison of the predictive characteristics of three biodata scaling methods.* Paper presented at the annual meeting of the American Psychological Association, New Orleans, LA.

Gammie, E. (2000). The use of biodata in the pre-selection of fully-accredited graduates for chartered accountancy training places in Scotland. *Accounting and Business Research, 31,* 19–35.

Gandy, J. A., Dye, D. A., & McLane, D. N. (1994). Federal government selection: The Individual Achievement Record. In G. S. Stokes, M. D. Mumford, & W. A. Owens (Eds.), *Biodata handbook: Theory, research and use of biographical information in selection and performance prediction* (pp. 275–310). Palo Alto, CA: Consulting Psychologists Press.

Gandy, J. A., Outerbridge, A. N., Sharf, J. C., & Dye, D. A. (1990). *Development and initial validation of the Individual Achievement Record (IAR).* Washington, DC: U.S. Office of Personnel Management.

Gessner, T. E., O'Connor, J. A., Clifton, T. C., Connelly, M. S., & Mumford, M. D. (1993). The development of moral beliefs: A retrospective study. *Current Psychology, 12,* 236–254.

Gessner, T. E., O'Connor, J. A., Mumford, M. D., Clifton, T. C., & Smith, A. (1995). Situational variables influencing the propensity for destructive acts: Taxonomy development and validation. *Current Psychology, 13,* 303–325.

Ghiselli, E. E. (1973). The validity of aptitude tests in personnel selection. *Personnel Psychology, 26,* 461–477.

Goldberg, L. R. (1972). Parameters of personality inventory construction and utilization: A comparison of prediction strategies and tactics. *Multivariate Behavior Research Monographs, 72*(2).

Gonter, R. (1979). *Comparisons of blacks and whites on background data measures.* Athens, GA: Institute for Behavioral Research.

Guion, R. M. (1966). *Personnel selection.* New York: McGraw-Hill.

Gustafson, S. B., & Mumford, M. D. (1995). Personal style and person-environment fit: A pattern approach. *Journal of Vocational Behavior, 46,* 163–188.

Harvey-Cook, J. E., & Taffler, R. J. (2000). Biodata in professional entry-level selection: Statistical scoring of common format applications. *Journal of Occupational and Organizational Psychology, 73,* 103–118.

Hein, M., & Wesley, S. (1994). Scaling biodata through subgrouping. In G. S. Stokes, M. D. Mumford, & W. A. Owens (Eds.), *Biodata handbook: Theory, research and use of biographical information in selection and performance prediction* (pp. 171–198). Palo Alto, CA: Consulting Psychologists Press.

Henry, E. R. (1966). *Research conference on the use of autobiographical data as psychological predictors.* Greensboro, NC: Creativity Research Institute, Richardson Foundation.

Hogan, J. B. (1994). Empirical keying of background data measures. In G. S. Stokes, M. D. Mumford, & W. A. Owens (Eds.), *Biodata handbook: Theory, research and use of biographical information in selection and performance prediction* (pp. 69–108). Palo Alto, CA: Consulting Psychologists Press.

Hough, L. M. (1984). Development and evaluation of the "accomplishment record" method of selecting and promoting professionals. *Journal of Applied Psychology, 69,* 135–146.

Hough, L. M., & Oswald, F. L. (2000). Personnel selection: Looking toward the future—remembering the past. *Annual Review of Psychology, 51,* 631–664.

Hough, L. M., & Paullin, C. (1994). Construct-oriented scale construction: The rational approach. In G. S. Stokes, M. D. Mumford, & W. A. Owens (Eds.), *Biodata handbook: Theory, research and use of biographical information in selection and performance prediction* (pp. 109–146). Palo Alto, CA: Consulting Psychologists Press.

Hunter, J. E., & Hunter, R. F. (1984). Validity and utility of alternative predictors of job performance. *Psychological Bulletin, 96,* 72–98.

Karas, M., & West, J. (1999). Construct-oriented biodata development for selection to a differentiated performance domain. *International Journal of Selection and Assessment, 7,* 86–96.

Katzell, R. A. (1994). Contemporary meta-trends in industrial and organizational psychology. In H. C. Triandis, M. D. Dunnette, & L. M. Hough (Eds.), *Handbook of industrial and organizational psychology* (Vol. 4, pp. 1–89). Palo Alto, CA: Consulting Psychologists Press.

Keinan, G., Friedland, N., Yitzhaky, J., & Moran, A. (1981). Biographical, physiological, and personality variables as predictors of performance under sickness inducing motion. *Journal of Applied Psychology, 66,* 233–241.

Kilcullen, R. N., White, L., Mumford, J. D., & Mack, H. (1995). Assessing the construct validity of rational biodata scales. *Military Psychology, 7,* 17–28.

Klein, S. P., & Owens, W. A. (1965). Faking of a scored life history blank as a function of criterion objectivity. *Journal of Applied Psychology, 49,* 452–454.

Kluger, A. N., & Colella, A. (1993). Beyond the mean bias: The effect of warning against faking on biodata item variances. *Personnel Psychology, 46,* 763–780.

Kolodner, J. L. (1984). *Retrieval and organizational strategies in conceptual memory.* Hillsdale, NJ: Lawrence Erlbaum Associates.

Koriat, A., Goldsmith, M., & Pansky, A. (2000). Toward a psychology of memory accuracy. *Annual Review of Psychology, 51,* 481–537.

Lautenschlager, G. J. (1994). Accuracy and faking of background data. In G. S. Stokes, M. D. Mumford, & W. A. Owens (Eds.), *Biodata handbook: Theory, research and use of biographical information in selection and performance prediction* (pp. 341–420). Palo Alto, CA: Consulting Psychologists Press.

Lawshe, C. H. (1985). Inference from personnel tests and their validity. *Journal of Applied Psychology, 70,* 237–238.

Lecznar, W. B., & Dailey, J. T. (1950). Keying biographical inventories in classification test batteries. *American Psychologist, 5,* 279.

Lefkowitz, J., Gebbia, M. I., Balsam, T., & Dunn, L. (1999). Dimensions of biodata items and their relationships to item validity. *Journal of Occupational and Organizational Psychology, 72,* 331–350.

Lerner, R. M., & Tubman, J. G. (1989). Conceptual issues in studying continuity and discontinuity in personality development across life. *Journal of Personality, 57,* 343–374.

Ligon, G. S. (2004). *Development of outstanding leadership: A life narrative approach.* Unpublished doctoral dissertation, University of Oklahoma, Norman.

Mael, F. A. (1991). A conceptual rationale for the domain and attributes of biodata items. *Personnel Psychology, 44,* 763–792.

Mael, F. A., Connerley, M., & Morath, R. A. (1996). None of your business: Parameters of biodata invasiveness. *Personnel Psychology, 49,* 613–650.

Mael, F. A., & Hirsch, A. C. (1993). Rainforest empiricism and quasi-rationality: Two approaches to objective biodata. *Personnel Psychology, 46,* 719–738.

Magnusson, D. (1988). Individual development from an interactional perspective. In D. Magnusson (Ed.), *Paths through life* (pp. 1–18). Hillsdale, NJ: Lawrence Erlbaum Associates.

Malone, M. P. (1978). *Predictive efficiency and discriminatory impact of verifiable biographical data as a function of data analysis procedure.* Unpublished doctoral dissertation, University of Minnesota, Minneapolis.

McAdams, D. P. (2001). The psychology of life stories. *Review of General Psychology, 5,* 100–122.

McClelland, D. C. (1975). *Power: The inner experience.* New York: Irvington.

McCrae, R. R., & Costa, P. T. (1988). Recalled parent-child relations and adult personality. *Journal of Personality, 56,* 417–433.

McManus, M. A., & Mitchell, T. W. (1987). *Test and retest reliability of the Career Profile.* Hartford, CT: Life Insurance Marketing and Research Association.

Messick, S. (1995). Validity of psychological assessment: Validation of inferences from persons' responses and performance as scientific inquiry into score meaning. *American Psychologist, 50,* 741–744.

Mitchell, T. W. (1994). The utility of biodata. In G. S. Stokes, M. D. Mumford, & W. A. Owens (Eds.), *Biodata handbook: Theory, research and use of biographical information in selection and performance prediction* (pp. 485–516). Palo Alto, CA: Consulting Psychologists Press.

Mitchell, T. W., & Klimoski, R. J. (1982). Estimating the validity of cross-validity estimation. *Journal of Applied Psychology, 71,* 311–317.

Morrison, R. F. (1994). Biodata applications in career development research and practice. In G. S. Stokes, M. D. Mumford, & W. A. Owens (Eds.), *Biodata handbook: Theory, research and use of biographical information in selection and performance prediction* (pp. 451–484). Palo Alto, CA: Consulting Psychologists Press.

Mount, M. K., Witt, L. A., & Barrick, M. R. (2000). Incremental validity of empirically keyed biodata scales over GMA and the five factor personality constructs. *Personnel Psychology, 53,* 299–323.

Mumford, M. D. (1994). *Report on the 1993 foreign service exam: The stability of background data measures.* Fairfax, VA: Author.

Mumford, M. D. (1999). Construct validity and background data: Issues, abuses, and future directions. *Human Resource Management Review, 9,* 117–145.

Mumford, M. D., Baughman, W. A., Threlfall, K. V., Costanza, D. P., & Uhlman, C. E. (1993). Personality, adaptability and performance: Performance on well-defined and ill-defined problem solving tasks. *Human Performance, 5,* 241–285.

Mumford, M. D., Baughman, W. A., Uhlman, C. E., Costanza, D. P., & Threlfall, K. V. (1993). Personality variables and skill acquisition: Performance at different stages of practice on a complex task. *Human Performance, 6,* 345–381.

Mumford, M. D., Connelly, M. S., Helton, W. B., Strange, J. M., & Osburn, H. K. (2001). On the construct validity of integrity tests: Individual and situational factors as predictors of test performance. *International Journal of Selection and Assessment, 9,* 240–257.

Mumford, M. D., Connelly, M. S., Scott, G. M., Espejo, J., Sohl, L. M., Hunter, S. T., et al. (2005). Career experiences and scientific performance: A study of social, physical, life, and health sciences. *Creativity Research Journal, 17,* 105–129.

Mumford, M. D., Costanza, D. P., Connelly, M. S., & Johnson, F. (1996). Item generation procedures and background data scales: Implications for construct and criterion-related validity. *Personnel Psychology, 49,* 361–398.

Mumford, M. D., Gessner, T. E., Connelly, M. S., O'Connor, A., & Clifton, T. C. (1993). Leadership and destructive acts: Individual and situational influences. *Leadership Quarterly, 4,* 115–148.

Mumford, M. D., O'Connor, J. A., Clifton, T. C., Connelly, M. S., & Zaccaro, S. (1993). Background data constructs as predictors of leadership behavior. *Human Performance, 5,* 241–285.

Mumford, M. D., & Owens, W. A. (1982). Life history and vocational interests. *Journal of Vocational Behavior, 21,* 330–348.

Mumford, M. D., & Owens, W. A. (1984). Individuality in a developmental context: Some empirical and theoretical considerations. *Human Development, 27,* 84–108.

Mumford, M. D., & Owens, W. A. (1987). Methodology review: Principles, procedures, and findings in the application of background data measures. *Applied Psychological Measurement, 11,* 1–31.

Mumford, M. D., Reiter-Palmon, R., & Snell, A. M. (1994). Background data and development: Structural issues in the application of life history measures. In G. S. Stokes, M. D. Mumford, & W. A. Owens (Eds.), *Biodata handbook: Theory, research and use of biographical information in selection and performance prediction* (pp. 555–584). Palo Alto, CA: Consulting Psychologists Press.

Mumford, M. D., Shaffer, G. S., Jackson, K. E., Neiner, A., Denning, D., & Owens, W. A. (1983). *Male-female differences in the structure of background data measures.* Athens, GA: Institute for Behavioral Research.

Mumford, M. D., Snell, A. N., & Hein, M. A. (1993). Varieties of religious experience: Continuity and change in religious involvement. *Journal of Personality, 61,* 69–88.

Mumford, M. D., Snell, R. M., & Reiter-Palmon, R. (1994). Personality and background data: Life history and self-concepts in an ecological system. In G. S. Stokes, M. D. Mumford, & W. A. Owens (Eds.), *Biodata handbook: Theory, research and use of biographical informational in selection and performance prediction* (pp. 553–625). Palo Alto, CA: Consulting Psychologists Press.

Mumford, M. D., & Stokes, G. S. (1992). Developmental determinants of individual action: Theory and practice in applying background data measures. In M. D. Dunnette & L. E. Hough (Eds.), *Handbook of industrial and organizational psychology* (Vol. 3, pp. 62–138). Palo Alto, CA: Consulting Psychologists Press.

Mumford, M. D., Stokes, G. S., & Owens, W. A. (1990). *Patterns of life adaptation: The ecology of human individuality.* Hillsdale, NJ: Lawrence Erlbaum Associates.

Mumford, M. D., Uhlman, C. E., & Kilcullen, R. N. (1992). The structure of life history: Implications for the construct validity of background data scales. *Human Performance, 5,* 104–137.

Nickels, B. J. (1994). The nature of biodata. In G. S. Stokes, M. D. Mumford, & W. A. Owens (Eds.), *Biodata handbook: Theory, research and use of biographical information in selection and performance prediction* (pp. 1–16). Palo Alto, CA: Consulting Psychologists Press.

Norman, W. T. (1963). Personality measurement, faking and detection: An assessment of a method for use in personnel selection. *Journal of Applied Psychology, 47,* 317–324.

Odegard, T., Lampinen, J. M., & Wirth-Beaumont, E. T. (2004). Organization and retrieval: The generation of event clusters. *Memory, 12,* 685–695.

Oswald, F. L., Schmitt, N., Kim, B. H., Ramsay, L. J., & Gillespie, M. A. (2004). Developing a biodata measure and situational judgment inventory as predictors of college student performance. *Journal of Applied Psychology, 89,* 187–207.

Owens, W. A. (1968). Toward one discipline of scientific psychology. *American Psychologist, 23,* 782–785.

Owens, W. A. (1971). A quasi actuarial basis of individual assessment. *American Psychologist, 26*, 992–999.

Owens, W. A. (1976). Background data. In M. D. Dunnette (Ed.), *Handbook of industrial and organizational psychology* (pp. 609–643). Chicago: Rand McNally.

Owens, W. A., & Schoenfeldt, L. F. (1979). Toward a classification of persons. *Journal of Applied Psychology, 64*, 569–607.

Pannone, R. D. (1984). Predicting test performance: A content valid approach to screening applicants. *Personnel Psychology, 37*, 507–514.

Pulakos, E. D., & Schmitt, N. (1996). An evaluation of two strategies for reducing adverse impact and their effects on criterion-related validity. *Human Performance, 9*, 241–258.

Reilly, R. A., & Chao, G. T. (1982). Validity and fairness of some alternative employee selection procedures. *Personnel Psychology, 35*, 1–62.

Reiser, B. J., Black, J. B., & Abelson, R. P. (1985). Knowledge structures in the retrieval and organization of autobiographical memories. *Cognitive Psychology, 17*, 89–137.

Reiter-Palmon, R. (1996, October). *Background data revisited: The stability of Owens*. Paper presented at the first annual Biodata Conference, Athens, GA.

Revo, B. (1976). Using biographical information to predict the success of men and women in the Army. *Journal of Applied Psychology, 61*, 106–118.

Roberts, K. V., Block, J., & Block, J. E. (1978). Relationship between personality and life history. *Journal of Personality, 46*, 223–242.

Robertson, I. T., & Smith, M. (2001). Personnel selection. *Journal of Occupational and Organizational Psychology, 74*, 441–472.

Robinson, J. A., & Swanson, L. (1990). Autobiographical memory: The next phase. *Applied Cognitive Psychology, 4*, 321–335.

Rothstein, H. R., Schmidt, F. L., Erwin, F. W., Owens, W. A., & Sparks, C. P. (1990). Biographical data in employee selection: Can validities be made more generalizable? *Journal of Applied Psychology, 75*, 175–184.

Russell, C. J., & Domm, D. R. (1990, April). *On the construct validity of biographical information: Evaluation of a theory-based measure of item generation*. Paper presented at the annual meeting of the Society for Industrial and Organizational Psychology, Inc., Miami Beach, FL.

Russell, C. J., & Kuhnert, K. W. (1992). New frontiers in management selection systems: Where measurement technologies and theory collide. *Leadership Quarterly, 3*, 109–135.

Russell, C. J., Mattson, J., Devlin, S. E., & Atwater, D. (1990). Predictive validity of biodata items generated from retrospective life experience essays. *Journal of Applied Psychology, 75*, 569–580.

Schaefer, C. E., & Anastasi, A. (1969). A biographical inventory for identifying creativity in adolescent boys. *Journal of Applied Psychology, 52*, 42–48.

Schmidt, F. L., Caplan, J. R., Bemis, S. E., Decuir, R., Dunn, C., & Antone, L. (1979). *The behavioral consistency method for unassembled examining*. Washington, DC: U.S. Office of Personnel Management.

Schmidt, F. L., & Hunter, J. E. (1998). The validity and utility of selection methods in personnel psychology: Practical and theoretical implications of 85 years of research findings. *Psychological Bulletin, 124*, 262–274.

Schmidt, F. L., & Rothstein, H. R. (1994). Application of validity generalization to biodata scales in employment selection. In G. S. Stokes, M. D. Mumford, & W. A. Owens (Eds.), *Biodata handbook: Theory, research and use of biographical information in selection and performance prediction* (pp. 237–260). Palo Alto, CA: Consulting Psychologists Press.

Schmitt, N., & Kunce, C. (2002). The effects of required elaboration of answers to biodata questions. *Personnel Psychology, 55*, 569–587.

Schmitt, N., Oswald, F. L., Kim, B. H., Gillespie, M. A., Ramsey, L. J., & Yoo, T. Y. (2003). Impact of elaboration on socially desirable responding and the validity of biodata measures. *Journal of Applied Psychology, 88,* 979–988.

Schmitt, N., & Pulakos, E. D. (1998). Biodata and differential prediction: Some reservations. In M. D. Hakel (Ed.), *Beyond multiple choice: Evaluating alternatives to traditional testing for selection* (pp. 167–182). Mahwah, NJ: Lawrence Erlbaum Associates.

Schoenfeldt, L. F. (1999). From dust bowl empiricism to rational constructs in biographical data. *Human Resource Management Review, 9,* 147–167.

Schoenfeldt, L. F., & Mendoza, G. C. (1994). Developing and using factorially derived biographical scales. In G. S. Stokes, M. D. Mumford, & W. A. Owens (Eds.), *Biodata handbook: Theory, research and use of biographical information in selection and performance prediction* (pp. 147–170). Palo Alto, CA: Consulting Psychologists Press.

Schooler, C. (1990). Psychological effects of complex environments during the life span: A review and theory. *Intelligence, 8,* 254–281.

Schuh, A. L. (1967). The predictability of employee tenure: A review of the literature. *Personnel Psychology, 20,* 133–152.

Shaffer, G. S., Saunders, V., & Owens, W. A. (1986). Additional evidence for the accuracy of biographical information: Long-term retest and observation ratings. *Personnel Psychology, 39,* 791–809.

Shermis, M. D., Falkenberg, B., Appel, V. A., & Cole, R. W. (1996). Construction of a faking detector scale for a biodata survey instrument. *Military Psychology, 8,* 83–94.

Stokes, G. S., & Cooper, L. A. (2001). Content/construct approaches in life history form development for selection. *International Journal of Selection and Assessment, 9,* 138–151.

Stokes, G. S., Mumford, M. D., & Owens, W. A. (1989). Life history prototypes in the study of human individuality. *Journal of Personality, 57,* 509–545.

Stokes, G. S., & Searcy, C. A. (1999). Specification of scales in biodata form development: Rational vs. empirical and global vs. specific. *International Journal of Selection and Assessment, 7,* 72–85.

Stokes, G. S., Toth, C. S., Searcy, C. A., Stroupe, J. P., & Carter, G. W. (1999). Construct/rational biodata dimensions to predict salesperson performance: Report on the U.S. Department of Labor sales study. *Human Resource Management Review, 9,* 185–219.

Stone, D. L., Stone-Romero, E. F., & Eddy, E. (1995, April). *Factors that influence the perceived invasiveness of biographical data.* Paper presented at the annual conference of the Society for Industrial and Organizational Psychology, Inc., Orlando, FL.

Stricker, L. J. (1989). *Assessing leadership potential at the Naval Academy with a biographical measure* (Research Report No. RR 89-14). Princeton, NJ: Educational Testing Service.

Strickler, L. J., & Rock, D. (1998). Assessing leadership potential with a biographical measure of personality traits. *International Journal of Selection and Assessment, 6,* 164–184.

Van Iddekinge, C. H., Eidson, C. E., Kudisch, J. D., & Goldblatt, A. M. (2003). A biodata inventory administered via interactive voice response (IVR) technology: Predictive validity, utility, and subgroup differences. *Journal of Business and Psychology, 18,* 145–156.

Wernimont, P. F. (1962). Reevaluation of a weighted application blank for office personnel. *Journal of Applied Psychology, 46,* 417–419.

West, J., & Karas, M. (1999). Biodata: Meeting clients' needs for a better way of recruiting entry-level staff. *International Journal of Selection and Assessment, 7,* 126–131.

Wilkinson, L. J. (1997). Generalizable biodata? An application to the vocational interests of managers. *Journal of Occupational and Organizational Psychology, 70,* 49–61.

CHAPTER NINE

Situational Judgment Tests

Michael A. McDaniel
Virginia Commonwealth University and Work Skills First, Inc

Deborah L. Whetzel
United States Postal Service

OVERVIEW

Situational judgment tests present applicants with scenarios that they might encounter on the job and ask applicants to evaluate various actions that might be taken in response to the situations. Thus, situational judgment tests are one type of job simulation that measures job knowledge. They rely on the principle that a person's behavior in past situations can predict how that individual is likely to behave in similar situations in the future. This means that one way to predict how effectively job applicants will perform on the job when they become employees is to measure how effectively they perform in a simulation of the job when they are applicants. People vary in the extent to which they acquire job knowledge from a series of events, and situational judgment tests are a method of assessing such differences.

Some job simulations are more realistic than others. For example, applicants for airplane pilot positions might be placed in a flight simulator that provides a very realistic reproduction of flying an airplane. Although such realistic simulations might be expected to have an advantage in their predictive potential, they can be so expensive to develop and administer that less realistic simulations often are an attractive alternative. Jobs for which high-fidelity simulations (e.g., flight simulators) are used to predict performance typically require some level of job experience. One advantage of low-fidelity simulations, such as situational judgment tests, is that they can be developed to predict performance in entry-level jobs in which no experience is required as well as in higher level jobs.

This chapter describes situational judgment tests in some detail and provides a brief history of their use. It then describes the characteristics along which situational judgment tests can vary, including test fidelity, cognitive complexity, and response instructions. The chapter then summarizes research evidence about their reliability, validity, and subgroup differences. Finally, the chapter describes procedures for developing situational judgment tests based on research findings.

WHAT IS A SITUATIONAL JUDGMENT TEST?

In a situational judgment item, a scenario is described and the applicant is required to evaluate several possible responses to the scenario. As mentioned earlier, situational judgment tests vary in their level of fidelity to the job. Typically, for entry-level selection (e.g., to an electrician apprenticeship training program), a situational judgment test might refer to general situations that might be encountered by employees. Such items might describe a problem with a boss or coworker. For higher level positions (e.g., promotion to journeyman), a situational judgment test might refer to circumstances that closely reflect issues or problems encountered in a specific job. An example of a situational judgment test item that might be used for promotion is shown here:

> You and another journeyman electrician from another crew are jointly responsible for coordinating a project involving both crews. This other person is not carrying out his share of the responsibilities. You would ...

1. Discuss the situation with your foreman and ask him to take it up with the other person's foreman.
2. Remind him that you need his help and that the project will not be completed effectively without a full team effort from both of you.
3. Tell him that he is not doing his share of the work, that you will not do it all yourself, and that if he does not start doing more, you will be forced to take the matter to his foreman.
4. Try to find out why he is not doing his share and explain to him that this creates more work for you and makes it harder to finish the project.
5. Get someone else from his crew to help with the project.

Motowidlo, Dunnette, and Carter (1990) used the term *low-fidelity simulation* to describe such an item. Sternberg et al. (2000) developed similar items and called them assessments of "practical intelligence." However, within the areas of human resource management and industrial psychology, these items typically are now referred to as "situational judgment."

Several situational judgment tests have been developed to predict job performance in managerial and supervisory positions (e.g., Bruce & Learner, 1958; Campbell, Dunnette, Lawler, & Weick, 1970; Corts, 1980; Mandell, 1950; Motowidlo et al., 1990; Wagner & Sternberg, 1991). They have also been developed to predict insurance agent turnover (Dalessio, 1992), success in engineer positions (Clevenger, Jockin, Morris, & Anselmi, 1999), performance in teams (Stevens &

Campion, 1999), success in telephone sales and collection positions (Phillips, 1992, 1993), and skill in managing conflict (Olson-Buchanan, Drasgow, Moberg, Mead, & Keenan, 1994). Thus, situational judgment tests are quite flexible and can be developed to predict performance in a variety of jobs.

A BRIEF HISTORY OF SITUATIONAL JUDGMENT TESTS

As noted by Weekley and Ployhart (2006), the earliest example of situational judgment tests depends on how they are defined. For example, a U.S. civil service exam used in 1873 for the Examiner of Trade-Marks, Patent Office contained the following: "A banking company asks protection for a certain device, as a trademark, which they propose to put upon their notes. What action would you take on the application?" (DuBois, 1970, p. 148). The 1905 Binet scale used to measure intelligence in children included questions such as, "When a person has offended you, and comes to offer his apologies, what should you do?" Although situations were presented, these early efforts did not include possible ways of handling the situation that were presented to the applicant.

As noted by McDaniel, Morgeson, Finnegan, Campion, and Braverman (2001), the first widely used situational judgment test that contained response options was likely the George Washington Social Intelligence Test. One of the subtests, called Judgment in Social Situations, required "keen judgment, and a deep appreciation of human motives, to answer correctly" (Moss, 1926, p. 26). Several solutions to each situation were offered in a multiple-choice format, only one of which was correct. In an early review of empirical studies, Thorndike and Stein (1937) criticized the test, claiming that correlations between the test and other tests of presumed social attributes were very low.

During World War II, Army psychologists attempted to assess the judgment of soldiers (Northrop, 1989). These judgment tests were comprised of scenarios and a number of alternative responses to each scenario. Solutions were based on the person's ability to use common sense, experience, and general knowledge, rather than logical reasoning. Starting in the 1940s, a number of situational judgment tests were developed to measure supervisory potential. These included the Practical Judgment Test (Cardall, 1942), How Supervise? (File, 1945; File & Remmers, 1948), Supervisory Practices Test (Bruce & Learner, 1958), Business Judgment Test (Bruce, 1965), Supervisory Judgment Test (Greenberg, 1963), and the Supervisory Inventory on Human Relations (Kirkpatrick & Planty, 1960). In the late 1950's and early 1960's situational judgment tests were also used by large organizations as part of selection test batteries to predict managerial success. For example, the Standard Oil Company of New Jersey designed a program of research called the Early Identification of Management Potential to identify employees who have potential to be successful in management (Campbell, Dunnette, Lawler, & Weick, 1970).

Recently, there has been renewed interest in the use of situational judgment measures for predicting job performance. For example, the United States Office of Personnel Management designed Test 905 to assess the human relations capacity and potential of applicants for promotion to first-line federal trades and labor supervisory positions (Corts, 1980). Motowidlo et al. (1990) examined the use of a situational judgment test, referred to as a low-fidelity simulation, for selecting entry-level managers. In validation studies with samples of managers from seven different companies, correlations between the test and various job performance criteria ranged from the .20s to the .40s. Wagner and Sternberg (1991) published a test called the Tacit Knowledge Inventory for Managers (TKIM). This measure is based on their theory of tacit knowledge, or "… practical know-how that usually is not openly expressed or stated and which must be acquired in the absence of direct instruction" (Wagner, 1987, p. 1236). The TKIM presents scenarios that require respondents to choose a course of action from a list of alternatives. These scenarios differ from those of previously mentioned tests in that the TKIM scenarios are considerably longer and more detailed. Wagner and Sternberg (1991) reported five studies examining the criterion-related validity of tacit knowledge measures in academic and business settings, although no validity was presented for the TKIM itself. They found moderate correlations between their measure and a variety of criteria, some of which would be considered job performance measures. Sternberg et al. (1995) also reported that these measures were unrelated to measures of general cognitive ability. This conclusion should be tempered by the fact that their samples (e.g., Yale undergraduate students) are likely to have substantial range restriction on measures of general cognitive ability, thus reducing observed relationships on the restricted predictor.

Finally, in investigating a situational judgment test, Smith and McDaniel (1998) found the largest correlates were with age and length of job experience. From this, they inferred that the test measured job-related knowledge and skills gained through life and work experiences. The test also correlated with the personality dimensions of conscientiousness ($r = .32$) and emotional stability ($r = .22$) as well as with measures of general cognitive ability (mean $r = .22$). Smith and McDaniel concluded that the situational judgment test assessed multiple job-related constructs.

THE STRUCTURE AND FORMAT OF SITUATIONAL JUDGMENT TESTS

Situational judgment items vary with respect to several characteristics (McDaniel & Nguyen, 2001; McDaniel, Whetzel, Hartman, Nguyen, & Grubb, 2006). Knowledge of the various situational judgment test formats can assist situational judgment test developers in making informed decisions. Also, some of the characteristics of situational judgment tests have implications for test validity and the degree of mean subgroup differences in test scores. Here, some of the major characteristics along which situational judgment tests vary are reviewed. These include test fidelity, cognitive complexity, and response instructions.

Test Fidelity

Test fidelity refers to the extent to which the test format mirrors how a situation would be encountered in a work setting. A higher fidelity situational judgment test may involve presenting situations using a short video, whereas a lower fidelity situational judgment test involves presenting situations in a written format (paper-and-pencil or computer presentation of text). Also, there are levels of fidelity within types of presentation. A situational judgment test with a written format might have more fidelity if the situation were described using technical terms common to the job. A situational judgment test with a video format might have less fidelity to the extent the item situation differs from aspects of the actual work situation. For example, if the work procedures shown in the video are not the most current procedures, then the situational judgment test may have less fidelity. This can happen when work procedures change over time but the video-based situational judgment test is not updated.

Video-based situational judgment tests are likely to reduce the reading and other cognitive demands relative to paper-and-pencil situational judgment tests. Consequently, video-based situational judgment tests typically produce lower correlations with cognitive ability, as well as smaller mean ethnic differences, when compared to paper-and-pencil situational judgment tests (Chan & Schmitt, 2002; Whetzel, McDaniel, & Nguyen, 2005). Although the smaller mean ethnic differences in video situational judgment tests are an advantage, the reduced correlations of such tests with cognitive ability may result in lower validities. Additional research is needed to evaluate this possibility.

Cognitive Complexity

Situational judgment items vary in their *cognitive complexity*. Cognitively complex items require more cognitive resources to understand than less cognitively complex items. One factor likely to influence the cognitive complexity of the items is the length of the stem. Some situational judgment test items have very short stems (e.g., "You have encountered a problem that you cannot solve and you cannot locate your supervisor to help you with the problem"). Other situational judgment test stems are much longer, such as those in the TKIM (Wagner & Sternberg, 1991) mentioned earlier. Longer item stems likely increase cognitive complexity in part through increased demands on reading comprehension. Thus, items with longer item stems tend to be more difficult to comprehend than items with shorter stems.

A second factor that is likely to influence the cognitive complexity of the items is the complexity of the situation presented. Consider this sample stem again: "You have encountered a problem that you cannot solve and you cannot locate your supervisor to help you with the problem." This stem describes a relatively low-complexity situation with obvious potential responses. For example, the employee could seek assistance from a different supervisor or a knowledgeable coworker, or the employee could gain knowledge of the assignment from reading. In contrast, an example of a high-complexity stem would be: "You are supervised by two electricians who are not getting along. The electricians give you conflicting instructions and each demands that the work each assigns be given the highest priority." This stem describes a more complex situation in which the potential responses also may be complex.

	One scoreable response	Two scoreable responses	As many scoreable responses as response options
Behavioral Tendency	What would you most likely do?	What would you most likely do? What would you least likely do?	Rate each response for the likelihood you would perform the response. Rank the responses from the most likely to the least likely.
Knowledge	Pick the best answer.What should you do?	Pick the best answer and pick the worst answer. Pick the best and second best.	Rate each response for effectiveness. Rank the responses from the best to the worst.

FIGURE 9.1   Taxamony of response instructions in situational judgement tests.

One can assess the cognitive complexity of a situational judgment test item by correlating that item with a cognitive ability test (McDaniel & Nguyen, 2001). This correlation might be based on data obtained from a pilot test or from operational use of the test. The cognitive complexity of a test has implications for mean racial differences and test validity. Given the large mean ethnic differences in cognitive ability (Roth, BeVier, Bobko, Switzer, & Tyler, 2001), a more cognitively complex test item is likely to increase the item's mean ethnic group differences. Because cognitive ability is one of the best predictors of job performance (Schmidt & Hunter, 1998), one might expect cognitively complex situational judgment tests to yield higher validities than less cognitively complex situational judgment tests. The implications of cognitive complexity for validity and subgroup differences as well as test development are discussed later in this chapter.

Response Instructions

There are many types of response instructions that can be used with a situational judgment test. McDaniel, Whetzel, and Nguyen (2006) offered a two-dimensional table of response instructions (see Fig. 9.1). The rows of the table are labeled "Behavioral Tendency" and "Knowledge." In a situational judgment test with behavioral tendency instructions, applicants are asked to report how they would typically behave in response to the situation. A situational judgment test with knowledge instructions asks applicants to evaluate the effectiveness of responses. The second dimension, defining the three columns of the table, lists the number of scoreable responses that can be obtained from the item. Some response instructions (e.g., "Pick the best answer") generate one scoreable response per item. Other response instructions yield two dichotomous responses per item (e.g., "Pick the best answer and pick the worst answer"). Still other response instructions yield as many scoreable responses as there are response options (e.g., "Rate each response for effectiveness").

Response instructions have been shown to influence the construct as well as the criterion-related validity of situational judgment tests. Due to their influence on construct validity (i.e., the extent to which the tests are correlated with g), response instructions also affect subgroup differences. The implications of response instructions for validity and subgroup differences as well as test development are discussed later in this chapter.

WHAT DO SITUATIONAL JUDGMENT TESTS MEASURE?

Situational judgment tests are best viewed as measurement methods. Some situational judgment tests might emphasize technical knowledge whereas others might emphasize knowledge of how to work as part of a team. Although situational judgment tests might be developed to measure specific personality or ability variables, their unique format (presenting a hypothetical work situation and eliciting a hypothetical response to that situation) lends itself especially well to measuring various forms of job knowledge. As mentioned, the predictive principle behind all simulations, including situational judgment tests, is that people's behavior in the past can predict how they will behave in similar situations in the future.

One reason that people behave somewhat consistently in similar situations is that through experience they develop beliefs or knowledge about the best thing to do in certain situations in order to achieve desired results. Some people have better opportunities to have these experiences and some people are better able to take advantage of their experiences and learn from them. As a result, people who have acquired this situational knowledge over time should know better how to deal with certain situations and should be consistently more effective in those situations than people who, for whatever reason, have not acquired that knowledge.

In their book, *Practical Intelligence in Everyday Life*, Sternberg et al. (2000) asserted that there is a general factor of practical or tacit intelligence that is substantively distinct from general cognitive ability. The items used in Sternberg et al.'s "practical intelligence" tests are situational judgment items. Thus, rather than measuring some unique and previously unknown construct using a relatively novel measurement tool, Sternberg et al. were actually using situational judgment tests. Reviews by Gottfredson (2003), McDaniel and Whetzel (2005), and Ree and Earles (1993) noted that there is no support for a construct of practical intelligence. The practical intelligence construct also is critiqued in chapter 5.

There are several methods for empirically identifying constructs measured by a selection instrument. One involves correlating scores on one instrument with scores on another. McDaniel, Hartman, and Grubb (2003) correlated situational judgment test scores with scores on cognitive ability and scores on the Big 5 personality dimensions (Digman, 1990; Goldberg, 1993; John, 1990). In general, the results showed that situational judgment tests are correlated with measures of cognitive ability and personality.

TABLE 9.1
An Example of the Multidimensionality of Situational Judgment Test Items (Scenario A)

Scenario A

You assigned a very high profile project to one of your project managers. During each of the project update meetings, your project manager indicates that everything is going as scheduled. Now, one week before the project is due, your project manager informs you that the project is less than 50% complete.

		Correlation with:	
Responses:	g (n = 448–450)	Conscientiousness (n = 1196–1222)	Agreeableness (n = 1196–1222)
Personally take over the project and meet with the customer to determine critical requirements.	.10*	.01	-.13*
Meet with the customer to extend the deadline. Talk with the project manager about how the lack of communication has jeopardized the company's relationship with the customer.	.11*	-.03	-.05
Fire the project manager and take over the project yourself.	.08	.00	-.16*
Coach the project manager on how to handle the project more efficiently.	-.17*	.01	.09
Do not assign any high profile jobs to this project manager in the future.	.13*	.07	-.08

* indicates statistically significant correlations.

TABLE 9.2

An Example of the Multidimensionality of Situational Judgment Test Items (Scenario B)

Scenario B

You lead a project that requires specific, accurate data to make decisions. The data-capturing method currently being used does not provide you with the information you need. Another department promised to provide you with the information, but failed to do so at the last minute. This setback delayed your project and you are certain that you will require the information to complete your project accurately.

Responses:	g (n = 448–450)	Correlation with:	
		Conscientiousness (n = 1196–1222)	Agreeableness (n = 1196–1222)
Do the time-consuming work yourself even though it is not tecnically your responsibility.	.07	.11*	-.08*
Temporarily allocate some member of your team to capture the data.	-.01	.11*	.00
Ask the customer for a deadline extension and explain that the other department failed to provide the necessary information.	.12*	.06	-.02
Ask your manager to pressure the other department to deliver the information.	.17*	.02	-.10*

* indicates statistically significant correlations.

McDaniel and Whetzel (2005) reported correlations between measures of *g* and personality and response options in a situational judgment test. The correlations are shown in Tables 9.1 and 9.2. These items were developed for professional positions in a Fortune 500 corporation and are presented here with permission. Each item presents a scenario and several response options. The respondents were asked to rate the effectiveness of each response option for resolving the problem depicted in the scenario. Each response option was individually correlated with other variables (e.g., cognitive ability and personality) collected on each respondent. In scenario A (Table 9.1), the first response option was judged effective by those higher in *g* (*r* = .10) and lower in agreeableness (*r* = –.13). The second and fifth options were judged effective by those high in *g* (*r* = .11 and .13). The third option was judged effective by those low in agreeableness (*r* = –.16). The fourth option was judged effective by those low in *g* (*r* = –.17). Other correlations were suggestive of relationships with the effectiveness ratings but were not statistically significant. The correlations are all relatively low because they represent correlations with a single item with limited reliability. In scenario B (Table 9.2), the first two options were found effective by those higher in conscientiousness (both *r* = .11), the third and fourth options found effective by those higher in *g* (*r* = .12 and .17), and the fourth option was found effective by those low in agreeableness (*r* = –.10). In summary, the response options for these scenarios, like most SJT scenarios and response options, are often construct heterogeneous. Tests made up of such items measure multiple constructs and have loadings on multiple factors.

A second method for empirically identifying constructs measured by situational judgments tests involves conducting factor analysis. However, factor analysis has seldom proved useful in specifying the content of situational judgment tests. Clause, Mullins, Nee, Pulakos, and Schmitt (1998) found that in situational judgment tests, multidimensionality often occurs within individual items. When items are multidimensional, it is very difficult to specify their content through traditional, empirical means such as factor analysis. McDaniel and Whetzel (2005) reviewed the sparse literature on factor analyses of situational judgment test items and concluded that instances of interpretable factors are rare.

In summary, both the correlational and factor analysis methods have shown situational judgment tests to be multidimensional, even at the item level. They appear to measure a variety of constructs including cognitive ability and the Big 5 (i.e., conscientiousness, agreeableness, extroversion, emotional stability, and openness to experience).

PSYCHOMETRIC CHARACTERISTICS
OF SITUATIONAL JUDGMENT TESTS

In this section psychometric properties of situational judgment tests, including reliability, construct validity, criterion-related validity, incremental validity beyond general cognitive ability, and subgroup differences, are discussed

Reliability

Computing the reliability of situational judgment tests is problematic for several reasons. First, the most readily available reliability estimate, Cronbach's alpha, may not be an appropriate reliability index because of the multidimensional nature of situational judgment tests (Cronbach, 1949, 1951). Test-retest reliability is rarely found in the literature on situational judgment tests because it requires at least two separate administrations of the same test to the same examinees. Parallel form reliability often is infeasible because it requires the use of different item content to measure the same constructs. Because it is difficult to isolate the particular constructs assessed using a situational judgment test, construct equivalence across forms can be problematic. Due to these test development and data collection problems, many researchers continue to provide internal consistency estimates while acknowledging that they underestimate the reliability (Chan & Schmitt, 1997; Pulakos & Schmitt, 1996; Pulakos, Schmitt, & Chan, 1996) of situational judgment tests. One notable exception is Chan and Schmitt (2002), who estimated parallel form reliability at .76. Clearly, more thought and research are needed on the appropriate methods for assessing reliability so that we have more and better estimates of the reliability of situational judgment tests.

Construct Validity

Three meta-analyses (McDaniel et al., 2001; McDaniel, Hartman, & Grubb, 2003; McDaniel & Nguyen, 2001) summarized the construct validity of situational judgment tests. McDaniel et al. (2003) provided the most comprehensive of these reviews. They found that situational judgment tests correlate in varying degrees with measures of three of the Big 5 personality traits (Digman, 1990) and with cognitive ability measures. The magnitude of these correlations is moderated by the situational judgment test response instructions, as shown in Table 9.3. Situational judgment tests with behavioral tendency instructions tend to be more correlated with personality than situational judgment tests with knowledge instructions. However, situational judgment tests with knowledge instructions correlate more highly with cognitive ability than do situational judgment tests with behavioral tendency instructions (.43 vs. .23).

As a result of these findings, McDaniel et al. (2003) suggested that it may be possible to change the construct validity of a situational judgment test by altering the response instructions. They could not empirically demonstrate this phenomenon because they had no studies in their sample that held the situational judgment test constant but varied the response instructions. However, since that time several researchers (Mary Doherty, personal communication, July 7, 2005; Hartman & Grubb, 2005; Nguyen, 2004; Nguyen, Biderman, & McDaniel, 2005; Vasilopoulos, Cucina, Hayes, & McElreath, 2005) found that when administering the same situational judgment test with varying response instructions, one can change the magnitude of correlations consistent with the findings of McDaniel et al. (2003).

TABLE 9.3

Meta-Analytic Correlations Between Situational Judgment Tests With Cognitive Ability and Big 5 Measures

	N	k	ρ
Cognitive ability	22,553	62	.39
Knowledge instructions	17,290	41	.43
Behavioral tendency instructions	5,263	21	.23
Agreeableness	14,131	16	.33
Knowledge instructions	8,303	5	.20
Behavioral tendency instructions	5,828	11	.53
Conscientiousness	19,656	19	.37
Knowledge instructions	13,754	8	.33
Behavioral tendency instructions	5,902	11	.51
Emotional stability	7,718	14	.41
Knowledge instructions	1,990	4	.11
Behavioral tendency instructions	5,728	10	.51
Extroversion	12,607	10	.20
Knowledge instructions	11,867	5	.21
Behavioral tendency instructions	740	5	.11
Openness to experience	874	5	.12
Knowledge instructions	160	1	.25
Behavioral tendency instructions	714	4	.09

Note. N is the number of subjects across all studies in the analysis; k is the number of studies; r is the population correlation. The first row in each analysis is the correlation between the situational judgment test and the Big 5 measure for both kinds of instruction.

Thus, test developers who are interested in assessing personality constructs may wish to use behavioral tendency instructions. However, one should note that behavioral tendency instructions are susceptible to faking (Nguyen et al., 2005). On the other hand, if one were interested in assessing cognitive ability, one might use knowledge instructions. The caution here is that a cognitively loaded situational judgment test is likely to result in greater subgroup differences. In summary, there are advantages and disadvantages to both kinds of response instructions and test developers need to carefully consider the consequences of their choices. Recommendations for test development resulting from these findings are provided later in this chapter.

Criterion-Related Validity

The criterion-related validity of situational judgment tests has been evaluated in many primary studies (Chan & Schmitt, 1997; Hanson & Borman, 1989; Motowidlo et al., 1990; Smith & McDaniel, 1998). Two meta-analyses examined the criterion-related validity of situational judgment tests (McDaniel et al., 2001; McDaniel et al., 2003). In the second and more recent meta-analysis, the overall validity of situational judgment tests across 84 coefficients was .32 (N = 11,809). In addition to overall validity, the study evaluated response instructions as a moderator of validity. As mentioned earlier, knowledge instructions ask examinees to determine the effectiveness of various responses to a situation and behavioral tendency instructions ask examinees what they would do in various situations. Situational judgment tests with knowledge response instructions yielded higher validity (.33) than situational judgment tests with behavioral tendency instructions (.27). Although this is not a large magnitude moderator, it does lead to implications about the design of situational judgment tests. To maximize criterion-related validity, a test developer should consider using knowledge instructions; however, as mentioned before, the use of knowledge instructions is more likely to result in subgroup differences than the use of behavioral tendency instructions. These validity results are almost entirely based on concurrent validity studies (e.g., research typically conducted using job incumbents, rather than applicants, as subjects). Conclusions about the magnitude of the response instruction moderator should be reexamined as estimates of predictive validity (e.g., research typically conducted using applicants as subjects) become available.

Incremental Validity

Two meta-analyses (McDaniel et al., 2001; McDaniel et al., 2003) and several primary studies (Chan & Schmitt, 2002; Clevenger et al., 2000; O'Connell, McDaniel, Grubb, Hartman, & Lawrence, 2002; Weekley & Jones, 1997, 1999) examined the incremental validity of situational judgment tests over measures of cognitive ability. The research is consistent in showing that situational judgment tests provide incremental validity over cognitive ability. As measurement methods, situational judgment tests can assess different constructs to varying degrees, and the degree of incremental validity over cognitive ability will vary depending on the correlation between the situational judgment test and the measure of cognitive ability. Situational judgment tests with high cognitive ability correlations likely will have less incremental validity over cognitive ability than situational judgment tests with low cognitive ability correlations.

Few studies have examined the incremental validity of situational judgment tests over both cognitive ability and personality. One study (O'Connell et al., 2002) reported incremental validity of the situational judgment test over cognitive ability but found little incremental validity over both cognitive ability and personality. However, Weekley and Ployhart (2005) discussed a situational judgment test that provided incremental validity beyond cognitive ability, personality, and experience. More research is needed before one can draw compelling conclusions about the incremental validity of situational judgment tests over both cognitive ability and personality.

Subgroup Differences

Whetzel et al. (2005) examined ethnic and gender subgroup differences in situational judgment test scores. Typically, African Americans scored lower on average

TABLE 9.4

Vector Correlations Between Ethnic and Gender Differences and Constructs Correlated With Situational Judgment Tests

	Cognitive Ability	Conscientiousness	Agreeableness	Emotional Stability
African American/ White difference	.88 (18)	.13 (9)	−.38 (9)	−.89 (6)
Male/female difference	−.05(19)	.36 (9)	.38 (10)	.37 (7)

Note. Numbers in parentheses are the numbers of coefficients contributing data to the vector correlations.

than Whites with a mean d of .39, where d is a standardized mean difference (a d of 0 indicates no mean difference between two groups). Differences were larger for situational judgment tests in a paper-and-pencil format ($d = .40$) in comparison to a video format ($d = .33$). These differences were almost entirely moderated by the extent to which the situational judgment tests were correlated with measures of cognitive ability. One can also compute the vector correlations (Jensen, 1998) between the effect size (i.e., difference between groups) and the cognitive loading of the test. As shown in Table 9.4, the vector correlation between the effect size for African Americans and Whites and the g-loading of the situational judgment test was .88. This suggests that as the correlation of the situational judgment test with a measure of general cognitive ability increases (i.e., as the cognitive complexity increases), the mean ethnic score difference also increases.

There also was a moderating effect related to the personality variables of agreeableness and emotional stability. As shown in Table 9.4, as the correlation of the situational judgment test with agreeableness and emotional stability increased, the magnitude of the mean African American versus White score difference decreased. In brief, situational judgment tests show larger ethnic differences when the situational judgment test is positively related to cognitive ability and negatively related to agreeableness and emotional stability.

Whetzel et al. (2005) also reported that the gender difference was small ($d = .14$) and favored females. This difference was moderated somewhat by the correlation of the situational judgment test with conscientiousness, agreeableness, and emotional stability. As shown in Table 9.4, as the correlation between these personality variables and the situational judgment test increased, the gender difference favoring females also increased. These findings suggest that females obtained

---

[1]Portions of this section of the chapter were taken directly, and with permission, from Motowidlo, Hanson, and Crafts (1997).

slightly higher situational judgment test scores to the extent that the tests were correlated with conscientiousness, agreeableness, and emotional stability.

HOW TO DEVELOP A SITUATIONAL JUDGMENT TEST[1]

Although situational judgment tests come in a variety of formats, they all have the common feature that they present a description of a situation representing a problem or challenge that might be encountered at work. The items ask applicants how they would respond to the situation. The rest of this chapter offers suggestions for developing a situational judgment test. This developmental strategy combines practices that have been successfully followed in the past to develop demonstrably valid situational judgment tests. A shortcut approach also is provided. Other ways to build situational judgment tests also are possible, and they might be as good or even better than the approach described in this chapter.

There are three general stages for developing a situational judgment test. First, a panel of subject matter experts (SMEs) generates descriptions of problem situations that might happen at work. Second, the SMEs write multiple-choice response alternatives for each problem situation. Third, a scoring key is developed.

Develop Situational Item Stems

Situational item stems should represent classes of events that actually happen on the job. They should represent classes of problems or challenges that people have to handle effectively or their job performance will suffer. They do not have to reflect matters of critical or monumental importance, but they should not be so minor or trivial that it does not matter how people deal with them. Furthermore, they should be difficult enough that there are meaningful differences in how effectively different people handle them.

The item stems should be described in enough detail to provide the cues necessary to distinguish more effective from less effective ways of dealing with the situations, but not in so much detail that the cues point to a single correct response that will be obvious to everyone. These cues should be general enough so that they can be correctly interpreted even by people who have never encountered the situation, as long as they have encountered similar situations in different contexts.

The first step is to assemble groups of SMEs into a workshop and ask them to write critical incidents (see chap. 3). Using the electrician example, groups of experienced electricians or journeymen would be assembled. If results of a job analysis (see chap. 3) are available, performance dimensions (i.e., the competencies, knowledge, skills, or abilities needed for successful performance) are shared with workshop participants. The SMEs would then be asked to think about occasions when they, or someone they knew, encountered a problem in a situation that involved one of the performance dimensions. Using a critical incident form, they would be asked to write about each situational critical incident by: (a) describing the problem in full detail, (b) briefly noting how the electrician in the incident dealt with it, and (c) describing the results of the electrician's actions. If performance dimensions are available, the participants also note which performance dimensions are related to the situation. Often a situation is related to several performance dimensions. An example of a critical incident, taken from chapter 3, is:

> The foreman of a job gave a print to an apprentice and said, "Tomorrow, lay this whole floor out and pipe it." The next day the apprentice realized that he did not know how to do the task and the foreman was not available. The apprentice reviewed available documentation until he learned what he needed to know. The apprentice successfully completed the job and felt proud.

The next step is to sort the critical incidents according to the content of the scenarios or problems that electricians must handle. Combining judgments of the different judges will show which situations tend to be grouped together most often and this will lead to definitions of situational categories. For instance, in the electrician example, two categories that could emerge might be Reading Blueprints and Completing Jobs on Time.

With these situational categories in hand, the next step is to select representative critical incidents from each one and edit them into situational judgment item stems. Selecting situations from each category helps to ensure that the final situational inventory will include examples of all the important kinds of situational problems that occur on the job. Normally, the final version of the situational judgment test will also contain multiple situations per situational category. The exact number of situations selected per category will be based on some rational procedure. For example, job experts may be asked to rate the importance of the situational categories, and situations from the more important categories will be more heavily represented on the test. Alternatively, individual situations may be mapped to the job performance categories, and importance ratings for these categories can be used to define a rule for selecting scenarios for the test. An example of a stem that could be developed from the previous critical incident is: "As an apprentice electrician you receive your work assignments and seek advice from your supervisor, the project foreman. You have encountered a problem that you cannot solve and you cannot locate your supervisor to help you." Note that some of the detail from the critical incident is omitted from the stem. The purpose is to make the stems general enough that most applicants will understand the content of the stem.

From a technical standpoint, the larger the number of situational judgment items in the final test the better, but practical considerations limit the number of items that can be included. Situational judgment items may take a minute or two to answer and the number of items in the final test should not exceed the time available to administer the test. If the final situational judgment test is to include no more than about 40 situational items, at least 50 to 60 problem situations should be prepared at this stage in the development process.

One can substantially shorten this process if a job analysis has been conducted that has identified performance dimensions. With verbally fluent incumbents, one can have the incumbents write item stems rather than critical incidents. Working from the list of performance dimensions, participants divide the dimensions among themselves and write situational judgment stems. This abbreviated process assumes that the performance dimensions provide good coverage of the job and that the participants are willing and competent to write item stems. If situational item stems can be developed in this manner, it is sometimes possible to write all the item stems needed for the test in less than a day.

Develop Response Alternatives

Response alternatives should represent classes of broadly different strategies for handling each situation. The alternatives should all seem reasonable but some have to be more "correct" for the situation than others. The more correct alternatives should be more attractive to applicants with the best potential for success on the job.

One way to develop response alternatives with these characteristics is to collect responses to the situational item stems from job incumbents. This can be done by assembling the situational item stems one to a page in a questionnaire. The questionnaire should be administered to incumbents who would be asked to complete the questionnaire by writing a short description in the space provided of how they or someone they know would handle each problem. The goal is to provide a range of possible responses that vary in effectiveness. If there are too many problems for people to answer all of them, the problems can be divided into two or more shorter questionnaires, but at least five people should answer each problem to ensure that many potentially different kinds of responses are collected. Examples of responses to the stem above are:

1. Review the available documentation and identify the best approach.
2. Seek out another foreman to help you.
3. Work on something else until the foreman is available.
4. Try various approaches until you find the solution.
5. Go on break until the foreman is available.

Note that Response 1 is similar to that provided in the original critical incident.

Taking one situational problem at a time, the responses should be reviewed to identify a variety of strategies, without worrying at this point about which are the best and worst responses to the problem.

Develop a Scoring Key

Finally, a scoring key is developed by collecting judgments from SMEs about the effectiveness of the alternative response options for each situational judgment item. Typically, the test developer prepares a questionnaire asking SMEs to rate each response on an effectiveness scale. The questionnaire should be completed by individuals who are very experienced and knowledgeable about the job. A common procedure is to ask the most knowledgeable individuals possible to complete

Very Ineffective	Ineffective	Effective	Very Effective
This action is inappropriate. It will make the problem worse.	This is a poor action. It will not help solve the problem.	This is a reasonable action that would go far in resolving the problem.	This is one of the best and most effective actions of all possible actions.

FIGURE 9.2   Example of effectiveness rating scale.

−1	Indicating that the keyed best response is the worst response
	Indicating that the keyed worst response is the best response
+1	Indicating that the keyed best response is the best response
	Indicating that the keyed worst response is the worst response
0	Any other response

FIGURE 9.3   Scoring pattern for selecting the best or worst response.

the questionnaire. In the present example, they would be experienced journeymen or very senior electricians. In general, the more SMEs who contribute to the ratings, the more stable the ratings will be (i.e., the ratings will be less subject to individual idiosyncrasies). That said, approximately five to seven raters often are used. A possible effectiveness rating scale that the SMEs might use is shown in Fig. 9.2.

Using these expert judgments, the test developer computes the mean and standard deviations of the rating of each response option. The standard deviation is an indication of expert judgment agreement. Situational items for which there is little agreement among experts on the relative effectiveness of alternatives should be dropped. For remaining items, the experts' judgments would be used to identify the effective and less effective response alternatives for each situational judgment item.

Once the test developers have obtained mean ratings on each response, they can determine the scoring key. If a response instruction is used that asks the applicant to select one choice (e.g., pick the best response, what would you most likely do), the developer should declare the response with the highest mean effectiveness rating to be the correct response. For example, if the instructions ask the applicant to choose the best or worst response, the simple scoring pattern shown in Fig. 9.3 is recommended (McDaniel, Whetzel, & Nguyen, 2006). Likewise, if the response instruction asks for two responses (e.g., pick the best response and then pick the worst response; what would you most likely do and what would you least likely do), the mean effectiveness ratings should be used to identify the most effective and least effective response for the keyed responses.

−1	Indicates that an effective behavior is ineffective or very ineffective
	Indicates that an ineffective behavior is effective or very effective
+1	Indicates that an effective behavior is effective or very effective
	Indicates that an ineffective behavior is ineffective or very ineffective

FIGURE 9.4 Scoring pattern for rating the effectiveness of possible responses.

On the other hand, if one seeks to have the applicant rate the effectiveness of each response, one could develop a scoring key based on the same 4-point scale shown in Fig. 9.2; however, the keying approach shown in Fig. 9.4 is recommended for several reasons (McDaniel, Whetzel, & Nguyen, 2006). First, it only requires that the incumbents who are providing ratings used to establish the key agree on whether the response option is an effective behavior or an ineffective behavior. Second, there are individual differences in how applicants understand relative statements (e.g., effective vs. very effective). Two incumbent raters might believe a given response option to be at the same level of effectiveness even though one rater describes it as "effective" whereas another describes it as "very effective." This difference is due to the rater's different interpretations of the word very. If the keying is based on this strategy, one can avoid dealing with the nuances of the word very.

However, McDaniel, Whetzel, and Nguyen (2006) recommended that a 4-point Likert rating scale, similar to the one shown in Fig. 9.2, be used in the actual situational judgment test instrument because applicants may feel constricted by 2-point, dichotomous rating scales. Thus, the use of a 2-point dichotomous rating scale is suggested (Fig. 9.4) for developing the answer key and a 4-point Likert scale (Fig. 9.2) is suggested for the actual situational judgment test instrument administered to examinees.

Another keying approach involves deviation scoring from the mean effectiveness rating (Legree, Psotka, Tremble, & Bourne, 2005). In this approach, the mean rating is used as the correct answer and ratings differing from the mean receive lower scores. For example, if the mean effectiveness rating of a response option is 1.5 and an applicant rates the response at "2," the applicant loses a half-point. Likewise, if the applicant rates the response a "1," the applicant also loses a half-point. Thus, the highest possible score is a 0 and the lowest possible is some negative number. One might want to add a positive number to all scores to make all scores positive.

SUMMARY

Situational judgment tests present descriptions of work situations that might happen on the job and ask applicants how they would handle them. They are based on the idea that people have different levels of knowledge about how best to handle various work situations. By measuring this knowledge, situational judgment tests can predict job performance. The literature on the reliability of situational judgment tests is deficient because the measures tend to have heterogeneous content but measures of homogeneity are typically offered as estimates of reliability. The criterion-related validity of situational judgment tests is at useful levels. Both the criterion-related and construct validity of situational judgment tests are moderated by response instructions. Response instructions fall into two general categories, knowledge and behavioral tendency, and the choice of one or the other affects validity and the likelihood of subgroup differences.

Developing a situational inventory involves three general stages: (a) preparing descriptions of problem situations, (b) preparing multiple response alternatives for each problem, and (c) identifying the effectiveness of each response option. A set of procedures that could be followed in each stage to develop an effective situational judgment test is provided.

REFERENCES

Bruce, M. M. (1965). *Examiner's manual: Business Judgment Test*. Larchmont, NY: Author.

Bruce, M. M., & Learner, D. B. (1958). A supervisory practices test. *Personnel Psychology, 11,* 207–216.

Campbell, J. P., Dunnette, M. D., Lawler, E. E., & Weick, K. E. (1970). *Managerial behavior, performance and effectiveness*. New York: McGraw-Hill.

Cardall, A. J. (1942). *Preliminary manual for the Test of Practical Judgment*. Chicago: Science Research Associates.

Chan, D., & Schmitt, N. (1997). Video-based versus paper-and-pencil method of assessment in SJTs: Subgroup differences in test performance and face validity perceptions. *Journal of Applied Psychology, 82,* 143–159.

Chan, D., & Schmitt, N. (2002). Situational judgment and job performance. *Human Performance, 15,* 233–254.

Clause, C. S., Mullins, M. E., Nee, M. T., Pulakos, E. D., & Schmitt, N. (1998). Parallel test form development: A procedure for alternative predictors and an example. *Personnel Psychology, 51,* 193–208.

Clevenger, J. P., & Haaland, D. E. (2000, April). *The relationship between job knowledge and situational judgment test performance*. Paper presented at the 15 annual convention of the Society for Industrial and Organizational Psychology, Inc., New Orleans, LA.

Clevenger, J. P., Jockin, T., Morris, S., & Anselmi, T. (1999, April). *A situational judgment test for engineers: Construct and criterion related validity of a less adverse alternative*. Paper presented at the 14th annual convention of the Society for Industrial and Organizational Psychology, Inc., Atlanta, GA.

Corts, D. B. (1980). *Development and validation of a test for the ranking of applicants for promotion to first-line federal trades and labor supervisory positions* (PRR-80-30). Washington, DC: U. S. Office of Personnel Management, Personnel Research and Development Center.

Cronbach, L. J. (1949). Statistical methods applied to Rorschach scores: A review. *Psychological Bulletin, 46,* 393–429.

Cronbach, L. J. (1951). Coefficient alpha and the internal structure of tests. *Psychometrika, 16,* 297–334.

Dalessio, A. T. (1992, May). *Predicting insurance agent turnover using a video-based situational judgment test.* Paper presented at the seventh annual conference of the Society for Industrial and Organizational Psychology, Inc., Montreal, Canada.

Digman, J. M. (1990). Personality structure: Emergence of the five factor model. *Annual Review of Psychology, 41,* 417–440.

Doherty, M. (2005, July). Personal communication.

DuBois, P. H. (1970). *A history of psychological testing.* Boston: Allyn & Bacon.

File, Q. W. (1945). The measurement of supervisory quality in industry. *Journal of Applied Psychology, 29,* 381–387.

File, Q. W., & Remmers, H. H. (1948). *How Supervise? Manual 1948 revision.* New York: The Psychological Corporation.

Goldberg, L. R. (1993). The structure of phenotypic personality traits. *American Psychologist, 48,* 26–34.

Gottfredson, L. S. (2003). Dissecting practical intelligence theory: Its claims and evidence. *Intelligence, 31,* 343–397.

Greenberg, S. H. (1963). *Supervisory Judgment Test Manual.* Technical Series No. 35. Personnel Measurement Research and Development Center. Bureau of Programs and Standards, Standards Division. Washington, DC: U.S. Civil Service Commission.

Hanson, M. A., & Borman, W. C. (1989, April). *Development and construct validation of a situational judgment test of supervisory effectiveness for first-line supervisors in the U.S. Army.* Paper presented at the symposium conducted at the 4th annual conference of the Society for Industrial and Organizational Psychology, Atlanta, GA.

Hartman, N. S., & Grubb, W. L., III. (2005, November). *Situational judgment tests and validity: It's a matter of instruction.* Paper presented at the Southern Management Association, Charleston, SC.

Jensen, A. R. (1998). *The g factor.* Westport, CT: Prager.

John, O. P. (1990). The "Big Five" factor taxonomy: Dimensions of personality in the natural language and in questionnaires. In L. A. Pervin (Ed.), *Handbook of personality: Theory and research* (pp. 66–100) New York: Guilford Press.

Kirkpatrick, D. L., & Planty, E. (1960). *Supervisory Inventory on Human Relations.* Chicago: SRA.

Legree, P. J., Psotka, J., Tremble, T., & Bourne, D. (2005). Using consensus based measurement to assess emotional intelligence. In R. Schulze & R. D. Roberts (Eds.), *Emotional intelligence: An international handbook* (pp. 155–180). Berlin, Germany: Hogrefe & Huber.

Mandell, M. M. (1950). The administrative judgment test. *Journal of Applied Psychology, 34,* 145–147.

McDaniel, M. A., Hartman, N. S., & Grubb, W. L., III. (2003, April). *Situational judgment tests, knowledge, behavioral tendency, and validity: A meta-analysis.* Paper presented at the 18th annual conference of the Society for Industrial and Organizational Psychology, Inc., Orlando, FL.

McDaniel, M. A., Morgeson, F. P., Finnegan, E. B., Campion, M. A., & Braverman, E. P. (2001). Use of situational judgment tests to predict job performance: A clarification of the literature. *Journal of Applied Psychology, 86,* 730–740.

McDaniel, M. A., & Nguyen, N. T. (2001). Situational judgment tests: A review of practice and constructs assessed. *International Journal of Selection and Assessment, 9,* 103–113.

McDaniel, M. A., & Whetzel, D. L. (2005). Situational judgment test research: Informing the debate on practical intelligence theory. *Intelligence, 33,* 515–525.

McDaniel, M. A., Whetzel, D. L., Hartman, N. S., Nguyen, N., & Grubb, W. L. (2006). Situational judgment tests: Validity and an integrative model. In J. A. Weekley & R. E. Ployhart (Eds.), *Situational judgment tests: Theory, measurement, and application* (pp. 183–203). Mahwah, NJ: Lawrence Erlbaum Associates.

256   MCDANIEL & WHETZEL

McDaniel, M. A., Whetzel, D. L., & Nguyen, N. T. (2006). *Situational judgment tests in personnel selection: A monograph for the International Personnel Management Association Assessment Council*. Alexandria, VA: International Personnel Management Assessment Council.

Moss, F. A. (1926). Do you know how to get along with people? Why some people get ahead in the world while others do not. *Scientific American, 135*, 26–27.

Motowidlo, S. J., Dunnette, M. D., & Carter, G. W. (1990). An alternative selection procedure: The low-fidelity simulation. *Journal of Applied Psychology, 75*, 640–647.

Motowidlo, S. J., Hanson, M. A., & Crafts, J. L. (1997). Low-fidelity simulations. In D. L. Whetzel & G. R. Wheaton (Eds.), *Applied measurement methods in industrial psychology* (pp. 241–260). Palo Alto, CA: Consulting Psychologists Press.

Northrop, L. C. (1989). The psychometric history of selected ability constructs. Washington, DC: U.S. Office of Personnel Management.

Nguyen, N. T. (2004, February). *Response instructions and construct validity of a situational judgment test*. Paper delivered at the 11th annual meeting of the American Society of Business and Behavioral Sciences, Las Vegas, NV.

Nguyen, N. T., Biderman, M. D., & McDaniel, M. A. (2005). Effects of response instructions on faking in a situational judgment test. *International Journal of Selection and Assessment, 13*, 250–260.

O'Connell, M. S., McDaniel, M. A., Grubb, W. L., III, Hartman, N. S., & Lawrence, A. (2002, April). *Incremental validity of situational judgment tests for task and contextual performance*. Paper presented at the 17th annual conference of the Society of Industrial and Organizational Psychology, Inc., Toronto, Canada.

Olson-Buchanan, J. B., Drasgow, F., Moberg, P. J., Mead, A. D., & Keenan, P. A. (1994, April). *The conflict resolution skills assessment: Model-based, multimedia measurement*. Paper presented at the ninth annual conference of the Society for Industrial and Organizational Psychology, Inc., Nashville, TN.

Phillips, J. F. (1992). Predicting sales skills. *Journal of Business and Psychology, 7*, 151–160.

Phillips, J. F. (1993). Predicting negotiation skills. *Journal of Business and Psychology, 7*, 403–411.

Pulakos, E. D., & Schmitt, N. (1996). An evaluation of two strategies for reducing adverse impact and their effects on criterion-related validity. *Human Performance, 9*, 241–258.

Pulakos, E. D., Schmitt, N., & Chan, D. (1996). Models of job performance ratings: An examination of ratee race, ratee gender, and rater level effects. *Human Performance, 9*, 103–119.

Ree, M. J., & Earles, J. A. (1993). g is to psychology what carbon is to chemistry: A reply to Sternberg and Wagner, McClelland, and Calfee. *Current Directions in Psychological Science, 2*, 11–12.

Roth, P. L., BeVier, C. A., Bobko, P., Switzer, F. S., III, & Tyler, P. (2001). Ethnic group differences in cognitive ability in employment and educational settings: A meta-analysis. *Personnel Psychology, 54*, 297–330.

Schmidt, F. L., & Hunter, J. E. (1998). The validity and utility of selection methods in personnel psychology: Practical and theoretical implications of 85 years of research findings. *Psychological Bulletin, 124*, 262–274.

Smith, K. C., & McDaniel, M. A. (1998, April). *Criterion and construct validity evidence for a situational judgment measure*. Paper presented at the 13th annual conference of the Society for Industrial and Organizational Psychology, Dallas, TX.

Sternberg, R. J., Forsythe, G. B., Hedlund, J., Horvath, J. A., Wagner, R. K., Williams, W. M., et al. (2000). *Practical intelligence in everyday life*. New York: Cambridge University Press.

Sternberg, R. J., Wagner, R. K., Williams, W. M., & Horvath, J. A. (1995). Testing common sense. *American Psychologist, 50*, 912–927.

Stevens, M. J., & Campion, M. A. (1999). Staffing work teams: Development and validation of a selection test for teamwork settings. *Journal of Management, 25,* 207–208.

Thorndike, R. L., & Stein, S. (1937). An evaluation of the attempts to measure social intelligence. *Psychological Bulletin, 34,* 275–285.

Vasilopoulos, N. L., Cucina, J. M., Hayes, T. L., & McElreath, J. A. (2005, April). *Effect of situational judgment test response instructions on validity.* Paper presented at the 20th annual conference of the Society for Industrial and Organizational Psychology, Inc., Los Angeles.

Wagner, R. K. (1987). Tacit knowledge in everyday intelligent behavior. *Journal of Personality and Social Psychology, 52,* 1236–1247.

Wagner, R. K., & Sternberg, R. J. (1991). *Tacit Knowledge Inventory for Managers: User manual.* San Antonio, TX: Psychological Corporation.

Weekley, J. A., & Jones, C. (1997). Video-based situational testing. *Personnel Psychology, 50,* 25–49.

Weekley, J. A., & Jones, C. (1999). Further studies of situational tests. *Personnel Psychology, 52,* 679–700.

Weekley, J. A., & Ployhart, R. E. (2005). Situational judgment: Antecedents and relationships with performance. *Human Performance, 18,* 81–104.

Weekley, J. A., & Ployhart, R. E. (2006). An introduction to situational judgment testing. In J. A. Weekley & R. E. Ployhart (Eds.), *Situational judgment tests.* Mahwah, NJ: Lawrence Erlbaum Associates.

Whetzel, D. L., McDaniel, M. A., & Nguyen, N. (2005). *Subgroup differences in situational judgment test performance: A meta-analysis.* Manuscript submitted for publication.

CHAPTER TEN

Assessment Centers

Suzanne Tsacoumis
Human Resources Research Organization (HumRRO)

OVERVIEW

An assessment center is a powerful methodology for evaluating one's job-related competence and capabilities. Through the implementation of multiple high-fidelity simulations (also referred to as exercises throughout this chapter), an assessment center offers an excellent opportunity to evaluate an applicant's strengths and weaknesses and to predict the applicant's potential to succeed in a particular position. The assessment center is an effective procedure because it is based on a standardized method by which applicants are provided an equal opportunity to perform and to be evaluated on the same job-related simulations. The underlying assumption in an assessment center is that potential for success can be predicted by having applicants perform under conditions that simulate the actual job. Well-developed assessment centers have sound psychometric proper-ties (Thornton & Byham, 1982), and any subgroup differences tend to be lower than those found with paper-and-pencil cognitive ability tests (Hoffman & Thornton, 1997). Assessment centers have withstood the test of time and have repeatedly been shown to be valid predictors of future job performance (Bray & Grant, 1966; Gaugler, Rosenthal, Thornton, & Bentson, 1987; Tziner, Ronen, & Hacohen, 1993).

High-fidelity simulations also provide an ideal opportunity to assess core job dimensions, such as relating to others, leadership, and problem solving (Thornton & Mueller-Hanson, 2004), that typically are difficult to measure by other means. As a consequence, assessment centers are an effective method for evaluating complex supervisory performance (Thornton & Byham, 1982). At the same time, assessment centers provide a method for evaluating both declarative

259

and procedural knowledge (Thornton & Mueller-Hanson, 2004). That is, in addition to determining whether a candidate possesses certain knowledge, assessors can observe the candidate performing a task that involves application of that knowledge. Given the realistic nature of the exercises, assessment centers tend to be more acceptable to candidates (Rynes & Connerley, 1993; Thornton, 1992) and are harder to fake (Thornton & Mueller-Hanson, 2004) than traditional paper-and-pencil tests. Finally, an organization's specific mission, needs, values, and goals can be incorporated into the simulations to yield a completely customized assessment center process (Thornton & Mueller-Hanson, 2004).

Nevertheless, given the time and resources required to develop, administer, and score high-fidelity simulations in an assessment center, some question the approach's utility. Although it is true that use of an assessment center may not be the best approach in all cases, there is ample evidence that implementing such simulations under the right circumstances can provide valuable information for a variety of human resource management applications.

The balance of this chapter presents the history and key components of assessment centers, and describes procedures for developing valid high-fidelity simulations. In addition, the chapter provides information about assessors, and describes training methods used to develop effective assessors.

WHAT IS AN ASSESSMENT CENTER?

An assessment center is a process that involves several standardized measures, which provide multiple opportunities for behavioral evaluations of applicants and employees by a number of assessors (International Task Force on Assessment Center Guidelines, 2000). The observations and the resulting judgments are pooled to yield a comprehensive assessment of an applicant's standing with regard to the targeted constructs. This approach of integrating information from a variety of sources evolved from numerous attempts to measure complex performance with a combination of evaluation techniques using multiple observers. These efforts involved multiple measures of an individual's performance and required the integration of information from these different measures to arrive at an overall evaluation.

The origins of assessment centers can be traced to the work of German psychologists in the early 1900s (Moses, 1977). German psychologists asserted that in order to assess leadership potential, an individual's total personality (rather than separate abilities) should be evaluated (Thornton & Byham, 1982). To obtain an accurate evaluation of the whole personality, they believed that a number of assessment approaches should be combined. In addition, they maintained that the assessment should occur in natural, everyday situations. Then, assessors should observe behavior elicited by situational techniques, and the judgments of several assessors should be pooled to obtain an objective appraisal of applicant performance.

The German officer assessment programs were among the first attempts to use both multiple assessment techniques and multiple assessors to evaluate complex behavior. The ultimate goal was to obtain behavioral samples of intellectual and personality characteristics rather than to rely solely on verbal responses or responses to paper-and-pencil tests (Thornton & Byham, 1982). This focus on measuring complex behaviors, as well as the use of multiple assessors and complex situational exercises, remain the key characteristics of modern assessment center processes.

Assessment centers were first used in the United States during World War II (Thornton & Byham, 1982). The Office of Strategic Services (OSS), the forerunner of the CIA, implemented a program to evaluate applicants for a variety of positions, including intelligence agents, saboteurs, propaganda experts, secretaries, and office workers. The OSS assessment program included both objective and subjective techniques, with an emphasis on situational tests (MacKinnon, 1977). Two of the more well-known situational tests, the "brook" and the "construction" exercises, were borrowed from the British Army's assessment program. As an example, the construction exercise involved one applicant and two assessors. The task required the applicant to use pieces of lumber to build a large wooden structure, using a model as an example to follow. The two assessors played the roles of two "farmhands," Kippy and Buster, who were available to help. Kippy, passive and sluggish, did nothing unless given explicit orders. Buster, aggressive and forward, rushed into impractical and incorrect solutions. Both assessors interfered with progress and criticized the applicant in many ways. The purpose of the exercise was to study the applicant's leadership abilities and emotional stability.

Most subsequent assessment efforts in the United States have drawn many of their ideas, methods, and points of view from the OSS program. The situational and performance exercises marked a significant shift away from primary reliance on paper-and-pencil instruments used in previous personnel selection work in the United States (Moses, 1977).

In the 1950s, the American Telephone and Telegraph company (AT&T) adapted the OSS concept to the selection and identification of management personnel. AT&T's Management Progress Study (MPS) represents a hallmark in the history of multiple assessment procedures. The purpose of the process was to trace the growth, development, and progress of young managers in the telephone business (Moses, 1977). Several assessment techniques were used, including a 2-hour background interview, an in-basket exercise, a business game, a leaderless group discussion, and various psychological tests (Bray & Grant, 1966).

The AT&T effort was unique in that the company processed individuals through an assessment center, made predictions about future management performance, and then sealed the predictions for several years. Thus, the assessment center results never influenced the individual's career progression. When AT&T compared the assessment center results with the actual promotional record of the individuals assessed, they found that 45% of those seen as suitable for middle management had attained this level, whereas only 7% of those given a low rating progressed to middle management (Huck, 1973).

In the early 1960s, the AT&T results were published and other organizations began to show great interest in them. By the late 1960s, a number of major corporations were using the assessment center to select managers and were generally pleased with the process and the results it produced. In the next section, the features that make assessment centers popular today are described.

ASSESSMENT CENTERS TODAY

Assessment centers remain an ideal method for evaluating job candidates or current employees on a wide range of knowledge, skills, abilities, and other characteristics (KSAOs), typically grouped into broader categories traditionally referred to as "dimensions." Although assessment centers may be rather costly and time consuming to develop, organizations often choose this evaluation strategy in lieu of or in addition to other testing methods, because it provides an opportunity to observe an individual's performance on job-relevant tasks and, in turn, to evaluate critical KSAOs. Also, as previously noted, the high-fidelity simulations tend to be well accepted by the participants and are resistant to faking.

The use of assessment centers has expanded to a wide range of settings, including private industry, government agencies, public safety departments, educational institutions, and the military. Most commonly, assessment centers serve as a key component of selection, promotion, and development programs primarily for supervisory, managerial, and executive personnel levels. However, this type of process also is useful for other occupations, such as sales positions, and proves beneficial when planning for succession and providing realistic job previews.

Although the purposes vary, the key elements of any properly designed assessment center include (International Task Force on Assessment Center Guidelines, 2000):

- KSAO dimensions based on a thorough and current job analysis.
- Job simulations developed to provide multiple opportunities for eliciting behaviors relevant to the dimensions being measured.
- Systematic and standardized procedures for recording assessor behavioral observations, classifying behavioral observations into the targeted dimensions, and converting classified observations into dimension scores.
- Multiple, trained assessors to evaluate the candidates.
- Standardized procedures for pooling behavioral observations, either by a consensual process or through statistical procedures.

These guidelines clarify the essential components of an assessment center, yet permit an organization to tailor the process to its specific needs. Some features on which assessment centers may vary are the type of consensual process used, the nature of feedback given to candidates, the mode of presenting simulations, and the types of exercises included.

Consensual Scoring Procedures

In a traditional assessment center model, different teams of assessors observe and document their observations of a candidate's performance on each simulation. Then, for each exercise, one assessor integrates the observations from all assessors, and prepares a summary of performance on that simulation. At a later time (e.g., end of the day), all the assessors gather to discuss each candidate. Assessors read their reports, which provide behavioral descriptions of the candidate's performance on each exercise. Once information regarding all exercises has been shared, and considering everything they have heard and observed about an applicant, each assessor then independently rates the candidate on each dimension, typically on a 5-point Likert scale. Assessors also often assign an overall assessment center score, which tends to be on a 4-point Likert scale. Then, assessors share their ratings. Any two ratings on a given dimension that differ by more than 1 point (e.g., 2 and 4) are discussed until all assessors have assigned ratings that either are the same or are within 1 point for the dimension. Finally, the overall assessment center score is discussed and any discrepancies are resolved so that all assessors have assigned the same overall score.

In response to concerns about the time and costs associated with the consensual approach described earlier, some assessment centers implement more streamlined approaches, which statistically integrate at least some of the scores. One such common approach is to have the team of assessors assign their ratings immediately after the candidate completes the simulation. In this case, assessors are given time after each exercise to review their notes, make independent dimension ratings for that simulation only, and then discuss their ratings with their assessor partner(s). Once again, assessor ratings must be within 1 point of each other on each dimension. Discrepancies are discussed by referring to behavioral observations and the rating scales until the assessors agree to modify their ratings. The overall assessment center score is the average of the dimension ratings provided for each simulation. In some cases, different weights are assigned (e.g., exercise or dimension weights) and applied during this statistical integration process.

Types and Amounts of Feedback

Assessment centers differ not only in the consensual process used, but also in the nature and specificity of feedback provided to candidates. In some cases, candidates receive limited feedback regarding their performance. For example, when the process is used for selection or promotion, applicants may only be provided with an overall score or simply informed that they passed or failed. If the process is used for promotion, which involves internal employees, some additional information typically is provided such as a rating or general indication of performance on each dimension. One method of depicting this information is to generate a profile of dimensional performance (see Fig. 10.1). This profile is based on raw dimension-within-exercise scores and displays the candidate's individual score profile, as well as: (a) the relative position of mean dimension-within-exercise scores for all candidates, and (b) the relative position of the highest and lowest score observed on each dimension-within-exercise across all candidates. These additional summary data are provided so candidates can determine how they performed relative to other candidates, and can diagnose areas of strength and developmental needs.

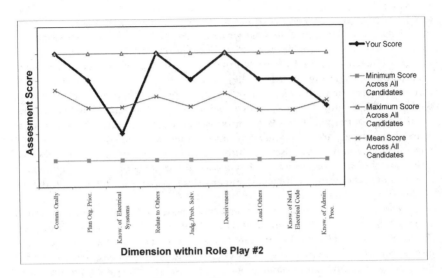

FIGURE 10.1   Sample candidate profile.

In contrast, when the ultimate goal of the assessment center is developmental, candidates usually are given more detailed feedback. Assessor observations are consolidated into a comprehensive report describing strengths and developmental needs, along with recommendations for enhancing the weaker KSAOs. At times, assessors provide face-to-face feedback to candidates, which may include reviewing clips of their videotaped performance on the simulations.

Modes of Simulation

In an assessment center, job simulations serve as the key evaluation method. Earlier assessment centers were based on simulations coupled with other instruments, such as personality measures, and tests of cognitive ability. Although one of these other types of measures, or a structured interview, may occasionally be incorporated into the process, current assessment centers place a heavy emphasis on job simulations. In fact, according to the *Guidelines and Ethical Considerations for Assessment Center Operations* (International Task Force on Assessment Center Guidelines, 2000), the techniques used as part of the process "must include a sufficient number of job-related simulations."

High-Fidelity Simulations

A job simulation presents situations that are very similar to the target job. In contrast to a work sample, which provides a nearly perfect duplication of some facet of the job (e.g., operating a forklift), simulations mirror the whole job as closely as possible (Thornton & Mueller-Hanson, 2004). They "simulate" several important job tasks to assess a number of important job-related KSAOs. These types of measures can be considered high-fidelity simulations because they closely resemble actual work situations. These high-fidelity simulations are distinct from low-fidelity simulations, such as situational judgment tests described in chapter 9. Low-fidelity simulations present either a written or oral scenario and ask applicants to rate various responses to the situation.

The underlying assumption of a high-fidelity job simulation is that the potential to perform successfully in a job can be best predicted by having candidates perform under conditions very similar to the actual job. This "behavioral consistency" model was proposed by Wernimont and Campbell (1968), who argued for a focus on meaningful and realistic samples of job behavior. The goal was to achieve point-to-point correspondence between predictor and criterion measures. Simulations approaching this idealized goal are generally viewed as having a potentially high degree of face validity (Cascio & Phillips, 1979; Schmidt, Greenthal, Hunter, Berner, & Seaton, 1977) and content validity, thereby reducing the possibility of unfair discrimination (Schmidt et al., 1977; Wernimont & Campbell, 1968). Job simulations also provide an equal opportunity for candidates to perform and be evaluated on the same job-relevant activities.

In many instances, the simulations associated with a particular assessment center are based on the same broad scenario. That is, in all exercises, the candidate assumes the role of the same individual who works in a particular office in a specific organization, and interacts with the same set of fictitious people. For example, if the assessment center is for a large electrical utility with several office locations, a fictitious office similar to the real offices is created, along with a detailed description of the people and issues associated with that office. Some organizations prefer that the simulations, and in turn the assessment center as a whole, be based on an entirely fabricated organization. In such cases, a company with a mission comparable to the target organization is created, along with its history, personnel, and any relevant issues. Regardless of the type of organization that serves as the framework for the assessment center, this thematic approach to simulation requires the candidate to assume the role of a particular person (e.g., supervisor or manager of an office or group) and then deal with a range of people and issues, all set within the same context, throughout all assessment center exercises.

Remote Simulations

In the traditional and still most common mode of implementing an assessment center, candidates and assessors gather at one location. However, with technological advances, and increasing concerns about the expense and time associated with the typical assessment center process, there has been movement toward the increased use of computers, video, and Internet or intranet resources. There are several variations on this theme, but essentially they all allow candidates to complete the process and assessors to evaluate their performance remotely, rather than at a centralized location.

Types of Exercises

The most common high-fidelity simulations are: oral presentation, role play, analysis exercise, in-basket, oral fact-finding exercise, and leaderless group discussion. Brief descriptions of each type of exercise or simulation are presented next.

Oral Presentation

Oral presentation exercises ask the candidate to review a packet of information regarding a specific issue, then prepare and give a formal presentation to an important person or organization. Depending on the complexity of the materials and resulting presentation, preparation time can vary from just a few minutes (e.g., 10 minutes) to 1 hour. Presentations rarely last more than 30 minutes.

Role-Play

Role-play exercises are one-on-one interactions with a person whom the incumbent of the targeted position deals with on the job. For example, if candidates assume the role of a supervisor, then the exercise could be designed for them to interact with a subordinate, their boss, another supervisor, a peer in another organization, a client or customer, or a member of the community. Prior to the interaction, candidates review information describing a specific situation, as well as any pertinent information associated with the individual involved in the role play. Candidates then proceed with the interactive portion of the simulation. The preparation time for this type of exercise tends to range from 10 to 45 minutes and the interactive portion usually is between 20 and 30 minutes long.

Analysis Exercise

During an analysis exercise, candidates are presented with detailed materials describing a complex situation. The information typically includes both qualitative information and data and requires in-depth analysis, integration, and interpretation of a multifaceted situation or issue. The instructions often provide a list of questions that candidates should address in their responses. The candidates usually prepare a written report, although in some cases candidates provide their responses orally. Occasionally, if an oral presentation is the mode of delivery, candidates may be asked to respond to additional questions at the conclusion of their presentation. The typical length of this exercise ranges from 45 minutes to 1.5 hours. The oral presentation, including any follow-up questions, takes 20 to 40 minutes.

In-Basket

The materials associated with an in-basket exercise are similar to those typically processed by an incumbent in the target position. The materials may include memos, e-mail messages, letters, phone messages, and reports. The materials may be presented in hard copy, electronically, or in some combination of modes. During the completion of this exercise, candidates read through the materials and provide a detailed explanation of how they would respond to each item. At the conclusion of the exercise, assessors review the written responses, and in some programs, meet with the candidates to obtain additional clarification of their responses. Following this interview, the assessors complete their final ratings. It can take from 1 to 3 hours for a candidate to document responses to each item and up to 45 minutes to interview each candidate to discuss the written responses.

Oral Fact Finding

The ultimate goal of an oral fact-finding exercise is for a candidate to gather information about a specific situation and make a recommendation regarding how to proceed. After reading a short description of the situation, the candidate meets with an assessor or role player to collect additional information and make a final recommendation. In some circumstances, once the decision has been made it is challenged by the assessor or role player. The candidate has 5 to 10 minutes to review the introductory information and prepare a list of questions. Then, there typically is a 15-minute period for questioning, followed by an approximate 10-minute period to formulate and present the final recommendation. An additional 10 to 15 minutes is needed if the candidate's recommendation is challenged.

Leaderless Group Discussion

In this type of simulation, candidates are presented with background information describing a particular problem and then are instructed to work with others to reach a resolution. Once candidates individually review the written materials, they are assembled in small groups (e.g., four to six candidates per group) to discuss the situation and generate a recommended solution. Leaderless Group Discussions (LGDs) can be classified into two broad categories: non-assigned role and assigned role. The more common form is the non-assigned role exercise in which candidates all work toward a common goal. In contrast, in the assigned role LGD, candidates are working toward different goals. Preparation for a LGD ranges from 5 to 60 minutes, with the interactive portion lasting from 30 to 90 minutes.

PSYCHOMETRIC CHARACTERISTICS OF ASSESSMENT CENTERS

Reliability

There are few published data on the reliability of assessment center exercises, most likely because no single type of estimate is ideal. Given the nature of the assessment technique, calculation of test-retest and split-half reliabilities is impractical or impossible. Other indices rely on an estimate of internal consistency obtained by looking at the dimensions measured within an exercise. However, because dimensions, by definition, measure different constructs or KSAOs, evaluating the consistency among dimension ratings within an exercise does not seem defensible. Other indices are based on the internal consistency of a dimension across exercises. This approach also seems problematic because different simulations often tap different aspects of the same dimension. Therefore, one would not necessarily expect consistency in dimension ratings across exercises.

Although limited information is available, reported interrater reliability estimates of assessment center exercises have been respectable. For in-basket exercises, Bray and Grant (1966) found a reliability estimate of .92. The interrater reliability estimates for management games and leaderless group tasks were found to be .60 and .69 for ratings and rankings, respectively (Bray & Grant, 1966). For the same types of simulations, Greenwood and McNamara (1967) reported estimates of .74 for ratings and .75 for rankings. For LGDs, Bray and Grant (1966) found interrater reliability estimates of .75 for ratings and Greenwood and McNamara (1969) found estimates ranging from .64 to .71. The interrater reliability estimates reported by Gatewood, Thornton, and Hennessey (1990) ranged from .66 to .99.

Tsacoumis, Putka, and Schantz (2005) described and evaluated various options for estimating the reliability of assessment center simulations. Within this context, reliability can be defined as the proportion of observed assessment score variance that is attributable to true score differences among candidates (as opposed to measurement error). Reliability estimates can be computed on dimensions within exercises, dimensions across exercises, exercises across dimensions, and on the overall assessment score. For more details on these options and the relative strength of each, the reader should refer to Tsacoumis et al. (2005).

For dimension-within-exercise scores, interrater reliability estimates index the degree to which candidates are rank ordered similarly by different assessors in terms of their performance on dimensions within exercises. Two indices of interrater reliability can be computed. The first is interpreted as the proportion of observed score variance in any single assessor's ratings that is attributable to true dimension-within-exercise score differences among candidates. The second index is interpreted as the proportion of observed score variance in mean dimension ratings (averaged across two assessors) that can be attributed to true dimension-within-exercise score differences among candidates.

As an example, both of these indices of interrater reliability were computed in two recent assessment centers (Tsacoumis, Katz, & Shultz, 2005; Tsacoumis, Putka, & Schantz, 2005). Each assessment center included four job simulations, each of which measured from 3 to 11 dimensions. Using pre-consensus ratings (i.e., prior to discussion with another assessor), the single assessor reliabilities ranged from .54 to .86, with the majority being above .70. The reliabilities stepped up for two assessors ranged from .76 to .93. These findings indicate that the assessor pairs who evaluated candidates provided similar rank orderings of candidates in terms of performance on dimensions within exercises.

Finally, Tsacoumis, Putka, and Schantz (2005) presented a methodology for computing the reliability of a statistically-derived overall assessment score (OAS). In this case, the individually weighted dimension-within-exercise scores were summed to obtain the OAS. Reliability was computed by using a formula for the reliability of the weighted composite of raw scores derived from Nunnally (1967). The reliability estimates for the OAS were very solid for two different assessment centers (Tsacoumis, Katz, & Schultz, 2005; Tsacoumis, Putka, & Schantz, 2005).

Validity

Content validity is a test development process that seeks to ensure that the resulting measure(s) cover all important aspects of the relevant content domain (e.g., defined by a job analysis) without testing KSAOs that are not relevant to that domain. A content validation strategy involves developing or selecting measures that reflect the content and are representative of the job for which candidates are to be selected. Evidence for content validity comes from following well-established and accepted job analysis and assessment program development steps and from data that demonstrate a direct link between the selection procedures and job requirements. The how-to portion of this chapter describes the steps required to demonstrate evidence of content validity.

In addition to the content validity evidence typically associated with simulations, assessment centers historically have been shown to have criterion-related validity. This chain of evidence began with the assessment centers administered by AT&T as part of the Management Progress Study (Bray & Grant, 1966; Moses, 1977). Assessment scores were evaluated in terms of career progression 8 years after participation in the process. The results revealed that 82% of those rated as having "excellent potential" had been promoted to at least middle management. In contrast, only 29.2% rated as having "low potential" progressed to middle-management or higher levels (Ritchie, 1994). The predictive validities of .44 and .71 for the college and non-college participants, respectively, spearheaded the popularity of the assessment center process (Huck, 1973). Subsequent research has continued to provide strong validity evidence for assessment centers. Hunter and Hunter (1984) reported median corrected correlations of .63 for ratings of potential and .43 for performance ratings. A 1987 meta-analysis obtained mean correlations of .53 and .36 for potential and performance, respectively (Gaugler et al., 1987). Schmidt and Hunter's (1998) meta-analytic work reported a mean validity coefficient of .37 for assessment centers. In its totality, this evidence suggests that assessment centers (i.e., high-fidelity job simulations) are valid measures of one's capabilities.

Subgroup Differences

Although many of the dimensions evaluated in an assessment center clearly have a cognitive component, the observed differences in performance between African

Americans and Whites are typically less than found on traditional cognitive ability tests. As an example, subgroup differences (White and African American) were computed using the d statistic in two different assessment centers (Tsacoumis, Katz, & Schultz, 2005; Tsacoumis, Putka, & Schantz, 2005). The d statistic indexes the difference between subgroup means in terms of standard deviation units (Cohen, 1988). Effect sizes at the exercise level ranged from .14 to .82, at the dimension level from −.17 to .92, and at the dimension-within-exercise level from −.36 to 1.05. It should be noted that the highest effect sizes in all categories were outlier values.

Also note the possibility that by the time applicants participate in an assessment center, they may have passed other selection hurdles that are correlated with cognitive ability (e.g., cognitive ability tests, interviews, situational judgment tests). This prescreening prior to the assessment center is likely to result in smaller subgroup differences in the assessment center. If the assessment center took place earlier in the selection process, the magnitude of subgroup differences may be larger (Roth, Van Iddekinge, Huffcutt, Eidson, & Bobko, 2002).

HOW TO DEVELOP AN ASSESSMENT CENTER

The core (and often sole) components of an assessment center are high-fidelity simulations. Thus, the remainder of this chapter describes development of job simulations following a content-oriented process, training of assessors to evaluate performance on the simulations, and thorough evaluation of the simulations themselves. The terms *simulation* and *exercise* are used interchangeably to refer to assessment center exercises.

Because it is unlikely that an assessment center would be implemented to select apprentice electricians, the context of the following discussion revolves around the evaluation of candidates for an electrician supervisor position.

Developing Assessment Center Exercises

When developing high-fidelity job simulations for an assessment center, the goal is to create measures that reflect the content of the target job, because the more closely selection measures simulate the actual job, the more content validity is enhanced (Society for Industrial and Organizational Psychology, 2003). Thus, industrial-organizational (I/O) psychologists adhere to a content-oriented development strategy. As noted in chapter 14, legal and professional guidelines have provided several principles for establishing the content validity of a selection measure or process. The ultimate goal is to ensure job-relatedness. This goal can be accomplished by using accurate job analysis data as the foundation for exercise development and by constantly referring back to the job analytic information throughout the development process.

Because assessment center simulations are intended to mirror the job, exercise developers must have sufficient knowledge of the job requirements. If the goal is to develop generic exercises that simulate typical supervisory or managerial situations, and to elicit behaviors associated with common supervisory and managerial KSAOs or dimensions, then it is less critical to rely on job experts to create the exercises. Trained I/O psychologists may develop these types of simulations on their own or may solicit input from current supervisors and managers. In other circumstances, the ultimate goal is to implement customized simulations that reflect the organization's environment, mission, values, and goals. In such cases it is important to present situations almost identical to those experienced by supervisors or managers in the specific organization. Customized simulations may be appealing because: (a) They allow the measurement of specific KSAOs, (b) they help participants feel as if they really are in the job, and (c) by definition, they are entirely unique to the organization. In turn, they can be a bit more time consuming to develop, and inherently, they require the involvement of subject matter experts (SMEs) from the organization.

Therefore, the first key step in developing high-fidelity simulations is to review current job analysis data. Specifically, the exercise developer reviews the task-KSAO linkages and generates ideas about possible exercises that simulate the job tasks. Development of simulations based on critical tasks enables an assessment of critical KSAOs linked to those tasks (Goldstein, Zedeck, & Schneider, 1992; Schmitt & Ostroff, 1986). Such assessment can best be accomplished by first organizing the important job tasks into groups that are similar in content, linked to the same KSAOs, or frequently performed together. The developers then carefully review these groups of tasks with an eye toward the practicality of simulating them in an exercise. For example, tasks that involve supervising a group of employees performing an activity are deemed difficult to simulate because a large number of personnel (i.e., confederate subordinates) would be required to conduct the simulation. As another example, some tasks involve activities that occur over a substantial time period, such as marketing and bidding on a project. Thus, it is not feasible to simulate them in a relatively short time period. The end result of this step is a list of different tasks or groups of important job tasks that can be simulated and measure a broad range of critical KSAOs.

Having selected the tasks that could be simulated and having mapped the critical KSAOs onto those tasks, the next step is to generate ideas about the types of simulations that might be developed. As previously noted, there are several standard types of exercises that frequently are used to evaluate supervisory and managerial skills. If the targeted tasks involve interaction between individuals or members of a group, then role-play or fact-finding exercises are often developed and structured around the specific content suggested by the tasks. As another example, if the tasks to be simulated involve activities such as scheduling, doing paperwork, and writing memos, then in-basket exercises are often useful for simulating these activities. One very important consideration when developing ideas for simulations is provision of multiple opportunities (i.e., exercises) to observe and assess a candidate's performance on the important job KSAOs. Multiple measures increase the reliability with which the KSAO can be assessed and provide an opportunity to observe performance on that KSAO in different contexts. In this respect, tasks that are linked to many KSAOs are excellent choices for exercise development.

Working closely with 8 to 10 SMEs, the developer generates ideas for different job simulations. Ideal SMEs are employees who are one level above the target position and have worked at the organization for a number of years, including some time in the target position. In the case of the electrician supervisor position, one simulation might be a role play during which the candidate, in the role of a supervisor, meets with an electrician employee to discuss a project. It could be a situation in which the employee is fairly inexperienced and needs technical guidance on how to proceed. As another example, an in-basket could be developed during which candidates review materials such as those found on an electrician supervisor's desk, indicate the action they would take for each item, and then discuss with an assessor team why they responded to each item as they did. An analysis exercise also might be useful for the electrician supervisor position. For example, this exercise could ask the candidate to review plans to install and modify various electrical systems and provide either a written evaluation of the plans or make a presentation regarding the best way to proceed.

Once the general concept for each exercise is solidified, SMEs and I/O psychologists create the content of the simulations. In many cases, materials must be developed to introduce the assessment center scenario and support each simulation. These materials provide the general context for and facts relevant to all simulations in the assessment center. The developer works with the SMEs to create the fictitious organizational background that will serve as the framework for all simulations. Then, for each simulation, specific materials and instructions are generated. These include: details on the purpose of the exercise; additional organizational or resource information not already included in the general background materials provided for all exercises; a description of the role to be played by the candidate; and information on how to serve as a role player, if a role-play exercise is developed. During the course of simulation development, the task-KSAO linkages, as well as other job analytic data such as critical incidents (see chap. 3) are reviewed. The job analysis data guide development of stimulus materials that elicit behaviors allowing assessment of a candidate's standing on relevant KSAOs.

To develop the exercise materials, SMEs are formed into small groups (e.g., two to three SMEs per group). They are asked to consider how an incumbent in the target position (the candidate in this case) would respond to the specific situation or incident. Details of the simulation evolve as the SMEs consider questions an actual supervisor would have about the scenario and options that might be pursued. Consider the electrician supervisor position. As previously noted, one potential role-play scenario could be a situation in which an inexperienced electrician has to lead a high-stakes project. An actual supervisor would want to know details about the status of the work, timelines, the number of employees assigned to the project, availability of resources, and any commitments the electrician had made regarding the project.

For the in-basket, memos, letters, and various other forms are developed to simulate actual types of materials that commonly appear in an electrician supervisor's in-basket, including e-mail messages. Materials from real supervisors' in-boxes are collected and used to guide development of the in-basket. An analysis exercise involves creating in-depth materials, including qualitative information and data. Fictitious documents are developed using actual job materials as a starting point. This helps ensure that the types of information and the formats of the material are consistent with the job-related materials. For example, the over-arching theme of an analysis exercise may be design of a project to install and modify various electrical systems. In this case, the candidate, playing the role of the supervisor, would be presented with detailed information about the request, the existing system including diagrams, and the availability of human and mone-tary resources.

One characteristic of high-fidelity simulations is that it is impossible to predict how a candidate will respond to the situation. Although all candidates receive stan-dardized preparatory materials, reactions to an exercise are highly individualistic. Although this response pattern contributes to the richness of the measurement tech-nique, it also adds to the complexity of the development process. It is important that the resulting scenarios elicit behaviors associated with the KSAO dimensions and that candidates have ample opportunity to display those behaviors. Therefore, it is necessary to ensure the candidate has sufficient information to respond to the situ-ation and understands that postponing an action or decision is not an effective response. In the same vein, in most cases, there should be no clearly correct or incorrect responses to an exercise, although there should be several better and worse responses. Exercises with these characteristics prevent candidates from pro-viding pat, textbook answers. Thus, it is incumbent on the SMEs during exercise development to consider how a wide range of candidates may respond to the sce-nario and how a role player can provide standardized responses.

Finalization of exercise content is an iterative process. Initial versions of the simulations are repeatedly reviewed and revised by small groups of SMEs (usually two or three in a group). The review process includes participation in the simu-lation (e.g., completing the in-basket simulation, participating in the role play), which helps solidify the exercise's content. Once the first group of SMEs com-pletes its revisions, a new group of two to three SMEs should complete the exer-cises. The second group would then review the materials to identify any conceptual problems and to evaluate the exercise's realism. During each review session, SMEs discuss their comments and suggested revisions with I/O psycholo-gists. All agreed-on changes are subsequently incorporated into the simulation. This repetitive process provides the opportunity to identify any inconsistencies in the materials, to ensure accuracy in the technical information presented in the exercises, and to confirm the relevance of the simulations.

Developing Rating Scales

Once the content of the simulations is finalized, rating scales are developed for each dimension that is measured by each simulation. Table 10.1 depicts a sample of the dimensions that could be tapped by each simulation for the electrician

TABLE 10.1
Sample Competency by Simulation Matrix

| KSAO Dimension | In-Basket | Simulation Method | | Analysis Exercise |
		Role Play 1	Role Play 2	
Knowledge of electrical systems	X		X	X
Knowledge of the National Electrical Code	X		X	X
Delegate activities	X	X		
Resources management	X			X
Judgment and problem solving	X	X	X	X
Decisiveness	X		X	X
Plan, organize, and prioritize	X		X	X
Communicate orally		X	X	X
Relate to others		X	X	
Lead others		X	X	

supervisor position. Recall that the dimensions are defined by various KSAOs grouped together based on conceptual similarity.

The first step in developing the simulation rating scales is to compile all important and entry-level (i.e., critical) KSAOs that are linked to all critical tasks on which each exercise is based. This process helps tailor the rating scales to the content of each exercise. For example, one task underlying a role-play exercise may be "plan and organize the work of subordinates." A review of job analysis results might indicate that the following KSAOs were linked to this task: (a) ability to organize information and activities, (b) ability to plan work of others; (c) ability to prioritize activities, (d) ability to manage multiple activities simultaneously, (e) ability to analyze and evaluate information, and (f) ability to distinguish relevant from irrelevant information. Given the conceptual similarity among the first four abilities, job analysts may group them into a KSAO dimension (e.g., Plan, Organize, and Prioritize).

I/O psychologists work with two to three SMEs to prepare guides to help raters determine how effectively applicants perform on each dimension. The SMEs review the materials (e.g., roles and in-basket memos) for each exercise and specify behaviors that define different levels of performance for each KSAO within the dimension that is measured by the simulation. The general practice is to develop behavioral benchmarks that define three levels (ineffective, moderately effective, and effective) of performance for each dimension within each exercise. The process of finalizing the rating scales is comparable to that used to create the exercises. Different teams of SMEs review and fine-tune the behavioral benchmarks. To facilitate this process, I/O psychologists repeatedly query the SMEs about how candidates may respond to the simulation and then discuss the effectiveness of those responses. In turn, that information is translated into the benchmarks for each level of performance. A sample rating scale that results from this process is show in Fig. 10.2.

As shown in Fig. 10.2, the dimension name is followed by a general definition, which includes the specific KSAOs associated with that dimension. Then, several behavioral benchmarks, anchoring each level of performance, provide a guide for evaluating applicant performance on each dimension.

Operationally, assessors observe a candidate's performance on an exercise and then consider how well the person performed in terms of the effective and ineffective behaviors defining each dimension rating scale. The assessors then rate each dimension on a 5-point scale, where a "1" means that the candidate's actions were nearly all ineffective (as defined by the behavioral examples on the low end of the dimension scale) with hardly any effective actions, and a "5" means that the candidate's actions were nearly all effective (as defined by the behavioral examples anchoring the high end of the scale) with hardly any ineffective actions. The general rules for using the rating scales are shown in Table 10.2.

Pilot Testing Exercises and Scales

After development of the simulations and rating scales is complete, the exercises and administration process are pilot tested. The major purposes of the pilot test are to check the clarity of instructions and other exercise materials, uncover any conceptual problems with the exercises or the information provided to candidates, gather information about the realism of the simulations, and evaluate the time limits.

A general rule of thumb is that 8 to 10 individuals should try out the simulations. This number is sufficient to evaluate several different reactions to the exercises, without exposing too many people to operational test materials. Nevertheless, various organizational factors, such as the limited availability of personnel or intense scrutiny of the program, may dictate decreasing or increasing the number of participants. Ideal participants are those who have recently been promoted to the target position. These individuals are very similar to the candidate pool, yet will never participate in the process. To the extent possible, these individuals should be diverse in terms of demographics, geographic location, and, if relevant, job responsibilities. In addition, it is desirable to select pilot participants who vary in terms of their capabilities, as reflected in their job performance.

Based on the results of the pilot test, I/O psychologists and the pilot test assessors (i.e., SMEs) discuss recommended modifications to the simulations and rating scales. In some cases, the performance of the pilot test participants may be videotaped. Videotaping enables SMEs who serve as assessors to review the performance

Role Play 2: Plan, Organize, and Prioritize

Plan, Organize, and Prioritize involves the ability to organize information and activities, plan the work of others, prioritize activities, and manage multiple activities simultaneously to complete all within prescribed times.

1	2	3	4	5
INEFFECTIVE		MODERATELY EFFECTIVE		EFFECTIVE
⋏ Failed to note that the safety issue is a priority.		⋏ Noted the importance of the safety issue, but handled all issues as priorities.		⋏ Recognized the potential safety issue needed to be addressed first, and then handled the other issues with the project.
⋏ Failed to provide any plan with regard to the potential safety hazard.		⋏ Noted the importance of dealing with the potential safety hazard, but only provided general guidance on how to proceed		⋏ Addressed the potential safety hazard immediately by proposing specific steps for addressing it, for example: • Dispatch experienced electrician to site immediately • Contact local authorities
⋏ Asked the electrician to determine a plan for proceeding or failed to Obtain more experienced provide a plan.		⋏ Suggested a general plan to the electrician that incorporated only the most obvious aspects of how to proceed in this situation.		⋏ Suggested a specific plan to the electrician regarding how to proceed: • Contact client to describe problem • Obtain more experienced electrician to go to site to help • Correct the problem • Call supervisor with status report

FIGURE 10.2   Sample rating scale.

TABLE 10.2
Scale Used to Evaluate Applicant Performance on Each Dimension

5 = High	If the candidate's responses were nearly all extremely effective, the candidate should be rated a "5."
4	If the candidate's responses were mostly very effective, the candidate should be rated a "4."
3 = Average	If the candidate's responses were moderately effective, the candidate should be rated a "3."
2	If the candidate's responses were mostly not effective, the candidate should be rated a "2."
1 = Low	If the candidate's responses were not effective, the candidate should be rated a "1."

of test participants and provide a final, comprehensive evaluation of the rating scales. Modifications of the rating scales typically involve additions to and clarifications of effective and ineffective behaviors used to anchor each rating scale.

The pilot test also provides insight regarding the time limits established for each exercise. Because simulations are designed to be power rather than speeded assessments, it is imperative to ensure that candidates have sufficient time to complete the exercises and to demonstrate their performance on the targeted dimensions.

HOW TO ENSURE QUALITY ASSESSORS

The ultimate success of an assessment center depends on the quality and competence of the assessors. Their job is to sort through all the information presented to them and select only the information that is directly relevant to rating the targeted dimensions. Toward this end, assessors proceed through a series of steps that guide them to a final rating. As a starting point, think about the repertoire of behaviors an individual could potentially exhibit while completing the simulations in an assessment center. Now recall that an assessment center is designed to elicit only that part of the repertoire that is related to job performance. Assessors are responsible for documenting the behaviors they observe, which narrows the potential scope from all job-related behaviors to only those demonstrated during the particular simulation. Then, the assessors review their notes and map their observations to the targeted dimensions. At this point, assessors can compare the relevant observed behaviors to the standardized benchmarks for each dimension. These steps guide assessors through the process of observing a wide range of behaviors to evaluating only those that are associated with a dimension being measured by the simulations. This systematic narrowing of focus ensures that assessors only rate relevant, observed behaviors. Ratings obtained in this manner help ensure the objectivity and validity of the process and minimize the potential for certain kinds of rating biases, such as halo effects (see chap. 11).

TSACOUMIS

It also is worth noting that an assessor's job is to observe and evaluate, but not to interact with the candidate in a job simulation. When an exercise requires interaction, trained role players interact with the candidate while assessors observe and record behaviors. Proponents of this approach believe that it is too challenging for one person to serve both as assessor and role player. This argument dictates that assessors focus solely on documenting observed behaviors.

Nevertheless, there are instances in which individuals have successfully served in both the assessor and role-player roles simultaneously. There are some situations that warrant the use of internal assessors, and these same situations also tend to require the use of internal personnel to serve as role players. In these cases, one assessor wears a dual hat and role plays with the candidates, taking as many notes as possible during the interaction. A second assessor observes the interaction, also taking copious notes. When the simulation is finished, the role player (assessor) takes a few minutes to complete the note-taking process prior to making dimension ratings. Although it may seem implausible that the dual-role approach can be effective and yield accurate evaluations, the approach has been successful (e.g., Tsacoumis, Katz, & Schultz, 2005; Tsacoumis, Putka, & Schantz, 2005; Tsacoumis, Schultz, Bayless, & Cuddy, 1994). The approach is compatible with environments in which specific job knowledge is required by both the role player and assessor. However, the dual-role approach also has been successfully implemented in assessment centers that are less dependent on in-depth knowledge of the job and organization (Tsacoumis, Schantz, Katz, Van Iddekinge, & Donsbach, 2003).

Selecting Assessors

In many situations, trained professionals external to the organization serve as assessors. This is beneficial because it avoids having to pull supervisors, managers, or executives from their jobs. In addition, external assessors are already trained on the assessment center process and understand the underlying concepts and principles. They only need training on any organization-specific policies and procedures, and on the specific simulations. The use of external assessors also eliminates the possibility of having a candidate evaluated by someone with whom they are familiar. Finally, some organizations believe that using external assessors enhances the credibility and perceived objectivity of the assessment center process.

Some research suggests that the use of external psychologists as assessors is preferable to using internal managers (e.g., Gaugler et al., 1987). However, upper management often wants the organization to be intimately involved, and ultimately in control, of the assessment process and, in turn, the results. Thus, they deem it imperative to use internal managers as assessors. In addition, some organizations maintain that an external assessor cannot fully comprehend the true effectiveness of behaviors in the specific work environment. In fact, there are situations in which the nature of the simulations essentially warrants the use of internal assessors. These instances are typically associated with simulations that require a significant amount of job knowledge in order to perform successfully.

TABLE 10.3
Familiarity and Objectivity Scales

Familiarity

5 =   I have supervised or worked with the candidate for at least 6 months and/or have known this candidate for a long time.

4 =   I have supervised or worked with this candidate for less than 6 months and/or have known this candidate fairly well.

3 =   I know this candidate somewhat, but I have not supervised or worked with him/her.

2 =   I do not know this candidate, but know of him/her.

1 =   I do not know this candidate at all.

Objectivity

3 =   I should not evaluate this candidate because I would not be objective or it would be perceived that I lack objectivity.

2 =   I may have some problems in evaluating this candidate because I may not be objective or I may be perceived as lacking objectivity.

1 =   I can objectively evaluate this candidate.

For example, a typical role-play exercise developed for a law enforcement agency often requires generating a course of action regarding a current case or operation. Or, in the case of an electrician supervisor, a scenario may involve reviewing the plan for an electrical system and providing guidance to a subordinate regarding how to proceed. Successful performance on these types of simulations mandates a demonstration of job- and occupation-specific knowledge. It is unlikely that external assessors will be able to evaluate accurately the effectiveness of a certain response in these types of situations. Therefore the use of internal assessors either is required or at the very least increases the overall credibility of the process.

The use of managers, however, introduces the possibility that the assessors know the candidates. In these circumstances it is good practice to administer a familiarity survey. The survey collects information on how familiar the assessor is with each candidate and how objective the assessor can be when making ratings. Examples of the scales used for this survey are presented in Table 10.3. When assigning candidates to assessor teams a general rule is that the familiarity rating should be ≤ 3 and objectivity must be a "1" for each assessor scheduled to evaluate a candidate. Reliance on this type of information helps prevent real or perceived bias from entering the process.

One solution to the issues just presented is to borrow assessors from another similar organization. For example, some state and local law enforcement agencies use senior-level police officers from other law enforcement agencies as assessors. This avoids potential familiarity problems, while ensuring the assessors are knowledgeable about the job-specific nuances.

Training Assessors

Once the assessors have been identified, it is crucial that they receive comprehensive training to ensure a thorough understanding of the simulations, dimensions, and procedures for evaluating candidates' responses. If assessors also serve as role players, they must be trained on how to perform objectively and consistently in the various simulations. Five basic training units can be organized as follows:

> Unit 1:Introduction to the Assessment Center Method
> Unit 2:Orientation to the Organization's Assessment Process
> Unit 3:Evaluation Training
> Unit 4:Review of Job Simulations
> Unit 5:Final Logistics

A brief description of the contents of each unit is presented next.

Unit 1: Introduction to the Assessment Center Method

Training begins with an explanation of the assessment center process and a description of the assessor's role. For new assessors, a brief history of the assessment center process and a description of high-fidelity simulations provide an overall context. Next, the trainer shifts focus to the assessor's role. This facet of training provides an overview of how assessors only focus on observed job-related behaviors associated with the targeted dimensions to obtain their final ratings.

Unit 2: Orientation to the Organization's Assessment Process

During this unit, trainers provide a thorough description of the organization's assessment center process and procedures. This includes an overview of the purpose, how it fits into the broader system, the use of scores, and the policies associated with the process. In addition, trainers briefly introduce the simulations and review the assessment center logistics and schedules. Figures 10.3 and 10.4 depict sample candidate and assessor schedules. As can be noted, these schedules provide the assessors with time after each simulation to generate and discuss their scores with their partners. There is no final consensus process with all assessors at the end of the day or at a later time. This assessor schedule reflects the assessment center model that relies on statistically combining scores to derive the overall assessment score.

Unit 3: Evaluation Training

This unit focuses on the process of making accurate ratings. First, a trainer provides a detailed description of the format of a rating scale (e.g., dimension name,

"A" Schedule	
8:00 – 8:15	Orientation
8:15 – 8:30	Background Material
8:30 – 8:50	Role Play #1 Prep
8:50 – 8:55	Escort to Room
8:55 – 9:15	Role Play #1
9:15 – 9:20	Break
9:20 – 11:55	In-Basket Prep
11:55 – 12:20	Lunch
12:20 – 12:25	Escort to Room
12:25 – 1:10	In-Basket Interview
1:10 – 1:15	Break
1:15 – 1:55	Role Play #2 Prep
1:55 – 2:00	Escort to Room
2:00 – 2:30	Role Play #2
2:30 – 2:35	Break
2:35 – 3:55	Analysis Exer. Prep
3:55 – 4:00	Escort to Room
4:00 – 4:40	Analysis Exercise
4:40 – 4:45	Check Out

"B" Schedule	
8:15 – 8:30	Orientation
8:30 – 8:45	Background Material
8:45 – 10:05	Analysis Exer. Prep
10:05 – 10:10	Escort to Room
10:10 – 10:50	Analysis Exercise
10:50 – 10:55	Break
10:55 – 11:15	Role Play #1 Prep
11:15 – 11:20	Escort to Room
11:20 – 11:40	Role Play #1
11:40 – 12:20	Lunch
12:20 – 2:55	In-Basket Prep
2:55 – 3:00	Escort to Room
3:00 – 3:45	In-Basket Interview
3:45 – 4:10	Break
4:10 – 4:50	Role Play #2 Prep
4:50 – 4:55	Escort to Room
4:55 – 5:25	Role Play #2
5:25 – 5:30	Check Out

FIGURE 10.3   Sample candidate schedules.

8:55–9:15	Role Play #1
9:15–9:30	Score Role Play #1
9:30–10:10	Break
10:10–10:50	Analysis Exercise
10:50–11:05	Score Analysis Exercise
11:05–11:20	Break
11:20–11:40	Role Play #1
11:40–11:55	Score Role Play #1
11:55–12:25	Lunch
12:25–1:10	In-Basket Interview
1:10–1:25	Score In-Basket Exercise
1:25–2:00	Break
2:00–2:30	Role Play #2
2:30–2:45	Score Role Play #2
2:45–3:00	Break
3:00–3:45	In-Basket Interview
3:45–4:00	Score In-Basket Exercise
4:00–4:40	Analysis Exercise
4:40–4:55	Score Analysis Exercise
4:55–5:25	Role Play #2
5:25–5:40	Score Role Play #2

FIGURE 10.4   Sample assessor schedule.

definition, behavioral anchors). Then, the training shifts to a discussion regarding the importance of describing behaviors in an objective manner. Behaviors are descriptions of what transpired; they are not judgments or inferences. To facilitate the understanding of this concept and to reinforce the importance of remaining objective at this stage of the process, the trainer may administer a behavior example exercise (see Table 10.4). This activity requires assessors to determine whether each statement is an objective observation or a subjective interpretation of observed behavior. Although it may seem a bit elementary, it tends to generate good discussion revolving around some of the items and it is an entertaining method for emphasizing the importance of only documenting observed behaviors.

The next step in training is to review how behaviors are observed in each of the simulations. Behavior is observed during an assessment center by watching candidates interact in various simulations (e.g., role-play, oral presentation, LGD) or by reviewing written materials generated by a candidate during a simulation. However, slightly different procedures are used to observe behaviors in the different types of exercises, as described next.

Observing Behavior in a Written Exercise.   Because assessors are given completed materials for evaluating written exercises, the assessment process for

TABLE 10.4
Sample Behavior Example Exercise

Following is a list of statements, some of which describe behavior and some of which do not. If you think that a statement describes behavior, place a plus (+) next to it. If you think that a statement is **NOT** a description of behavior, place a minus (–) next to it. If you are unsure or think it is in a "gray area," put a question mark (?) next to it.

___   1.   Chris made poor decisions in the Analysis Exercise.

___   2.   In response to a suggestion by the role player, Chris asked "Do you think that would be effective?"

___   3.   Chris delegates all tasks that do not have an immediate deadline.

___   4.   Chris quickly perceived and defined the problem.

___   5.   During the role play, it seemed like Chris would be a good leader.

___   6.   Chris did not respond to questions.

___   7.   Chris acted interested.

___   8.   Chris was hesitant to make any recommendations during the Analysis Exercise.

___   9.   Chris concluded the role play by saying "clean up your act or else."

---

these simulations simply involves looking through the written materials for actions that are relevant to each dimension being rated. The necessity for a follow-up interview is dictated by the nature and purpose of the simulation. For example, in some instances a follow-up interview is conducted subsequent to the completion and review of in-basket materials. The purpose of this interview is to obtain a clear understanding of the candidates' thought processes associated with their responses. This is particularly beneficial if one component of the simulation is to prioritize items.

Observing Behavior in the Interactive Portion of Simulations.   All assessors involved in or observing a simulation must record behaviors exhibited by a candidate as they occur. It is extremely difficult to recall precisely what behaviors candidates exhibit if observations are not documented during the simulation. As noted earlier, information recorded during the observation stage of the rating process must be limited to behaviors, and should not reflect an interpretation of those behaviors. Also, at the observation stage, all behaviors should be documented. Assessors should not be concerned at this point about whether the behaviors are relevant to the dimensions being assessed, nor should they consider the effectiveness of the behaviors.

Once trainers review the principles associated with observing behaviors, they move on to a description of how to sort observed behaviors into the dimensions based on their content. At this point, assessors identify the dimension with which

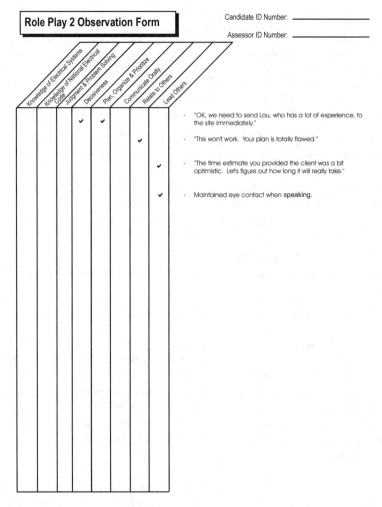

FIGURE 10.5   Sample observation form.

each documented behavior best fits based on its content. In some programs, assessors complete this categorization process on the observation form by reviewing each behavior recorded and then placing a check next to the dimension measured by the behavior (see Fig. 10.5).

Assessors are trained to review all of the observed behaviors relevant to each dimension. When deciding on an overall dimension rating, assessors must determine the performance level that best matches the candidate's responses. One way to capture the rating is to record it onto a scannable sheet as depicted in Fig. 10.6. For some programs, assessors enter their ratings directly into a computer.

Role Play 2 Rating Sheet

Candidate

Assessor
ID Number

Initial Individual Ratings	Low	Moderate		High
Role Play 2	1	2	3	4	5
Knowledge of Electrical Systems	①	②	③	④	⑤
Knowledge of National Electrical Code	①	②	③	④	⑤
Judgment & Problem Solving	①	②	③	④	⑤
Decisiveness	①	②	③	④	⑤
Plan, Organize & Prioritize	①	②	③	④	⑤
Communicate Orally	①	②	③	④	⑤
Relate to Others	①	②	③	④	⑤
Lead Others	①	②	③	④	⑤

Final Individual Ratings	Low	Moderate		High
Role Play 2	1	2	3	4	5
Knowledge of Electrical Systems	①	②	③	④	⑤
Knowledge of National Electrical Code	①	②	③	④	⑤
Judgment & Problem Solving	①	②	③	④	⑤
Decisiveness	①	②	③	④	⑤
Plan, Organize & Prioritize	①	②	③	④	⑤
Communicate Orally	①	②	③	④	⑤
Relate to Others	①	②	③	④	⑤
Lead Others	①	②	③	④	⑤

FIGURE 10.6   Sample scannable rating sheet.

Training then proceeds with an explanation of how assessors compare and discuss their independent ratings. Typically, once assessors have made their independent ratings, they compare the scores assigned to each dimension. If two ratings for a dimension differ by more than 1 point, then assessors discuss the rationale for their assigned ratings. The discussion continues until one (or more) of the assessors agrees to change their scores so that the different scores for each dimension are the same or within 1 scale point. One way to document the final score is shown in Fig. 10.6, where assessors record their final individual rating at the bottom of the form. For some assessment centers, assessors also provide an overall assessment rating (OAR), often on a 4-point scale. In other programs, this overall score is computed by combining the individual dimension scores.

Assessor training proceeds with an overview of common rating tips and errors (see chap. 11). This discussion addresses: stereotyping, contrast effect, first impressions, leniency-severity, central tendency, and halo. Even though it is likely that the assessors are familiar with these concepts, it is beneficial to remind them of the potential traps and to encourage them to evaluate their own rating tendencies.

Unit 4: Review of Job Simulations

Once the dimension definitions have been thoroughly reviewed and the assessors understand how to make ratings, training should proceed with a comprehensive review of each job simulation. In general, the steps associated with training each simulation are:

- Assessors read through candidate materials.
- Trainer reviews the facts.
- Assessors read through role-play materials (if relevant).
- Trainer reviews additional facts associated with the role-player's role.
- Trainer discusses how to play the role.
- Assessors read through rating scales for each targeted dimension.
- Trainer reviews benchmarks associated with each rating scale.
- Assessors watch videotaped performance or review written materials of a mock candidate and document observed behaviors.
- Assessors rate mock candidate.
- Trainer reviews the ratings for each dimension and provides guidance on appropriate rating given the candidate's performance.
- A second mock candidate is viewed or reviewed, rated, and discussed.
- Assessors practice playing the assigned role if appropriate.

Several training exercises are used to facilitate understanding of some of the topics listed. For example, a Fact Quiz can be administered after the final review of all the facts associated with a particular simulation. This is a closed-book exercise that is reviewed as a large group once everyone has completed it. Examples of items used in this type of exercise are presented in Table 10.5. This exercise is an excellent tool for reinforcing the facts that the assessor or role player must know during administration of the simulation. It breaks the monotony often associated with reading or listening to the trainer speak. In addition, it highlights the facts that need more review.

Another useful training tool is an exercise that encourages the role-player to think about how to respond to unanticipated questions or reactions from the

TABLE 10.5
Sample Job Simulation Fact Quiz Items

True-False

_____ 1. Pat Jennings informed Chris Lawrence that he does not have any information he can provide.

_____ 2. Chris Lawrence was the group's first choice for the supervisor position.

Multiple Choice

1. How much money was the contractor paid for the purchase of five ceiling mounted lighting fixtures on November 2nd?
a. $50
b. $500
c. $1000
d. $1500

2. How much time did the electrician tell the client it would take to complete the rewiring job?
a. 1 week
b. 2 weeks
c. 3 weeks
d. 4 weeks

Short Answer

1. What is the purpose of the meeting between Electronics USA and the client to take place on November 4th?

2. What role would Pat like the contractor to take in the project?

candidates. The "What Would You Say?" exercise offers several potential candidate responses and invites the role players to indicate how they would reply. A few sample items are listed in Table 10.6. This exercise invariably generates in-depth discussion regarding the most appropriate responses, as well as other potential candidate reactions. It serves as a useful stimulus for encouraging the role players to think through their roles.

To facilitate a thorough understanding of the rating scales for each targeted dimension, a "Categorization" exercise can be administered. This activity provides a list of "observed behaviors" for the specific simulation (see Table 10.7 for a few examples). The assessors indicate the dimension into which each behavior can be classified. This exercise is extremely beneficial in helping assessors to learn the dimensions and their associated anchors, to understand how to categorize behaviors, and to keep the dimensions independent. One key point that should be emphasized is that the evaluation process should be based solely on behaviors that can be categorized into dimensions. In addition, the importance of the independence of the dimensions should be stressed. For example, poor performance on a given dimension should not be considered when evaluating performance on

TABLE 10.6
Sample "What Would You Say?" Exercise Questions

1. Let's start from the beginning. How did you become involved in this project?
2. Have you learned anything more about how the errors were made and who made them?
3. What do you think we need in terms of supplies, equipment, and personnel?
4. Who do you plan to bring with you to the meeting today?

TABLE 10.7
Sample Role Play 2 Categorization Exercise Items

In the space before each statement, write the competency to which the statement *best* applies. You should refer to the simulation rating scales and use the following codes:

A. Communicate Orally   E. Decisiveness
B. Plan, Organize, and Prioritize F. Lead Others
C. Relate to Others   G. Knowledge of Electrical Systems
D. Judgment and Problem Solving   H. Knowledge of National Electrical Code

_____ 1. "This project has a lot of potential. I'm going to see what I can do to rearrange things and make some of the journeyman electricians available to you."
_____ 2. "What were you thinking? There are a lot of holes in this project plan you've put together."
_____ 3. "We need to get the inspectors involved. They should be on site this afternoon for the meeting."
_____ 4. "We need to concentrate on getting things in place so the project can start on time as planned. We'll handle the paperwork corrections after that."
_____ 5. Candidate continually clicked pen throughout the role play.

other dimensions. That is, to avoid halo error, the observed behaviors that contributed to the rating of poor performance on one dimension should not be considered when evaluating performance on other dimensions.

One final point is the importance of providing realistic mock candidates to evaluate and then leading a thorough discussion of the ratings of the candidate's performance. When reviewing the ratings, it is useful for all assessors to state their assigned rating for each dimension. If there is disagreement about the appropriate rating, the trainer should ask the assessors to defend their ratings by describing the observed behaviors considered in the rating process and noting the scale anchors associated with those behaviors. Another effective approach is to walk through the behavioral anchors and ask the assessors to indicate, based on their observations, the candidate's performance for each anchor. A strong trainer walks through each anchor on a dimension and helps the trainee assessors to determine the effectiveness of performance in terms of the anchors, and ultimately to assign the final dimension score.

Unit 5: Final Logistics

Assessor training concludes with a description of all administrative procedures. This includes assessor team assignments, guidance on room setup, and review of the schedule.

HOW TO EVALUATE THE SIMULATIONS

Once the simulations are implemented, it is important to evaluate them. One way to assess their quality is to evaluate the distributional characteristics of the assessment scores. This can include dimension, exercise, dimension within exercise, and overall assessment scores. This information provides an indication of the difficulty of the simulations and an insight into the variance, which is critical for identifying differences among candidates. Given sufficient sample sizes, subgroup differences (e.g., males vs. females) are computed. One common method for investigating differences is to compute the effect size (d statistic; Cohen, 1988). The d statistic indexes the difference between subgroup means (e.g., means for Whites and African Americans) in terms of standard deviation units.

Additional evaluation criteria include reliability estimates and validity evidence. If there are good criterion measures and sufficient sample sizes, criterion-related validity coefficients may be computed. Because a content-oriented development strategy typically is followed when creating simulations, the evaluation process should also include the collection of content validity ratings. The purpose in doing so is to verify which dimensions the job simulations measure. This step is taken to ensure a direct connection between the dimensions and the simulations. As previously noted, each simulation is designed to capture specific dimensions.

In many cases, the trained assessors serve as the ideal SMEs for making content validity judgments. These individuals are trained on the simulations and the corresponding evaluation criteria, which ensures that they are very familiar with the exercises and cognizant of the knowledges and abilities that potentially could be measured. Of course, other SMEs or trained test developers can serve as the raters. The prerequisite is simply in-depth knowledge of the simulations and associated rating scales.

Following the procedures outlined by Goldstein et al. (1992), the first step in collecting the content validity rating data is to distribute an instruction and rating booklet that describes the content validity rating task to each rater. Then, raters are asked to carefully review each exercise and dimension definitions and rate the extent to which each dimension could be measured by the exercise just reviewed. These ratings are made using a 3-point scale, where 3 = the exercise directly measures the dimension, 2 = the exercise indirectly measures the dimension, and 1 = the exercise does not measure the dimension.

For each simulation, means and standard deviations are calculated for each dimension to determine the extent to which the dimension is perceived as being measured by the exercise. The results are evaluated by reviewing the mean ratings for the dimensions specifically targeted by each simulation. A possible cutoff is that the mean should be greater than 2.0.

The content validity judgments, coupled with the direct linkages between the simulations and the job analysis data (i.e., critical tasks and KSAOs) established during the exercise development process, provide clear content validity evidence for the measures.

SUMMARY

As a method of performance evaluation and prediction, the assessment center provides individuals with opportunities to participate in multiple situational exercises that serve as snapshots of the job. These exercises commonly take the form of an in-basket simulation, role play, oral presentation, written exercise, and leaderless group exercise. Because assessment centers are known to predict supervisory and managerial performance, they often are used to select or promote employees into first-level supervisor, mid-level manager, or executive positions. In other instances, assessment centers serve as an evaluation tool for selecting candidates into a career development or succession planning program.

Most assessment centers rely solely on several high-fidelity simulations. However, in some cases, structured interviews or paper-and-pencil personality or cognitive ability tests also are implemented. Overall, research studies have shown that assessment centers are a valid means of selecting qualified applicants for a variety of jobs. If strict content-oriented development procedures are followed, then job simulations can serve as a rich source of information regarding a candidate's potential job performance.

REFERENCES

Bray, D. W., & Grant, D. L. (1966). The assessment center in the measurement of potential for business management. *Psychological Monographs, 80*(17, Whole No. 625), 1–27.

Bray, D. W., & Moses, J. L. (1972). Personnel selection. *Annual Review of Psychology, 23*, 545–576.

Cascio, W. F., & Phillips, N. F. (1979). Performance testing: A rose among thorns? *Personnel Psychology, 32*, 751–766.

Cohen, J. (1988). *Statistical power analysis for the behavioral sciences* (2nd ed.). Hillsdale, NJ: Lawrence Erlbaum Associates.

Gatewood, R., Thornton, G. C., III, & Hennessey, H. W., Jr. (1990). Reliability of exercise ratings in the leaderless group discussion. *Journal of Occupational Psychology, 63*, 331–342.

Gaugler, B. B., Rosenthal, D. B., Thornton, G. C., III, & Bentson, C. (1987). Meta-analysis of assessment center validity. *Journal of Applied Psychology, 74*, 611–618.

Goldstein, I. L., Zedeck, S., & Schneider, B. (1992). An exploration of the job analysis-content validity process. In N. Schmitt & W. C. Borman (Eds.), *Personnel selection in organizations* (pp. 3–34). San Francisco: Jossey-Bass.

Greenwood, J. M., & McNamara, W. J. (1967). Interrater reliability in situational tests. *Journal of Applied Psychology, 51,* 101–106.

Greenwood, J. M., & McNamara, W. J. (1969). Leadership styles of structure and consideration and managerial effectiveness. *Personnel Psychology, 22,* 141–152.

Hoffman, C. C., & Thornton, G. C., III. (1997). Examining selection utility where competing predictors differ in adverse impact. *Personnel Psychology, 50,* 455–470.

Huck, J. R. (1973). Assessment centers: A review of the external and internal validities. *Personnel Psychology, 26,* 191–212.

Hunter, J. E., & Hunter, R. F. (1984).Validity and utility of alternate predictors of performance. *Psychological Bulletin, 96,* 72–98.

International Task Force on Assessment Center Guidelines. (2000). Guidelines and ethical considerations for assessment center operations. *Public Personnel Management, 29,* 315–331.

MacKinnon, D. W. (1977). From selecting spies to selecting managers: The OSS assessment program. In J. L. Moses & W. C. Byham (Eds.), *Applying the assessment center method* (pp. 13–30). New York: Pergamon Press.

Moses, J. L. (1977). The assessment center method. In J. L. Moses & W. C. Byham (Eds.), *Applying the assessment center method* (pp. 3–11). New York: Pergamon Press.

Nunnally, J. C. (1967). *Psychometric theory.* New York: McGraw-Hill.

Ritchie, R. J. (1994). Using the assessment center method to predict senior management potential. *Consulting Psychology Journal, 46,* 16–23.

Roth, P. L., Van Iddekinge, C. H., Huffcutt, A. I., Eidson, C. E., Jr., & Bobko, P. (2002). Corrections for range restriction in structured interview ethnic group differences: The values may be larger than researchers thought. *Journal of Applied Psychology, 87,* 369–376.

Rynes, S. L., & Connerley, M. L. (1993). Applicant reactions to alternative selection procedures. *Journal of Business and Psychology, 7,* 261–277.

Schmidt, F. L., Greenthal, A. L., Hunter, J. E., Berner, J. G., & Seaton, F. W. (1977). Job sample versus paper-and-pencil trades and technical tests: Adverse impact and examinee attitudes. *Personnel Psychology, 30,* 187–197.

Schmidt, F. L., & Hunter, J. E. (1998). The validity and utility of selection methods in personnel psychology: Practical and theoretical implications of 85 years of research findings. *Psychological Bulletin, 124,* 262–274.

Schmitt, N., & Ostroff, C. (1986). Operationalizing the "behavioral consistency" approach: Selection test development based on a content oriented approach. *Personnel Psychology, 39,* 91–108.

Society for Industrial and Organizational Psychology, Inc. (2003). *Principles for validation and use of personnel selection procedures.* (4th ed.). College Park, MD: Author.

Thornton, G. C., III. (1992). *Assessment centers in human resource management.* Reading, MA: Addison Wesley.

Thornton, G. C., III, & Byham, W. C. (1982). *Assessment centers and managerial performance.* New York: Academic Press.

Thornton, G. C., III, & Mueller-Hanson, R. A. (2004). *Developing organizational simulations: A guide for practitioners and students.* Mahwah, NJ: Lawrence Erlbaum Associates.

Tsacoumis, S., Katz, B. D., & Schultz, S. R. (2005). *Development and implementation of an assessment center* (Tech. Rep. No. FR-05-02). Alexandria, VA: Human Resources Research Organization.

Tsacoumis, S., Putka, D. J., & Schantz, L. (2005). *Development and implementation of an assessment center* (Tech. Rep. No. FR-05-01). Alexandria, VA: Human Resources Research Organization.

Tsacoumis, S., Schantz, L., Katz, B., Van Iddekinge, C., & Donsbach, J. (2003). *Development of an assessment center for applicants to the 2002 Social Security Administration SES career development program* (Tech. Rep. No. FR-03-16). Alexandria, VA: Human Resources Research Organization.

Tsacoumis, S., Schultz, S. R., Bayless, J. A., & Cuddy, S. (1994). *Revision and administration of promotion processes for 1994.* (Tech. Rep. No. FR-95-04). Alexandria, VA: Human Resources Research Organization.

Tziner, A., Ronen, S., & Hacohen, D. (1993). A four-year validation study of an assessment center in a financial corporation. *Journal of Organizational Behavior, 14,* 225–237.

Wernimont, P. F., & Campbell, J. P. (1968). Signs, samples, and criteria. *Journal of Applied Psychology, 52,* 372–376.

CHAPTER ELEVEN

Performance Measurement

Elaine D. Pulakos
Personnel Decisions Research Institutes, Inc.

OVERVIEW

Rewarding and promoting effective performance in organizations, as well as identifying ineffective performers for developmental programs or other personnel actions, are essential to effective human resource management. The ability to perform these functions relies on evaluating employee performance in a fair and accurate manner. However, performance management is the Achilles' heel of human resources management. A recent survey by Watson Wyatt showed that only 30% of employees felt that their company's performance management system helped improve performance, and less than 40% said they had clear performance goals and received honest feedback. Although these results suggest that there may be many ineffective performance management systems in organizations, it typically is not poorly developed performance appraisal tools and processes that cause problems. Rather, difficulties arise because performance management is an inherently threatening process for both managers and employees.

Many managers are uncomfortable discussing performance with employees for fear of reprisal or damaging relationships. Often, employees feel that their managers are unskilled in providing feedback and developmental coaching. Managers and employees frequently complain that performance management systems are bureaucratic and too time-consuming. This leads managers and employees to treat performance management as an administrative burden rather than as a process that helps achieve important organizational goals. In spite of the difficulties, performance management can result in important outcomes for an organization, its managers, and its employees. Specifically, effective and accurate performance assessment is essential for appropriately developing employees,

293

rewarding employees, and evaluating the effectiveness of an organization's selection practices. Accordingly, this chapter focuses on developing and implementing effective performance management systems in organizations. It is organized into four sections, as follows:

1. How to develop an effective performance management process.
2. How to develop effective evaluation tools.
3. How to evaluate and improve performance rating quality.
4. How to implement effective performance systems.

HOW TO DEVELOP AN EFFECTIVE PERFORMANCE MANAGEMENT PROCESS

Performance management processes should be defined, understandable, and consistent. Especially in organizations that use performance management as a basis for pay and other important decisions, it is important to ensure that all employees are treated fairly. Most appraisal processes begin with a performance planning process, in which managers and employees discuss expectations and results to be achieved for the upcoming rating period. During the rating period, job performance is observed and feedback provided. At the end of the rating period, performance is formally evaluated. In an effective system, employees will be appraised against standardized, job-relevant rating factors and standards. The formal evaluation process typically concludes with a formal performance review and feedback session that occurs between managers and employees.

Performance Planning

At the beginning of the rating period, managers should review their performance expectations with employees and agree on results the employee will concentrate on achieving during the rating period. The research literature has shown several guidelines to be important for establishing effective goals (Hillgren & Cheatham, 2000; Locke & Latham, 1990). First, to the extent possible, goals should have a direct and obvious link to organizational success factors. Second, performance goals need to be difficult but achievable to have a motivating effect on employees. Finally, expectations should be set in no more than a few areas, because attempting to achieve too many different goals at once will impede success.

Ongoing Feedback

Feedback should be provided to employees whenever they have exhibited exceptional or ineffective performance. There are several principles associated with providing effective feedback that have been discussed in the literature (Cederblom, 1982; Wexley, 1986). Managers should provide actionable feedback in a timely manner and employees should seek feedback if they do not feel they are receiving sufficient input from their managers. For feedback to have a positive impact, it needs to be delivered immediately following the performance event. If a manager needs to give developmental feedback to an employee, it is important to ask for the employee's view about what could have been done differently. Managers should be specific about what actions were effective or ineffective and why; not what is effective or ineffective about the person. Managers should work collaboratively with and help employees address any development needs.

Performance Evaluation

The importance of accurate evaluation in a performance management process cannot be overemphasized. This is because evaluation data are used as a basis for making important personnel decisions as well as evaluating the effectiveness of organizational systems and processes. For example, evaluation information is used to make decisions about employee rewards and advancement. If incorrect decisions are made, employee motivation will decrease and the best talent will not be advanced and retained in the organization. In addition, the ability to evaluate the usefulness of an organization's selection practices also relies on developing effective evaluation tools for ongoing appraisal of employee performance. The resulting data are invaluable in assessing and continuously improving the quality of those hired.

There are different types of measures that can be used to evaluate employee performance, most of which can be classified into two general categories: (a) objective performance measures and (b) subjective performance measures. Objective performance measures include such things as dollar volume of sales, number of words typed per minute, number of pieces produced, number of errors made, number of days absent from work, and so forth. While useful information can be obtained from objective performance indices, there are some inadequacies associated with these types of measures that preclude their use in many jobs (Dunnette, 1966; Guion, 1965). One problem is that objective measures often are deficient, that is, they do not provide an assessment of all aspects of the job that contribute to performance. Consider, for example, the job of an electrician. Although the number of construction tasks completed on time may be a useful indicator of one's performance effectiveness, the ability to complete tasks on time is only one aspect of the electrician's job. There are other important aspects of performance, such as maintaining good team relations, for which no objective measures of performance may exist. If one were to focus only on the objective number of tasks completed on time criterion, other aspects of performance would be neglected, leaving an incomplete picture of the electrician's effectiveness. Thus, number of tasks completed on time would be a deficient performance measure—a common problem with many objective performance indices.

A second major problem associated with objective performance measures is that they are often affected by factors that are outside of the employee's direct control. Again using the number of tasks completed on time example, there are many factors beyond the electrician's ability or motivation to perform effectively that may impact the number of tasks completed on time. For example, some of these factors might include the effectiveness of suppliers or the knowledge level of teammates. An electrician who happens to have good material suppliers and knowledgeable team members may be more likely to complete tasks on time than an electrician with poor suppliers and peers who do not understand the business. Such unequal circumstances create difficulties in comparing the performance of different electricians using the number of tasks completed on time criterion.

The problems associated with objective performance measures have led researchers and managers to place more emphasis on subjective measures of job performance. Subjective measures of performance usually are some type of performance rating tool. In fact, the most common measures used in organizations to provide developmental feedback to subordinates, make personnel decisions, or validate testing or other human resource programs are performance rating scales. One important advantage of using ratings to collect information about an individual's job performance is that all of a job's performance requirements can be described on a set of rating scales (Borman, 1987). Thus, subjective rating measures are not plagued by the deficiencies discussed above that often are inherent in objective performance measures. Further, subjective measures can be developed to focus on behaviors that lead to effective performance, which helps to alleviate the problems imposed by unequal opportunities to perform effectively. Using the example discussed above, an electrician who happens to have poor suppliers and inexperienced teammates could be expending as much time and effort completing tasks on time as the electrician with good suppliers and knowledgeable peers. Using rating scales, both electricians would be given credit for behaviors on a scale that dealt with effort expended completing tasks on time, even though the number of tasks completed would be fewer for the electrician with poor suppliers and inexperienced team members. Because job performance rating scales mitigate against some of the problems inherent in objective performance measures, they are the instrument most commonly used in organizations to evaluate employee performance.

Performance Review and Feedback

The final step of most performance management processes consists of the formal feedback and review session. Managers owe employees explanations of why they were evaluated as they were, and they should be coaching employees to address their developmental needs. Unfortunately, this usually does not happen to the extent that it should in organizations because many managers are not skilled in the development and coaching process. A key problem is that many managers avoid providing feedback because they do not know how to deliver feedback productively, in way that will minimize employee defensiveness. Because the exchange of feedback information is inherently difficult for both managers and employees, managers typically need training in this area.

For the performance review and feedback process to work well, it must be a two-way communication process and the joint responsibility of managers and employees, not just the manager's responsibility. Helping managers and employees to understand their roles and responsibilities in the performance management process through training, mentoring, or other interventions is important for the system to operate effectively. In organizations where the inherent tension between giving and receiving feedback has been effectively addressed, performance development and coaching are much more effective. In fact, addressing this very issue is probably the single most important determinant of whether a performance management system will achieve its maximum benefits from a coaching and development perspective.

HOW TO DEVELOP EFFECTIVE EVALUATION TOOLS

Over the years, many different types of rating tools have been developed in both research studies and practice. The motivation behind much of this work was based on the assumption that certain rating format characteristics would lead to more accurate ratings. In fact, some research has shown that rating scales anchored with specific job behaviors yield higher quality ratings than other types of rating scales (Borman & Dunnette, 1975; Campbell, Dunnette, Arvey, & Hellervick, 1973; Keaveny & McGann, 1975). However, literature reviews of format comparison studies (Bernardin, 1977; DeCotiis, 1977; Landy & Farr, 1980; Schwab, Heneman, & DeCotiis, 1975; Zedeck, Kafry, & Jacobs, 1976) have led researchers to conclude that no one rating format consistently produces superior ratings (e.g., more reliable, valid, or accurate). In fact, Landy and Farr (1980) estimated that as little as 4% of the rating variance in rating quality is accounted for by the rating format used, leading them to call for a moratorium on rating format research.

Although the rating format may have little impact on the quality of performance ratings, there are other aspects of the performance appraisal process for which format issues are relevant. For example, one issue is the ease with which managers are able to understand and use the format. Another is the extent to which managers and employees accept the rating instrument and view it as appropriate. A third issue is how well the rating format supports provision of meaningful developmental feedback to employees. The final issue is the degree to which the rating format meets legal standards. In the following sections, five of the more common rating formats are discussed: (a) graphic rating scales (Paterson, 1922–1923), (b) behaviorally anchored rating scales (Smith & Kendall, 1963), (c) behavioral summary scales (Borman, 1979), (d) behavioral observation scales (Latham & Wexley, 1981), and (e) mixed standard scales (Blanz & Ghiselli, 1972). It should be noted that there has recently been a great deal of attention on competency modeling as a basis for developing performance evaluation tools in organizations (Lievens, Sanchez, & DeCorte, 2004; Shippmann, Ash, Battista, et al., 2000). Any of the procedures described below for developing different types of rating formats can be used to develop competency-based rating scales by simply focusing on identifying key job competencies as the rating dimensions.

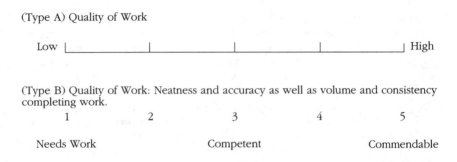

FIGURE 11.1   Examples of graphic rating scales.

Graphic Rating Scales

One of the more widely used rating formats is the graphic rating scale (Paterson, 1922–1923). Graphic rating scales are designed to elicit ratings on dimensions of performance relevant to a job. Performance dimensions typically are identified through a job analysis in which job experts describe the major aspects of performance for their job(s). The scale developer must decide how many rating scale points will be included on the scales. A generally accepted guideline is between 4 and 9. Use of fewer than 4 rating scale points tends to provide insufficient discrimination among employees, while more than 9 yields unimportant distinctions. The scale points are usually defined on a continuum, but the scale developer must decide how these points will be anchored, for example, with verbal anchors, numerical anchors, or a combination of both. Two examples of a graphic rating scale are shown in Fig. 11.1.

The first graphic rating scale shown in Fig. 11.1 (Type A) contains qualitative end anchors only, while the second (Type B) includes both numerical and verbal anchors. A major problem with many rating scales of this type is that the scale points are not thoroughly defined, leaving managers to develop their own interpretations of what is meant by the different rating levels. One consequence of allowing managers to apply their own standards to the rating task is that they often do not agree about the types of behavior or performance that constitute different effectiveness levels. Consider this example. Two managers observe an electrician performing a series of job tasks. Using Scale B in Fig. 11.1, one manager may evaluate the performance as a 3, whereas the other manager may evaluate that exact same performance as a 5. Because the anchors on the rating scales are not well defined, there are no guidelines presented for what types of behavior should be rated a 3 versus a 4 or a 5. The main problem, then, with graphic rating scales is that they do not adequately define the meaning of different performance levels. Not only does this make the manager's job of distinguishing between the different effectiveness levels very difficult, but also the standards applied by different managers are not consistent across employees.

It also is difficult to provide feedback using graphic rating scales. A manager can inform employees that their quality of work is a 3, but why that rating was given versus another rating can be difficult to explain. Graphic rating scales also provide little, if any, information about what the employee must do to achieve a more effective rating.

Behaviorally Anchored Rating Scales

Behaviorally anchored rating scales (BARS; Smith & Kendall, 1963) are used to assess performance dimensions that represent major requirements of a job. Actual examples of behaviors that incumbents may exhibit on the job are used to anchor different levels of performance effectiveness within each dimension. These behaviors help managers make accurate assessments of performance by matching their observations of employee performance to an appropriate effectiveness level on each dimension.

The development of BARS relies on input from job incumbents, their supervisors, or both. These subject matter experts (SMEs) provide the information necessary to construct the rating scales (e.g., rating dimensions and behaviors that define different levels of effectiveness for each dimension). The behaviors are derived from critical incidents (Flanagan, 1954), as described in chapter 3. After the critical incidents are collected from SMEs and edited by psychologists, SMEs are asked to sort the critical incidents into dimensions and rate their effectiveness. Often, a 7-point scale is used, where 1 is highly ineffective and 7 is highly effective. The percentage of SMEs sorting each incident into a particular dimension and the means and standard deviations of the effectiveness ratings for each incident are computed. Examples of results from an analysis of critical incidents are provided in Appendix B of chapter 3.

The scale developer must then decide which reliably rated incidents will be used as anchors for each performance dimension. Two criteria typically are used to select incidents to anchor each dimension: (a) each incident should have a low standard deviation for the effectiveness rating (indicating high agreement among raters); and (b) each incident should be placed in a particular dimension by a high percentage of the raters. If a 7-point scale is used to make the effectiveness ratings, a standard deviation of 1.5 is often used as a cutoff for retaining behavioral incidents (any incident with a standard deviation greater than 1.5 would be eliminated). A frequently used cutoff for the percentage of raters agreeing that a given incident belongs in a particular dimension is 60%–70%. Behavioral incidents that meet these criteria are used to anchor the rating scale points.

Usually between 5 and 12 representative incidents are selected to anchor the different levels of effectiveness for rating dimension. Figure 11.2 shows an example of BARS developed for apprentice electricians for the dimension Planning, Preparing and Organizing Work. Notice that in chapter 3, the fifth incident in Appendix B about piping school rooms for lighting using shallow boxes was categorized into the dimension Planning, Preparing and Organizing Work by 12 of the 20 respondents (60%). The mean effectiveness rating was 2.45 with a standard

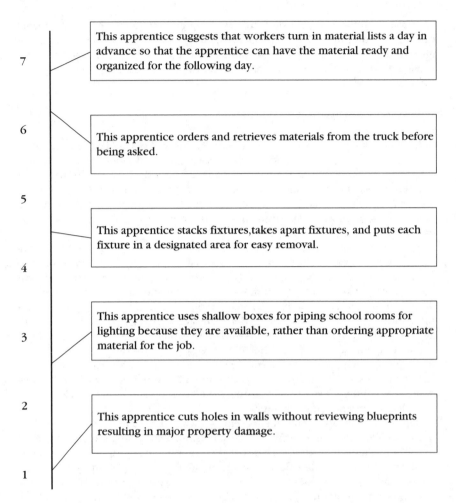

FIGURE 11.2   Example of a Behaviorally Anchored Rating Scale for the dimension Planning, Preparing, and Organizing Work for apprentice electricians.

deviation of .66. Since this incident is within the limits described above, it was chosen to anchor the scale shown in Fig. 11.2 near the low end.

To evaluate a worker's performance using BARS, managers are first asked to record behavioral observations of employee performance relevant to each performance dimension. Because these observations may occur over a 6-month to 1-year time period, managers are encouraged to keep notebooks in which they record performance examples as they occur. At the end of the rating period, managers compare the effectiveness of the employee behaviors they have observed with the effectiveness levels represented in the scaled behavioral examples. A rating is then assigned based on this comparison process. Thus, in using BARS, managers are encouraged to attend to and record actual behaviors rather than relying on general impressions as a basis for making their ratings. Further, the scaled behavioral anchors serve as comparison points against which an employee's observed performance can be evaluated.

Behavioral Summary Scales

Although the BARS rating format was an important step in the development of well-defined rating scales, a potential limitation with BARS is that managers may have trouble matching an employee's actual performance to the specific behavioral examples used to anchor the rating scales (Borman, 1979). Using the BARS rating scale shown in Fig. 11.2, imagine the difficulty a manager might have comparing an employee's performance to the very specific scale anchors shown there. Even though employees may be performing at an effectiveness level represented by one of the anchors, it is unlikely that they will have exhibited the exact behavior depicted on the rating scale. This puts the manager in the position of having to decide which of the relatively few scaled behaviors best matches the employee's actual job performance. Such judgments can be very difficult to make, leaving managers unsure about how to use the scaled effectiveness levels to guide their ratings.

In response to this problem with BARS, the behavioral summary scale (BSS) rating format was developed by Borman, Hough, and Dunnette (1976). BSS are similar to a BARS because both scales are anchored with behavioral descriptions of effective and ineffective performance that guide managers' evaluations of employee job performance. However, rather than using a few specific behaviors to anchor the different scale points, BSSs contain anchors that are more general descriptions of effectiveness at the different performance levels. To develop these more general behavioral anchors, the highly specific behavioral incidents that were assigned to a specific dimension and effectiveness level, using the criteria outlined earlier, are examined for similar underlying content. Statements are then written to represent a wider range of behaviors that are characteristic of the specific incidents scaled at each effectiveness level. Formulating broader scale anchors that capture the content of several behavioral incidents enables the scale developer to include information on the rating scales that will be relevant to the performance of a larger number of employees.

To develop a BSS, one would collect and analyze critical incidents using the process described in chapter 3. Then, as mentioned, rather than anchoring the rating scales with a few specific behavioral examples, the scale developer writes statements that capture as much content as possible of all of the behavioral incidents that were reliably sorted into each performance dimension. Several

Please rate the apprentice on the following scale by reading the descriptions of each performance level and selecting the number that most closely corresponds to the behavior exhibited by the apprentice.

LOW	MEDIUM	HIGH
Starts to perform tasks without checking blueprints/plans; uses inappropriate, but available materials for jobs; hurries through work before considering additional tasks that need to be performed before job is completed; misjudges time to complete tasks.	Plans tasks before performing them; organizes tools and materials so that they are easily retrievable when needed; writes down information needed for jobs so that work is completed efficiently; makes adjustments to material before starting jobs so that work is completed efficiently.	Reviews blueprints/plans before starting tasks; makes suggestions about organizing material so that preparation time is minimized; creates lists of tasks to be completed and orders material on own initiative; keeps foreman informed of progress of jobs; anticipates needs for jobs and retrieves tools and materials before they are requested.
1 2	3 4 5	6 7

FIGURE 11.3   Example of a behavioral summary scale for the dimension Planning, Preparing, and Organizing Work for apprentice electricians.

hundred behavioral incidents typically are categorized into dimensions and rated for effectiveness using a 1 (highly ineffective) to 7 (highly effective) rating scale. To develop summary statements, the incidents are categorized as follows: Incidents rated between 1.00 and 2.49 are considered low-level behaviors; incidents rated from 2.50 to 5.49 are considered average-level behaviors; and incidents rated from 5.50 to 7.00 are considered high-level behaviors. Behavioral statements are written to capture the content of the behavioral incidents in each dimension and at each effectiveness level.

Figure 11.3 shows an example of a BSS for the same dimension of electrician performance (Planning, Preparing, and Organizing Work) measured by the BARS shown in Fig. 11.2. As shown in Fig. 11.3, the BSS anchors cover more of the behavioral domain of the dimension than the specific behavioral incidents used to anchor the BARS (Fig. 11.2). For example, the anchor for high performance states, "Reviews blueprints/plans before starting tasks." This statement could summarize several incidents, including the third and fourth incidents in Appendix B in chapter 3. By providing a more comprehensive definition of the behaviors that constitute different levels of effectiveness, it is more likely that one of the anchors will describe an employee's observed performance on each dimension. Accordingly, the manager's task of matching observed behaviors to the scaled behavioral anchors is facilitated. Although research comparing different rating formats has shown no consistent differences in the quality of ratings obtained using one versus another rating format (Landy & Farr, 1980), managers react more favorably to the BSS format than to the BARS format, because they feel it is easier to see the relevance of the BSS anchors for the employees they are evaluating.

Behavioral Observation Scales

Behavioral observation scales (BOS; Latham & Wexley, 1981) contain a large number of very specific, effective and ineffective behaviors on which each employee is evaluated. There are no average behaviors included on the rating scales. For each behavioral incident on the scale, raters are asked to evaluate the frequency with which they have observed each employee exhibit the behavior. Latham and Wexley recommended that a 1 indicate "almost never (performs the behavior)" and a 5 indicate "almost always (performs the behavior)." Thus, rather than evaluating the effectiveness of an employee's performance on each of several job-relevant dimensions (as is the case when using BARS or BSS), a BOS requires managers to evaluate the frequency with which they have observed several specific behaviors listed on the rating scales.

BOS performance dimensions and behavioral incidents are obtained during a series of workshops to generate performance dimensions and incidents, as described in chapter 3. However, rather than only using selected incidents (as one would when developing BARS) or summarizing the content of many incidents into more general behavioral anchors (as one would when developing BSS), the procedure for developing BOS retains all of the behavioral statements generated for use on the scales. One difference between the BOS and BARS or BSS development procedures is that participants in BOS incident generation workshops are instructed to write only ineffective and effective behavioral examples. The rationale is that average behaviors do not help supervisors make distinctions between effective and ineffective performers, nor do they effectively pinpoint employee actions that should be rewarded or those that should be remediated.

The behavioral statements are placed into a format similar to that shown in Fig. 11.4. Behavioral examples are typically organized under the title of the performance dimension for which they are relevant. Employees can be scored on each performance dimension by summing their ratings across all of the items contained in each dimension and then dividing this total by the number of items listed under each dimension. Note that negatively worded statements would need to be scored such that high rating values would lower the individual's overall

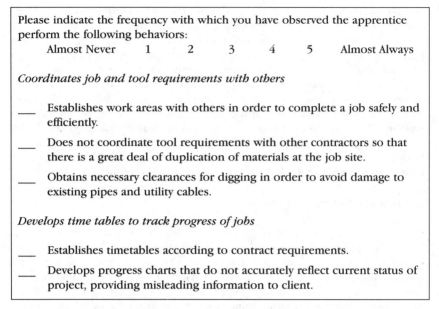

Please indicate the frequency with which you have observed the apprentice perform the following behaviors:

Almost Never   1   2   3   4   5   Almost Always

Coordinates job and tool requirements with others

___   Establishes work areas with others in order to complete a job safely and efficiently.

___   Does not coordinate tool requirements with other contractors so that there is a great deal of duplication of materials at the job site.

___   Obtains necessary clearances for digging in order to avoid damage to existing pipes and utility cables.

Develops time tables to track progress of jobs

___   Establishes timetables according to contract requirements.

___   Develops progress charts that do not accurately reflect current status of project, providing misleading information to client.

FIGURE 11.4   Example of a Behavioral Observation Scale for the dimension Planning, Preparing, and Organizing Work for apprentice electricians.

rating score. It is then possible to give feedback to employees that is structured around their performance on each major dimension of performance as well as on more specific aspects of that performance.

Latham and Wexley (1981) argued that an important feature of a BOS is that managers are required to focus on relatively specific behaviors and to record the frequency with which they have observed those behaviors. They argued that this relatively straightforward rating process should result in more accurate ratings because raters are not required to make complex evaluative judgments about performance effectiveness, as when a BARS or BSS format is used. Research has shown that managers may experience some difficulty integrating complex performance information to arrive at an accurate assessment of performance (Cooper, 1981; Feldman, 1981), suggesting that appraisal formats like BOS, which make fewer cognitive demands on managers, might be advantageous. However, other research has shown that a BOS measures traits like judgments rather than simply frequency of performance data (Murphy, Martin, & Garcia, 1982). Thus, the expected major advantage of the BOS format may not be realized in practice.

Mixed Standard Rating Scales

Mixed standard scales (MSS), developed by Blanz and Ghiselli (1972), are similar to the scales described earlier in that they contain performance dimensions and examples of ineffective, average, and effective behaviors. Again, behavioral incidents for these rating scales can be identified and dimensions generated using the procedures described in chapter 3. Similar to the BARS format, only a few incidents are selected for each MSS performance dimension. Specifically, three incidents are selected per dimension: one effective, one average, and one ineffective. The scale developer must take care to ensure that the content of the rating dimension is represented as well as possible by the incidents selected. Once all of the items are selected (e.g., three times the number of dimensions), they then are randomly arranged to form a single list of behaviors. An example of this format for the electrician's job is shown in Fig. 11.5.

To use these rating scales, managers are instructed to read each behavioral statement and decide whether the employee's performance exceeds the performance described in the statement ("+"), falls below the performance described in the statement ("–"), or is accurately described by the statement ("0"). MSS dimensions are scored from 1, indicating that all "minuses" were received, to 7, indicating that all "pluses" were received. The rules for deriving dimensional scores using MSS are shown in Fig. 11.6. For example, to obtain a rating of 7, one would be rated as performing better (+) than all three statements (Effective, Average, and Ineffective) for each dimension; to obtain a rating of 4, one would be rated as lower (–) than the effective statement, equal (0) to the average statement, and better (+) than the ineffective statement for a given dimension. Thus, these scoring procedures not only produce a final evaluation score but also enable an assessment of "logical" evaluation errors. One example of a logical error would be when, within a given dimension, an employee receives a "+" on the average performance statement and a "–" on the ineffective performance statement. Consistent errors of this type indicate either that a manager is incapable of using the rating scales or that there are problems with the effectiveness levels represented by the behavioral statements.

One major impetus behind the design of MSS was to minimize halo error, which is one of the most pervasive errors made when one individual evaluates another. It occurs when a rater assigns ratings based on a global, overall impression of an employee rather than distinguishing the employee's strengths and weaknesses on different performance dimensions. Halo error results in ratings that are at about the same level across different dimensions when the employee's performance is, in fact, variable across these dimensions. By randomizing the behavioral statements relevant to the different dimensions, and requiring that raters rate each behavior in the manner described earlier, Blanz and Ghiselli (1972) hypothesized that halo error would be minimized when using MSS compared to other rating formats in which the evaluation(s) for each dimension were clearly discernible to raters. Unfortunately, research has shown that MSS have not resulted in the reductions in halo that had been anticipated (Finley, Osburn, Dubin, & Jeanneret, 1977; Saal & Landy, 1977). MSS may, however, be somewhat easier to use than BARS or BSS. The rater must simply compare observed behavior to the effectiveness reflected in single behavioral statements, rather than integrate performance information to arrive at a rating on a continuum of effectiveness.

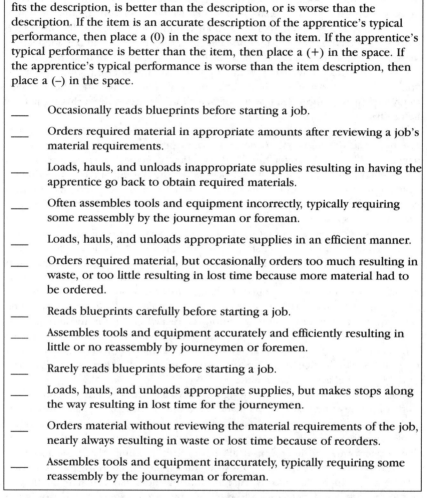

Read each item and decide if the typical behavior of the apprentice to be rated fits the description, is better than the description, or is worse than the description. If the item is an accurate description of the apprentice's typical performance, then place a (0) in the space next to the item. If the apprentice's typical performance is better than the item, then place a (+) in the space. If the apprentice's typical performance is worse than the item description, then place a (–) in the space.

_____ Occasionally reads blueprints before starting a job.

_____ Orders required material in appropriate amounts after reviewing a job's material requirements.

_____ Loads, hauls, and unloads inappropriate supplies resulting in having the apprentice go back to obtain required materials.

_____ Often assembles tools and equipment incorrectly, typically requiring some reassembly by the journeyman or foreman.

_____ Loads, hauls, and unloads appropriate supplies in an efficient manner.

_____ Orders required material, but occasionally orders too much resulting in waste, or too little resulting in lost time because more material had to be ordered.

_____ Reads blueprints carefully before starting a job.

_____ Assembles tools and equipment accurately and efficiently resulting in little or no reassembly by journeymen or foremen.

_____ Rarely reads blueprints before starting a job.

_____ Loads, hauls, and unloads appropriate supplies, but makes stops along the way resulting in lost time for the journeymen.

_____ Orders material without reviewing the material requirements of the job, nearly always resulting in waste or lost time because of reorders.

_____ Assembles tools and equipment inaccurately, typically requiring some reassembly by the journeyman or foreman.

FIGURE 11.5   Example of a Mixed Standard scale for the dimension Planning, Preparing, and Organizing Work for apprentice electricians.

Selecting a Rating Format

In deciding what type of rating format is most appropriate, consideration should be given to several factors, including adherence to legal standards, rater acceptance, and ease of providing feedback. These factors are discussed here.

Effective Statement	Average Statement	Ineffective Statement	Derived Rating
+	+	+	7
0	+	+	6
–	+	+	5
–	0	+	4
–	–	+	3
–	–	0	2
–	–	–	1

FIGURE 11.6   Mixed standard scale (MSS) dimension scoring guidelines.

Adherence to Legal Standards.   A number of factors have been considered by the courts when evaluating the adequacy of different rating formats and performance appraisal systems, in general. Some of these relate to technical standards outlined in the *Uniform Guidelines on Employment Selection Procedures* (1978), whereas others can be considered personnel practices that help safeguard against discrimination in employment decisions. There are four major characteristics of performance rating formats that researchers have concluded are important based on legal defensibility and fairness criteria: (a) performance standards should be based on an appropriate job analysis, (b) performance evaluation should be based on a set of specific job dimensions rather than on a global or overall measure, (c) ratings should be made on behaviorally based performance dimensions rather than on vague personality traits or personal characteristics, and (d) supporting evidence for the ratings given should be accurately and comprehensively documented (Bernardin & Beatty, 1984; Cascio & Bernardin, 1981; Nathan & Cascio, 1986). Scale developers should ensure that these criteria are met when selecting a rating format.

Rater Acceptance.   Certainly, another important factor to consider when selecting a rating format is rater acceptance. One advantage of all of the behavioral instruments described previously is that they tend to be well liked by both employees and their supervisors. This is likely due to scale development processes that incorporate a high level of organizational member involvement. Because the scales are based on performance dimensions and behavioral examples generated by organizational members (e.g., electricians), the final instrument is customized for both the job and the specific organization for which it was developed. Not only are the scales written in the user's language, but they also reflect the organization's specific values and orientation.

Another issue that impacts on rater acceptance is the type of rating format organizational members prefer. It is important for the scale developer to lead decision makers through the scale format selection process, outlining the advantages and disadvantages associated with different options. For example, one issue concerns the number and type of ratings managers prefer to make. With formats such as BARS or BSS, managers are required to make one effectiveness rating for each performance dimension. Thus, if there are 10 performance dimensions, then a total of 10 ratings will be made per employee. With a BOS or MSS format, managers will be required to make ratings of several behavioral examples for each rating dimension. Another issue when considering a BARS or MSS format is how comfortable managers will feel extrapolating employee performance levels from a relatively small number of very specific behavioral examples that may or may not describe what they have observed employees do on the job.

Ease of Providing Feedback. The extent to which provision of feedback about performance will be facilitated by various formats also should be considered. For instance, BSS and BOS formats provide more information that can be used as the basis for a performance discussion than BARS or MSS. A BSS contains comprehensive descriptions of the behaviors that are associated with different levels of effectiveness for each rating dimension. A BOS lists numerous effective and ineffective behaviors relevant to each dimension. Using either a BSS or a BOS, supervisors have a guide not only for describing what has been observed (and thus a rationale for their ratings), but also for giving guidance to subordinates about what behaviors must be exhibited to achieve a higher rating. BARS and MSS formats are less useful when providing feedback because these formats contain only a few very specific behaviors describing each dimension. In addition, these behaviors may or may not be relevant for a given employee's performance. BARS and MSS formats thus provide employees and their supervisors with less information on which to base a performance feedback discussion or to design a developmental action plan than BSS or BOS formats.

HOW TO EVALUATE AND IMPROVE PERFORMANCE RATING QUALITY

Evaluation of the statistical properties of ratings is important to ensure that managers are providing high quality ratings. This involves examining descriptive statistics (e.g., means and standard deviations) and rating reliabilities. Researchers also frequently examine the underlying factor structure of a set of ratings to better understand the dimensions measured by the instrument.

Rating Distributions

Examination of the means and standard deviations for a set of ratings provides important information about their adequacy. One frequently observed problem, especially when performance ratings are used to make operational decisions (e.g., pay, promotion) is a relatively high rating mean and low variability in the ratings, indicating managers' tendencies to evaluate most employees using the high end of the rating scale. One reason for this is that managers are reluctant to give low or even moderate ratings that they will then need to explain and justify to the very individuals they count on to get work done. If one is using a 7-point scale, a mean rating between 4.00 and 5.00 and a standard deviation between 1.00 and 1.50 are reasonable and indicative of an adequate rating distribution. It is reasonable to expect rating distributions to be somewhat skewed, because extremely ineffective performers are likely to have left the organization.

Rating Reliability

There are several different ways that reliability of a set of ratings can be evaluated. One is to assess the internal consistency of ratings, which measures the extent to which ratings across different dimensions of performance are similar within employees. However, many raters are prone to committing halo error, rather than distinguishing among the employees' strengths and developmental areas. If employees are evaluated at roughly the same level of effectiveness across all of the performance dimensions, a high internal consistency reliability will result, but it may simply be the result of halo error. For this reason, a more appropriate means for assessing the reliability of a set of ratings is interrater reliability. Interrater reliability assesses the level of agreement between two or more raters regarding employee performance levels.

There have been many studies investigating the reliability of ratings. Two meta-analytic reviews, in which large numbers of studies were quantitatively cumulated, are described here. Rothstein (1990) presented empirical evidence from 79 organizations, in which ratings on 9,975 employees were collected. She found that as the opportunity to observe performance (as measured by the number of years supervised or observed) increased, the interrater reliability increased, but the level of reliability reached an asymptotic maximum of .60 at about the 2-year point. This is consistent with King, Hunter, and Schmidt (1980), who conducted a meta-analysis of the reliability of ratings and found that the value of .60 represents the upper bound on reliability of supervisor ratings made by a single rater. Rothstein's results suggested that ratings made of employees who have been observed for less than 12 months are likely to be fairly unreliable, and thus recommended that organizations not use the ratings of one supervisor to evaluate the performance of employees with less than 1 year of job experience.

Viswesvaran, Ones, and Schmidt (1996) compared various kinds of reliability estimates. They found that supervisory ratings appeared to have higher reliability than peer ratings and that the mean interrater reliability of supervisory ratings was .52 (using 40 reliability coefficients and a total sample of 14,650 participants) for the Overall Job Performance rating dimension. They also found that interrater reliability (the extent to which different raters agree on the performance of different individuals) was lower than intrarater reliability (the extent to which there is single rater agreement across dimensions or over time).

In summary, the primary means for assessing the psychometric properties of ratings involves examining descriptive statistics and rating reliabilities. Rating distributions are likely to be skewed, as managers are reluctant to provide low ratings to employees and truly ineffective performers usually do not remain in their jobs. Interrater reliability is the most appropriate form of reliability to compute with rating data. Reliability estimates in the .50 to .60 range are typical for performance ratings.

Rater Training to Improve Rating Quality

One intervention that can improve the quality of performance ratings is training. There are two basic types of training programs that have been used for this purpose: error training and accuracy training. Error training programs (e.g., Latham, Wexley, & Pursell, 1975) focus on teaching managers to eliminate common rating errors. To eliminate halo error, for example, trainees are taught not to give employees the same rating across multiple performance dimensions but instead to spread their ratings out across the different performance dimensions. As another example, raters are trained to diagnose whether they tend to be lenient or severe raters overall, irrespective of ratees' true performance level, and to avoid this. Finally, raters are trained to avoid any personal biases and stereotypes that may influence their ratings. These certainly include potential biases against different racial or gender groups, but also more subtle biases based, for example, on where someone went to school.

Although error training programs have been successful in reducing rating errors, as they are defined statistically (e.g., Bernardin & Buckley, 1981; Latham et al., 1975), they have not been shown to significantly increase the accuracy of ratings. The reason is that rater training primarily focuses on teaching particular response sets (e.g., do not give an employee all the same ratings across dimensions, do not rate too leniently or severely), rather than teaching managers how to accurately observe and evaluate performance. For instance, some employees may actually perform at about the same level on several rating dimensions. In an attempt to reduce halo, however, rater error training may actually lead a rater to provide inaccurate ratings of these employees.

Rather than focus on eliminating rating errors, accuracy training attempts to improve managers' observational skills and teach them the appropriate use of the rating scales. Researchers (e.g., DiNisi, Cafferty, & Meglino, 1984; Feldman, 1986; Pulakos, 1984, 1986) have argued that managers should be trained to make the particular types of judgments required by the rating tool. As an example, Pulakos (1986) developed a training program for increasing accuracy with the BARS format. Recall that the rater's task in using BARS is to select a level of effectiveness on each rating dimension by matching observations of the employee's job behavior to the most similar scaled behavioral anchor. In order to perform the BARS rating task accurately, raters need to have a thorough knowledge of the rating dimension content as well as the different types of behaviors that constitute the various effectiveness levels within each dimension. Accordingly, rater training focused on teaching raters about the performance dimensions and the types of behaviors associated with different effectiveness levels. This training strategy was shown to be more effective for increasing rating accuracy than either no training or error training (McIntyre, Smith, & Hassett, 1984; Pulakos, 1984).

One important caveat regarding rater training interventions is that there are often environmental and interpersonal factors that may negatively impact managers' motivation to provide accurate ratings, even if they have the knowledge and ability to rate accurately. For example, if others are rating their employees at the high end of the scale, managers may not want to disadvantage their staff in terms of the rewards they will receive by rating them lower than employees in other groups. Likewise, as previously discussed, managers may be hesitant to confront performance issues with employees for fear of damaging relationships or creating defensiveness, so they may not be motivated to provide less than exceptional ratings. Thus, even if training is provided to managers, it may be insufficient to yield accurate ratings that effectively discriminate between more and less effective performers. Other interventions and strategies for dealing with the interpersonal, environmental, and organizational factors that can impact ratings may be necessary. Several of these are discussed in the next section, which focuses on how to implement performance management systems effectively.

HOW TO IMPLEMENT EFFECTIVE PERFORMANCE MANAGEMENT SYSTEMS

Attention has thus far been directed to developing effective performance management processes and tools. However, having quality processes and tools in place is a necessary but not sufficient condition for having an effective performance management system. What really matters in any performance management system is how it is used by managers and employees. This is why both the most challenging and the most important part of developing an effective performance management system is successful implementation. The cornerstones of successful implementation include: getting organizational members on board, communicating, automating, testing, training, and evaluating and improving.

Getting Organizational Members on Board

For any performance management system to be effective, managers and employees must be motivated to use it properly. Effective performance management systems are characterized by a high level of support from the very top levels of management (Rogers, Hunter, & Rogers, 1993). A committed CEO and leadership team, who model effective performance management and make direct reports accountable for effective performance management, are required for any performance management system to work well. Plainly and simply, without high-level management support, the system will fail.

Because a performance management system's success relies so much on the effectiveness with which managers and employees use the system, it is essential to get organizational members committed to the new system. The most productive way to accomplish this is to involve stakeholders in the design and implementation process (Engelmann & Roesch, 2001). Although performance management design teams are typically led by human resource representatives or consultants who are experienced in implementing performance management systems, design team participants should be organizational members. These individuals are used to provide input that represents different constituencies, to disseminate information about the system, to serve as champions to get others on board, and to try out the system.

Communicating

An effective communications and change management process is necessary to clearly and simply explain to employees the advantages of and rationale for the system. Organizational members should be provided with ample opportunities to comment on any new system and their comments should be responded to, if not actually addressed. Some organizations have been known to undertake full-blown advertising campaigns, with slogans, marketing materials, and massive communication campaigns, to "sell" a new performance management system to employees. It is important to understand that extensive change management work may be required to implement performance management successfully (Mohrman, Resnick-West, & Lawler, 1989).

Automating

Performance management systems involve a considerable amount of paperwork and exchange of documents. When the administrative demands are great, both employees and managers end up spending their performance management time dealing with paper rather than interacting with each other. Automation can greatly facilitate the performance management workflow and substantially reduce the paperwork and time associated with this process. In fact, many organizations look to automated systems to decrease the workload, ensure widespread access to performance management tools, and provide a standardized, structured approach to collecting and storing performance data. When making decisions about the extent of performance management system automation, it is important to balance time, resource, development, and maintenance costs. For example, database development and maintenance can represent extensive costs beyond applications development. Additionally, features such as information security, archiving, and records management represent additional areas for consideration.

Testing

Another important factor in ensuring a successful implementation is to pilot test any new process on smaller groups prior to large-scale implementation. Pilot testing will show if the system functions smoothly and efficiently and if users understand and support the new system. Most importantly, a pilot test allows for an assessment of reactions to the system and the ability to make improvements that will better meet users' needs.

Training

The importance of training managers and employees in proper use of the performance management system has been discussed throughout this chapter. There are a number of training formats that can be used, including classroom training, job aides, or Web-based training, each of which has advantages and disadvantages. The training format that should be used depends on how experienced raters are in conducting performance management and what resources the organization is willing to devote to their training. For example, classroom training is preferable when the training content requires hands-on practice or interactive discussions, such as training about how to provide and receive feedback effectively. Although written performance management aids can be useful for experienced managers, they tend to be less effective for new managers, who may need hands-on practice and more information than is typically provided in an aid. An advantage of Web-based training is that it allows participants to complete the program at their own pace. However, this type of training also can be easily ignored and may require significant policing to ensure participation.

In addition to the error and accuracy training to improve rating quality discussed earlier, there are several other topics that deal with the broader performance process for which training should be provided. These include: (a) roles and responsibilities of employees and managers, (b) how to engage in performance planning and set goals, (c) how to seek feedback from others, (d) how to react to and act on feedback in a constructive manner, (e) how to give feedback while minimizing defensiveness and maintaining self-esteem, and (f) how to identify and address development needs.

Evaluating and Improving

Performance management systems need to be evaluated and continually improved over time. There are several metrics that can be tracked to monitor how effectively a system is operating. Such metrics include the extent to which managers and employees are completing performance management activities, the quality of the ratings produced by the system, the alignment between performance ratings and other human resource decisions such as pay and promotion, and user satisfaction.

SUMMARY

This chapter discussed the development and implementation of effective performance management systems. The following are offered as general conclusions:

- Effective performance management processes typically include four key steps: performance planning, ongoing feedback, performance evaluation, and performance review.

- There is no one rating format that will consistently provide ratings with psychometric qualities that are superior to those of other formats. However, behavioral rating formats better meet legal defensibility criteria than vague and ill-defined rating scales. One can also expect higher levels of user acceptance when these types of rating formats are used. In addition, due to their comprehensive definition of different performance effectiveness levels, behavioral rating formats can facilitate providing feedback and conducting developmental planning with employees.
- To evaluate the quality of performance ratings, their statistical properties (distributions and reliabilities) should be examined. Rater training programs that focus on teaching managers how to accurately observe and evaluate performance have been shown to enhance the quality of ratings.

It is important to recognize, however, that even the most well-developed systems, tools, and rater training programs may not yield high quality performance management processes. This is because managers and employees must also be motivated to use the performance management system properly. In operational performance management situations, there are numerous factors that can profoundly affect performance management (Pulakos, 1991). Some of these include manager–employee (i.e., rater–ratee) interpersonal relationships; the purpose of the appraisal (e.g., whether it will be used for human resource decision making versus employee development); time constraints for completing ratings; the opportunities managers have to observe employee performance; political and union pressure on managers; and the extent to which managers are accountable for their ratings. To gain the maximum benefits from a performance management system, broader implementation issues also must be addressed:

- Support from upper management for the performance management process and involvement of organizational members in developing the system are crucial for acceptance and effective implementation.
- Communications, change management, and training initiatives will be necessary to "sell" the benefits of performance management to managers and staff and to promote proper use of the system.
- Managers need to be made accountable and rewarded for providing high quality, accurate appraisals rather than punished for doing so by the organization or employees.
- Managers need to be trained on how to provide useful feedback to subordinates and how to deal effectively with performance problems.
- Employees need to be trained on how the system operates and how they can effectively participate in their own appraisal process.
- To facilitate the process and focus attention on manager–employee interaction rather than paperwork, automation should be used to the extent feasible to route documents and collect and store performance management information.
- The system should be thoroughly tested to ensure that any problems have been resolved prior to large-scale implementation.

• The performance management system should be regularly evaluated and continuously improved.

REFERENCES

Bernardin, H. J. (1977). Behavioral expectation scales versus summated scales: A fairer comparison. *Journal of Applied Psychology, 62,* 422–428.

Bernardin, H. J., & Beatty, R. W. (1984). *Performance appraisal: Assessing human behavior at work.* Boston, MA: Kent-Wadsworth.

Bernardin, H. J., & Buckley, M. R. (1981). Strategies in rater training. *Academy of Management Review, 6,* 205–212.

Blanz, R., & Ghiselli, E. E. (1972). The mixed standard scale: A new rating system. *Personnel Psychology, 25,* 185–200.

Borman, W. C. (1979). Format and training effects on rating accuracy and rating errors. *Journal of Applied Psychology, 64,* 410–421.

Borman, W. C. (1987). Behavior-based rating scales. In R. A. Berk (Ed.), *Performance assessment: Methods and application.* Baltimore: John Hopkins University Press.

Borman, W. C., & Dunnette, M. D. (1975). Behavior-based versus trait-oriented performance ratings: An empirical study. *Journal of Applied Psychology, 60,* 561–565.

Borman, W. C., Hough, L. M., & Dunnette, M. D. (1976). *Development of behaviorally based rating scales for evaluating U. S. Navy Recruiters.* (Tech. Rep. No. TR-76-31). San Diego, CA: Navy Personnel Research and Development Center.

Campbell, J. P., Dunnette, M. D., Arvey, R. D., & Hellervick, L. V. (1973). The development and evaluation of behaviorally based rating formats. *Journal of Applied Psychology, 57,* 15–22.

Cascio, W. F., & Bernardin, H. J. (1981). Implications of performance appraisal litigation for personnel decisions. *Personnel Psychology, 34,* 211–216.

Cederblom, D. (1982). The performance appraisal interview: A review, implications, and suggestions. *Academy of Management Review, 7,* 219–227.

Cooper, W. H. (1981). Ubiquitous halo. *Psychological Bulletin, 90,* 218–244.

DeCotiis, T. A. (1977). An analysis of the external validity and applied relevance of three rating formats. *Organizational Behavior and Human Decision Processes, 19,* 247–266.

DiNisi, A. S., Cafferty, T. P., & Meglino, B. M. (1984). A cognitive view of the performance appraisal process. *Organizational Behavior and Human Performance, 33,* 360–369.

Dunnette, M. D. (1966). *Personnel selection and placement.* Belmont, CA: Brooks-Cole.

Engelmann, C. H., & Roesch, R. C. (2001). *Managing individual performance: An approach to designing an effective performance management system.* Scottsdale, AZ: World at Work.

Feldman, J. M. (1981). Beyond attribution theory: Cognitive processes in performance appraisal. *Journal of Applied Psychology, 66,* 127–148.

Feldman, J. M. (1986). Instrumentation and training for performance appraisal: A perceptual-cognitive viewpoint. In K. M. Rowland & J. R. Ferris (Eds.), *Research in personnel and human resource management.* (Vol. 4). Greenwich, CT: JAI Press.

Finley, D. M., Osburn, H. G., Dubin, J. A., & Jeanneret, P. R. (1977). Behaviorally based rating scales: Effects of specific anchors and disguised scale continua. *Personnel Psychology, 30,* 658–669.

Flanagan, J. C. (1954). The critical incident technique. *Psychological Bulletin, 51,* 327–358.

Guion, R. M. (1965). *Personnel testing.* New York: McGraw-Hill.

Hillgren, J. S., & Cheatham, D. W. (2000). *Understanding performance measures: An approach to linking rewards to the achievement of organizational objectives.* Scottsdale, AZ: World at Work.

Keaveny, T. J., & McGann, A. F. (1975). A comparison of behavioral expectation scales. *Journal of Applied Psychology, 60,* 695–703.

King, L. M., Hunter, J. E., & Schmidt, F. L. (1980). Halo in a multidimensional forced-choice performance evaluation scale. *Journal of Applied Psychology, 65,* 507–516.

Landy, F. J., & Farr, J. (1980). Performance rating. *Psychological Bulletin, 87,* 72–107.

Latham, G. P., & Wexley, K. N. (1981). *Increasing productivity through performance appraisal.* Reading, MA: Addison-Wesley.

Latham, G. P., Wexley, K. N., & Pursell, E. D. (1975). Training managers to minimize rating errors in the observation of behavior. *Journal of Applied Psychology, 60,* 550–555.

Lievens, F., Sanchez, J. I., & DeCorte, W. (2004). Easing the inferential leap in competency modeling: The effects of task-related information and subject matter expertise. *Personnel Psychology, 57,* 881–904.

Locke, E. A., & Latham, G. P. (1990). *A theory of goal setting and task performance.* Englewood Cliffs, NJ: Prentice Hall.

McIntyre, R. M., Smith, D., & Hassett, C. (1984). Accuracy of performance ratings as affected by rater training and perceived purpose of rating. *Journal of Applied Psychology, 69,* 147–156.

Mohrman, A. M., Jr., Resnick-West, S. M., & Lawler, E. E., III. (1989). *Designing performance appraisal systems: Aligning appraisals and organizational realities.* San Francisco: Jossey-Bass.

Murphy, K. R., Martin, C., & Garcia, M. (1982). Do behavioral observation scales measure observation? *Journal of Applied Psychology, 67,* 562–567.

Nathan, B. R., & Cascio, W. F. (1986). Technical and legal standards. In R. A. Berk (Ed.), *Performance assessment: Methods and application* (pp. 1–50). Baltimore: Johns Hopkins University Press.

Paterson, D. G. (1922–1923). The Scott Company graphic rating scale. *Journal of Personnel Research, 1,* 351–376.

Pulakos, E. D. (1984). A comparison of rater training programs: Error training and accuracy training. *Journal of Applied Psychology, 69,* 581–588.

Pulakos, E. D. (1986). The development of training programs to increase accuracy with different rating tasks. *Organizational Behavior and Human Decision Processes, 38,* 76–91.

Pulakos, E. D. (1991). Rater training for performance appraisal. In J. W. Jones, B. D. Steffy, & D. W. Bray (Eds.), *Applying psychology in business: The manager's handbook.* New York: Lexington Books.

Rogers, R., Hunter, J. E., & Rogers, D. L. (1993). Influence of top management commitment on management program success. *Journal of Applied Psychology, 78,* 151–155.

Rothstein, H. R. (1990). Interrater reliability of job performance ratings: Growth to asymptote level with increasing opportunity to observe. *Journal of Applied Psychology, 75,* 322–327.

Saal, F. E., & Landy, F. J. (1977). The mixed standard rating scale: An evaluation. *Organizational Behavior and Human Performance, 18,* 19–35.

Schwab, D. P., Heneman, H. G., III, & DeCotiis, T. (1975). Behaviorally anchored rating scales: A review of the literature. *Personnel Psychology, 28,* 549–562.

Shippmann, S., Ash, R.A., Battista, M., Carr, L., Eyde, L. D., & Hesketh, B. (2000). The practice of competency modeling. *Personnel Psychology, 53,* 703–740.

Smith, P. C., & Kendall, L. M. (1963). Retranslation of expectations: An approach to the construction of unambiguous anchors for rating scales. *Journal of Applied Psychology, 47,* 149–155.

Uniform guidelines on employment selection procedures. (1978). *Federal Register, 43,* 38290–38309.

Viswesvaran, C., Ones, D. S., & Schmidt, F. L. (1996). Comparative analysis of the reliability of job performance ratings. *Journal of Applied Psychology, 81,* 557–574.

Wexley, K. N. (1986). Appraisal interview. In R. A. Berk (Ed.), *Performance assessment* (pp. 167–185). Baltimore: Johns Hopkins University Press

Zedeck, S., Kafry, D., & Jacobs, R. (1976). Format and scoring variations in behavioral expectation evaluations. *Organizational Behavior and Human Performance, 17,* 171–184.

CHAPTER TWELVE

Tests of Job Performance

Daniel B. Felker and Patrick J. Curtin
Caliber, an ICF International Company

Andrew M. Rose
American Institutes for Research

OVERVIEW

This chapter describes the assessment of job performance. In contrast to the previous chapters, which describe ways to predict how well job applicants would perform on a job if they were actually hired or selected, here we are explicitly concerned about criterion performance—the job performance of workers who already have been hired to do the job. Organizations rely on measures of job performance to help them determine how well employees are performing. Such measures of criterion performance are useful for supporting a variety of operational personnel decisions and related research (Borman, 1991; Siegel, 1986). Measures of job performance provide an objective basis for deciding which workers to promote, reassign, certify, or retain. In research, they are essential as criteria for establishing the validity of selection instruments and evaluating the effectiveness of job training programs.

The most complete and, in a sense, truest picture of job performance would involve continuously observing and evaluating incumbents as they complete their assigned job tasks under all possible working conditions at their job sites. This, of course, is not feasible for many practical and obvious reasons: job disruption, cost, inconvenience, infrequency of occurrence of some tasks, the time and resources needed to make the observations, to name several. A step back from this true ideal would be to observe and evaluate job incumbents as they work on a sample (rather than all) of their assigned tasks under selected working conditions.

319

Although this approach may be logistically feasible, it still intrudes on work routines and is inefficient. Moreover, because conditions of performance—both in terms of environmental conditions and in terms of specific job-task requirements—could vary substantially from one set of observations to the next, this observational approach is unlikely to produce reliable or generalizable measures.

One step removed from observing and evaluating actual on-the-job performance would be to measure job performance using tests. Tests can be developed that cover a representative and generalizable sample of work tasks and they can be administered to job incumbents in controlled and standardized test settings that permit meaningful comparison of worker proficiency. This type of assessment can be accomplished using two kinds of tests: work sample tests, in which examinees perform tasks using the same equipment, materials, and procedures required to perform tasks on the job; and performance-based job knowledge tests, in which examinees answer items that demonstrate that they know how to complete job tasks. We describe how to develop, administer, and score both of these kinds of tests in the rest of this chapter.

CHARACTERISTICS AND USES OF JOB PERFORMANCE TESTS

Background

Job performance tests, which include both work sample tests and performance-based job knowledge tests, are ways to measure work performance. These job performance tests share many characteristics of lower fidelity simulations (e.g., situational judgment tests and assessment centers discussed in chaps. 9 and 10, respectively), but are distinguished from them by the intent of measurement—job performance tests are used to measure the work proficiency of job incumbents, not to predict how well job applicants might perform if hired. Work sample tests require job incumbent examinees to perform tasks under conditions that are identical or highly similar to those they encounter in the workplace and to make decisions comparable to those they make at work. Performance-based job knowledge tests require examinees to apply the knowledge, skills, and abilities found in their work when answering test questions. When both kinds of job performance tests are properly constructed and administered, performance on a relatively small number of tests can provide an assessment of how well incumbents perform job tasks. Both work sample tests and performance-based knowledge tests have been developed and administered in many work contexts, including electrician, vehicle maintenance, electronic installation, clerical and administration, regulation writing, nursing, law enforcement, physicians, pilots, and sales, among many others (Campbell et al., 1990; Felker et al., 1988; Felker et al., 1992).

Interest of organizations in performance testing has stemmed from the need to know how well workers can apply job knowledge to their work and the degree to which they have requisite job skills. This interest historically has led to the use of performance tests as predictor measures more commonly than as criterion measures (Knapp & Campbell, 1993). For example, Asher and Sciarrino (1974) reviewed the predictive validity of performance tests for selection into various jobs and Siegel (1986) described the use of work sample tests as predictors of trainability for selected jobs. Nevertheless, because performance tests elicit virtually the same type of behavior required in job settings, their value as a method of criterion measurement also has long been recognized.

Several studies have demonstrated the usefulness and validity of work sample tests as criterion measures. Hedge and Teachout (1992) compared a traditional work sample test with an interview-based work sample test that required examinees to verbally describe the tasks and processes of a work activity. The study concluded that both forms of the work sample test produce similar results and similar correlations with several other performance criteria used in the investigation. Jackson, Harrris, Ashton, McCarthy, and Tremblay (2000) demonstrated the value of using a work sample test as the criterion to validate a selection battery. They administered selection tests and a work sample test that required incumbent security officers to produce written incident reports. They found strong correlations between scores on the work sample test and scores on predictor measures. Guion (1998) noted that an effective use of performance tests is to provide proficiency-related feedback during performance evaluations.

The widely accepted prescription to develop, administer, and score performance tests has been significantly advanced by research and development undertaken by the U.S. military. For instance, the Army, as part of its program to key training to specific performance requirements, changed its approach to soldier evaluation in 1973 by moving from norm-referenced paper-and-pencil tests to criterion-referenced performance tests. This change meant that soldiers' proficiency would be based on whether they met specific standards of performance rather than on their test scores relative to test scores of other soldiers.

In the performance-based training approach implemented by the Army, soldier proficiency was measured on carefully selected tasks contained in Skill Qualification Tests (SQTs). The overriding requirement of SQTs was that they be job relevant. Test content was tied to critical tasks of military jobs that were identified through job and task analysis (e.g., as described in chap. 3). Much of the seminal research to assist the Army in its transition to performance testing was done by Osborn and his colleagues at the Human Resources Research Organization (e.g., Osborn, 1974; Osborn, Campbell, & Ford, 1976). This research program specified the requirements and procedures for developing performance tests, and their guidance still is widely followed today.

A distinguishing characteristic of job performance tests is that they are measures of actual (or nearly equivalent) job performance. As such, they require demonstration and application of the knowledge, skills, and abilities needed to complete the task being tested. It is because of this feature that work sample tests especially have been touted as being the highest fidelity form of performance measurement available and the most valid indicator of job performance (e.g., Green & Wing, 1988). Although not all personnel psychologists may totally agree with this assertion, they nonetheless would agree that work sample tests have excellent face validity and utility and can be more objective than other types of performance measures (Borman & Hallam, 1991; Knapp & Campbell, 1993; Sackett, Zedeck, & Fogli, 1988; Schmidt & Hunter, 1998). Moreover, because these tests are based on actual job tasks, they are focused on integrated components of whole task performance, rather than on relatively molecular components of job performance. For example, if we wanted to test an electrical lineman's proficiency in climbing wooden utility poles, we would present the electrical linemen with all the necessary materials and observe actual pole climbing rather than only some component of the task, such as putting on safety belts.

Applications of Job Performance Tests

Job performance tests have a variety of human resources applications, when there is a need to understand how well employees are performing on the job or are prepared to perform a specific job. For example, job performance tests can play a key role in organizational performance appraisal systems to support personnel decisions about issues such as salary increases and promotions. This entails using tests to collect information about incumbents' current proficiency on critical job tasks. Test results then provide an empirical basis for determining whether individuals meet expected work standards and for rank ordering individuals by their levels of proficiency. Using such a system, management can give salary increases or promotions to job incumbents who demonstrate the highest levels of job proficiency.

Tests that measure job performance also may be used to decide whether an employee is qualified to hold or retain a job. This especially applies to occupations that affect the safety and well-being of others. In these instances, incumbents require certification to ensure they are qualified to perform critical tasks within their jobs. Some obvious examples include aircraft pilots, medical specialists, nuclear power plant operators, and law enforcement officers. In these situations, it is critical to establish that incumbents are able to perform their jobs at specified levels of proficiency. Clearly, it is not sufficient for pilots to demonstrate only that they have the knowledge necessary to land a plane; they need to demonstrate actual performance before they can be certified as pilots. These are criterion-referenced testing situations. That is, the test requires the examinee to demonstrate proficiency at or above specified standards that have been established by some professional association or accreditation agency.

In another human resource application, performance tests can be used to evaluate the effectiveness of training programs. If the terminal objectives of a training program are to teach specific job tasks, then job performance tests administered at the completion of training can provide evidence of whether the terminal objectives were achieved. If the objectives were achieved, the training program can be judged effective; if they were not, the training may be deemed deficient and in need of revision.

Training effectiveness can also be evaluated by administering job performance tests to job incumbents after they have been working for several months (or some other meaningful time frame) following training. If performance on the tests demonstrates that incumbents can perform the tasks at the desired level of competence, then there is evidence that transfer of training has occurred (i.e., that the knowledge and skills taught in training are being applied in the work setting).[1] The evaluation of training based on performance tests reflects use of a higher and more desirable level of evaluation. Kirkpatrick (1994) suggested that training can be evaluated on a continuum of increasing levels of rigor—evaluating reactions, learning, behavior, and results. Performance tests represent the evaluation of job behavior and results.

Job performance tests also can play a critical role in personnel selection research. Performance tests often serve as the criterion—or more likely, as one of several criteria—for validating personnel selection instruments and procedures. This application typically involves having job applicants and job incumbents complete selection (predictor) instruments and job performance tests. The job performance test scores are then correlated with scores on selection instruments to determine whether the selection instruments can predict who will perform well on the job (i.e., on the job performance tests). Validation designs and procedures are described in detail in chapter 13.

In all of the personnel applications we have described, the value of job performance tests is that they measure how well individuals can perform actual job tasks. More specifically, as Siegel (1986) noted, these tests are most useful for assessing the proficiency of job-experienced persons or those who have already been trained to do a job. Job performance tests have high physical fidelity and, consequently, high face validity.

Limitations of Job Performance Tests

As with any type of measurement approach, there are technical and practical constraints on the development and use of job performance tests. Work sample tests can be especially expensive to develop and, depending on the equipment and materials involved in performing the task being tested, they can be relatively complex to administer and score. Often, they can only be administered to one person at a time. Aircraft pilot simulators are extreme examples of expensive performance tests.

In addition, others have noted (e.g., Borman, 1991; Sackett et al., 1988) that what workers actually do on the job may not reflect what they can do as much as what they are willing to do. Job performance tests are considered can do measures of performance because the testing situation measures what people are able to do (can do), rather than what they actually will do on the job. Workers who are capable of performing a task well in a testing situation may not do so on the job because they lack motivation, have poor supervision, or are working with defective

---

[1]The presentation of these two training applications is an oversimplification. When evaluating training effectiveness, proper care must be taken to obtain performance data from comparable contrasting groups, such as an untrained control group and trained groups. The main point is that job performance tests can play an important role in evaluating training effectiveness.

equipment. Also, job performance tests (in which examinees perform under controlled circumstances) usually contain some degree of reactivity in which the testing process itself affects what is being measured. If examinees know they are being tested, it may affect how they perform. Thus, restricting the measurement of job effectiveness to only job performance tests could miss information about typical worker performance. For this reason, it is important to use more than one kind of measure to assess job performance, such as supervisor ratings, job knowledge tests, and work sample tests, so that all aspects of job performance are covered.

Performance Tests: Measuring Job Processes and Job Products

Job performance tests can measure both the processes needed to complete a job task and the products that result from performing a task. Work sample tests and performance-based job knowledge tests accommodate both aspects of performance. Whether task processes, task products, or both should be measured depends on the task and what is deemed important to assess. For tasks in which the end result is important but how it is attained is not, the quality of the product is critical and should be measured. Examples include:

- Identifying an applicable legal statute: This can be accomplished in different ways, including searching a database, looking at a print source, or from memory; the result is important for the job not the method of obtaining the result.
- Installing an electrical alarm system that meets electrical code specifications: Within safety constraints, this can be done using different tools in a variety of ways; whether the installed system meets code specifications is important, not how it was installed.
- Diagnosing a mechanical problem: This can be accomplished using different sequences of diagnostic tests, examining different components and system elements, and using different troubleshooting strategies; finding the problem is the important measure.
- Finding the distance and location of a road junction on a map: Several methods of determining distance and location are acceptable, including using a compass, a measuring stick, or some other informal technique; the correct answer is critical, not the method used.
- Producing a technical report: Writing and assembling a technical report can be done in a variety of ways with different combinations of writers and technical staff; the process used is less important than producing a complete, accurate, and readable written report.

On the other hand, when the process by which a task is accomplished is inherently important, we want to measure each step required to complete the task. In these cases, the correct process may be essential to ensure safety, to prevent damage to equipment or material, or to enable proper operation at the end of the process. Examples include:

- The process used to land a passenger plane: It is essential for the pilot to read the right gauges correctly at the right time, operate the right switches and controls in the proper sequence and time, and follow all prescribed safety procedures; the process of performing the task is critical to achieving the desired end.
- The process followed in drawing blood: It is vital that sterilized needles are used, the syringe is held in the proper manner, and that the needle is inserted, not jabbed, into the donor's arm.
- The process used to shut down a nuclear plant in an emergency: Steps must be precisely followed in the prescribed order to ensure quick and safe shutdown.
- The process used by an electrician outdoor lineman to move "hot wires" on a pole to different positions: It is critical that proper insulated tools be used in specified ways to prevent serious injury.
- The process used to handcuff and arrest criminal suspects: The arresting officer must position the suspect in the proper way, put handcuffs on by following procedures prescribed to ensure safety and security, and inform the suspects of legal rights prior to booking.

There can be occasions when it is desirable to measure both task processes and the task product. This might happen when the quality of the product is inextricably linked to the procedures used to produce the result—when variations in methods to achieve a product are not equivalent—or when safety is critical to attaining the desired result. Landing aircraft or handling high-voltage electrical wires are examples. It might be possible to land an airplane or move a hot electrical wire without following prescribed procedures, but to do so would represent an inferior level of proficiency and would put others at great risk. The nature of the task and specifics of the testing situation will dictate whether testing the process or product of a task or both is appropriate.

PSYCHOMETRIC CHARACTERISTICS OF JOB PERFORMANCE TESTS

The quality of job performance tests is assessed by the same general psychometric considerations as any other type of personnel measure: reliability and validity. Psychometric properties of job sample tests are of special interest because of the added need to justify the relatively high costs to develop these tests. The military's extensive work on job performance measurement is a major source of research that speaks to the psychometric quality of job performance tests when used as criterion measures. Other psychometric evidence is available from research done by business and industry examining job performance tests used as predictors. In this section we highlight evidence drawn from the military's use of performance tests as criterion measures. A third consideration, measurement bias, has rarely been examined in the context of criterion measurement. Oppler, Campbell, Pulakos, and Borman (1992) discussed results of several approaches to investigating subgroup differences in performance, primarily based on Army data (Project A). In these analyses, however, the focus was on supervisor and peer ratings rather than on hands-on performance measurement.

Reliability

Establishing the reliability of work sample tests is complicated by the logistic complexities involved in administering and scoring these tests. Typically, work sample tests require one or more scorers to observe an examinee perform a task in real time and to score the performance as it is being done. When steps of the task being performed are hard to detect, are supposed to be completed in a prescribed sequence, or are accomplished quickly, scoring can be further complicated. Variability in scoring can easily arise due to the need for one or more scorers to directly observe test performance, interpret the quality of performance, and make on-the-spot decisions about the adequacy of performance.

The military services have reported consistently high interrater agreement scores for work sample tests (Knapp & Campbell, 1993). This is noteworthy because the military services have developed and administered job sample tests to thousands of examinees across a wide range of occupational specialties and have used different types of scorers. For example, Carey (1990) and Felker et al. (1988) reported agreements exceeding 90% between test scorers and "shadow" scorers for a variety of Marine Corps job sample tests. Hedge, Lipscomb, and Teachout (1988) reported pairwise agreements ranging from almost 75% to 90% across three different teams of test administrators and three Air Force occupations; moreover, interrater agreement tended to improve over time. Doyle and Campbell (1990) reported comparable interrater indices for Navy radioman tests.

The generally high interrater agreement reported by the military has led to speculation about the reasons for this outcome (e.g., Wigdor & Green, 1986). Plausible explanations lie in the serious approach taken to develop, administer, and score job sample tests. In much of the research that has been reported, the military services treated job sample tests as benchmark criterion measures and devoted substantial effort and resources to their design and administration. The care taken during task analysis and test construction had an obvious impact on the level of interrater agreement attained. As will be described in more detail later in this chapter, careful analysis and segmentation of tasks into small, individually observable units of performance, and pilot testing to ensure that all steps could be consistently scored, were typical procedures followed in developing work sample tests.

In addition, the military services assigned or recruited competent job experts as test scorers-administrators. Although the approaches differed in details, test administrator training was a rigorous process that involved demonstrations of the task to be scored, emphasized ways to standardize test conditions, and provided extensive practice scoring tests. The important lesson from this for any organization—military, business, or government—is that experienced and well-trained test administrators can dependably score well-constructed proficiency tests across time, different examinees, and varying test content.

Test-retest reliability evidence also is available from military job performance measurement research. A sample of 188 Marine Corps infantrymen was retested after 7 to 10 days with an alternate work sample test form. This yielded a test-retest reliability estimate of .77 (Mayberry, 1990). In other Marine Corps research, reported test-retest reliabilities were .79 for a sample of 88 automotive mechanics and .88 for a sample of 67 helicopter mechanics (Mayberry, 1992).

In addition to the research done on work sample tests, the military services also have examined the reliability of performance-based job knowledge tests. These multiple-choice tests resemble other multiple-choice knowledge tests with the distinction that the test items are based on job tasks and performance requirements and ask questions about what, how, and when to do task activities. Pictures and drawings often are used to enhance the fidelity of test items to the job setting. These tests can be reliable, as shown by reported internal consistency reliability estimates ranging from .89 to .92 for Army performance-based job knowledge tests (Campbell, 1988) and from .91 to .97 for Marine Corps tests (Mayberry, 1990). Mayberry (1992) also reported split-half reliability estimates for automotive and helicopter mechanic tests ranging from .92 to .97.

Validity

Referring to the validity of the criterion may seem an odd thing to do at first because validity is most often used to describe a certain quality of a predictor. However, because a performance measure should be reliable and valid, it makes sense to consider the reliability and validity of a criterion. Both the *Uniform Guidelines on Employee Selection Procedures* (1978) and the *Principles for the Validation and Use of Personnel Selection Procedures* (Society for Industrial and Organizational Psychology, 2003, pp. 16–17) make reference to the importance of establishing and describing such qualities of the criterion in order to justify the use of the criterion as a reliable and representative (i.e., valid) indicator of performance. Because performance measures such as work samples directly measure the ability of a person to do a given type of work, work samples are a logical choice for use as an assessment of performance. As such, work samples are subject to the same standards as are any other assessment method with regard to reliability and validity.

Schmidt and Hunter's (1998) review of eight decades of personnel selection research addressed the overall validity and utility of work sample tests. Schmidt and Hunter observed that because work sample tests are only used meaningfully with examinees who already know the content of the job, work sample tests are an appealing and valid performance assessment method for current employees. Other research (Schmidt, Hunter, & Outerbridge, 1986) suggests that the observed validity of work sample tests is influenced by job experience. The more experience an employee has in a position the more likely that employee is to perform well on work sample tests. This relationship between experience and work sample performance is, however, influenced by the abilities of the employees, the complexity of their work, and the nature of their past work experience (Quiñones, Ford, & Teachout, 1995; Schmidt et al., 1986).

Establishing the validity of job performance tests is a more oblique process than it is for predictor tests. Indeed, it is difficult to think about criterion validity of job performance measures themselves, because they normally are the standard against which predictor tests, training programs, and other personnel interventions are validated. It is generally acknowledged (e.g., Borman & Hallam, 1991) that job sample tests have excellent face validity. That is, most observers who look at work sample tests or performance-based job knowledge tests can readily see the relevance of the tests to the job. Face validity of a test is enormously important for acceptance by managers and decision makers who are not test specialists versed in psychometrics. A test that does not "look" like it is suited for the measurement task at hand is a hard sell in almost any organization.

Fortunately, a strong case for content validity can usually be made for job performance tests. The general argument for content validity centers on the relevance and representativeness of the test to performance required on the job. As pointed out by Guion (1979a, 1979b, 1979c, 1979d) and by Borman (1991), the determination of content validity relates to how closely the test shares important content, such as tasks and performance conditions, with the content of the job. Tests requiring performance that is highly similar to the performance required on the job are content valid tests. Content validity is almost automatic if the performance test is developed on the basis of a systematic analysis of job requirements, working conditions, and equipment and materials used. The importance of content validity for test instruments and prescriptions for developing them are discussed in guidelines such as the *Standards for Educational and Psychological Testing* (American Educational Research Association, American Psychological Association, & National Council on Measurement and Evaluation, 1999) and *Uniform Guidelines on Employee Selection Procedures* (1978). The process by which test content is identified is critical. Evidence of test and job domain content similarity can be based on logical and empirical analyses as well as on judgments of subject matter experts. Relationships between test and job content ensure the test is representative of the job it measures. The importance of job and task analysis for identifying the content domain of a job and for selecting test content that reflects the domain is discussed later.

Subgroup Differences

Work sample tests produce smaller subgroup differences than other forms of performance assessment (Gatewood & Feild, 1994; Morath, Curtin, Brownstein, & Christopher, 2004; Schmidt, Greenthal, Hunter, Berner, & Seaton, 1977), possibly because examinees tend to view work sample tests as more job relevant (i.e., face valid) and fair than other forms of assessment (Robertson & Kandola, 1982; Smither, Reilly, Millsap, Pearlman, & Stoffey, 1993; Steiner & Gilliland, 1996). In addition, work sample tests allow examinees to make self-assessments of their ability to perform the job (Cascio & Phillips, 1979; Harvey, Perkins, & McGonigle, 2003) and this, too, might contribute to perceptions of test relevance and fairness. However, Bobko, Roth, and Buster (2005) cautioned that the possible advantages of work sample tests might be inflated in the literature, because the nature of the constructs being assessed might affect the degree of adverse impact. Bobko et al. suggested that using a work sample test to assess more cognitively loaded constructs than, say, procedural knowledge, is more likely to produce levels of subgroup differences similar to those on cognitive ability tests.

McKay and McDaniel (2006) conducted a meta-analysis of African American and White mean differences in work performance and found that mean racial differences in performance favor Whites (d = .27). Similar to Bobko et al.'s suggestion, effect sizes were most strongly moderated by cognitive loading of criteria (e.g., job knowledge tests), data reported in unpublished sources (e.g., technical reports), and for performance measures consisting of multiple-item scales. McDaniel, McKay and Rothstein (2006) examined these data for evidence of publication bias (Rothstein, Sutton, & Bornstein, 2005) and concluded that journals systematically underestimate the magnitude of mean racial differences in job performance.

HOW TO SELECT TEST CONTENT

The first decision when constructing performance tests is to determine what parts of the job's total performance domain should be tested. Ideally, all tasks would be tested under all significant working conditions. However, several factors limit the tasks that realistically can be tested:

1.   There are too many tasks in the performance domain of the job to test. For example, one job analysis revealed that the performance domain for inside wireman electricians contains over 200 tasks requiring over 150 different types of knowledge, skills, and abilities (Williams, Peterson, & Bell, 1994). Testing the performance requirements for all 200 tasks would take too long, be too expensive, and require training a very large number of test administrators.
2.   Some tasks are more important to the job, more difficult to perform, more frequently performed, and more representative of the job than others. These task characteristics may be used to help determine which tasks to select for testing. For instance, tasks that are unrepresentative, unimportant, and infrequently performed clearly are unlikely candidates for testing.
3.   Practical and logistic considerations limit what can be tested. Tasks that put examinees at risk of injury, damage expensive equipment, or cannot be administered in a standardized manner are not suitable for testing.

The challenge is to select a small number of tasks to assess job proficiency from a larger pool of job tasks so that test performance can be generalized to the job. Therefore, representativeness and generalizability of test content to the entire performance domain are critical. To select representative and generalizable tasks, we must accomplish two steps: (a) specify the total performance domain for the job and (b) devise a valid and defensible sampling strategy for selecting tasks from that domain. The remainder of this section describes methods for achieving these steps. We then describe two applied research projects in which different procedures were used to select test content.

Specifying the Job Performance Domain

The job performance domain documents the totality of tasks that are performed in that job. A performance domain typically describes how the tasks are organized under major job functions. A complete enumeration of tasks is the necessary first step to provide an empirical basis for selecting representative and generalizable tasks to test. Job and task analysis methods used to develop job performance domains are based on such procedures as observing job incumbents while they work, interviewing job incumbents and their supervisors about what is done on the job, and reviewing existing task descriptions and inventories of tasks. Typically, job and task analysis uses several procedures to compile the tasks of a job domain, as described in chapter 3.

To support the development of performance tests, the results of a job and task analysis should consist of more than just a complete listing of tasks in the domain. It is critical that the contextual conditions of task performance also be identified. These contextual conditions include the circumstances (e.g., environmental conditions) in which the tasks are performed, chronological dependencies of a task (e.g., when a task is performed in a sequence of activities), and interaction requirements (e.g., where other people's performance affects task performance conditions). Test developers use this information to determine suitable testing conditions and logistical support needed to administer the test.

Sampling Strategies for Selecting Tasks

Test developers have a long history of selecting tasks that are related to job performance. Among these efforts, the branches of the U.S. military have been instrumental in developing structured methods for selecting test content that have been adapted and widely applied to civilian occupations. These methods are described in detail in various research technical reports (e.g., Guion, 1979a, 1979b, 1979c, 1979d) and military documents (e.g., the U.S. Army's TRADOC PAM 351-4[T], 1979). We describe two of these methods next.

Method 1: The Four- and Eight-Factor Models. In the first method, analysts and test developers rate (or collect data for) each task in the domain on up to eight of the following descriptors:

1. Percent of the workforce performing the task (e.g., what proportion of electricians splice wire?).
2. Task delay tolerance (e.g., how much flexibility is there in terms of time before this task must be performed?).

3. Consequences of inadequate performance of the task (e.g., how much damage will occur to equipment, workers, or the completion of the job if this task is not performed adequately?).
4. Task learning difficulty (e.g., how long will it take to learn how to do this task?).
5. Percent of time spent performing (e.g., what proportion of time is spent performing this task on the job?).
6. Probability of deficient performance (e.g., what are the chances that the worker cannot perform the task?).
7. Immediacy of performance (e.g., how urgent is task performance?).
8. Frequency of performance (e.g., how often is this task performed?).

The first four of these descriptors comprise the four-factor model; the entire set makes up the eight-factor model. Job analysts and subject matter experts (SMEs) rate each task in the domain on each of the four or eight factors. For example, in rating frequency of task performance, job experts might rate a task on a scale ranging from "once a week or less" to "10 times a week or more." The ratings could be provided by job incumbents or their supervisors, or both, or compiled from task descriptions previously generated by the organization's job analysts. After each factor has been rated, SMEs decide which factors are most important. They then set cutoffs for each of these relevant factors. Example cutoff scores might be:

1. Percent of the workforce performing the task: 40% or more
2. Task delay tolerance (1 = high tolerance, 7 = no tolerance): 3
3. Consequences of inadequate performance (1 = minor, 7 = major): 5
4. Task learning difficulty (1 = low, 7 = high): 4

Tasks in the performance domain that meet all of these criteria are selected for testing.

Method 2: The DIF Model. Another method for selecting test content is the DIF (Difficulty, Importance, and Frequency) model. The basic procedures are the same as those used for the four- or eight-factor models. Analysts and SMEs rate each task on the following descriptors:

1. Difficulty: Either task learning difficulty or probability of deficient performance or both.
2. Importance: The consequences of inadequate performance, task delay tolerance, and time spent performing (importance has often been rated for different scenarios, such as peak and nonpeak production periods).
3. Frequency: How often the task is performed as well as the percent of people in the job performing the task.

If simple yes-no responses are provided for each of the three DIF dimensions, then there are eight potential outcomes for each task, as shown in Table 12.1:

TABLE 12.1
Decision Rules Regarding Tasks to Be Tested

Difficult?	Important?	Frequent?	Decision
Yes	Yes	Yes	Select
Yes	Yes	No	Select
Yes	No	Yes	Select
Yes	No	No	Do not select
No	Yes	Yes	Select
No	Yes	No	Select
No	No	Yes	Do not select
No	No	No	Do not select

The last column in Table 12.1 presents a particular decision rule. Decision rules to identify the tasks to test typically are agreed on by test developers or organization managers. In the previous example, the decision rule is to select all tasks judged important and, in addition, all tasks that are rated both difficult and frequently performed even if not rated important. This rule eliminates easy and unimportant, and infrequently performed. Different and more elaborate decision rules can be used, depending on the purposes of testing and resource constraints. For example, when considering tasks to select for initial training, the yes-yes-no tasks (difficult, important, not frequently performed) are possible appropriate candidates.

Variants on this primarily judgmental DIF approach occasionally appear in the literature. For example, Rose, Radtke, and Shettel (1984) were concerned with predicting tasks that were likely to be forgotten if not practiced. They developed a method to determine difficulty based on 10 task characteristics, such as number of steps in the task, its cognitive demands, and the presence and adequacy of job aids. Thus, a task that is comprised of 20 steps, involves rapid calculations and decisions, and has no job aids would be judged very difficult and prone to forgetting. Tasks identified by such procedures could be singled out for special treatment, such as giving them additional training time.

Selecting Test Content: Two Examples

Perhaps the largest effort ever initiated that involved the measurement of job performance was the Joint Services Job Performance Measurement (JPM) Project, commissioned by the Department of Defense (Harris, 1987). The scope and content of this initiative reflect both traditional and innovative approaches to developing job performance tests. In 1980, the Department of Defense directed each branch of the Armed Services (i.e., Army, Navy, Marine Corps, Air Force) to develop and validate procedures for measuring job performance. These measures were to be used as criterion measures to determine the validity of military selection and classification procedures. The challenge facing each service was to select from their respective task domains a relatively small number of tasks to test. In this section, we describe two of these efforts: the U.S. Army's Project A and the U.S. Marine Corps' JPM Project.

The U.S. Army's Project A.   As described by Campbell et al. (1990), Project A defined the total domain of performance for entry-level enlisted personnel in several Army jobs, or military occupational specialties (MOS), such as infantryman and vehicle driver. Reliable and valid measures of the major tasks and duty areas of each MOS then were developed. These measures were used as criteria against which to validate both existing and project-developed selection and classification tests.

Major components of the Project A job performance measures included work sample tests and performance-based job knowledge tests. Because the procedures for selecting test content for Project A were fairly typical and are applicable to civilian performance domains, we discuss these steps in detail:

1. Specify the entire task domain for a particular job. As mentioned before, this is a necessary requirement for selecting test content, especially when we are concerned with estimating the representativeness of the test. During Project A, tasks of the job (or MOS) domain were identified and enumerated within each job (or MOS) domain by using three sources of information: (a) Army doctrine (e.g., soldier's manuals and technical manuals), which consists of policy statements regarding what soldiers should know and be able to do; (b) survey data from soldiers concerning what they actually do on the job; and (c) interviews with representatives from the Army agencies responsible for training in the specific jobs.

2. Edit and describe tasks uniformly. Task lists generated from different sources often result in task descriptions that vary in level of specificity. For example, one infantryman task was "Move individually." This task involves several different activities, such as "Perform low crawl" (on elbows and knees) and "Move through barbed wire." Another task was "Take immediate action on the Light Antitank Weapon," itself consisting of several procedures to follow if the weapon failed to fire. The goal of this editing step is to describe all tasks at a comparable level of specificity, so that the tasks can provide essentially equivalent amounts of information about the domain. For Project A, after the complete task list was generated, it was reviewed and edited by project staff and then reviewed by SMEs for consistency and uniformity of scope. Occasionally, overly inclusive "supertasks" were separated into several tasks of comparable scope.

3. Rate or judge task characteristics. Practically all test content selection procedures involve sampling tasks (or subtasks) from the performance domain. To aid in this sampling, a typical procedure is to rate each task on a number of characteristics (e.g., the four- and eight-factor or DIF models),

and then to use the ratings systematically when selecting content. For Project A, a relatively large number of SMEs—between 15 and 30 for each job—performed three rating activities. First, they grouped all of the tasks according to similarity of behavior described in the task. That is, they sorted tasks into an unspecified number of clusters, with the instructions to make the tasks within a cluster as similar as possible and to make the clusters as dissimilar as possible. Next, the SMEs rated the importance of each task on a 7-point scale ranging between "Not at all important to unit success" to "Absolutely essential for unit success." Finally, the SMEs rated each task on task performance difficulty: They were asked to judge the level of performance that a typical group of soldiers would reach on a task. The range of levels within the typical group of soldiers was used as the measure of expected performance variability, which in turn was used as an indirect measure of task difficulty; more variable tasks tend to be more difficult.

4.   Select tasks to be tested. Using the task importance and difficulty ratings from the previous step, tasks were selected by panels of military experts and project staff. As described in Campbell et al. (1990), "No strict rules were imposed on the analysts in making their selections, although they were told that high importance, high performance variability, a range of difficulty, and frequently performed tasks were desirable and that each cluster should be sampled" (p. 282). Following initial selections, the panels developed a consensual list of the most representative and critical tasks. The consensual list was reviewed by several committees and review panels as the final step in selecting the tasks to be tested.

The Marine Corps' JPM Project.   In this project, researchers attempted to improve on consensual procedures for selecting test content (Felker et al., 1988). The approach focused on representativeness and generalizability of the tests and the desire to include aspects of random selection in the process, rather than solely relying on SME consensus. The guiding theory was that each task consists of a series of "behavioral elements," which are general behaviors that are included in and performed across many other tasks or subtasks. Performance of these elements was presumed to be transferable if Marines who can perform the elements in one task can also perform the same elements in other tasks. Behavioral elements are the task components that are sufficiently similar in two tasks to lead one to predict that performance on the two tasks will be correlated.

Figure 12.1 shows the behavioral elements derived for a Marine Corps electrician job (Felker et al., 1992). In the Marine Corps, individuals receive training and qualify to work on specific pieces of electrical equipment (e.g., linear actuator, controllable spotlight). They perform three types of activities on these pieces of equipment: Troubleshoot and Test (T/T), Remove and Replace (R/R), and Align and Adjust (A/A). In Fig. 12.1, these activities are displayed across the top of the matrix. The electrician task-behavioral element matrix shown as Fig. 12.1 is part of the Marine Corps electrician performance domain.

Having defined the performance domain, we then specified the behavioral elements that comprised each activity. For example, "Connect/disconnect wires/cables" (Fig. 12.1, 4) is a behavioral element that occurs in many of the task activities electricians were expected to do. Of course, electricians connect and disconnect different wires and cables in different activities. Nonetheless, if a person could perform "Connect/disconnect wires/cables" for troubleshooting one piece of equipment (e.g., the linear actuator), we considered it likely that the person could also "Connect/disconnect wires/cables" when troubleshooting other pieces of equipment (e.g., the trim actuator). Similarly, further down the list in Fig. 12.1, the behavioral element "Set switch to proper position" (10) is embedded in fewer task activities, but the thinking was the same: This element would transfer across the different tasks that included it.

Behavioral element matrices also helped identify the testable units that comprised the electrician performance test. Because many Marine Corps electrician tasks were very comprehensive, testable units served as the uniform level of description, and generally corresponded to a column of the matrix (e.g., "troubleshoot/test trim actuator"). Conceptually, a testable unit is roughly equivalent to a subtask (i.e., a meaningful segment of performance that is relatively independent, while maintaining its overall fidelity to the task, and can be performed in a reasonable time period; Mayberry, 1987). Using these matrices, test content was selected on the basis of coverage of behavioral elements. Essentially, columns of the matrix—that is, testable units—weighted by the number of elements they contained, were randomly sampled. Thus, a testable unit with 20 behavioral elements was weighted more heavily than a testable unit with 12 behavioral elements. After a column was selected, the weights were regenerated by deleting the behavioral elements from those sampled and randomly sampling the domain for another column. This process was repeated until all testing time—the chief logistic constraint—was accounted for. This procedure enabled documentation of the representativeness of the test and generation of hypotheses regarding the likelihood of performance success for any task in the domain. More specifically, the hypothesis was that performance on behavioral elements transferred across tasks; performance on tasks that had more elements in common would be more highly correlated, a hypothesis that was generally supported in analyses of the Marine Corps data.

HOW TO CONSTRUCT JOB PERFORMANCE TESTS

All of the methods described previously—four-factor, eight-factor, DIF, SME consensus, behavioral elements approach—have the same goal. They are used to provide test developers with an empirical and defensible approach for the selection of test content that represents the entire job performance domain. Once this content is selected, test development can begin. In this section, we discuss methods for developing work sample tests and performance-based job knowledge tests.

Behavioral Element	Linear Actuator			Controllable Spotlight			Power Lever Control Quad.			RPM Limit Detector			Master Switch Control Panel			Trim Actuator		
Task	T/T	R/R	A/A	T/T	R/R	A/A	T/T	R/R	A/A	T/T	R/R	A/A	T/T	R/R	A/A	T/T	R/R	A/A
1 Read technical manual	X	X	X	X	X		X	X		X	X		X	X		X	X	X
2 Follow safety procedures	X	X	X	X	X		X	X		X	X		X	X		X	X	X
3 Remove-replace screws, nuts, bolts	X	X	X	X	X		X	X		X	X		X	X		X	X	X
4 Connect/disconnect wires/cables	X	X	X	X	X		X	X		X	X		X	X		X	X	X
5 Visually inspect for physical damage	X	X	X	X	X		X	X		X	X		X	X		X	X	X
6 Remove/replace cover/panel assembly	X	X	X	X	X		X	X		X	X		X	X		X	X	X
7 Read/interpret schematics	X	X	X	X	X		X	X		X	X		X	X		X	X	X
8 Read/observe indicators	X			X			X			X			X			X		
9 Connect probes across items	X			X			X			X			X			X		
10 Set switch to proper position	X			X			X			X			X			X		
11 Remove/replace components		X								X		X	X					
12 Align mechanical/electrical parts		X	X		X				X	X			X					
13 Clean parts													X					
14 Tag wires											X							
15 Align/adjust screws using turning tool	X																	
16 Remove/replace module /PCB							X		X			X						
17 Apply lubricating/sealing/cleaning compo																X		
18 Release switch										X		X		X	X			
19 Remove/replace wire/lead								X							X			
20 Read/interpret oscilloscope																		
21 Engage/hold switch				X	X		X		X			X						
22 Remove/replace sealing compound																		
23 Remove/replace gasket/seals																		
24 Remove/replace safety/lock wire																	X	
25 Measure time using stopwatch						X												

FIGURE 12.1 Electrician task-behavioral elements matrix; T/T = test and troubleshoot, R/R = remove and replace, A/A = align and adjust.

Troubleshoot: Trim Actuator

Equipment/Materials Required

1 Trim Actuator
1 Multimeter (AN/PSM-4C)
1 DC Power Supply (0-30VCD, LH-125)

Procedure to Set Up Station

1. Open retract switch (Item #52) by disconnecting wire.
2. Remove sealing compound.

Procedures to be Performed Before Testing Each Marine

1. Open retract switch (Item #52) by disconnecting wire.

Testable Units

1. Calibrate Multimeter (Steps 1–5)
2. Troubleshoot Actuator (Steps 6–12)

FIGURE 12.2   Setup sheet for electrician task.

Constructing Work Sample Tests

A work sample test requires examinees to perform a task or an essential part of a task (e.g., a subtask or testable unit) under conditions similar to how the task is performed on the job. As with all types of tests, it is essential that work sample tests be administered in the same way and under the same testing conditions so that all examinees have the same opportunity to demonstrate their ability to perform without any undue advantage from the test setting. As with any other form of testing, the instructions for administering work sample tests are of the utmost importance for standardizing how the test is administered and scored.

Drawing on the task-behavioral element matrix detailed in Fig. 12.1, an example of a work sample test is shown in Figs. 12.2 and 12.3. The illustrative work sample test is a Marine Corps electrician task that required examinees to troubleshoot a trim actuator, an aircraft electrical component. Because the process of troubleshooting is critical to proficiency on this task, the test was developed so that each step of the process could be observed and scored by the test administrator as it was performed.

Figure 12.2 shows the setup sheet for the test, which helped to standardize the test conditions for each person tested. The setup sheet gives specific instructions to the test administrator for preparing the test station. It lists the materials and equipment required for the test, the procedures to set up the test station, and the procedures to be performed before testing each examinee. Because work sample tests often require elaborate setup procedures, test administrators need to be trained in how to both prepare the test station and administer and score the test. The score sheet for the test is shown in Fig. 12.3. The score sheet includes space for biographical information about the examinee, and lists the steps of the process that must be followed that will be scored (work sample tests often use some type of go-no-go or pass-fail format for scoring steps of the task). It also includes the exact words that the test administrator should say during the testing and when they should be said.

Figure 12.3 demonstrates why task analysis results are crucial for the development of work sample tests. A good task analysis used to develop work sample tests will indicate not only what tasks are performed on the job but also how they are done, any materials and equipment used, what constitutes acceptable performance, and the mandatory or preferred sequence of performing task steps. All this information is used in constructing draft and final versions of work sample tests and in deciding what performance conditions to incorporate into the test setting. Although the intent always is to make these tests as real as possible, compromises often have to be made in the degree of authenticity to accommodate practical considerations. Decisions to compromise reality in testing are affected by the issues described next.

Degree of Physical Fidelity. It may not always be possible to duplicate the exact working conditions for all tasks. Thus, some conditions may need to be simulated; however, these simulated conditions must still elicit use of the same essential skills and knowledge needed to perform the actual task. For example, it is infeasible, if not impossible, to test truck drivers in all possible driving conditions in a standardized way. But requiring examinees to maneuver around portable obstacles at certain speeds and braking at different speeds (based on job analysis) may adequately simulate skills needed in many driving conditions like wet roads and heavy traffic.

Whole or Part-Task Testing. Some job tasks may be too long to test or consist of steps that are repetitive or trivial. In such cases, testing may be restricted to the portion of the task that involves the use of critical skills or the key steps or behavioral elements of the task. For example, the task of "Replacing brakes" on a car encompasses jacking up the car, removing hubcaps, and other steps that are peripheral to the essence of replacing brakes. In the interest of saving testing time and focusing on critical skills, testing only that part of the task that actually relates to replacing brakes would be prudent and adequate.

Equipment and Material Needs. Some job tasks may require the use of equipment and materials that can be adapted for testing only with great difficulty,

---

Troubleshoot: Trim Actuator

Test Date: _____
Scorer: _____   Examinee: _____
Scorer ID: _____   Examinee ID: _____

Say: The Trim Actuator before you is not working properly. You are to find the problem or problems. You may use the test equipment provided. Do you have any questions? Begin.

PERFORMANCE STEPS	GO	NO-GO
1. Removed all power to the Trim Actuator.	____	____
2. Set AC/DC switch to + DC on multimeter.	____	____
3. Set function selector switch to R × 1k on multimeter.	____	____
4. Touched two leads of multimeter together.	____	____
5. Read O on multimeter.	____	____
Note. Ask examinee for what was read.		
6. Touched first lead to Pin C of connector.	____	____
7. Touched second lead to Pin A of connector.	____	____
8. Touched first lead to pin C of connector.	____	____
9. Touched second lead to Pin B of connector.	____	____
10. Engaged retract switch.	____	____
11. Performed steps 6-10 in sequence.	____	____
Note: Ask examinee what he/she found.		
12. Indicated there is an open in the retract circuit.	____	____

FIGURE 12.3   Score sheet for electrician task.

or at great expense, or are only found in the work setting. The use of these materials or equipment would have to be carefully planned and justified. For example, testing avionics specialists on their skill in removing electronic equipment from actual aircraft would involve the use of a very expensive airplane. Similarly, testing maintenance technicians on their skill in assembling a part by shutting down a factory production line may not be feasible. Testing requirements like these need to be planned in advance or the testing situation must be altered so that such testing conditions are unnecessary.

Safety.   A paramount consideration for many work sample tests is the safety of the examinee. Some job tasks are dangerous and some working situations cannot be safely simulated under standardized conditions. Examples include cleaning up toxic materials, controlling fires, quelling riots, and caring for patients with highly contagious diseases.

Expense and Time.   Work sample tests often are costly to develop and administer. With enough money and support, very elaborate and expensive work sample tests can be developed and administered under standardized conditions (e.g., flight simulators). However, for most work environments, compromises are often necessary to develop and administer reasonable tests that approximate some working conditions. Test developers almost always have to balance the cost of developing good work sample tests that measure critical knowledge and skills with the time available for testing and the proportion of the performance domain that is covered by the sample of tasks tested. It often is useful to supplement these measures with performance-based job knowledge tests and various types of rating scales to reduce cost and increase comprehensiveness of assessment.

Scoring Work Sample Tests

Devising objective and reliable schemes for scoring work sample tests is both a creative and challenging exercise. The results of job and task analyses are critical inputs for scoring, too, because they will specify how tasks are performed and describe the level of competency and quality expected.

Score Task Processes.   Developing procedures for scoring task processes requires familiarity with how the task is performed. This is because scoring is done in real time as the task is being performed step by step by the examinee. At times, task steps might be very quickly performed and other task steps might be legitimately completed in different sequences, both of which complicate observing and scoring performance. To ensure that the performance steps of a task are accurately and reliably scored, the test must require the test administrator to make as few subjective decisions as possible. Several principles should be followed when developing scoring procedures for process-based work sample tests:

- Make performance steps observable. Because performance on each step of the task process is to be scored, the steps must consist of observable behavior. For example, Step 3 in Fig. 12.3, "Set function selector switch to R x 1k on multimeter," is a behavior that can be observed and is therefore scorable. Steps that call for "checking," "inspecting," "reading," and "observing" something are unobservable behaviors. The scorer does not know if the examinees are really "inspecting" or "reading" and, if they are, what they are inspecting for or what they are actually reading. Step 5 in Figure 12.3 avoids this problem by having the test administrator prompt examinees to verbalize what they read on the multimeter.

- Specify performance step beginning and ending points. Each performance step should be a behavioral unit such that observers can tell when it begins and when it ends. The Step 3 example fits this description. The step has a clear starting point ("Set function switch") and ending point ("to R x 1k on multimeter").

- Use objective standards of performance. For steps that can be performed at different levels of proficiency, the standard of performance should be objective and quantitative rather than subjective. For example, the first-aid task step "Ties bandage on arm adequately" is not particularly useful for a performance test because there is no standard for assessing "adequacy." Different scorers can interpret "adequacy" in different ways. But saying, "Ties bandage on the arm so you can insert your little finger under the edge of the bandage" provides an objective standard of performance that can be accurately and reliably scored.

- Score special performance conditions. For tasks that require certain steps to be performed in sequence or to be accomplished in a certain amount of time, the conditions should be scored as separate performance steps. Step 11 in Fig. 12.3 provides for scoring steps in proper sequence. In the case where the time to perform a step (or number of steps) is important, the score sheet could include separate performance steps for scoring the task steps and for scoring the time taken to complete the task steps. That is, some steps on the score sheet would be for scoring individual task steps (e.g., "adjusted xyz correctly") and a separate one would be included for scoring the time taken to perform the task steps (e.g., "adjusted xyz within two minutes"). This would distinguish examinees who knew how to perform a task from those who not only knew how to do the task but could do it within the specified time as well.

- Avoid testing trivial steps. Some task steps that are tangential to the core requirements of tasks should not be tested or scored. For example, removing the protective cap of a needle before administering an injection tells very little about the ability to give an injection and is better left unscored.

- Incorporate job aids in tests. Job aids are typically used in work when incumbents are not expected to memorize lengthy or complicated tasks or to perform certain procedures unaided. Examples include steps to follow when making a medical diagnosis, or repairing complicated equipment, or performing mathematical transformations or calculations. Tests that require examinees to look up answers in manuals, use checklists, or follow procedures in the order shown on a schematic, just as they would on the job, can be very realistic. An example is a task to troubleshoot an electrical component where the job aid graphically depicts the proper sequence to follow. At defined points in the troubleshooting process, some kind of decision or interim action may be required. By incorporating the job aid, a test can measure an examinee's ability to follow the proper sequence and make the appropriate decision. Examinees

---

Electrician Task: Installation of Service Entrance Conductors

---

Test Date: _____

Scorer: _____   Examinee:

_____

Scorer ID: _____   Examinee ID:

_____

Read to examinee: *Your supervisor has told you to use the tools that have been given to you to bring electrical power from poles and lines in this neighborhood into the residence identified. Any questions? Your work will be checked after you finish. Begin.*

PERFORMANCE STEPS   GO   NO-GO

1. Maintained at least three feet of clearance over
    house roof.   _____   _____

2. Installed service line where the pitch of the roof
    was at least 4/12.   _____   _____

3. Terminated conductors from main supply line at
    a through-the-roof raceway.   _____   _____

4. Installed so that at least 18 inches clearance is
    maintained above the overhanging portion of the roof. _____   _____

FIGURE 12.4   Score sheet for product scoring.

either can be required to say what they would do at the decision points or to perform the expected interim activity.

- Train test administrators. Administering work sample tests that measure task processes and scoring them are intricate procedures and require competent test administrators. This is particularly true when many steps are performed rapidly. It is always beneficial for test administrators to practice performing the tasks they will score as well as to observe others performing the task as part of scorer training.

Score Task Products.   Figure 12.4 shows an example of a score sheet for scoring a task product. This particular test required an electrician apprentice to bring electrical power into a residence from electrical poles and lines running through a residential neighborhood. Examinees were scored by how well they "dropped service entrance" (i.e., brought electrical power into the house) and met electrical code standards. Because the method of installation was less important than meeting electrical code, only the end product was scored. The scorer did not need to be present when the apprentice examinee performed the task.

Scoring task end products typically is easier than scoring a task as it is performed. Most task products—for example, a completed form, a finished letter, a manufactured ball bearing, an installed electrical outlet, the result of a calculation—have definite specifications and these can be used to assess quality of performance. To illustrate, certain parts of a form need to be completed to be correct, or ball bearings must meet precise specifications for size and smoothness, or there is a correct answer to a mathematical application. All have precise specifications. As such, these products can be determined and scored with some certainty. Sometimes decisions need to be made about the acceptability of products that do not meet perfection and whether they should be scored as "failures" or "partially correct." Decisions on scoring exceptions also will be guided by task analysis results and input of job experts.

Constructing Performance-Based Job Knowledge Tests

Another approach to measuring job performance is the specialized form of written test called performance-based job knowledge tests. These tests resemble multiple-choice tests that are typically administered in paper-and-pencil or computer-based formats. Although they have the same format and look like any other knowledge tests, they differ in that the test items ask examinees how they would perform a task rather than just their knowledge about the task. Indeed, Osborn et al. (1976) pointed out that the key requirement for these tests is that the test questions be methodically anchored in task procedures. When adequately constructed, these tests can provide wider coverage of the job domain at less cost as compared to work sample tests, although at a lower level of fidelity.

Different levels of job knowledge obviously are important for job performance. As DuBois (1996) noted, job knowledge consists of the concepts, procedures, principles, and other information that support job performance. Because job knowledge conceptually includes both declarative knowledge and procedural knowledge (McCloy, Campbell, & Cudeck, 1994), information about what to do and how to do it affects performance by guiding which tasks get performed and how these tasks are completed. Research has shown job knowledge to be a link between abilities and performance (Borman, White, Pulakos, & Oppler, 1991). Research also has shown that knowledge tests, designed to tap knowledge and skills required in jobs, predicted apprentice performance in a large manufacturing firm (Hattrup & Schmitt, 1990).

By focusing on procedural knowledge, performance-based job knowledge tests are likely to tell us how an examinee would perform on a work sample test and on the job. To distinguish the typical job knowledge test item from a performance-based test item, consider the example shown in Fig. 12.5 for one item for a vehicle maintenance troubleshooting task.

The job-knowledge test item shown in Fig. 12.5 tests whether the examinee recognizes a particular part of a fuel pump. The item asks for knowledge, not

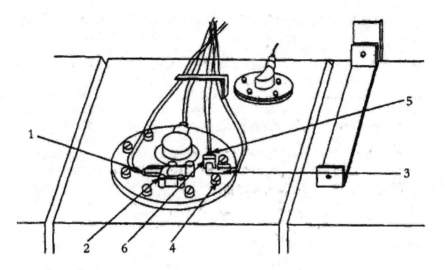

Your first step is to take the electrical connector off the fuel pump receptacle.
What numbers in the figure refer to those items?

    A. 3 and 4
    B. 5 and 6
    C. 4 and 6
    D. 1 and 2

FIGURE 12.5   Job-knowledge test item for a vehicle maintenance troubleshooting task.

performance. Someone who has memorized the names of all parts of a fuel pump could correctly answer this item and still not know how to replace the pump. In contrast, a performance-based item would get at the performance aspect, the "how to." For example, the same job-knowledge item shown in Fig. 12.5 could be made performance-based by asking the test question in the following way, still using the same options: "If you must replace this fuel pump, what parts should you remove first?" Although a correct answer to this item would not guarantee that examinees could actually physically replace the fuel pump, it at least demonstrates that they know the first thing they should do to replace the pump.

A performance-based job knowledge test can tap into the performance aspects of a task in a number of ways. Test items using words such as those in the following list reflect different ways of measuring whether someone knows how to perform a task:

What is the first step to install the ...
After you have ... you next should ...

If you have tried ... and it didn't help, you then should ...
To replace the ... you should first ...
If the customer objects to ... you should say ...
If ... is damaged, what must be replaced?
Before removing the ... you should ...
If the decision is to ... you must notify ...
The work team did ... and ... and ... so they now need to ...
The gauge reads ... in what sequence should the four switches be operated?
If part 1 shown in the figure malfunctions, you should first ... and then ...
Given the conditions of the accompanying scenario, you should ...

The preceding phrases illustrate that performance-based test items often require action of some kind as the correct answer. The examinee needs to know what to do given certain conditions, when to perform a step in a sequence of steps, and how different task steps relate to each other. To create realistic contexts for examinees, performance-based items often use pictures and other graphic material and detailed scenarios to set up the decision or performance requirement the examinee is to demonstrate.

For both work sample tests and performance-based job knowledge tests, the examinee's performance is typically scored by some variant of the number of things done right. In the case of work sample tests, each test is built around a set of task steps (see Fig. 12.3). Because each step of a task—process or product—is individually observable and scorable, we can compile the pass-fail (or go-no-go) status of each step. The individual step scores can then be aggregated to produce total task pass-fail scores, or proportion of steps passed by task or across tasks. In the case of performance-based job knowledge tests, the number of test items answered correctly is usually calculated and summed over all items to derive a performance score.

SUMMARY

Job performance tests are relatively direct and higher fidelity measures of what people can do at their work. Work sample tests, one type of job performance test, attempt to duplicate the essential working requirements of the job setting. These tests measure examinees' proficiency in performing representative job tasks under standardized but realistic working conditions. Work sample tests have often been proposed as a benchmark measure of job performance. In contrast, performance-based job knowledge tests, another type of job performance test, are typically formatted as paper- or computer-based multiple-choice tests. Performance-based job knowledge tests differ from other job knowledge tests in that the test items ask about how to carry out job tasks rather than just facts about tasks. Job performance tests have proven useful as criteria for validating predictor tests and evaluating training effectiveness. They can support personnel promotion, retention, and compensation decisions when used in performance appraisal and certification.

REFERENCES

American Educational Research Association, American Psychological Association, & National Council on Measurement and Education (Joint Committee). (1999). *Standards for educational and psychological testing*. Washington, DC: American Educational Research Association.

Asher, J. J., & Sciarrino, J. A. (1974). Realistic work sample tests: A review. *Personnel Psychology, 27*, 519–533.

Bobko, P., Roth, P., & Buster, M. (2005). Work sample selection tests and expected reduction in adverse impact: A cautionary note. *International Journal of Selection and Assessment, 13*, 1–10.

Borman, W. C. (1991). Job behavior, performance, and effectiveness. In M. D. Dunnette & L. M. Hough (Eds.), *Handbook of industrial and organizational psychology* (pp. 271–376). Palo Alto, CA: Consulting Psychologists Press.

Borman, W. C., & Hallam, G. L. (1991). Observation accuracy for assessors of work-sample tests: Consistency across task and individual-differences correlates. *Journal of Applied Psychology, 76*, 11–18.

Borman, W. C., White, L. A., Pulakos, E. D., & Oppler, S. H. (1991). Models of supervisory job performance ratings. *Journal of Applied Psychology, 76*, 863–872.

Campbell, C. H., Ford, P., Rumsey, M. G., Pulakos, E. D., Borman, W. C., Felker, D. B., et al. (1990). Development of multiple job performance measures in a representative sample of jobs. *Personnel Psychology, 43*, 277–300.

Campbell, J. P. (Ed.). (1988). *Improving the selection, classification, and utilization of Army enlisted personnel: Annual report, 1985 fiscal year* (ARI TR 792). Alexandria, VA: U.S. Army Research Institute for the Behavioral and Social Sciences.

Carey, N. B. (1990). *An assessment of surrogates for hands-on tests: Selection standards and training needs* (CRM 90-47). Alexandria, VA: Center for Naval Analyses.

Cascio, W., & Phillips, N. (1979). Performance testing: A rose among thorns. *Personnel Psychology, 32*, 751–766.

Doyle, E. L., & Campbell, R. C. (1990, November). *Navy: Hands-on and knowledge tests for the Navy radioman*. Paper presented at the 32nd annual conference of the Military Testing Association, Orange Beach, AL.

DuBois, D. A. (1996, April). *The construct validity of job knowledge: A meta-analytic review and critique*. Paper presented at the annual convention of the Society for Industrial/Organizational Psychology, Inc., San Diego, CA.

Felker, D. B., Bowler, E. C., Szenas, P., Rose, A. M., Barkley, P., Helgerman, D., et al. (1992). *Analysis of job requirements and development of model job performance measures for Marine Corps electronic maintenance occupational areas* (AIR-89500-6/92-FR). Washington, DC: American Institutes for Research.

Felker, D. B., Crafts, J. L., Rose, A. M., Harnest, C. W., Edwards, D. S., Bowler, E. C., et al. (1988). *Developing job performance tests for the United States Marine Corps infantry occupational field* (AIR-47500-9/88-FR). Washington, DC: American Institutes for Research.

Gatewood, R., & Feild, H. (1994). *Human resource selection* (3rd ed.). Fort Worth, TX: Dryden Press.

Green, B. F., & Wing, H. (1988). *Analysis of job performance measurement data: Report of a workshop*. Washington, DC: National Academy Press.

Guion, R. M. (1979a). *Principles of work sample testing: I. A non-empirical taxonomy of test uses* (ARI TR-79-A8). Alexandria, VA: U.S. Army Research Institute for the Behavioral and Social Sciences.

Guion, R. M. (1979b). *Principles of work sample testing: II. Evaluation of personnel testing programs* (ARI TR-79-A9). Alexandria, VA: U.S. Army Research Institute for the Behavioral and Social Sciences.

Guion, R. M. (1979c). *Principles of work sample testing: III. Construction and evaluation of work sample tests* (ARI TR-79-A10). Alexandria, VA: U.S. Army Research Institute for the Behavioral and Social Sciences.

Guion, R. M. (1979d). *Principles of work sample testing: IV. Generalizability* (ARI TR-79-A11). Alexandria, VA: U.S. Army Research Institute for the Behavioral and Social Sciences.

Guion, R. M. (1998). *Assessment, measurement, and prediction for personnel decisions.* Mahwah, NJ: Lawrence Erlbaum Associates.

Harris, D. A. (1987). Job performance measurement and the joint-service project: An overview. In *Proceedings of the Department of Defense/Educational Testing Service conference on job performance measurement technologies.* San Diego, CA.

Harvey, J., Perkins, L., & McGonigle, T. (2003, June). *Managing applicant reactions in the selection process.* Paper presented at the 27th annual conference of the International Public Management Association Assessment Council, Baltimore.

Hattrup, K., & Schmitt, N. (1990). Prediction of trades apprentices' performance on job sample criteria. *Personnel Psychology, 43,* 453–466.

Hedge, J. W., Lipscomb, M. S., & Teachout, M. S. (1988). Work sample testing in the Air Force job performance measurement project. In M. S. Lipscomb & J. W. Hedge (Eds.), *Job performance measurement: Topics in the performance measurement of Air Force enlisted personnel* (AFHRL-TP-87-58). Brooks Air Force Base, TX: Air Force Human Resources Laboratory.

Hedge, J., & Teachout, M. (1992). An interview approach to work sample criterion measurement. *Journal of Applied Psychology, 77,* 453–461.

Jackson, D., Harris, W., Ashton, M., McCarthy, J., & Tremblay, P. (2000). How useful are work samples in validational studies? *International Journal of Selection and Assessment, 8,* 29–33.

Kirkpatrick, D. L. (1994). *Evaluating training programs: The four levels.* San Francisco: Berrett-Koehler.

Knapp, D. J., & Campbell, J. P. (1993). *Building a joint-service classification research roadmap: Criterion-related issues* (AL/ HR-TP-1993-0028). Brooks Air Force Base, TX: Armstrong Laboratory, Manpower and Personnel Research Division.

Mayberry, P. W. (1987). *Developing a competency scale for hands-on measures of job proficiency* (CRC 570). Alexandria, VA: Center for Naval Analyses.

Mayberry, P. W. (1990). *Validation of the ASVAB against infantry job performance* (CRM 90-182). Alexandria, VA: Center for Naval Analyses.

Mayberry, P. W. (1992). *Reliability of mechanical maintenance performance measures* (CRM 91-246). Alexandria, VA: Center for Naval Analyses.

McCloy, R., Campbell, J., & Cudeck, R. (1994). A confirmatory test of a model of performance determinants. *Journal of Applied Psychology, 79,* 493–505.

McDaniel, M. A., McKay, P., & Rothstein, H. (2006, May). *Publication bias and racial effects on job performance: The elephant in the room.* Paper presented at the 21st annual conference of the Society for Industrial and Organizational Psychology Inc., Dallas, TX.

McKay, P., & McDaniel, M. A. (2006). A re-examination of Black-White mean differences in work performance: More data, more moderators. *Journal of Applied Psychology, 91,* 538–554.

Morath, R., Curtin, P., Brownstein, E., & Christopher, C. (2004). *Situational judgment tests: Recent innovations in development and scoring.* Fairfax, VA: Caliber Associates.

Oppler, S. H., Campbell, J. P., Pulakos, E. D., & Borman, W. C. (1992). Three approaches to the investigation of subgroup bias in performance measurement: Review, results, and conclusions [Monograph]. *Journal of Applied Psychology, 77,* 201–217.

Osborn, W. C. (1974). *Process versus product measures in performance testing* (HumRRO Professional Paper No. 16-74). Alexandria, VA: Human Resources Research Organization.

Osborn, W. C., Campbell, R. C., & Ford, J. P. (1976). *Handbook for development of skill qualification tests* (HumRRO Final Rep. No. FR-CD(L)-77-1). Alexandria, VA: Human Resources Research Organization.

Quiñones, M., Ford, K., & Teachout, M. (1995). The relationship between work experience and job performance: A conceptual and meta-analytic review. *Personnel Psychology, 48,* 887–910.

Robertson, I., & Kandola, R. (1982). Work sample tests: Validity, adverse impact, and applicant reaction. *Journal of Occupational Psychology, 55,* 171–183.

Rose, A. M., Radtke, P., & Shettel, H. H. (1984). *User's manual for predicting military task retention.* Washington, DC: American Institutes for Research.

Rothstein, H. R., Sutton, A. J., & Borenstein, M. (2005). *Publication bias in meta-analysis: Prevention, assessment, and adjustments.* West Sussex, England: Wiley.

Sackett, P. R., Zedeck, S., & Fogli, L. (1988). Relations between measures of typical and maximum job performance. *Journal of Applied Psychology, 73,* 482–486.

Schmidt, F. L., Greenthal, A. L., Hunter, J. E., Berner, J., & Seaton, F. (1977). Job sample vs. paper-and-pencil trades technical tests: Adverse impact and examinee attitudes. *Personnel Psychology, 30,* 187–197.

Schmidt, F. L., & Hunter, J. E. (1998). The validity and utility of selection methods in personnel psychology: Practical and theoretical implications of 85 years of research findings. *Psychological Bulletin, 124,* 262–274.

Schmidt, F. L., Hunter, J. E. & Outerbridge, A. (1986). Impact of job experience and ability on job knowledge, work sample performance, and supervisory ratings of job performance. *Journal of Applied Psychology, 71,* 432–439.

Siegel, A. I. (1986). Performance tests. In R. A. Berk (Ed.), *Performance assessment: Methods and applications* (pp. 121–142). Baltimore: Johns Hopkins University Press.

Smither, J. W., Reilly, R. R., Millsap, R. E., Pearlman, K., & Stoffey, R. W. (1993). Applicant reactions to selection procedures. *Personnel Psychology, 46,* 49–76.

Society for Industrial and Organizational Psychology, Inc. (2003). *Principles for the validation and use of personnel selection procedures* (4th ed.). College Park, MD: Author.

Steiner, D., & Gilliland, S. (1996). Fairness reactions to personnel selection techniques in France and the United States. *Journal of Applied Psychology, 81,* 134–141.

Uniform guidelines on employee selection procedures. (1978). *Federal Register, 43,* 38290–38315.

U.S. Army. (1979). *Job and task analysis handbook* (TRADOC Pam 351-4[T]). Fort Monroe, VA: U.S. Army Training Developments Institute.

Wigdor, A. K., & Green, B. F. (Eds.). (1986). *Assessing the performance of enlisted personnel: Evaluation of a joint-service research project.* Washington, DC: National Academy Press.

Williams, K. M., Peterson, N. G., & Bell, J. A. (1994). *Job analysis of three electrical worker positions for the National Joint Apprenticeship Training Committee.* Washington, DC: American Institutes for Research.

CHAPTER THIRTEEN

Strategies for Test Validation and Refinement

Fritz Drasgow
University of Illinois at Urbana-Champaign

Deborah L. Whetzel
United States Postal Service

Scott H. Oppler
American Institutes for Research

OVERVIEW

As mentioned in chapter 1, one of the purposes for conducting job analysis and then developing predictor instruments and measures of job performance is to validate selection measures. In this chapter, we describe validation designs, and discuss issues related to collecting and analyzing validity data. For purposes of test refinement, we discuss issues related to item analysis. Item analysis is described both in terms of classical test theory and item response theory (IRT). Because of the complexity of IRT, we only provide an introduction to this topic, assisting the reader in understanding some of the issues related to item analysis when using this theory.

The objective of a validation study is to obtain evidence to support the interpretation and use of predictor scores. Note that in this chapter, we discuss validating inferences made from test scores (e.g., a cognitive ability test as described in chap. 5). But pencil-and-paper multiple-choice tests are only one kind of predictor; inferences from other predictors, such as innovative computerized assessments (see Drasgow & Olson-Buchanan, 1999, for examples), measures of training and experience (see chap. 6), interviews (as described in chap. 7), background data (as described in chap. 8), situational inventories (as described in chap. 9), and assessment centers (see chap. 10) also should be validated. According to the *Standards for Educational and Psychological Testing*:

> [Validity] refers to the degree to which evidence and theory support the interpretations of test scores entailed by proposed uses of tests. Validity is, therefore, the most fundamental consideration in developing and evaluating tests. The process of validation involves accumulating evidence to provide a sound scientific basis for the proposed score interpretations. It is the interpretations of the test scores required by proposed uses that are evaluated, not the test itself. (American Educational Research Association, American Psychological Association, & National Council on Measurement in Education, 1999, p. 9)

This definition emphasizes the idea that validity is not a characteristic of a test or assessment procedure, but, instead, of inferences made from test or assessment information (Binning & Barrett, 1989). As Nunnally (1978) stated, "One validates not a measuring instrument but rather some use to which a measuring instrument is put" (p. 87).

This definition also emphasizes that valid inference must be supported by sound evidence. The collection and analysis of such evidence are discussed in this chapter. The definition also implies that predictor validation is a special case of hypothesis testing and theory development. In employment testing, the hypothesis is that test scores can be used to predict job performance. In testing for achievement and licensing, the hypothesis is that test scores can be used to describe mastery of relevant skills.

Historically, validity evidence was defined by three types of validity: content, criterion-related, and construct (*Uniform Guidelines on Employee Selection Procedures*, 1978). Content validity is based on professional judgments about the relevance of the predictor content to the content of a particular behavioral domain of interest (i.e., job performance) and about the representativeness with which the predictor items cover that domain. A careful job analysis should first be conducted to identify the knowledge and skills constituting the domain, and then a test blueprint should be developed that specifies how many items should be included on the test from each knowledge or skill area identified in the job analysis. In summary, content validity provides evidence in support of the relevance of the content of the predictor to the domain it assesses, which then provides support for assertions based on test scores such as "a person who passes the Uniform Certified Public Accountant licensing exam is competent to practice as a CPA."

Criterion-related validity is based on the degree of empirical relationship, usually expressed in terms of correlations and regressions, between predictor scores and criterion scores. This approach focuses on specific relationships with measures used for an applied purpose (i.e., predicting job performance). Construct validity is based on an integration of evidence that supports the interpretation or meaning of predictor scores. Almost any kind of information about a predictor can contribute to an understanding of construct validity, but the contribution becomes stronger if the theoretical rationale underlying the predictor scores is evaluated.

Many researchers have supported a unified conception of validity (American Educational Research Association [AERA] et al., 1999; Binning & Barrett, 1989; Dunnette & Borman, 1979; Guion, 1977, 1978, 1980; Messick, 1980; Tenopyr, 1977; Tenopyr & Oeltjen, 1982). The argument is that content evidence and criterion-related evidence offer an incomplete understanding of validity. Binning and Barrett (1989) argued that validation is theory building, and the various strategies provide different, but complementary, sources of evidence to support understanding and interpretation of constructs. Therefore, the different strategies cannot be logically separated. In the next section of this chapter, we describe how to develop a research plan for validating the inferences made from predictor measures.

HOW TO DEVELOP A VALIDATION RESEARCH PLAN

Insofar as possible, research projects should be designed and carried out according to the *Principles for the Validation and Use of Personnel Selection Procedures* (Society for Industrial and Organizational Psychology, 2003) and the *Standards for Educational and Psychological Testing* (AERA et al., 1999). Although neither document is legally binding, it is important to follow the guidance in these documents because they summarize the best practices of the profession. (Adherence to the *Uniform Guidelines*, 1978, which is a legally binding document, is described in chap. 14.) Whereas the *Principles* primarily address the problems of making decisions in the workplace (e.g., employee selection, placement, promotion), the *Standards* address psychometric issues in a wide range of settings. This section describes psychometric and methodological issues to consider when planning to conduct validation research in accordance with both documents.

Specify Objectives

All validation efforts should begin with a research plan. Such a plan should state the purpose for conducting the study and the steps to be followed. The purpose for conducting the validity study must be based on an understanding of the work performed on the job, the needs of the organization, and the rights of current and prospective employees. Of primary importance in the decision-making process is the validity of the final selection decision.

An important step for describing the objectives of the research plan is to conduct a literature review to determine what studies already have been conducted on the construct in question for predicting performance on the job(s). It is important to determine whether the objectives have already been met by previous research or how the new effort might build on previous research. Conducting the literature review was described in chapter 2.

Describe Validation Strategy

If an objective of the validation strategy is to assess the accuracy of predictions of job performance from test scores, then a criterion-related validation approach is required. There are two kinds of strategies that can be categorized according to the timing of the collection of predictor and criterion data. When predictor data (e.g., test scores) and criterion data (e.g., performance ratings or scores) are collected from job incumbents at or around the same time, the design is referred to as a *concurrent* design. On the other hand, when predictor data are collected at Time 1, usually when individuals are applying for a job, and criterion data are collected at a later time (Time 2) when the individuals have been hired and become experienced in their jobs, then the design is referred to as a *predictive* or *longitudinal* design. The most important difference between concurrent and longitudinal designs is the timing of the collection of predictor and criterion information.

Concurrent Designs.   Designs of this type use a sample of examinees who are currently performing the job that is the focus of the study. Once the job analysis is conducted and the predictor(s) are developed, each predictor (e.g., test or interview) is administered to a sample of job incumbents. Around the same time, performance data (e.g., ratings, measures of task or course proficiency) are also collected from these incumbents. There are several advantages and disadvantages associated with this design. An important practical advantage is that this design often produces relatively timely results. The predictor administration is economical, because the total number of people to be tested is known or can be determined in advance. An important disadvantage of this design is that current job incumbents may be quite strong in the constructs measured by the predictors and, therefore, there will likely be restriction in the range of scores on the predictor. This restriction in range will cause the correlation between the predictors and the criterion to appear lower than if there were a greater amount of variance in the predictor scores (as might be observed in an applicant population). In addition, the knowledge or skills assessed by the predictors may be affected by learning on the job and hence incumbents' test scores may differ from what their performance would have been when they were applicants. To the extent that performance on the predictors is affected by experience on the job, the correlation between predictor scores and criterion scores may misrepresent the ability of the test to predict the job performance of applicants. Another disadvantage is that it may prove difficult to obtain examinees. Employers often are reluctant to take workers off the job for the necessary test administration. A related concern is the motivation of current employees. Because they are taking the tests "for research purposes only," incumbents may not exert their maximal effort to obtain high scores.

Longitudinal Designs.   The basic distinguishing feature of the longitudinal validation design is the separation in time between the collection of predictor and criterion data. In a study using a longitudinal design, the sample usually consists of applicants tested at the time they apply for a job. An advantage of this design is that the selection situation closely parallels the operational situation, because the sample is drawn from the same population of applicants on which the predictors will be used for selection purposes, and the entire range of predictor scores is represented. Another advantage is that the predictor scores obtained from untrained individuals are used in the prediction of performance (i.e., this design rules out any possibility of the predictor scores being influenced by job-specific training and experience, because the sample is tested before acquiring that training and experience).

Note that use of a longitudinal design does not necessarily eliminate the problems associated with range restriction because the correlation between predictor scores and criterion scores can only be estimated using data from job applicants who were actually hired and remained on the job long enough for criterion data to be collected. These applicants will often have higher scores on the constructs being measured than applicants who were not selected, even when the tests being validated are not being explicitly used to make the hiring decisions. Later in this chapter we provide a formula that adjusts a correlation from the value computed in a restricted sample (e.g., those job applicants who were hired) to the value that would be expected for the entire group of job applicants.

Other disadvantages of the longitudinal design are practical. Typically, the time lag between predictor and criterion data collection ranges from 6 months to 1 year, and many companies may not wish to wait that long for study results. Furthermore, in many cases, applicants who were tested do not remain on the job long enough for suitable criterion data to be obtained, and it is seldom possible to determine if their reason for leaving was related to job performance. Thus, it is important to assess the level of turnover, so that rates of attrition can be analyzed and sample sizes can be estimated. Another disadvantage is that the accumulation of samples of sufficient size usually requires long periods of time during which job applicants are tested and some are hired and added to the sample.

It should be noted that empirical comparisons of validity estimates for cognitive ability tests using both longitudinal and concurrent designs indicate that the two types of designs do not yield substantially different estimates (Barrett, Phillips, & Alexander, 1981; Schmitt, Gooding, Noe, & Kirsch, 1984). On the other hand, there is evidence that the same cannot be said of scores from personality or biodata instruments. Specifically, Oppler, Peterson, and Russell (1992) found that the validities of such measures were considerably lower when estimated using a longitudinal design, rather than a concurrent design. The response options scored as correct can be particularly obvious on personality instruments and consequently evidence of validity obtained from a concurrent sample of employees who were told their responses would be used "for research only" should not be assumed to generalize to a longitudinal sample of job applicants who know that their chances of being hired depend on their responses.

Develop the Sampling Plan

The sampling plan describes who will be included in the study. It must address two important issues. The first issue is the sample size. How many examinees will be required to meet the study's objectives? The second issue is specification of the characteristics of the sample to be selected. How will examinees be selected to be representative of the population of interest? The validation design will dictate the general characteristics of those to be tested (e.g., whether they are applicants, trainees, or employees), but further specification is required to ensure a sample that is representative with respect to demographic characteristics, experience, and the nature of the job or work setting.

Sample Size.   The first issue in deciding on the appropriate sample size is to identify the statistics that will be computed and to determine the level of reliability desired for these statistics. (Statistical reliability refers to the consistency, or repeatability of measurement.) Generally, the larger the sample of examinees included in the validation study, the more dependable the statistics will be, provided that the sample is representative of the target population. The analysis of the relationship between sample size and statistical reliability for hypothesis testing is termed *power analysis*. In a power analysis, the probability that a null hypothesis will be rejected is specified as a function of the true (population) value of the statistic of interest and the size of the sample. Generally, it is desirable that the sample size be selected so that there is a 90% or greater chance that differences of practical significance will be found to be statistically significant. Schmidt, Hunter, and Urry (1976) provided the power of a significance test of a correlation for various sample sizes. Later in this chapter, we discuss the use of confidence intervals for evaluating study results.

Decisions about sample size reflect a practical trade-off between statistical reliability and the cost of conducting the research. The sample size is related to costs in a number of ways, beginning with the resources required to obtain the participation of study participants and continuing on to the administration and scoring of both the predictor and criterion measures.

Sample Characteristics.   It is important for the sample to be representative of the target population (i.e., the applicant pool). From a scientific perspective, the greater the similarity between the sample and the population, the more likely it will be that the results of the study will continue to be applicable when the predictor scores are used operationally. For instance, if a test is to be used to predict performance in training, then it would be inadvisable to include individuals in the sample who have many years of job experience. On the other hand, if a test is to be used to predict long-term performance, then it is important for examinees participating in a concurrent validity study to have at least a minimum amount of experience, perhaps defined as successfully completing a probationary period or working at a job for 6 months. Employees who have just begun a job may not yet be performing at their optimum level. If criterion data are collected on relatively inexperienced employees, then the criterion scores may be lower than they would be if the employees had more job experience. This would affect the correlation obtained (e.g., if employees who had high predictor scores performed poorly on the criterion due to minimal job experience, the coefficient would likely be artificially low). Furthermore, if employees at one site do not perform the same tasks as employees at another site (even if they have the same job title), then the job requirements may be different and the predictor may be more valid for one job site than for another.

From a legal perspective, it is important to have proportions of minorities and women in the study sample comparable to the proportions that are likely to apply for the job. If the selection system is challenged, one question likely to be asked concerns the makeup of individuals in the validation study. Of course, if certain statistics (e.g., correlations between predictor and criterion scores) are to be computed separately for members of different subgroups, it may be necessary to oversample from these subgroups to obtain results that are statistically reliable.

Select the Criterion Measurement Instruments

The criterion-related validation of a predictor battery for use in selection requires evaluation of the ability of the test(s) to predict performance on the job or task. The criteria used in such a validation study are the measures of performance that are used to infer true performance. Obtaining satisfactory measures of performance is a difficult problem and one that requires attention during the planning phase of the study. Detailed discussions of how to develop measures of job performance are provided in chapters 11 and 12. In this section, we describe issues regarding the choice of criterion measures.

There are several characteristics that make criteria useful for a validation study. Some of these are:

1. Validity or relevance: A criterion measure is relevant when the knowledge, skills, and basic aptitudes related to the measure are the same as those required to perform the job duties.
2. Reliability: When evaluating the reliability of a criterion such as ratings, one can investigate the amount of agreement between the ratings provided by two different raters or between the ratings provided by one rater at two different times. Rothstein (1990) found that the reliability of supervisor ratings increased with opportunity to observe, but reached a maximum of only about .55 to .60 with 10 to 20 years of experience.
3. Freedom from bias: Bias may occur whenever individuals or subgroups of a sample are evaluated in systematically different ways. Brogden and Taylor (1950) classified the various types of criterion bias in raw criterion data as either the omission of pertinent elements from the criterion (criterion deficiency) or the introduction of extraneous elements into the criterion (criterion contamination).
4. Practicality: There are very real limits to the effort that may be exerted or the disturbance of routine procedures that will be tolerated during data collection. Unless the validity study is being well supported by management and operating personnel, any program for gathering criterion information that

calls for additional work on their part may be resisted. It is important to provide supervisors with a realistic evaluation of the burden imposed by the collection of criterion data.

One should guard against using data from operational performance appraisal systems where performance ratings were made for administrative purposes such as determining salary increases or bonuses. Although relatively easy to collect, ratings of performance made for administrative purposes are subject to a variety of contaminating factors. For example, employees given below average ratings in one year might receive above average ratings the next year so that they can catch up. Note that such ratings are probably unrelated to job performance. Wherry and Bartlett (1982) hypothesized that ratings collected solely for research purposes would be more accurate than ratings collected for administrative purposes. Several studies have demonstrated that ratings collected for administrative purposes are significantly more lenient and exhibit more halo than ratings collected for research purposes (Sharon & Bartlett, 1969; Taylor & Wherry, 1951; Veres, Field, & Boyles, 1983; Warmke & Billings, 1979).

Whenever possible, more than one set of criterion measures should be obtained in validation studies. One reason for collecting more than one set of criterion data is the multidimensionality of jobs. For example, in a study conducted by the U.S. Army, known as Project A, Campbell, McHenry, and Wise (1990) showed that supervisor ratings were more highly indicative of will do or motivational aspects of job performance, and work sample and job knowledge tests were more indicative of can do or maximal proficiency aspects of job performance. Hence, it is important to consider a wide variety of criteria when designing validation studies.

HOW TO COLLECT DATA

Several kinds of data must be collected in a validation study. These include personnel data, predictor data, and criterion data. Each of these kinds of data is described next. In addition, we describe methods for preparing data to ensure their quality.

Collect Personnel Data

It is necessary to collect background data for two key reasons: (a) professional and scientific research practices require thorough documentation of the nature of the sample of individuals studied and (b) selection methods are subject to public and legal scrutiny. In the event that the research practices are questioned, information regarding sample representation must be made available. In addition, if subgroup analyses are conducted, one must be able to differentiate among various groups.

Typical personnel data include some type of personal identification (e.g., employee number or social security number), age, education, gender, ethnicity, and amount of work experience. Other data may be specified by the research plan, such as information concerning specific types of work experience, training, or equipment operated. Other subsample information may include data collection site name, and the *Dictionary of Occupational Titles* (U.S. Department of Labor, 1991) or O*NET (Hubbard et al., 2000; Peterson, Mumford, Borman, Jeanneret, & Fleishman, 1999) code number for the job being studied.

Personnel data collected directly from examinees should be placed on various research forms specified by the research plan. These forms should be designed for the convenience of the examinees completing them and for ready, efficient entry into electronic form for data analysis. Note that one of the most important forms for examinees to complete is a privacy or confidentiality agreement. Such agreements, signed by examinees, usually state that participation in the research is voluntary and that their data will be reported as part of group statistics only, not individually. It may be very difficult to obtain applicant or employee information if these conditions are not communicated and maintained. Under no circumstances should the researcher release individual data to organizational officials after confidentiality has been promised to participants.

Collect Predictor Data

When collecting predictor data on instruments that can be administered to groups, several issues must be considered to ensure standardization across data collection sites. These include organizing the physical facilities of the testing room, ensuring that there are adequate supplies, maintaining security of test materials, and writing clear instructions to examinees.

Physical Facilities of Testing Room.   A well-lighted and properly ventilated room with tables, chairs, and adequate space for testing is required. Preferably, the room should have no telephone and be situated so that there will be no distracting noises, so that the testing session can be conducted without interruption. Also, the room should have sufficient space to allow the test monitor easy access to all examinees. If testing at a site for the first time, it is a good idea to arrive at the site prior to testing to ensure that the facility is adequate for testing.

For paper-and-pencil testing, all booklets and answer sheets should be examined prior to the testing session for misprints, pencil marks, and missing pages. Also, if there are several forms of each booklet, the examiner must check to see that answer sheets match the appropriate book. Sharpened pencils with erasers should be provided to each examinee. Scratch paper also should be provided to examinees, if necessary. If any of the predictor instruments are to be completed within a specific time limit, the examiner should have a backup timing device (e.g., a stopwatch) in case one malfunctions. Also, if more than about 20 examinees are being tested at once, it may be useful to have an assistant to help distribute materials and monitor examinees during the session.

For computer-based testing, it is important that the hardware and software do not disadvantage some examinees relative to others. For example, a test of reading comprehension may ask questions about paragraphs. If some examinees have small monitors running at low resolution, the paragraphs may not fit on the screen, whereas other examinees with high-resolution, large monitors may have the entire text passage on their screen. Bridgeman, Lennon, and Jackenthal (2003), for example, found that scores on a test of reading comprehension were higher by about .25 standard deviations for examinees with large, high-resolution displays compared to examinees with small, low-resolution displays. Note that these authors found no difference for a math test; there are usually no problems fitting such items on screen. Analogously, the speed of Internet connections should be held constant for all examinees. Drasgow, Luecht, and Bennett (2006) provide further discussion of hardware and software issues for computer-based testing.

Test Security. Testing materials should be kept secure at all times. In preparation for testing sessions, testing personnel should consider setting up ahead of time. This may be especially useful if special equipment or apparatus is required for testing (computers, pegboards, etc.). Written test materials should always remain under tight control. Numbering test booklets is one way to ensure that all test booklets are retrieved at the end of a session. When the testing session is completed, the test administrator must count booklets and answer sheets to ensure that all test materials are accounted for.

Instructions to Examinees. All examinees participating in test research should understand the purpose of their participation for ethical reasons and to ensure cooperation. Typically, a presentation by a researcher immediately prior to test administration will put the examinees at ease and will enable them to understand the purpose of their participation. When job incumbents are tested, it may be desirable for management to distribute a specially prepared statement to employees who are asked to take the tests. When validity data are being collected, the written or oral statement should include the following points:

1. Describe the exact purpose of the study and who is sponsoring the research, for example, "ABC Company is conducting this research in order to identify procedures for selecting people who have a good chance of succeeding on the job."
2. Tell the examinees exactly what will be done with their predictor scores, for example, "Your scores will be compared to other data describing your job performance. Your scores will not be seen by your supervisors or anyone else outside the Research Department."
3. Inform them that their participation is voluntary and not participating will have no effect on their chances of getting or keeping a job.
4. Encourage examinees to do their best on the predictors so that the research will be meaningful.
5. Tell the examinees about how long it will take to complete the tests or other instruments.
6. Ask whether examinees have any remaining questions and address any concerns that are voiced.

Following such a statement, the tests should be administered using the specific instructions developed for each test. Adherence to the specific test administration procedures published and prepared for each test is crucial to ensure standardized data collection across sites and sessions. See chapter 5 for a discussion of such instructions.

Collect Criterion Data

The procedures used for collecting criterion data depend on the type of criterion measures used. If a job knowledge test is used as a criterion, the procedures may be similar to those described earlier for collecting predictor data. If on-the-job criterion data are collected (e.g., productivity rate or error rate), procedures need to be developed to ensure their accuracy. Such data should reflect individual rather than group performance, because these scores will be correlated with individual performance on predictors. It is important that employees have approximately equal opportunity to perform the criterion behavior (i.e., employees must have been on the job long enough to be accurately measured by the criterion or to have had equal access to and equal time on any machines used). Procedures for collecting criterion data will be specific to the organization and criterion measure. For example, when collecting data using work sample measures, as described in chapter 12, one must ensure that those who score such measures are knowledgeable enough about the task to be able to distinguish correct from incorrect performance. Often, graders will need to be trained to score such measures uniformly.

If subjective criterion data are collected (e.g., peer or supervisor ratings), it is useful to collect more than one rating for each examinee in order to assess reliability. To collect ratings, it is advisable to meet with each rater individually, or in small groups, to provide instructions for making ratings. Rater training techniques, including error training and accuracy training, are described in chapter 11.

Prepare Data to Ensure Quality

Quality control of the data begins with the data collector. The data collector is in the best position to detect any significant departure from the validation research plan and data collection standards. Irregularities in test administration or in examinee behavior may not be detectable until after the data collection is complete, which makes it especially important for the data collector to conscientiously monitor all phases of data collection. Irregularities should be documented so that questionable data can be excluded from the study (e.g., data from examinees responding randomly). However, clear justification must be demonstrated before data can be excluded. Careful monitoring and documentation of the data collection effort are necessary to provide such justification.

To the extent that the data collected are inaccurate, the data analyses and the conclusions drawn from the analyses will be flawed. Inaccurate data are defined as follows: (a) data that are not valid measures of the variables being measured or data that are not representative of the individuals or jobs being studied, or

(b) data that are irregular due to administration problems (e.g., insufficient lighting in a testing room or computer malfunction) or due to individual performance on the measure that may be exaggerated or attenuated.

A form for documenting data collection should be developed and used to document the date, location, and circumstances of data collection, and to provide descriptive information about each subsample to enable researchers to decide whether data should be included in data analysis. The exact form of these records should be specified during development of the validation research plan.

Preparing the database prior to conducting analyses is another important step for ensuring quality research. Preparing the database involves specifying how data are to be entered (e.g., using scannable forms or manually entering the data), editing the data (e.g., for out-of-range values), and resolving issues surrounding missing data (e.g., eliminating an examinee's data on an instrument or statistically imputing the missing values). Resolving these issues will require a number of decisions that will impact on how the data are analyzed. We now turn to methods for analyzing data.

HOW TO ANALYZE VALIDITY DATA

This section of the chapter describes a wide range of statistical techniques that are routinely used by analysts to examine the psychometric properties of tests and their validity. It covers topics ranging from the computation of means and standard deviations to regression and bias and includes methods based on classical test theory and IRT. The more complex topics are discussed at a conceptual level. In the event that more thorough understanding of these topics may be useful, references are made to appropriate texts.

Compute Basic Descriptive Statistics

Descriptive statistics are used to describe the characteristics of the data and to make appropriate inferences based on statistical measures. In this section, we focus on three common types of descriptive measures: measures of central tendency, measures of variability, and correlations.

Measures of Central Tendency. There are three commonly used measures of central tendency: the median, the mode, and the mean. The *median* of a set of scores is defined as the middle value when the scores are arranged in order of magnitude. The median is most often used to measure the midpoint of a large set of measurements, such as the median age of all people providing criterion data in the study. This is a useful statistic because it is not influenced by extreme data points (known as outliers). The *mode* of a set of scores is defined as the measurement value that occurs most often. The mode is commonly used to determine the most frequently occurring test score. Outliers do not influence this measure of central tendency. The *mean*, or arithmetic average, is a third measure of central tendency. The mean of a set of scores on a variable (e.g., ages of workers, scores on a predictor, ratings on a dimension of job performance) is simply the sum of all the scores divided by the number of scores. The mean is the most frequently used measure of central tendency and is used in the calculation of other more complex statistics. We provide an example of a set of reading comprehension and job knowledge test scores for currently employed electricians participating in a validation study for which a mean was computed. The formula used to calculate the mean for a set of scores is:

$$M_x = \frac{\sum_{i=1}^{n} X_i}{n}$$

where: M_x = the mean of the scores on the variable X,
X_i = the score of the ith person in the set,
$\sum_{i=1}^{n}$ = sum of observations $i = 1, 2, \ldots n$, so that $\sum^{n} X1 + X2 + \ldots + Xn$,
n = the total number of individuals in the sample who provided scores.

By way of illustration, assume that predictor data (reading comprehension scores) and criterion scores (job knowledge test scores) have been collected from a sample of 10 electricians. The reading comprehension scores and the job knowledge test scores of the electricians are shown in Table 13.1.

To compute the mean predictor test and criterion scores for this sample, the following calculations are performed.

Let: X_i = the test score of the ith examinee
Y_i = the criterion score of the ith examinee
n = the number of electricians = 10
Compute: ΣX_i = the sum of reading comprehension scores = 106
ΣY_i = the sum of job knowledge scores = 73

Substitute the appropriate values in the formula for the mean:

The mean reading comprehension score for this sample is 10.6; the mean job

$$M_x = \frac{\Sigma X_i}{n} = \frac{106}{10} = 10.6$$

$$M_y = \frac{\Sigma Y_i}{n} = \frac{73}{10} = 7.3$$

knowledge test score for this sample is 7.3. The primary disadvantage of the mean as a measure of central tendency is that outlier values may greatly affect the value of the mean. For example, if we changed the 10th worker's score on the criterion from 3 to 60, M_y would increase from 7.3 to 13.0, a value greater than any of the other nine actual observations.

TABLE 13.1
Reading Comprehension Scores and Job Knowledge Test Scores of
Electricians: An Example

Examinee	Reading Comprehension Scores (X_i)	Job Knowledge Test Scores (Y_i)
1	16	9
2	12	6
3	14	12
4	10	5
5	11	12
6	7	4
7	9	3
8	12	9
9	7	10
10	8	3
Sum	106	73

Measures of Variability.   Just as there is more than one measure of central tendency, so are there multiple measures of variability. Among these are the range, the interquartile range, and the standard deviation. The *range* is a rough measure of dispersion that is determined by the lowest and highest values in a distribution of scores. Computing the range of a set of scores is a simple way to check whether the scores are within the expected limits. For example, if a researcher found that the range of scores for a sample was 7 to 25 and knew that it was not possible to obtain a score above 20, the researcher would be alerted to the fact that at least one score must be incorrect and could take steps to correct it. Related to the range is the *interquartile range*. This is expressed by ranking the observations from lowest to highest and referring to the values occurring at the 25th and 75th percentiles of the distribution. For example, if there are 20 scores ordered from lowest to highest, the 5th score would represent the 25th percentile, and the 15th score would represent the 75th percentile.

Whereas the interquartile range is the measure of variability most closely aligned with the median, the measure of variability associated with the mean is the *standard deviation*. Specifically, the standard deviation is a measure of dispersion that describes the extent to which scores scatter or vary about the mean score. It is defined as the square root of the average squared deviations of a set of scores from their mean. A small standard deviation suggests that scores tend to cluster closely around the mean; a large standard deviation suggests that scores tend to range from very high to very low and there is greater dispersion around the mean. Note that the square of the standard deviation is the variance. The formula for calculating the standard deviation of a set of scores is:

$$SD_x = \sqrt{\frac{\sum_{i=1}^{n}(X_i - M_x)^2}{n}}$$

where Σ, X_i, M_x, and n were previously defined.

To compute the standard deviation of the reading comprehension scores in our example, we would make the calculations shown in Table 13.2.

Substituting the appropriate values into the formula as follows, the result is a standard deviation of 2.84:

$$SD_x = \sqrt{\frac{\sum(X - M_x)^2}{n}} = \sqrt{\frac{80.40}{10}} = 2.84$$

After similar calculations, the standard deviation of the criterion scores (Y) reported earlier is found to be 3.35.

Compute Standard Scores from Raw Scores

It often is inappropriate to compare the raw score on one measure with the raw score on another measure because of differences in the units of measurement. For example, a score of 30 on an aptitude test with a mean of 50 and a standard

TABLE 13.2
Calculations Needed to Compute the Standard Deviation of the Reading Comprehension Scores

Examinee	Reading Comprehension Scores (X_i)	X_i-M_x	$(X_i$-$M_x)^2$
1	16	5.4	29.16
2	12	1.4	1.96
3	14	3.4	11.56
4	10	−0.6	0.36
5	11	0.4	0.16
6	7	−3.6	12.96
7	9	−1.6	2.56
8	12	1.4	1.96
9	7	−3.6	12.96
10	8	−2.6	6.76
Sum	106	0	80.40

deviation of 10 is not equivalent to a score of 30 on a different test that has a mean of 20 and a standard deviation of 5. Transforming raw scores to a particular type of scaled score, known as *standard scores*, permits comparisons to be made across scores from different tests. By comparing standard scores, it can be determined whether examinees' performance on the first measure is better or worse than their performance on the second measure. Standard scores are typically expressed in *standard deviation units*. That is, to transform an examinee's raw score on a given measure to a standard score, the raw score is subtracted from the average test score (as computed in the previous example) and this difference is divided by the test's standard deviation. The distribution of a set of standard scores, so defined, will always have a mean of 0 and a standard deviation of 1.

For example, suppose one wanted to compare the reading comprehension test score of one electrician from the previous sample to the criterion score. To do so, one would first calculate the standard scores of each. The formula for converting raw scores on a variable to standard scores on the same variable is:

$$Z_x = \frac{X - M_x}{SD_x}$$

where: Z_x =   the standard score in a set of scores
          X =   the raw score in the original set of scores,
          M_x =   the mean of the original set of scores, and
          SD_x =   the standard deviation of the original set of scores.

Substituting the appropriate values for electrician 1 into the formula yields:

$$Z_x = \frac{X - M_x}{SD_x} = \frac{16 - 10.6}{2.84} = 1.90,$$

and

$$Z_y = \frac{Y - M_y}{SD_y} = \frac{9 - 7.3}{3.35} = 0.51$$

Based on these calculations, electrician 1's standard reading comprehension score is 1.90, which is higher than Electrician 1's standing on the criterion, represented by a standard score of 0.51. That is, Electrician 1's reading comprehension score is 1.9 standard deviations greater than the mean, whereas this electrician's criterion score is only 0.51 standard deviations greater than the mean.

Compute Correlation Coefficients

Correlational methods are used in predictor validation work to analyze the relationships between variables. The size and direction of the relationship between two variables can be expressed in terms of a correlation coefficient computed from data obtained from a sample. Although there are many types of correlational indices, the most appropriate one for use in validation work is the Pearson product-moment correlation coefficient, r_{xy} (Kutner, Nachtsheim, & Neter, 2004). Correlation coefficients can have values ranging from –1.00 to 1.00. A positive correlation coefficient indicates that two variables are related in such a way that high scores on one variable tend to be associated with high scores on the other variable, and that low scores on one variable tend to be associated with low scores on the other variable. In contrast, a negative correlation coefficient indicates that high scores on one variable tend to be associated with low scores on the other variable. The size of the correlation coefficient (regardless of the sign) is an index of the degree of linear relationship, with a value of 0 indicating no linear relationship between the two variables, and a value of 1.00 or –1.00 indicating a perfect linear relationship. Hence, the correlation between a set of predictor and criterion scores indicates the degree to which individuals' relative standing on the predictor corresponds to their relative standing on the criterion.

The formula for computing the product-moment correlation between any two variables is:

$$r_{xy} = \frac{Cov_{xy}}{SD_x \times SD_y},$$

where

r_{xy} =   the Pearson product-moment correlation between predictor scores (X) and criterion scores (Y),

SD_x =   the standard deviation of X,

SD_y =   the standard deviation of Y, and

Cov_{xy} =   the covariance between X and Y.

The covariance is defined as:

$$Cov_{xy} = \frac{\sum_{i=1}^{n}(X_i - M_x)(Y_i - M_y)}{n}$$

The covariance is a measure of the degree to which scores on X and Y covary. It reflects the extent to which people have scores above the mean on both X and Y or below the mean on both X and Y. Covariances are not easily interpreted because they are affected by the scale of the X and the Y measures. However, dividing the covariance by the standard deviations of X and Y yields the correlation coefficient r_{xy}, which is more easily interpreted. If one squares the correlation coefficient, one can assess the amount of variance accounted for in one variable by another.

Today, most statistical software packages (and even many hand calculators) include programs for computing the product-moment correlation coefficient between two variables. The example in Table 13.3, using the small sample of electricians described earlier, is provided for illustrative purposes.

TABLE 13.3
Calculations Needed to Compute the Correlation Between Reading
Comprehension Scores and Job Knowledge Test Scores

Examinee	Reading Comprehension Scores (X_i)	Job Knowledge Test Scores (Y_i)	$(X_i\text{-}M_x)$	$(Y_i\text{-}M_y)$	$(X_i\text{-}M_x)(Y_i\text{-}M_y)$
1	16	9	5.4	1.7	9.18
2	12	6	1.4	−1.3	−1.82
3	14	12	3.4	4.7	15.98
4	10	5	−0.6	−2.3	1.38
5	11	12	0.4	4.7	1.88
6	7	4	−3.6	−3.3	11.88
7	9	3	−1.6	−4.3	6.88
8	12	9	1.4	1.7	2.38
9	7	10	−3.6	2.7	−9.72
10	8	3	−2.6	−4.3	11.18
Sum	106	73	0	0	49.20

Substituting the appropriate values in the formulas yields:

$$Cov_{xy} = \frac{49.2}{10} = 4.92$$

and then:

$$r_{xy} = \frac{4.92}{2.84 \times 3.35} = .517$$

By squaring the correlation $(.517)^2$, one can say that approximately 27% of the variance in variable Y is accounted for by variable X, or vice versa.

A correlation coefficient is meaningful only when it is computed using accurate measurements for a representative sample from the total population. Correlation coefficients computed using data obtained from samples are subject to chance error, known as sampling error, with the result that, in general, the values of the obtained correlation coefficients differ to some degree from the value of the population correlation coefficient. The degree of confidence that can be placed in a correlation coefficient computed from sample data depends on the number of cases in the sample. The larger the sample, the more confidence one can have that the value of the obtained correlation coefficient approaches the value of the population correlation coefficient. It is a general rule in statistical analysis that the stability of any statistic is greater for large samples than for small samples. For this reason, validation studies should be based on samples that are as large as possible (Schmidt & Hunter, 1978).

Because of the inaccuracy of sample-based correlation coefficients, it is helpful to consider a sample correlation coefficient not as a single value, but as a range of values. For this purpose, it is useful to calculate a confidence interval, which is a range of values that has a given probability of containing the population value. The formula for calculating a 95% confidence interval is:

$$r_{xy} - (1.96 \times SE_r) \leq \rho_{xy} \leq r_{xy} + (1.96 \times SE_r)$$

where ρ_{xy} is the unknown correlation of X and Y in the population, and SE_r is the standard error of the sample correlation r_{xy}.

To calculate the confidence interval for a given correlation, one must first compute the standard error for that correlation. The formula for the standard error of a correlation is:

$$SE_r = \frac{1 - r_{xy}^2}{\sqrt{n - 1}}$$

In our example, the standard error of the correlation would be calculated as:

$$SE_r = \frac{1 - .517^2}{\sqrt{9}} = .244$$

Using this value in the formula for the confidence interval presented before, the confidence interval is calculated as follows:

$$.517 - (1.96 \times .244) \leq \rho_{xy} \leq .517 + (1.96 \times .244)$$
$$.039 \leq \rho_{xy} \leq .995$$

Note that the confidence interval does not contain 0, indicating that we can be confident, with 95% accuracy, that the population correlation r_{xy} is greater than 0. However, the size of the interval encompasses nearly the entire range of positive correlations, from 0 to 1. This indicates that little confidence can be placed in the precision of .517 as a point estimate of the correlation in the population. The reason for this was alluded to earlier: The accuracy of a sample correlation is highly dependent on the number of cases included in the analysis, which, in our example, was only 10.

Tests of statistical significance also are used to determine whether the obtained correlation coefficient is significantly different from 0 (or from some other specified level). Tables for testing the significance of correlation coefficients can be found in most statistical textbooks (Hays, 1981, Appendix D). Although tests of statistical significance are quite frequently used to evaluate predictor validity (i.e., the correlation between a predictor and criterion measure), statistical significance tests of correlations are susceptible to large Type II error, defined as accepting the null hypothesis (e.g., that the predictor is not valid) when it should be rejected (e.g., the predictor really is valid; Murphy & Myors, 2003; Schmidt & Hunter, 1977). Now we describe reasons why observed correlations may be artificially low.

Correct for Factors Affecting the Correlation Coefficient

Previously, we noted that sample correlation coefficients are meaningful only when they are computed using valid predictor and criterion scores for large and representative samples, and that large samples are needed to provide hypothesis tests with adequate power. In this section, we discuss deleterious effects of non-representative samples and unreliable scores.

Range Restriction. The intent of validation research is to determine the true validity of a predictor for members of the applicant population. However, concurrent validation studies use employee samples (e.g., current workers, screened by some form of operational selection procedure). If the operational selection procedure happens to be correlated with the predictor being validated, then the distribution of predictor scores in the employee population will differ from the distribution of predictor scores in the applicant population. Specifically, employees' predictor scores will be less variable than applicants' scores. This phenomenon is known as *range restriction.* The effect of range restriction is to artificially reduce the size of the correlation coefficient. As a consequence, the correlation between predictor scores and criterion scores for the examinee sample will underestimate the correlation for the applicant population at large. To estimate the correlation for the population, we need to know: (a) the correlation between the predictor and criterion scores in the job incumbent sample (r^*_{xy}), (b) the standard deviation of predictor test scores in the job incumbent sample (SD^*_x), and (c) the standard deviation of predictor test scores in the applicant population (SD_x). Note that a star (*) is used to indicate statistics that have been computed from data obtained from a nonrepresentative sample.

The formula for estimating the correlation between the test and the criterion in the applicant population $\hat{\rho}_{xy}$ is:
where $\hat{\rho}_{xy}$ is the estimate of the population correlation, and r^*_{xy}, SD^*_x, and SD_x are defined as before.

$$\hat{\rho}_{xy} = \frac{r^*_{xy}\dfrac{SD_x}{SD^*_x}}{\sqrt{1 - (r^*_{xy})^2 + (r^*_{xy})^2\left(\dfrac{SD_x}{SD^*_x}\right)^2}}$$

As calculated in the preceding section, the correlation between the reading comprehension scores and the criterion scores for the sample of 10 electricians is 0.517. Suppose that the standard deviation of reading comprehension scores is 5.0 for the applicant population, and the standard deviation of test scores for this sample of job incumbents is only 2.84. To estimate the validity of the test in the applicant population, the formula is used in the following way:

$$\hat{\rho}_{xy} = \frac{.517\left(\dfrac{5}{2.84}\right)}{\sqrt{1 - .517^2 + .517^2\left(\dfrac{5}{2.84}\right)^2}} = .728$$

Using the correction formula, the correlation between the reading comprehension test and the criterion would be estimated at 0.728 for the population of job applicants. This procedure is referred to as correcting the correlation coefficient for the effects of range restriction.

The primary problem associated with use of the range restriction correction formula concerns the estimation of the standard deviation of test scores for the population. Only in situations where test scores are available for applicants who were rejected, as well as for those who were accepted, can the standard deviation of the applicant population be estimated. In concurrent validation research, this value must be estimated from other sources of information. When conducting longitudinal test validation research, it is important to collect predictor test data on all applicants, not just those selected for the job.

Criterion Unreliability. When a test validation study is conducted, the correlation to be determined is that between a given predictor measure and a particular performance measure. However, because pure measures of performance do not exist, criterion measures that contain some amount of random error must be used. This random error is referred to as *criterion unreliability*. The more random error that a criterion measure contains, the more unreliable it is. The correlation obtained between a test and a criterion will tend to decrease as the reliability of the criterion decreases, and will tend to increase as the reliability of the criterion increases. As a result, the effect of criterion unreliability is to cause the correlation computed in a test validation study to underestimate the size of the relationship between test scores and perfectly measured job performance.

However, if the reliability of the criterion is known, the correlation obtained between any test and that criterion can be corrected for criterion unreliability. Scores on the criterion that contain no measurement error are called *true scores* and are denoted τ_y. The correlation between test scores X and criterion true scores τ_y can be computed by the following formula:

$$r_{x\tau_y} = \frac{r_{xy}}{\sqrt{r_{yy}}}$$

$r_{x\tau_y}$ = the correlation between scores on a test that is not perfectly reliable and criterion true scores, and

r_{yy} = the reliability of the criterion.

For example, suppose, for the sample of 10 electricians described earlier, that the criterion has a reliability of 0.60. The correlation between the test scores and the criterion scores, as calculated earlier in this chapter and corrected for the effects of range restriction, is 0.728. The preceding formula can be used as follows to estimate the predictor-criterion correlation ($r_{x t_y}$) that would have been obtained if the criterion were perfectly reliable:

$$r_{x t_y} = \frac{0.728}{\sqrt{.60}} = .940$$

Thus, it is estimated that if the criterion were perfectly reliable, the predictor-criterion correlation in the applicant population would have been 0.940, instead of 0.728.

It is important to remember that a coefficient corrected for criterion unreliability represents the correlation that would be obtained between a perfectly reliable criterion and a predictor that is not perfectly reliable. The obtained predictor-criterion correlation is usually not corrected for the lack of perfect reliability of the predictor, because under normal circumstances, the same imperfect predictor will be used in both the validation and operational situations.

For a more detailed discussion of both the range restriction and criterion unreliability corrections, a good source is *Measurement Theory for the Behavioral Sciences* by Ghiselli, Campbell, and Zedeck (1981).

Conduct Regression Analysis

In the previous section, we discussed the use of correlations to assess the strength of the relationship between a set of predictor scores and a set of criterion scores. Correlation is often used to describe the relationship between the two sets of scores. Regression, on the other hand, is used to predict an individual's score on one measure (e.g., the criterion) using that individual's score on one or more other measures (e.g., the predictors). The term *simple linear regression* refers to the special case where there is only one predictor measure. The adjective *linear* refers to the description of the relationship as a straight line. That is, in a positive linear relationship, as the values of one variable (e.g., scores on a test of reading comprehension) increase, so do the values of the other variable (e.g., scores on a job knowledge test), and they do so in the same proportion at any level of the first variable (Nunnally, 1978).

The basic equation for simple linear regression is:

$$\hat{Y} = a + bX_i$$

where: $\hat{Y}$ =   individual i's predicted score on the criterion measure, such as a job knowledge test,

X_i =   individual i's score on the predictor measure,

a =   The y-intercept (the value of the criterion when the value of the predictor measure is zero), and

b =   the slope of the straight line (the unit change in the criterion for a unit change in the predictor score).

Using the regression equation $\hat{Y}_i = 10 + .9X_i$, a person with a predictor score (X_i) of 50 would be expected to have a Y score of $10 + .9(50) = 55$. In actual practice, a group of individuals, each with an X score of 50, would likely have Y scores scattered above and below 55, but 55 would be the best guess for any one of them, if all we knew was their performance on X.

Multiple regression techniques differ from simple linear regression in that more than one predictor is used to predict performance on a criterion variable. For example, performance on a test of job knowledge may be related to cognitive ability, grade point average in college, and years of experience on the job. Multiple regression techniques can be used to determine both the unique and combined contribution of these variables to the prediction of performance on that criterion.

Various outcomes may be obtained in a multiple regression analysis. For example, regression techniques may reveal that all three variables contribute to the prediction of performance, or regression techniques may reveal that once the contribution of one variable is taken into account (e.g., cognitive ability), most of the variance in performance on the criterion is explained, and the contributions of the other variables are minimal. Similarly, one can assess the extent to which a measure predicts performance on several criterion variables, such as a job knowledge test, a work sample measure, and supervisor or peer ratings. Because different predictors are likely to predict performance on different criteria, one would conduct these analyses separately. If there are different measures of the same criterion construct, one may create a combined score and conduct the analyses on that measure as well. A good description of the concept of regression is provided in Ghiselli et al. (1981) and in Cohen, Cohen, West, and Aiken (2003).

Assess Predictive Bias

The term test bias has been used to refer to a wide range of test issues, including differences between groups in average scores, language demand, validity, content relevance, content offensiveness, and selection rates (Flaugher, 1978). In employment testing, these issues are embedded in a history of complex and emotionally charged debates regarding the purposes of testing, the constitutional legality of certain testing procedures and employment selection policies (Bolick, 1988), as well as the appropriateness of a variety of analytic procedures used for designing tests, evaluating outcomes, and distinguishing the fine line between adverse impact and reverse discrimination (Baldus & Cole, 1980). Adverse impact is defined as a substantially different rate of selection in hiring, promotion, or other employment decision that works to the disadvantage of members of a racial, gender, or ethnic group (Cascio, 1987). This is different from test bias, which focuses on differences in subgroup regression lines.

The commonly accepted definition of test bias, described in the *Uniform Guidelines on Employee Selection Procedures* (1978) and the *Standards for Educational and*

Psychological Testing (AERA et al., 1999), focuses not on mean subgroup differences in test scores, but rather on subgroup differences in the relationship between test scores and performance on the criterion that the test is being used to predict. This definition, known as the Cleary (1968) definition of test bias, states:

> A test is biased for members of a subgroup of the population if, in the prediction of a criterion for which the test was designed, consistent nonzero errors of prediction are made for members of the subgroup. In other words, the test is biased if the criterion score predicted from the common regression line is consistently too high or too low for members of the subgroup. (p. 115)

According to this regression model, a test is considered to be biased if use of an overall regression equation results in systematic underprediction or overprediction for one or more subgroups. A generally accepted method used to assess whether a particular measuring instrument meets this definition of bias has been the comparison of the regression line of some criterion on the test scores for members of one subgroup with the regression line of the same criterion on the test scores for another group. If significant differences between the two regression lines exist, then prediction based on a common regression line for the total group will result in systematic errors of prediction.

A source of some confusion concerns the distinction between test bias and fairness of test use. Although often used interchangeably, the notions of test bias and fairness of test use are conceptually different. Whereas test bias is exclusively concerned with the equality of the prediction error across subgroups for each test score level, fairness of test use is concerned with equality across subgroups regarding a wider variety of outcomes resulting from the use of test scores in selection. Because people have differed in their opinions regarding which specific outcomes of selection should be equated, different definitions of fairness of test use have been proposed. One approach to fairness that has received widespread acceptance is Cleary's (1968) regression definition. As Jensen (1980) pointed out, fairness of test use is a subjective concept that is affected by moral, legal, and philosophical ideas, rather than scientific or statistical analyses. In addressing the distinction between bias and fairness, Cole (1981) wrote:

> Testing scholars and the courts must clearly recognize that test validity and the appropriateness of social or educational policies are separate issues. Thus, even as the scholarly community affirms its concern with (and belief in the value of) validity-type evidence about test bias, it must not be blinded to the limitations of this evidence in answering the essentially different question of the relative desirability of alternate social policies. (p. 1069)

For a more extensive discussion of test bias and fairness, see Petersen and Novick (1976) and Hartigan and Wigdor (1989).

TABLE 13.4
Hypothetical Results for a New Test of Electrical Knowledge

Item	Item Difficulty $\hat{p}_j$	Corrected Item-Total Correlation	Alpha if Item Deleted
1	.97	.12	.77
2	.91	.27	.75
3	.78	.35	.74
4	.89	.28	.76
5	.61	.34	.74
6	.79	.03	.80
7	.67	.29	.75
8	.27	.04	.79
9	.33	.21	.76
10	.61	.42	.74
11	.52	.45	.74
12	.21	.19	.77
13	.52	.37	.75
14	.96	.09	.77
15	.17	−.15	.80
16	.73	.39	.74
17	.31	.27	.75
18	.91	.40	.74
19	.76	.32	.74
20	.61	.37	.73

Assess Item Characteristics: Classical Item Statistics

In the test development process, item writers are well advised to write twice as many items as the final test form will require (Nunnally, 1978, p. 261). It is advisable to administer the new items in a pilot study; many items will be found to be too easy, too difficult, or poorly discriminating. Hypothetical results for a new test of electrical knowledge are provided in Table 13.4.

In this table, $\hat{p}_j$ is the proportion of people answering item j correctly. For example, $\hat{p}_{18}$ is .91; this means that 91% of the examinees answered Item 18 correctly. For Item 18, the corrected item-total correlation is .40. The term *corrected item-total correlation* needs a bit of explanation. First, an item-total correlation is the correlation of scores on Item 18 with total test scores; it tells us whether people who did well on the total test also tended to do well on a particular item (Item 18 here). Item-total correlations provide useful information about whether an individual item is measuring the same thing as the rest of the test; an item-total correlation near 0 indicates that it is not, whereas a correlation of, say, .40 indicates that the item is likely measuring the same thing. A problem with simply computing the item-total correlation is that the item is part of the total. The total score is the sum of the scores on the individual items, including Item 18. Consequently, an item-total correlation is subject to a part-whole confound, and would be expected to have a positive correlation regardless of whether the item is validly measuring the underlying skill or ability assessed by the other items. To eliminate this confound, we can compute a total score based on the other 19 items and correlate Item 18 with this "corrected" total score. Because Item 18 has a corrected item-total correlation of .40, we can be confident that it is measuring the same skill as the other items and contributes to the assessment of electrical knowledge.

The column titled by "Alpha if Item Deleted" is based on coefficient alpha. Coefficient alpha is probably the most widely used measure of the reliability r_{xx} of a test. It is computed from the variance of the total test score and the sum of the variances of the item scores:

$$\alpha = \frac{J}{J-1} \left(1 - \frac{\sum_{j=1}^{J} \sigma_j^2}{\sigma_x^2} \right)$$

where:

α	=	coefficient alpha,
J	=	the number of items on the test,
σ_j^2	=	the variance of scores on item j, and
σ_x^2	=	the variance of scores on the test X.

Suppose that the coefficient alpha for this 20-item test is .77. The column "Alpha if Item Deleted" shows the reliability for 19-item tests obtained by deleting each of the 20 items in turn. Like the corrected item-total correlation, this column is useful for evaluating whether an item measures the same skill as the other items. If the "alpha if item deleted" increases when an item is deleted, the test can be made more reliable by deleting that item. Clearly, such items do not contribute to valid measurement of the underlying skill assessed by the rest of the items on the test.

The three types of statistics in Table 13.4 are useful for understanding the measurement properties of the items on the test. For example, it is apparent that Item 1 is very easy: The $\hat{p}$ value is .97, which means that virtually every examinee answered correctly. Such an item is not very useful for measuring electrical knowledge and if the test developer is most concerned with efficiency, Item 1 should be deleted. On the other hand, it often is desirable to begin a test with an easy item to help test takers warm up. Consequently, the test developer may decide to retain Item 1 because it can help test takers get started on the right foot. Item 14 also is very easy, but has a lower corrected item-total correlation than Item 1. In all likelihood, this item would be deleted.

In contrast to Item 1, Item 12 is very difficult: The $\hat{p}$ value is .21. Assuming the items on this test have four multiple-choice options, the chance of answering correctly simply by guessing is .25. Some test developers delete any item with a $\hat{p}$

below the chance level. Note, however, that the corrected item-total correlation for Item 12 is .19, which indicates that this item is contributing to the assessment of electrical knowledge. On the other hand, Item 15 is very difficult, with a p of .17, but its corrected item-total correlation is −.15. The combination of a low p and a negative but large item-total correlation suggests that this item has been miskeyed. That is, the response option that the test developer designated as the correct answer probably is not truly the correct answer.

Items 6 and 8 have very low item-total correlations: .03 and .04. In addition, the reliability of the test (alpha if item deleted) would increase if each item were deleted. These items do not appear to contribute to the assessment of electrical knowledge and would be deleted from the test.

In summary, based on the data in Table 13.4, many test developers would delete Items 6, 8, 14, and 15. The reliability of the test would increase from .77 to perhaps .83.

Assess Item Characteristics: Item Response Theory (IRT)

The item statistics described in the preceding section (p the corrected item-total correlation, and the alpha if the item is deleted) are easy to interpret and relatively straightforward to compute. Consequently, they are routinely examined by test developers and test users. However, a more sophisticated approach is sometimes needed. For example, in computer adaptive testing (CAT), the computer branches to a more difficult item following a correct answer and to an easier item following an incorrect answer. As a result, high-ability examinees are administered items that are more difficult than the items administered to low-ability examinees. How should a CAT be scored? Proportion correct is unsatisfactory because high- and low-ability examinees might both answer 60% correct, but the high-ability examinees answered difficult items and the low-ability examinees answered easy items.

IRT provides a means of solving complex measurement problems. Introductions to IRT were provided by Hulin, Drasgow, and Parsons (1983) and Hambleton, Swaminathan, and Rogers (1991). More advanced treatments are given in Van der Linden and Hambleton (1996) and Van der Linden and Glas (2000).

IRT assumes that all of the items on a test assess a single, underlying ability, usually denoted by the Greek letter theta (θ). This underlying ability is called the *latent trait* because it is not directly observable. The responses to the test items, in contrast, are observed, and they are used to estimate the latent trait.

Latent trait scores are usually expressed as standard scores (see the section on computing standard scores from raw scores). A person with a latent trait score θ of +2.0 would have a score two standard deviations above the mean and consequently be very high on the skill assessed by the test. A person with a θ of −1.0, on the other hand, would be a standard deviation below the mean and hence be relatively low on the latent trait.

Fundamental to IRT is the item characteristic curve (ICC). It describes the probability of a correct response as a function of the latent trait and one or more

ICCs for 1PL Items

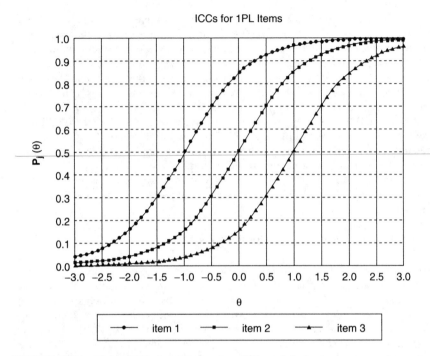

FIGURE 13.1.   Three ICCs for the simplest IRT model, the one-parameter logistic (1PL, sometimes called the Rasch model).

item parameters. This probability is denoted $Pj(\theta)$, which means "the probability of a correct answer on item j among examinees with ability θ." Figure 13.1 shows three ICCs for the simplest IRT model, the one-parameter logistic (which is sometimes called the Rasch model). Each curve represents a single item.

The equation for the one-parameter logistic model is:

$$P_j(\theta) = \frac{1}{1 + e^{-1.7(\theta - b_j)}},$$

where: $P_j(\theta)$ =   the probability of a correct answer on item j among examinees with ability θ,

e =   a mathematical constant, e is an irrational number approximately equal to 2.718,

1.7   =   a scaling constant used for historical reasons, and

b_j =   the item difficulty parameter for item j.

Note that the IRT item difficulty parameter b_j is analogous to the classical item statistic p. As described later, b_j is a parameter that reflects the location of the ICC on the latent trait continuum.

The item difficulty parameters of the three items in Figure 13.1 are $b_1 = -1.0$, $b_2 = 0$, and $b_3 = 1.0$. Note that when examinees' ability levels are substantially lower than an item's difficulty parameter (e.g., at θ values below -2.0 for the three items in Fig. 13.1), examinees have very little chance of answering correctly.

When $\theta = -1.0$, the probability of answering the easiest item, Item 1, correctly is .50, which can be seen by:

$$P_1(-1) = \frac{1}{1 + e^{-1.7[(-1)-(-1)]}} = \frac{1}{1 + e^{-1.7[0]}} = \frac{1}{1 + 1} = .5$$

At this same ability level ($\theta = -1.0$), the probability of answering Item 2 correctly is:

$$P_2(-1) = \frac{1}{1 + e^{-1.7[(-1)-0]}} = \frac{1}{1 + e^{-1.7[-1]}} = \frac{1}{1 + 5.47} = .15$$

and the probability of answering Item 3 correctly is near 0.

The ICCs for these three items increase for higher values of θ. When $\theta = 2.0$, the probability of answering Item 1 correctly is nearly 1.0, the probability for Item 2 is very high, and for Item 3:

$$P_3(2) = \frac{1}{1 + e^{-1.7[2-1]}} = \frac{1}{1 + e^{-1.7}} = \frac{1}{1 + 0.18} = .85$$

For items with k multiple-choice options, we might expect low-ability examinees to be able to guess the answers to difficult items with probability approximately $1/k$. In other words, on a multiple-choice item having four options, the probability of getting the correct answer by guessing alone is .25. Hence, ICCs that decrease to a low value of about $1/k$ seem more realistic than one-parameter logistic ICCs, which decrease to 0 as in Fig. 13.1. Moreover, some items are more discriminating than others. For example, in Table 13.4, Item 3 has a corrected item-total correlation of .35 whereas Item 8 has a corrected item-total correlation of .04; this leads us to say that Item 3 is more discriminating than Item 8. In IRT, the steepness of the ICC indexes an item's ability to discriminate among higher and lower ability examinees, but the one-parameter logistic ICCs are all equally steep. Thus, in the one-parameter logistic model, all items are assumed to be equally discriminating.

The three-parameter logistic model adds two additional parameters to the one-parameter model so that we can model items with varying discriminations and nonzero guessing (i.e., the fact that examinees can sometimes guess the correct answer to multiple-choice items). This model is given by the formula:

$$P_j(\theta) = c_j + \frac{1 - c_j}{1 + e^{-1.7[a_j(\theta - b_j)]}},$$

where: $P_j(\theta)$ =   the probability of a correct answer on item j among
                                 examinees with ability θ,

             e =   a mathematical constant, e is an irrational number
                                 approximately equal to 2.718,

             1.7   =   a scaling constant used for historical reasons,

             c_j =   the lower asymptote parameter for item j,

             b_j =   the item difficulty parameter for item j,

             a_j =   the item discrimination parameter for item j.

Here, c_j is the lower asymptote (the lowest value) of the height of the ICC as $\theta \to$
$-\infty$ and a_j is termed the discrimination parameter because it reflects the steepness
of the ICC above the point $\theta = b_j$ (see later for more explanation).

Figure 13.2 shows ICCs for three items. The first has $a_1 = 1.0$, $b_1 = 0.5$, and c_1
$= 0.2$; the second has $a_2 = 0.9$, $b_2 = -0.5$, and $c_2 = 0.5$; and the third has $a_3 = 0.2$,

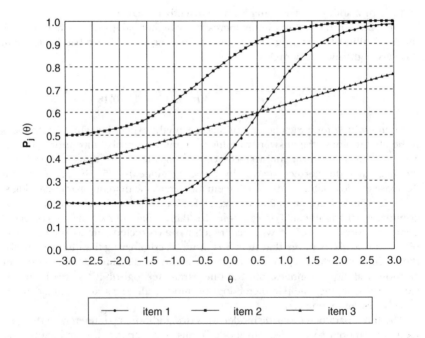

FIGURE 13.2   Item characteristic curves for three items in the three-parameter
logistic (3PL) model; Item1 has $a_1 = 1.0$, $b_1 = 0.5$ and $c_1 = 0.2$; Item 2 has $a_2 = 0.9$,
$b_2 = -0.5$, and $c_2 = 0.5$; Item 3 has $a_3 = 0.2$, $b_3 = 0.0$, and $c_3 = 0.15$.

$$P_1(-2) = 0.2 + \frac{(1 - 0.2)}{1 + e^{-1.7[1.0(-2-0.5)]}}$$

$$= 0.2 + \frac{0.8}{1 + e^{-1.7[-2.5]}} = 0.2 + \frac{0.8}{1 + 70.1} = .21$$

$b_3 = 0.0$, and $c_3 = 0.15$. The figure shows that the probability of a low-ability examinee (e.g., $\theta = -2.0$) correctly answering the first item is near the value of the lower asymptote parameter. Note that for Item 3, due to the flatness of the curve, the c_3 parameter (0.15) is not on the graph. To show how the probability is computed, note that:

The fact that the ICC for Item 1 rises sharply in the range –0.5 to 1.5 means that it is a "good" item. Specifically, this item is said to be "discriminating" because an examinee with $\theta = -0.5$ has a much lower chance of answering correctly than someone with $\theta = 1.5$.

The most prominent feature of Item 2 is the fact that its lower asymptote is not very low. Because $c_2 = 0.5$, even low-ability examinees have a 50% chance of answering correctly. This item seems like a true-false item, rather than a four-option multiple-choice item.

Note that the ICC for Item 3 is nearly flat: Its ICC rises from about .50 at $\theta = -1$ to just .62 at $\theta = 1$. In contrast, Item 1's ICC rises from about .25 to .75 in this same interval. Thus, Item 3 is not discriminating in the sense that an examinee with $\theta = -1.0$ has nearly the same probability of answering correctly as an examinee with $\theta = 1.0$; Item 1, in contrast, is much more discriminating because an examinee with $\theta = -1.0$ will answer incorrectly three times in four whereas an examinee with $\theta = 1.0$ will answer correctly three times in four. Another interesting feature of Item 3 is that its ICC is so flat that the lower asymptote c_3 is not on this graph. The reason the ICC is so flat is that the item discrimination parameter is small: $a_3 = 0.2$. Items with low discrimination parameters are ordinarily eliminated during the test development process.

Computer Adaptive Testing (CAT).   Although the technical details of CAT are beyond the scope of this chapter, it is possible to provide an overview. A CAT begins by assuming that an examinee is of average ability (i.e., $\theta = 0$) and the computer selects an item from a pool of items that has a difficulty parameter (b_j) near 0. The reason for selecting an item with a difficulty parameter near an examinee's ability level can be seen in Figs. 13.1 and 13.2. The ICCs in both figures rise most steeply near their b_j values and, therefore, are most discriminating near their difficulty parameter. (The exception is Item 3 in Fig. 13.2, which exhibits a relatively flatter ICC across values of θ and consequently would be deleted during the test development process.)

Suppose that an examinee answers the first item on a CAT correctly. The assumption that the examinee is of average ability (i.e., $\theta = 0$) would be updated based on this information. A sophisticated statistical method (e.g., expected a posteriori

Bayesian estimation; Bock & Mislevy, 1982) is used to estimate examinees' abilities based on their responses. Suppose that this process yields an updated ability estimate of $\hat{\theta} = 0.45$ for a particular test taker. The computer would now examine the item pool, select an item with a difficulty parameter (b_j) near 0.45, and administer it to the examinee. After the examinee answers, their ability would be estimated based on the answers to the two items.

The process of selecting an item from the item pool near the examinees' current ability estimates, administering the item to the examinees, and updating the ability estimates after the examinees have answered continues until a fixed number of items has been administered or the examinees' ability estimates have reached a predetermined level of accuracy. Many CATs being used operationally administer 15 to 35 items. Research has shown that a CAT provides ability estimates that are about as precise as a conventional test (i.e., a test where all examinees answer the same set of items) that is twice as long. A CAT can be much shorter than a conventional test because it selects items that are appropriately difficult for examinees; we learn little about the ability of a high-ability examinee by administering an easy item (it will be answered correctly) or administering a very difficult item to a low-ability examinee (the examinee will just guess).

Differential Item Functioning (DIF).   Earlier, we described the Cleary (1968) definition of test bias and the use of regression analysis to examine possible test bias. IRT provides another approach for examining the possible bias of a test.

Consider the following two examples:

1. Suppose a test of electrical knowledge is given to a large number of applicants for jobs as electricians. The initial analysis of the data shows that the average score of male applicants is about one standard deviation higher than the average score of female applicants. Is this test biased against females?
2. Suppose the test of electrical knowledge is translated into Spanish so that Hispanic applicants can be offered the choice of taking the test in either English or Spanish. Is the translation correct? Do the Spanish versions of the items assess electrical knowledge in the same way as the English versions?

Provided that the sample sizes are adequate, IRT can answer these questions.

In these two examples, as well as in many other situations, the questions can be boiled down to a matter of whether the J items on the test measure equivalently across two groups. To answer this question, the data from the first group would be analyzed by a computer program such as BILOG-MG (Zimowski, Muraki, Mislevy, & Bock, 2002), and then data from the second group would be analyzed similarly. In these analyses, BILOG would estimate item parameters: Let ($\hat{a}_j$, $\hat{b}_j$, $\hat{c}_j$) denote the discrimination, difficulty, and lower asymptote parameter estimates for the first group and let $(\tilde{a}_j, \tilde{b}_j, \tilde{c}_j)$ denote the estimates for the second group. Item j measures differently for the two groups if $(\hat{a}_j, \hat{b}_j, \hat{c}_j)$ and $(\tilde{a}_j, \tilde{b}_j, \tilde{c}_j)$ differ more than expected on the basis of random sampling fluctuations (see Hulin et al., 1983, pp. 173–175; for an improved approach to testing DIF, see Stark, Chernyshenko, & Drasgow, in press).

A DIF analysis proceeds, item by item, to examine whether the items measure the latent trait in the same way across groups. If an item measures differently (i.e., its ICC differs significantly across the two groups), the item should be examined for content to determine if it should be removed from the test. When the DIF analysis is complete, and all items exhibiting differences across groups have been reviewed and possibly removed, the revised test provides equivalent measurement across groups. Thus, scores can be compared across groups and used to make hiring decisions.

It is important to note that mean differences in test scores can still remain after all items with DIF have been eliminated. The educational and life experiences of different groups certainly differ and so there is no reason to believe that the amount of electrical knowledge (or any other skill assessed by a test) should be the same across diverse groups. The virtue of the DIF analysis is that it allows us to examine the measurement properties of the items and identify any that measure differently across groups. After eliminating items with DIF, any remaining differences in test scores across groups can be attributed to preexisting group differences rather than any flaws in the test.

Document the Research Design and Study Results

As described earlier, conducting a validity study requires making many research design decisions (e.g., sampling, data collection, and data analysis). The rationale underlying these decisions needs to be documented so that their effects on the results can be considered. Furthermore, study results should be documented so that, if challenged, the use of a measure for predicting performance of an individual on a particular job is defensible, both legally and scientifically.

SUMMARY

In this chapter, we have discussed various methodological and statistical techniques used to conduct a validation study. These techniques included how to develop a validation research plan, procedures for collecting data, and methods of data analysis. We recognize that portions of this chapter are written at different levels of technical sophistication. Although sufficient information is probably provided for relatively simple statistical processes (i.e., descriptive statistics), more information may be required about advanced kinds of analyses. Toward that end, we have made reference to more technical texts.

REFERENCES

American Educational Research Association, American Psychological Association, & National Council on Measurement in Education. (1999). *Standards for educational and psychological testing*. Washington, DC: American Educational Research Association.

Baldus, D. C., & Cole, J. W. L. (1980). *Statistical profile of discrimination*. New York: McGraw-Hill.

Barrett, G. V., Phillips, J. S., & Alexander, R. A. (1981). Concurrent and predictive validity designs: A critical analysis. *Journal of Applied Psychology, 25,* 499–513.

Binning, J. F., & Barrett, G. V. (1989). Validity of personnel decisions: A conceptual analysis of the inferential and evidential bases. *Journal of Applied Psychology, 74,* 478–494.

Bock, R. D., & Mislevy, R. J. (1982). Adaptive EAP estimation of ability in a microcomputer environment. *Applied Psychological Measurement, 4,* 431–444.

Bolick, C. (1988). Legal and policy aspects of testing. *Journal of Vocational Behavior, 33,* 320–330.

Bridgeman, B., Lennon, M. L., & Jackenthal, A. (2003). Effects of screen size, screen resolution, and display rate on computer-based test performance. *Applied Measurement in Education, 16,* 191–205.

Brogden, H. E., & Taylor, E. K. (1950). The theory and classification of criterion bias. *Educational and Psychological Measurement, 3,* 159–186.

Campbell, J. P., McHenry, J. J., & Wise, L. L. (1990). Modeling job performance in a population of jobs. *Personnel Psychology, 43,* 313–334.

Cascio, W. F. (1987). *Applied psychology in personnel management*. Englewood Cliffs, NJ: Prentice Hall.

Cleary, T. A. (1968). Test bias: Prediction of grades of Negro and White students in integrated colleges. *Journal of Educational Measurement, 5,* 115–124.

Cohen, J., Cohen, P., West, S., & Aiken, L. (2003). *Applied multiple regression/correlation analysis for the behavioral sciences* (3rd ed.). Hillsdale, NJ: Lawrence Erlbaum Associates.

Cole, N. (1981). Bias in testing. *American Psychologist, 36,* 1067–1077.

Drasgow, F., Luecht, R., & Bennett, R. (2006). Technology and testing. In R. L. Brennan (Ed.), *Educational measurement* (4th ed.). Washington, DC: American Council on Education.

Drasgow, F., & Olson-Buchanan, J. B. (Eds.). (1999). *Innovations in computerized assessment*. Mahwah, NJ: Lawrence Erlbaum Associates.

Dunnette, M. D., & Borman, W. C. (1979). Personnel selection and classification. *Annual Review of Psychology, 30,* 477–525.

Flaugher, R. L. (1978). The many definitions of test bias. *American Psychologist, 33,* 671–679.

Ghiselli, E. F., Campbell, J. P., & Zedeck, S. (1981). *Measurement theory for the behavioral sciences*. New York: Freeman.

Guion, R. M. (1977). Content validity, the source of my discontent. *Applied Psychological Measurement, 1,* 1–10.

Guion, R. M. (1978). "Content validity" in moderation. *Personnel Psychology, 31,* 205–213.

Guion, R. M. (1980). On trinitarian doctrines of validity. *Professional Psychology, 11,* 385–398.

Hambleton, R. K., Swaminathan, H., & Rogers, H. J. (1991). *Fundamentals of item response theory*. Newbury Park, CA: Sage.

Hartigan, J. A., & Wigdor, A. K. (1989). *Fairness in employment testing: Validity generalization, minority issues and the General Aptitude Test Battery*. Washington, DC: National Academy Press.

Hays, W. L. (1981). *Statistics* (3rd ed.). New York: CBS.

Hubbard, M., McCloy, R., Campbell, J., Nottingham, J., Lewis, P., Rivkin, D., et al. (2000). *Revision of O*NET data collection instruments*. Raleigh, NC: National O*NET Consortium.

Hulin, C. L., Drasgow, F. & Parsons, C. K. (1983). *Item response theory: Application to psychological measurement*. Homewood, IL: Dow Jones-Irwin.

Jensen, A. R. (1980). *Bias in mental testing*. New York: Free Press.

Kutner, M. H., Nachtsheim, C. J., & Neter, J. (2004). *Applied linear regression models* (4th ed.). Chicago: McGraw-Hill.

Messick, S. (1980). Test validity and the ethics of assessment. *American Psychologist, 35,* 1012–1027.

Murphy, K., & Myors, B. (2003). *Statistical power analysis: A simple and general model for traditional and modern hypothesis tests* (2nd ed.). Mahwah, NJ: Lawrence Erlbaum Associates.

Nunnally, J. C. (1978). *Psychometric theory*. New York: McGraw-Hill.

Oppler, S. H., Peterson, N. G., & Russell, T. (1992). Basic validation results for the LVI sample. In J. P. Campbell & L. M. Zook (Eds.), *Building and retaining the career force: New procedures for accessing and assigning Army enlisted personnel. Annual report, 1991 fiscal year* (pp. 155–193). Alexandria, VA: U.S. Army Research Institute for the Behavioral and Social Sciences.

Petersen, N. S., & Novick, M. R. (1976). An evaluation of some models for culture-fair selection. *Journal of Educational Measurement, 13,* 3–29.

Peterson, N. G., Mumford, M. D., Borman, W. C., Jeanneret, P. R., & Fleishman, E. A. (Eds.). (1999). *An occupational information system for the 21st century: The development of O*NET*. Washington, DC: American Psychological Association.

Rothstein, H. R. (1990). Interrater reliability of job performance ratings: Growth to asymptote level with increasing opportunity to observe. *Journal of Applied Psychology, 75,* 322–327.

Schmidt, F. L., & Hunter, J. E. (1977). Development of a general solution to the problem of validity generalization. *Journal of Applied Psychology, 62,* 529–540.

Schmidt, F. L., & Hunter, J. E. (1978). Moderator research and the law of small numbers. *Personnel Psychology, 31,* 215–232.

Schmidt, F. L., Hunter, J. E., & Urry, V. W. (1976). Statistical power in criterion-related validity studies. *Journal of Applied Psychology, 61,* 473–485.

Schmitt, N., Gooding, R. Z., Noe, R. A., & Kirsch, M. (1984). Meta-analysis of validity studies published before 1964 and 1982 and the investigation of study characteristics. *Personnel Psychology, 37,* 407–422.

Sharon, A. T., & Bartlett, C. J. (1969). Effect of instructional conditions in producing leniency on two types of rating scales. *Personnel Psychology, 23,* 251–263.

Society for Industrial and Organizational Psychology, Inc. (2003). *Principles for the validation and use of personnel selection procedures* (4th ed.). Bowling Green, OH: Author.

Stark, S., Chernyshenko, O. S., & Drasgow, F. (in press). Are CFA and IRT equally viable methods for detecting biased items? Toward a unified strategy for DIF detection. *Journal of Applied Psychology*.

Taylor, E. L., & Wherry, R. J. (1951). A study of leniency in two ratings systems. *Personnel Psychology, 4,* 39–47.

Tenopyr, M. L. (1977). Content-construct confusion. *Personnel Psychology, 30,* 47–54.

Tenopyr, M. L., & Oeltjen, P. D. (1982). Personnel selection and classification. *Annual Review of Psychology, 33,* 581–618.

U.S. Department of Labor (1991). *Dictionary of occupational titles* (4th ed.). Washington, DC: U.S. Government Printing Office.

Uniform Guidelines on Employee Selection Procedures (1978). *Federal Register, 43,* 38290–38315.

Van der Linden, W. J., & Glas, C. A. W. (Eds.). (2000). *Computerized adaptive testing: Theory and practice.* Boston: Kluwer.

Van der Linden, W. J., & Hambleton, R. (1996). *Handbook of modern item response theory.* New York: Springer.

Veres, J. G., III, Field, H. S., & Boyles, W. R. (1983). Administrative versus research performance ratings: An empirical test of rating data quality. *Public Personnel Management, 12,* 290–298.

Warmke, D. L., & Billings, R. S. (1979). Comparison of training methods for improving the psychometric quality of experimental and administrative performance ratings. *Journal of Applied Psychology, 64,* 124–131.

Wherry, R. J., Sr., & Bartlett, C. J. (1982). The control of bias in ratings. *Personnel Psychology, 35,* 521–551.

Zimowski, M., Muraki, E., Mislevy, R. J., & Bock, R. D. (2002). *BILOG-MG* [Computer software]. Lincolnwood, IL: Scientific Software International.

CHAPTER FOURTEEN

Developing Legally Defensible Content Valid Selection Procedures

Lisa W. Borden
Baker, Donelson, Bearman, Caldwell, and Berkowitz, P.C.

James C. Sharf
Sharf and Associates, Employment Risk Advisors, Inc.

OVERVIEW

Title VII of the Civil Rights Act of 1964, 42 U.S.C. § 2000e *et seq.*, has been interpreted by the courts as requiring that procedures used to make decisions about the hiring and promotion of employees must either: (a) have no adverse impact against legally protected groups or (b) be job-related and consistent with business necessity (e.g., *Griggs v. Duke Power Co.*, 1971). Selection professionals and courts frequently define the latter requirement as demanding that selection procedures having adverse impact be valid. In fact, demonstrated validity has been held to satisfy both prongs of the requirement—a valid selection process is considered to be both job-related and consistent with business necessity (e.g., *Hamer v. City of Atlanta*, 1989). This chapter discusses legal requirements and the litigation process as they affect the work of those involved in developing content valid selection procedures. We note that there are other methods for assessing validity. As stated in chapter 13, criterion-related validity is based on the degree of empirical relationship between predictor scores and criterion scores and construct validity is based on an integration of evidence that supports the interpretation or meaning of predictor scores. Both of these methods for assessing validity involve highly technical and sophisticated statistical issues, some of which are briefly described in chapter 13, and many of which are beyond the scope of this chapter.

385

The chapter is presented from the perspective of those who develop, use, and wish to defend the content validity of the selection procedure. (For simplicity, we refer to all of them as the *user*.) Those wishing to challenge content validity, however, may apply the principles and practices discussed in this chapter to identify issues to attack. The chapter is divided into three major sections. The first section provides an introduction to litigation issues, including the definition of the applicant pool, recruiting and advertising, the description of jobs in observable terms, and the search for alternative predictors. Second, we describe issues involving the development and validation of minimum qualifications and the advent of Internet recruiting. Third, we describe procedures that test developers should consider prior to developing content valid selection and promotion procedures.

INTRODUCTION TO LITIGATION: CHALLENGING CONTENT VALIDITY

Litigation challenging both content- and criterion-related validity arises when a class of applicants or employees (or, less frequently, an individual applicant or employee), claims that the procedures used by the employer to make hiring and promotion decisions have adverse impact on the group to which they belong. Initially, the burden is on the plaintiffs to demonstrate that the procedures at issue do, indeed, have adverse impact. As we discuss subsequently, litigation concerning that question alone can be complex and protracted and involves primarily, but not exclusively, statistical evidence. Once plaintiffs succeed in showing that adverse impact exists, the burden shifts to the user who must demonstrate the validity of its procedures in order to avoid liability (e.g., *Griggs*, 1971; *Dothard v. Rawlinson*, 1977). The *Uniform Guidelines on Employee Selection Procedures* (1978) spell out how validity is to be determined and documented.

Statistical arguments of adverse impact generally involve statisticians and labor economists as experts, but industrial psychologists also may be asked for their expert opinion. Litigation concerning the presence or absence of adverse impact may include disputes over issues such as:

- Properly defining the applicant pool.
- The extent to which applicant or workforce data are aggregated across jobs or facilities.
- The inclusion or exclusion of variables such as minimum qualifications.
- Which statistical tests should be applied.

We note that issues involving definition of the applicant pool often are central, and the absence of a defined meaning for the term *applicant* has led to a significant amount of litigation and to myriad difficulties for employers. Regarding the definition of the applicant pool, the *Uniform Guidelines* (1978) do not actually define the term *applicant*. However, the Q&A 15 states:

> The precise definition of the term "applicant" depends on the user's recruitment and selection procedures. The concept of an applicant is that of a person

who has indicated an interest in being considered for hiring, promotion, or other employment opportunities. This interest might be expressed by completing an application form, or might be expressed orally, depending upon the employer's practice. (EEOC, 1979, p. 11998)

When adverse impact is established and validity evidence is required, the user may rely on one or more of the following lines of defense: already existing, locally developed validity evidence; conducting a validity study to develop such evidence; or transporting and generalizing validity evidence developed elsewhere. The user typically will need testimony and other assistance from expert witnesses both to support validity and to rebuff attacks by plaintiffs on issues of compliance with the *Uniform Guidelines* (1978). The expert witnesses also may have to demonstrate that users have met the generally accepted principles and practices of industrial psychology as described in the *Principles for the Validation and Use of Employee Selection Procedures* (Society for Industrial and Organizational Psychology [SIOP], 2003), refereed journal articles and texts, and possibly also the *Standards for Educational and Psychological Testing* (American Educational Research Association, American Psychological Association, National Council on Measurement in Education, 1999).

Aspects of the selection process that may be subject to challenge are not limited to the test or assessment. Plaintiffs may also challenge other decisions such as:

- Recruiting and advertising.
- The means of applying (paper and pencil, online).
- Minimum qualifications or other prerequisites (education, experience, certification, licensure).
- Weighting of the selection procedure components.
- Scoring procedures (ranking, cut score, banding).
- Final selection decisions.

Recruiting and advertising processes have always been subject to criticism. For example, one potential criticism is that recruiting efforts may be targeted in such a way that minority candidates are not likely to be reached. Another potential criticism is that aspects of the advertisements may discourage protected groups from applying. As discussed in the next section, however, heightened scrutiny of the recruiting and advertising stage of selection is on the horizon.

The weights assigned to various components of a selection procedure also may be challenged. For example, if one were to highly weight a procedure that tends to have large subgroup differences over a procedure that has lower levels of subgroup differences, then that weighting procedure might be questioned.

Various scoring procedures have been the subject of some controversy in the industrial psychology literature. Specifically, the practice of banding has received some attention (Campion et al., 2001; Schmidt, 1995; Schmidt & Hunter, 1995). Although it is not our intention to recreate the arguments in this chapter, the choices made regarding how tests are scored and the justifications for those choices should be very carefully documented.

Final selection decisions also should be described in detail. That is, the methods for integrating the information provided by predictors in arriving at a final selection decision should be documented.

Disputes over the content validity of the selection process may include:

- Qualifications of person(s) developing the selection procedure.
- Sampling plan (test specification).
- Qualifications of subject matter experts (SMEs).
- Selection and training of SMEs.
- Documentation of SMEs' judgments (questionnaires, rating scales).
- Documentation of observable behavior.
- Decision rules regarding use of SME data.
- Translation of SME data to selection procedure.
- Item bias.
- Compensatory versus noncompensatory use of components.
- Consideration of valid alternatives with lesser adverse impact.
- Documentation.

Many of these topics are described in detail in preceding chapters. Here, we emphasize the importance of describing jobs in terms of observable behavior as well as investigating use of alternative predictors.

Concerning the observability of job behavior, the *Uniform Guidelines* (1978) stress extensive documentation of the following elements (among others) of content validity studies:

15(C)(3) *Job analysis—Content of the job.* A description of the method used to analyze the job should be provided (essential). The work behavior(s), the associated tasks, and, if the behavior results in a work product, the work products should be completely described (essential). Measures of criticality and/or importance of the work behavior(s) and the method of determining these measures should be provided (essential). Where the job analysis also identified the knowledges, skills, and abilities used in work behavior(s), an operational definition for each knowledge in terms of a body of learned information and for each skill and ability in terms of *observable behaviors and outcomes,* and the relationship between each knowledge, skill, or ability and each work behavior, as well as the method used to determine this relationship, should be provided (essential). The work situation should be described, including the setting in which work behavior(s) are performed, and where appropriate, the manner in which knowledges, skills or abilities are used, and the complexity and difficulty of the knowledge, skill, or ability as used in the work behavior(s). (p. 38305)

Definitions, Sec. 16:

16(A). *Ability*. A present competence to perform an *observable behavior* or a behavior which results in an *observable product*.

16(K). *Job analysis*. A detailed statement of work behaviors and other information relevant to the job.

16M). *Knowledge*. A body of information applied directly to the performance of a function.

16(O). *Observable*. Able to be seen, heard, or otherwise perceived by a person other than the person performing the job.

16(T). *Skill*. A present, *observable competence* to perform a learned psychomotor act.

16(Y). *Work behavior*. An activity performed to achieve the objectives of the job. Work behaviors involve observable (physical) components and unobservable (mental) components. A work behavior consists of the performance of one or more tasks. Knowledges, skills, and abilities are not behaviors, although they may be applied in work behaviors (pp. 38307–38308, emphasis added).

Concerning the investigation of alternative predictors with less adverse impact, if the employer proves that the challenged requirements are job-related, the plaintiff may then show that other selection devices without a similar discriminatory effect would also "serve the employer's legitimate interest in efficient and trustworthy workmanship" (*Albemarle Paper Co. v. Moody*, 1975, *quoting McDonnel Douglas Corp. v. Green*, 1973).

THE PROBLEM OF MINIMUM QUALIFICATIONS AND THE ADVENT OF INTERNET RECRUITING

Although legal challenges may arise at any stage of the selection process, use of minimum qualifications or other prescreening procedures (collectively referred to here as MQs) can present unique problems for the user. An example of an MQ is requiring applicants to have a high school diploma or some number of years of experience. There is a relative dearth of professional literature and very few reported legal opinions concerning the validation and use of MQs. Notable exceptions include an article that directly addressed the subject of MQ validation (Levine, Maye, & Gordon, 1997). A handful of other articles have discussed MQ topics (e.g., Ash, Levine, Johnson, & McDaniel, 1989; Gatewood & Feild, 2001). A recent article detailed an MQ validation procedure that the user successfully defended in federal court (Buster, Roth, & Bobko, 2005). The federal court case in which the procedure outlined by Buster et al. was approved is *Reynolds et al. v. Alabama Department of Transportation et al.*, (2003). Except for these few articles, the user of MQs may be without much guidance regarding generally accepted principles and practices of industrial psychology.

It appears that the users of MQs will soon be shouldering a new and somewhat murky set of additional regulatory burdens. Moreover, others who had no intent to develop and defend MQs will find that, for all practical purposes, they too will be burdened with doing so for the following reason. In March 2004, the EEOC and the Department of Labor's Office of Federal Contract Compliance Programs (OFCCP) separately proposed the adoption of "Additional Questions and Answers to Clarify and Provide a Common Interpretation of the *Uniform Guidelines on Employee Selection Procedures* as They Relate to Internet and Related Technologies." According to these enforcement agencies, the intent of the proposed Q&As is to "guide users in their efforts to comply with requirements of Federal law prohibiting employment practices which discriminate" against protected groups (29 C.F.R. 1607.1[B]), and "to clarify how the *Uniform Guidelines on Employee Selection Procedures* apply in the context of the Internet and related technologies" (EEOC, 2004, p. 10152). The OFCCP issued a final rule in November, 2005, regarding "obligation to solicit race and gender data for Agency enforcement purposes" dealing with the "e-applicant" (EEOC, 2005, p. 58945). The new Q&As would create a separate category of "Internet applicants," so that "if an employer's recruitment processes for a particular job involve both electronic data technologies, such as the Internet, and traditional want ads and mailed, paper submissions, the proposed rule would treat these submissions differently for that particular job" (EEOC, 2004, p. 16445).

According to Proposed Q&A 8, "Internet applicants" would be defined as follows:

In order for an individual to be an applicant in the context of the Internet and related electronic data processing technologies, the following must have occurred:

1) The employer has acted to fill a particular position;
2) The individual has followed the employer's standard procedures for submitting applications; and
3) The individual has indicated an interest in the particular position. (EEOC, 2004, p. 10155)

The EEOC's proposed guidance also addressed search criteria employers use to screen Internet applications. An employer who uses specific qualifications to search a database, and then contacts some individuals to solicit their applications, will be required to assess whether the qualifications for which it searches have an adverse impact on protected groups. The OFCCP's (EEOC, 2005) guidance on the definition of an Internet applicant goes further, adding a fourth prong: whether the job seeker's expression of interest in a position indicates that the individual possesses the "advertised, basic qualifications" for the job. The OFCCP (EEOC, 2005) specified that the advertised, basic qualifications must be "job related."

The agencies would rely on labor force statistics "or other relevant data" when determining whether the user's recruitment processes arguably might result in adverse impact. As noted by the OFCCP (2004), the courts have recognized that application data alone might not adequately reflect the applicant pool because "otherwise qualified people might be discouraged from applying because of a self recognized inability to meet the very standards challenged as being discriminatory" (EEOC, 2004, p. 16445). In the case of Internet recruitment, advertised basic qualifications may well have the effect of causing otherwise qualified individuals to refrain from applying. Certainly, the same may be said of advertised basic qualifications that appear in traditional printed or other non-electronic recruiting announcements. Therefore, once enforcement agencies and courts begin to make adverse impact and validity determinations concerning advertised, non-MQ qualifications in the Internet recruiting context, those types of analyses are almost certain to trickle down to the more traditional types of recruitment as well. Thus, enforcement agencies would agree to omit those who do not satisfy the advertised qualifications from the potential applicant pool (and thus from adverse impact calculations) only if those qualifications are demonstrably valid.

Although this procedure may make some sense on its face, it effectively blurs the distinction between selection practices (i.e., employment decisions), which have always been burdened under the *Uniform Guidelines* (1978), and recruitment practices, which have not. To put the proposed Q&A guidance into practice, recruiting announcements that are intended to attract a pool of qualified applicants will be subjected to analysis of their adverse impact comparing labor market statistics to the employer's applicant flow. Should adverse impact be found (which is highly likely), the user will have to demonstrate the validity of the specific, prerequisite qualification in the recruiting announcement in order to overcome the presumption that such MQs are discriminatory.

DEVELOP PROCEDURES BEFORE DEVELOPING AN MQ OR OTHER SELECTION PROCESS

How can the user of a selection process be ready to meet the wide variety of legal challenges that may arise? The answer is to carry out and document the test development and validation process with the potential for litigation in mind. Each step of the process must be meticulously planned, executed, and documented.

The first and possibly most important step in developing a defensible selection process is to plan to document the procedures that will be followed. The user, through an industrial psychologist or other professional with comparable qualifications, should develop standard operating procedures to be followed and should document those procedures in a manual. A procedures manual serves a number of important purposes:

- Written procedures ensure that all who are involved in the project have the same instructions, the same understanding of how the process is to work, and what they are supposed to document.
- Written procedures corroborate the statements of a witness who testifies about how the work was done.

- The manual helps to refresh the memory of a witness who may have worked on a project months, or even years, before being called to testify about it.
- A documented set of generally accepted practices, if properly developed and followed, enhances the court's confidence in the process. Generally accepted practices that are followed and documented tend to be viewed as enhancing credibility.

In preparing written, generally accepted validation procedures, users (in this case, the I/O psychologist) should draw on a variety of sources. Their professional experience, of course, should play an important role. Courts typically have a healthy respect for the exercise of professional judgment by practitioners and any standard operating procedures should leave room for the exercise and documentation of such judgment at every stage (where, of course, such judgment does not conflict with any expressed requirement, such as a consent decree, to the contrary).

The *Uniform Guidelines* (1978), the SIOP *Principles* (2003), and other peer-reviewed articles and texts will also inform any such effort. It may be tempting for the industrial psychologist to pay little attention to certain details in the *Uniform Guidelines*; after all, they were written at a rather general level and have remained unchanged since their adoption in 1978. Many consider that the *Uniform Guidelines* have been eclipsed by the cumulative knowledge of the profession and are therefore of little practical utility. Although the generally accepted principles and practices of industrial psychology have evolved considerably since 1978, the user must bear in mind that the *Uniform Guidelines* still are the federal enforcement agencies' interpretation of burdens under Title VII and Executive Order 11246. Therefore, the *Uniform Guidelines* continue to be applied by many courts as a legal standard that must be met. The generally accepted principles and practices of industrial psychology also are relevant. The user must consider both when developing and documenting selection procedures by following the documentation section (Section 15) of the *Uniform Guidelines*. Also, when exercising professional judgment that may be at odds with the *Uniform Guidelines*, it will be useful to explain specific provisions that are no longer supported by the generally accepted principles and practices of industrial psychology.

In addition, a review of professional literature is very important. Literature supporting the chosen procedure should be cited as part of the user's documentation. Ideally, standard operating procedures should follow the generally accepted principles and practices of industrial psychology wherever possible. In situations where the potential for litigation is a concern, procedures lacking support in the *Principles* (SIOP, 2003) or peer-reviewed articles and texts should be avoided unless there is no other reasonable option.

The user also must consider applicable legal precedent and should consult with legal counsel for assistance in interpreting and complying with such precedents, because there exists a respectable amount of case law addressing the specifics of a validation study. When a particular circuit court has not ruled on an issue itself, it is likely to consider rulings on the topic from other circuit courts to be persuasive. It is important, then, to be familiar with any court opinions that may relate to issues in the validation work being done, to understand how precedents support or confound the proposed methodology, and to be prepared to articulate how conflicting precedents can be distinguished from the situation at issue.

In situations where litigation is anticipated, it also may be wise to involve outside experts early so that those experts can contribute to the preparation of the methodology to be followed and documented in the development process. As we discuss later, experts will play a key role in litigation and it is essential that their opinions about the methodology underlying the selection process be favorable. By involving experts in preparing that methodology, the user is assured of the experts' support.

Staffing the Development Project

It sometimes is difficult to gather and maintain adequate staffing for a test development project. When the project is very large or will continue for a lengthy period of time, there may be a temptation to assign some responsibility to anyone who is available to help. Giving in to such temptation can lead to trouble. Keep in mind that every person who contributes to development of a selection process is a potential fact witness who may be called to testify about the project in court.

The number of staff members who work on development should be limited. The user should select a small number of trained, well-qualified people to perform most development work. To the extent that less experienced assistants must be used, they should be closely supervised and should not be permitted to make significant judgment calls.

The background of each staff member must be carefully reviewed. Ideally, individuals who have significant responsibilities on the project will have prior experience in selection procedure development and an educational background that has prepared them for this kind of work. In court, the opposing party will attempt to criticize the development work that was done by picking apart the credentials of those who performed the work. The lack of relevant education or work experience will be pointed to as indicating a lack of professional competence.

Relevant education, training, and experience are necessary, but are not the end of the inquiry into a potential staff member's suitability for a project with litigation potential. The user must also consider the ability of each staff member to act as a witness. A person who has very good technical skills may still make a terrible witness, so personal characteristics in addition to professional competence must also be taken into account. Some characteristics to consider include:

- Attention to detail: Is the staff member a big-picture person who may consider small details insignificant? When lawyers are able to take the witness through a laundry list of items that were ignored or not completed, they can make the entire process look sloppy and, ultimately, unacceptable. The court may not understand or care that those items were minor details that did not necessarily undermine the final product.

- Temperament: Is the person defensive and easily rattled, or can this person remain calm and composed under pressure? Does the person have a quick temper? Will this person snap at someone who criticizes, or come back with a sarcastic retort? A good opposing lawyer will quickly recognize and take advantage of such tendencies and make the witness look bad, even if the person's work is very good.
- Communication skills: Is the individual articulate, or is it sometimes difficult to have a conversation with this person that is understandable to a lay person (judge or jury)? Can the witness be expected to explain clearly both the witness's actions and the reasons for making certain decisions? Is the person direct and plain spoken? Again, technically competent work may not be adequate if the person who performed it is unable to describe and to explain clearly that work to the court.

Selecting the Right Expert

The expert witness plays a crucial role in selection procedure litigation, not just at trial, but throughout the process. As previously mentioned, if the experts' involvement can begin early, perhaps even before the procedures are developed, they will be in a better position to influence and then to support the methods that are used. The level of confidence a court or even another party to litigation has in the procedures under review may be greatly enhanced by the knowledge that a competent outside expert was paying attention from the outset. When experts are able to testify that they either contributed to the procedures or reviewed and approved them before they were used to develop tests, a higher level of confidence is likely to be engendered.

Obviously, the user wants to select experts who have the right qualifications including a good educational background with relevant degrees and a substantial amount of experience. At best, this experience will include both practical, hands-on test development experience as well as previous deposition and courtroom testimony. Just as with staff members, the experts' abilities as a witness must be considered in addition to their professional selection experience.

When considering a potential expert, there is another important factor in addition to those previously mentioned. Any potential expert comes with a body of work on record that must be reviewed and compared to the issues at hand. The individual's prior work, previous testimony, and writings should be reviewed to determine whether they reveal actions or opinions that bear on the current project. The revelation of previous testimony or writings that conflict with the opinion being expressed, or are critical of a method that has been used in the current project, is not a matter that any party wants to be surprised with during their expert's cross-examination at trial. If something of concern is found during a careful pre-engagement review, the expert will have the opportunity to think through how to explain it. Alternatively, another expert can be hired.

Review all court opinions that have been issued in cases in which the prospective expert previously testified. Of course, it is important to have a thorough understanding of the opinions that have been expressed by the expert in prior cases. It is equally important, though, to know how the expert's testimony has been received in other cases. Again, courts often find the opinions of other courts to be persuasive. If a prospective expert has been criticized by a court, that criticism will almost certainly be brought to the attention of the court in later cases and could be very damaging. When the user discovers that the prospective expert has been criticized by a court for being sloppy or careless or, worse, for having been less than candid or even dishonest, it is time to move on to other candidates. The user and counsel should conduct the same sort of review with respect to any opposing expert. If this investigation reveals that the opposing expert has a record of contrary writings or criticism by courts, do not be shy when it comes to cross-examination.

A careful interview of prospective experts, in addition to a review of their prior work, is essential. The developer, ideally together with legal counsel, should create a list of questions designed to elicit the experts' opinions on, and prior experiences with, all aspects of the project. This list should cover, at a minimum, the following topics:

- Experience in developing or critiquing selection procedures of the types that are contemplated for the project at hand, and for jobs similar to those under consideration.
- Opinions and previous experience, research, or writings concerning any potentially controversial issues that are expected to arise during the design, administration, and scoring of the procedures.
- Experience with and knowledge of other people who are expected to be involved in the project including the development staff, experts from other disciplines who might also be involved, and lawyers or experts for any interested party (to the extent they have already been identified).
- A thorough review of prior litigation including identification of all prior depositions, trial testimony, and expert reports the person has produced.
- A discussion of how the experts view their role in such a project also is essential. The user, the expert, and the attorney, if applicable, should have a clear and common understanding of how the expert is to participate in the process and what decision-making authority, if any, the expert will be able to exercise.

When selection procedures are developed in implementing a consent decree, experts for both sides may be expected to work together in the development process. Both the user and the expert must understand the extent to which the expert has the authority to make representations to or agreements with the other side concerning the project.

Documenting the Development Process

Once personnel are in place and the development process begins, all of the resulting work should go through a formal sign-off procedure. Although there may be a number of staff members in the field doing background research, conducting SME panels, and developing draft items and instruments, all of their work products should ultimately be reviewed by one or two highly qualified people. These may include the in-house psychologists or project managers, the outside experts, or both. It is reasonable to presume that these final reviewers will be called to testify concerning their review and approval of what was done.

All of the work performed on the project should be meticulously documented. The opposing party in litigation may raise the smallest, most seemingly insignificant detail as a problem, so it is vital that the user be able to both recall and document what was done with respect to that detail and why. The user should consider relying on the provisions in Section 15 of the *Uniform Guidelines* (1978) as a point-by-point outline of the documentation that should be compiled and maintained. It also may be helpful to use such an outline, with the documentation relating to each point spelled out, as an appendix to the final validation report. Thorough documentation may prevent a lengthy period of testimony with the witness being required to identify each item in a report that satisfies each provision of the *Uniform Guidelines*.

There is, however, one very important exception to the general rule of meticulous documentation: Those involved in the development project should try to avoid corresponding in writing, especially via e-mail, about questions or problems that arise. Such matters should be handled in face-to-face meetings or by phone whenever possible. The resolution of a problem can always be documented in a memo after it has been discussed in person.

The user should understand that correspondence relating to the project, whether between staff members or with the expert, is generally discoverable in litigation. Even minor difficulties that are memorialized in e-mails are likely to be subjected to scrutiny and blown out of proportion by an opposing party due to the predictable tendency of most people to treat e-mail as if it were a conversation and not a written document. People make remarks in e-mail that they would not likely write in a letter or a memo, and they seem to forget that e-mail is forever (or, at least, for a very long time). The judicious use of correspondence in general and e-mail in particular should be made a part of the pre-project training for development staff.

The procedures that were created and documented before the project began should be followed as closely as possible. Of course, there will be occasions when a situation arises that either was not anticipated by the standard operating procedure or that calls for some variance from that procedure. As with other aspects of the work, these matters should be carefully documented. When a departure from the written procedure is called for, the user should provide an explanation for the decision to change the procedure and should include references from the professional literature to support the exception.

The documentation should include a description of the process for conducting job analysis, including the SMEs who provided information, data collection procedures (e.g., workshops, surveys), the data collected (e.g., task or work behavior frequency and importance, task-KSAO linkages, needed-at-entry information). Processes for conducting job analysis are described in Chapter 3 and need to be carefully documented.

Similarly, development of the measurement plan must be documented. Specifically, the user must document: the choice of predictors for a particular job(s) and how the measurement methods were evaluated (e.g., conducting a literature review, using qualified experts to make choices among various predictors); and what criteria were used to evaluate them (e.g., validity, reliability, likelihood of subgroup differences, practical considerations such as cost). Methods for developing a measurement plan are described in detail in chapter 4. Research on the psychometric characteristics of a variety of predictors is provided in chapters 5 through10.

If a criterion-related validity study is conducted, the development and administration of the criterion measures also must be documented. Methods for developing such instruments are described in chapters 11 and 12. A brief description of statistical techniques for documenting criterion-related validity is provided in chapter 13.

The process of careful documentation should culminate in a comprehensive report that describes the work performed and the resulting product as well as the decisions made and the professional judgment exercised. When a number of selection procedures are to be developed, resulting in a number of reports to be written, it is advisable to create a template that outlines the topics that must be covered. By doing so, the user will ensure consistency across the validation reports that may be authored by different staff members and reduce the likelihood that someone will omit important information from a report.

Additional Considerations in Developing and Documenting the Process

The potential for litigation should be a consideration throughout the development and validation process and should focus attention on specific areas that are likely to be challenged. This section discusses several such points that traditionally may not have received the attention they deserve.

SME Selection. Obviously, SMEs should be people who are sufficiently knowledgeable about the duties of the job under consideration. They should not include persons who have only been in the job for a very short time (ideally, not less than 6 months). To the extent possible, a reasonable balance between job incumbents and supervisors should be sought—the use of too many supervisors in the process can lead to accusations that the selection procedures are too difficult because supervisors, it is sometimes argued, have an inflated view of what the job requires.

Just as obviously, it is very important to have significant representation from both genders and from various minority groups, unless it is not possible to do so. Again, failure to include these groups can contribute directly to allegations that the procedures are biased or are too difficult. The user may wish to err on the side of overrepresentation.

On a related note, those involved in SME selection should take the time to identify potential problems that may militate against the inclusion of particular individuals, even though those individuals are otherwise qualified. For example, the user should consider excluding, if possible, persons who have a history of being accused of discriminatory conduct. Where persons with a demonstrable bias against the protected group are permitted to play a role in selection procedure development, the procedure may be vulnerable to allegations of bias.

Use of Scores.   Plaintiffs may contend that even though a selection procedure is valid, the way in which the procedure is being used is discriminatory. Again, this issue can arise in somewhat different contexts.

When a selection process has multiple components, the weighting of the various component scores may be challenged, with plaintiffs contending for a weighting scheme that will somehow reduce between-group differences in the selection rates. Careful documentation of the rationale for the chosen weighting procedure should be prepared based on generally accepted principles and practices and on peer-reviewed articles and professional texts.

The presence of multiple components may also give rise to contentions concerning the compensatory versus non-compensatory use of the candidates' scores on each component. Where component scores are used in a non-compensatory, multiple-hurdle manner (in other words, a high score on one component would not help to compensate, or make up for, a low score on another component), plaintiffs may argue that using the scores in a compensatory manner instead would reduce adverse impact and maintain the validity of the procedure. This type of dispute typically arises when the exam contains some components that test "hard" skills such as technical job knowledge, whereas others deal with "soft" interpersonal skills such as communication and management. The user should be prepared for such contentions by having considered both compensatory and non-compensatory uses, and by being able to articulate the bases for selecting one over the other. Job analysis information may be quite useful in this regard.

Rank ordering of scores on an examination also is likely to bring challenges. The *Uniform Guidelines* (1978) provides the bases on which rank-order use can be justified, but the user must take the appropriate steps during the development process to rely on those provisions. The *Uniform Guidelines* stated, "If a user can show, by a job analysis or otherwise, that a higher score on a content valid selection procedure is likely to result in better job performance, the results may be used to rank persons who score above minimum levels" (29 C.F.R. § 1607). During development, in order to provide data supporting the rank-ordered use of scores, the user should ask SMEs to rate the extent to which each exercise distinguishes between levels of performance on the job. Including such questions with other item ratings will allow the user to develop data that may be helpful when making decisions about the use of scores, as well as when defending those decisions in court.

Recruiting and Advertising. Frequently, the recruiting and advertising process is overseen by persons who are not part of the test development process. Indeed, those who are developing the selection procedures that follow the recruiting and application stage may not even be aware of the way job openings are announced. Failure to pay attention to recruiting and advertising issues, however, may lead to liability for the entire selection process. This will be a particularly acute problem once the newly proposed Internet applicant guidance discussed earlier takes effect. The user should be sure that the content of recruiting announcements and other advertising does not set forth "minimum qualifications" that are not valid and would arguably result in adverse impact when comparing applicants to the labor market.

The user would also be well advised to review the scope of recruiting to ensure that it is not focused in ways that could later be found to be discriminatory. Reliance on word-of-mouth referrals, announcements only placed in media that are unlikely to be viewed by adversely affected candidates, or only placed in geographic areas that are low in minority representation may result in an unrepresentative applicant pool that raises liability issues.

Consideration of Alternative Selection Procedures. Pursuant to the *Uniform Guidelines* (1978), the user is required to give adequate consideration to alternatives to the chosen selection procedure that may be of substantially equal validity and have less adverse impact. Even though the Civil Rights Act of 1991 placed the burden of advocating any specific alternative on the plaintiff, the user should nevertheless be careful to undertake a reasonable investigation into the availability and feasibility of other equally valid, less adverse procedures or less adverse uses of a procedure. This does not have to be an exhaustive study, but should include consideration of professional literature in the area, and other procedures that have previously been used for the same or similar jobs. If any available alternatives are identified that appear likely to have substantially equal validity and less adverse impact, but such alternatives are ultimately not adopted, the justification for adopting the chosen procedure instead of the alternative should be carefully documented.

Once in litigation, the issue of consideration of suitable alternatives can arise in two slightly different ways. First, plaintiffs may complain that the user has failed to consider equally valid, less adverse alternatives as called for in the *Uniform Guidelines* (1978). Documentation showing a reasonable process of consideration of alternatives should easily dispatch this argument. Second, plaintiffs are permitted to proffer a specific alternative that they allege is of substantially equal validity and has less adverse impact: "If an employer does meet the burden of proving

that its tests are 'job related,' it remains open to the complaining party to show
that other tests or selection devices, without a similarly undesirable racial effect,
would also serve the employer's legitimate interest" (*Albemarle*, 1975). Only if
plaintiffs put forth such "other tests or selection devices" must the court consider
"whether adequate alternatives with a lesser adverse impact would serve the
employer's needs" (*Giles v. Ireland*, 1984). The burden is on plaintiffs in litigation
to prove that the proffered alternative is of substantially equal validity and that it
would have less adverse impact.

The Final Selection Process.   A well-developed, valid selection process can
still be successfully challenged in practice when a subjective, undocumented final
selection is made. Many organizations put a great deal of care and resources into
developing the recruitment and application process, pre-screening, and using
valid selection procedures only to permit untrained decision makers to make subjective, undocumented selections from among the candidates that remain at the
end of the process. Plaintiffs (or, more accurately, plaintiffs' lawyers) are sophisticated enough to challenge unstructured interviews and other undocumented procedures that follow use of valid procedures. Therefore, the basis for the final
selection decision also should be documented.

SUMMARY

Employment is one of the most active areas in litigation today. Selection procedure litigation, in particular, was once focused almost exclusively on public
employers and very large corporations. Increasingly, however, selection procedures used by employers of all types and sizes are coming under scrutiny. For all
of the reasons identified in this chapter, those involved in developing selection
procedures must think defensively in order to be prepared to meet legal challenges. Hopefully, this chapter will be instructive in meeting the realities of making
employment decisions in a litigious society.

REFERENCES

Albemarle Paper Co. v. Moody, 422 U.S. 405, 425 (1975).
American Educational Research Association, American Psychological Association, & National
    Council on Measurement in Education (Joint Committee). (1999). *Standards for educa-
    tional and psychological testing.* Washington, DC: American Educational Research
    Association.
Ash, R., Levine, E., Johnson, J., & McDaniel, M. A. (1989). Job applicant training and work
    experience evaluation in personnel selection. In G. R. Ferris & K. M. Rowland (Eds.),
    Research in personnel and human resources management (pp. 183–226). Greenwich,
    CT: JAI Press.
Buster, M. A., Roth, P. L., & Bobko, P. (2005). A process for content validation of education
    and experience-based minimal qualifications: An approach resulting in federal court
    approval. *Personnel Psychology, 58,* 771–800.

Campion, M. A., Outtz, J. L., Zedeck, S., Schmidt, F. L., Kehoe, J. F., Murphy, K. R., et al. (2001). The controversy over score banding in personnel selection: Answers to 10 key questions. *Personnel Psychology, 54,* 149–185.

Civil Rights Act of 1964, 42 U.S.C. § 2000e (1964).

Civil Rights Act of 1991, 42 U.S.C. § 2000e (1991).

Dothard v. Rawlinson, 433 U.S. 321, 329 (1977).

Equal Employment Opportunity Commission. (1979, March 2). Adoption of question and answers to clarify and provide a common interpretation of the Uniform Guidelines on Employee Selection Procedures. *Fed. Reg.,* 11996.

Equal Employment Opportunity Commission. (2004–2005). Additional questions and answers to clarify and provide a common interpretation of the Uniform Guidelines on Employee Selection Procedures as they relate to Internet and related technologies. *Federal Register, 64*(43), March 4, 2004, p. 10152; *Federal Register, 70*(194), November 2, 2005, p. 58945.

Gatewood, R. D., & Feild, H. S. (2001). *Human resource selection.* Fort Worth, TX: Harcourt.

Giles v. Ireland, 742 F.2d 1366 (11th Cir. 1984).

Griggs v. Duke Power Co., 401 U.S. 424 (1971).

Hamer v. City of Atlanta, 872 F.2d 1521, 1534 (11th Cir. 1989).

Levine, E. L., Maye, D. M., & Gordon, T. R. (1997). A methodology for developing and validating minimum qualifications (MQs). *Personnel Psychology, 50,* 1009–1023.

McDonnel Douglas Corp. v. Green, 411 U.S. 792, 801 (1973).

Reynolds et al. v. Alabama Department of Transportation et al. CV-85-T-665-N (2003).

Schmidt, F. L. (1995). Why all banding procedures in personnel selection are logically flawed. *Human Performance, 8,* 165–177.

Schmidt, F. L., & Hunter, J. E. (1995). The fatal internal contradiction in banding: Its statistical rationale is logically inconsistent with its operational procedures. *Human Performance, 8,* 203–214.

Society for Industrial and Organizational Psychology, Inc. (2003). *Principles for the validation and use of personnel selection procedures* (4th ed.). Bowling Green, OH: Author.

Uniform Guidelines on Employee Selection Procedures (1978). *Federal Register, 43,* 38290–38315.

Author Index

Subject Index

Note: *f* indicates figure, *t* indicates table.

A

Abilities needed to perform job successfully, 2–3, 31*f*
Ability, 130, 387
  to perform, 211
  requirements, 16
"Ability to Plan and Organize Tasks and Meet Deadlines," 194*f*, 194
Academic intelligence, 131
Accomplishment record(s), 6, 164, 172–174
  rating scale for written communication, 175*f*
Accuracy training, 308
Achievement tests, 100, 102
Adverse impact, 98, 100, 384–385
Advertising, 385, 397
African American students
  college graduation rate of, 165–166
  high school graduation rate of, 165
Alternative selection procedures, 397–398
American Psychological Association (APA), 137
American Psychological Society, 137
Analysts, 19
Applicant (*see also* Internet applicants)
  definition of, 384–385
  reactions, 182
Applied measurement
  key issues in, vii
Appraisal system, 3
Applied Measurement Methods in Industrial Psychology, vii
Aptitude tests, 100, 102
Archival item approach to developing background data items, 218
Aristotle, 130
Army Air Force Elimination Board, 59
Army Alpha and Beta Tests, 130
Assembling Objects Test (AO), 109–110*f*

Assessment
  center(s), ix, 5, 104, 258–265
    consensual scoring procedures of, 260–261
    developing exercises for, 268–275
    ensuring quality assessors, 275–287
    evaluating simulations, 287–288
    feedback provided from, 261–262
    methods, 2–3
    origins of, 258–259
    overview of, 257–258
    psychometric characteristics of, 268
  tests, 97
Assessors
  selecting, 276–277
  training, 278–287
Association of Test Publishers, The, 137
Attention to detail, 391
Autobiographical recall, 206
Aviation Psychology Program, 59

B

Background data, viii, 5–6, 199–200
  alternative formats of, 207
  developing, 212–219
  empirical scaling procedures, 208
  factorial scaling approach, 208
  faking answers, 201–203
  gathering, 59–60
  instruments, 98
  interpreting responses to, 205
  item content of, 203–205
  psychometric characteristics of, 208–212
  rational scaling approach, 208
  subgrouping procedures, 208,212
  used to identify destructive tendencies, 200
  validating, 219–223
Basic Math Test, 110–112
Before-hire requirements, 100
Behavior description interview (BDI), 183–184, 192–194
  moderators of the validity of, 186–188
Behavioral